Schools as Communities provides a deep look at the DNA of Christian schools—a look that will be transformational for many. For example, my views of leadership will never be the same again. And struggling to help schools become communities of grace is a powerful idea that will likely find itself in my own writing. Jim Drexler and his contributing authors have skillfully prepared a manuscript with a level of coherence rarely found in an edited book. This book will be widely read.

—Thomas J. Sergiovanni
Lillian Radford Professor of Education
Trinity University, San Antonio, Texas

The authors of this very fine book have written about Christian school leadership in thoughtful, helpful, interesting ways. Seasoned superintendents and principals as well as newcomers to school leadership will find the book very worthwhile. My hope is that this book will be required reading in every Christian college and university graduate program in leadership.

—Gloria Stronks
Director of Continuing Education for Teachers Worldwide Christian Schools
Whitworth College Scholar in Residence, Professor of Education Emerita
Calvin College, Grand Rapids, Michigan

Christian school leaders will want to keep this book close at hand throughout the school year. The authors use an impressive range of ideas from Christian and other educational thinkers to work out how we can effectively shape schools to be communities of grace. Many chapters are worthwhile for staff and board discussions.

—Harro Van Brummelen,
Dean, School of Education
Trinity Western University, Langley, BC, Canada

Finally, a comprehensive treatment of possibly the greatest challenge confronting Christian schools: effective educational leadership in Christian perspective. The book examines the key aspects of leadership, reflects a holistic and coherent biblical worldview, addresses some of the most pernicious spirits of the age (such as a lingering dualism), and offers many practical recommendations. Required reading for all who are or aspire to be principals.

—John Van Dyk,
Professor of Education and Director of Center for Educational Services
Dordt College, Sioux Center, Iowa

Christian educational leaders face an overwhelming number of issues as they try to apply their faith to the actual *process* of leading a school rather than merely giving the school a Christian veneer. *Schools as Communities* addresses those issues in ways that may sometimes challenge your current practices. It will also open your eyes to new possibilities. In both cases you will find careful biblical thought applied to the issues as well as practical questions and suggestions to help you move forward in your quest to become an effective, God-honoring leader.

—Donovan Graham
Covenant College
Lookout Mountain, Georgia

The authors of *Schools as Communities* have provided valuable information that can assist schools in becoming a positive witness by how they are organized and how they minister within the organization and to those they serve. One of the great challenges for the Christian school is to be a "living curriculum," providing a life witness for the staff, parents, and students. This book should be a valuable tool in helping schools become what God intends.

—James Braley
Christian Schools Consultant
Cottonwood, Arizona

James Drexler is to be congratulated for being the editorial force behind this fine ACSI collection of integrated chapters on central issues in Christian educational leadership and administration. Drexler sets forth the book's central themes: Christian schools are to be characterized by true community and a grace-based perspective, governed according to biblical principles, and relevantly engaged with the culture. Over 20 contributing authors ably flesh out these themes as they discuss the central issues of school leadership. The authors are thoroughly conversant with current research and engage major secular and Christian authors in a knowledgeable and insightful manner. Highly recommended for undergraduate education courses, as a primary text for graduate courses in educational leadership, and as a resource for current educational leaders in Christian schools.

—Robert Bruinsma
Professor of Education and Associate Vice President (Academic)
The King's University College, Edmonton, AB, Canada

Many voices speaking calmly and clearly toward one end: Christian school leadership. Good balance of research, "been there, done that," and biblical models. Good advice on all aspects of leadership: curriculum, guiding staff and students, and building communities of grace. No prospective principal should leave school without it. Any current Christian school leader will be better with it.

—Daniel R. Vander Ark
Former Executive Director
Christian Schools International

Educational Leadership,

Relationships,

and the Eternal Value of

Christian Schooling

SCHOOLS AS COMMUNITIES

Educational Leadership,

Relationships,

and the Eternal Value of

Christian Schooling

SCHOOLS AS COMMUNITIES

James L. Drexler, Editor

purposeful design
p u b l i c a t i o n s
A Division of ACSI

Colorado Springs, Colorado

Purposeful Design Publications is the publishing division of the Association of Christian Schools International (ACSI) and is committed to the ministry of Christian school education, to enable Christian educators and schools worldwide to effectively prepare students for life. As the publisher of textbooks, trade books, and other educational resources within ACSI, Purposeful Design Publications strives to produce biblically sound materials that reflect Christian scholarship and stewardship and that address the identified needs of Christian schools around the world.

All Scripture quotations, unless otherwise indicated, are taken from the HOLY BIBLE, NEW INTERNATIONAL VERSION®. NIV®. Copyright © 1973, 1978, 1984 by International Bible Society. Used by permission of Zondervan. All rights reserved.

Scripture quotations marked (NASB) are taken from the New American Standard Bible®, © 1960, 1962, 1963, 1968, 1971, 1972, 1973, 1975, 1977, 1995, by the Lockman Foundation. Used by permission. Scripture quotations marked (NKJV) are taken from the Holy Bible, New King James Version, © 1982 by Thomas Nelson, Inc. Used by permission. All rights reserved. Scripture quotations marked (*The Message*) are taken from *The Message*, © 1993, 1994, 1995, 1996, 2000, 2001, 2002. Used by permission of NavPress Publishing Group. Scripture quotations marked (KJV) are taken from the King James Version.

Printed in the United States of America
15 14 13 12 11 10 09 08 07   1 2 3 4 5 6 7

Library of Congress Cataloging-in-Publication Data

Schools as communities : educational leadership, relationships, and the eternal value of Christian schooling
         p. cm.
     Edited by James L. Drexler
     Includes bibliographical references and indexes.
     ISBN 978-1-58331-083-0
1. Church schools--United States. 2. Christian education--United States--Philosophy. 3. Communities--Religious aspects--Christianity. I. Drexler, James L.
     LC621.S36 2007
     371.0710973--dc22
                         2006037623
Catalog #6551

Editorial team: John Conaway, Karen Friesen, Christina Nichols
Design Team: Scot McDonald, Jocelyn Chan

Purposeful Design Publications
A Division of ACSI
PO Box 65130 • Colorado Springs, CO 80962-5130
Customer Service: 800-367-0798 • Website: www.acsi.org

CONTENTS

ACKNOWLEDGMENTS

It is more than appropriate that a book on community and leadership be the product of many people. In addition to the twenty other authors in this volume, the editor gratefully acknowledges the support, ideas, and encouragement of the members of the education department of Covenant College, especially those involved with the master of education programs. The editor also thanks Jane Brooks Young, Mary Belz Kaufmann, and Heidi Jean Kaufmann for their invaluable help in editing the first drafts of each chapter. Finally, special and loving thanks to Sara and the children for their support and patience through the process. Sara is a trophy of God's grace and living proof of the eternal value of Christian education, something we have had the privilege of passing on to our four children. To God be the glory.

—James L. Drexler

FOREWORD

I WAS SITTING around a table with a small group of North American educators, each of us a guest of a prominent Ivy League graduate school of education. We were crystallizing our best thinking on the key characteristics of quality instruction. One can't talk quality instruction without pushing the word *rigor* to the surface. As we worked toward a common understanding of rigor, we found it difficult to separate program *relevance* from any common understanding of program *rigor*. Today those two words are dominating the vocabulary of school leaders as they describe their classrooms to an interested public.

In the context of Christian schooling, one can't speak of a rigorous or relevant program without recognizing the powerful role that *relationships* play in the learning process. Teachers, students, parents, and the external community are all woven together in delicate ways, and either the relationships among these groups add energizing fuel as the school seeks to accomplish its mission, or those relationships bog down growth as they sap the school community of critical energy.

Jim Drexler has orchestrated scholarly thought that helps the reader better understand both the complexities and the potential power of seeing the school as a community. As you work your way through this book, replace the traditional three Rs of education (reading, writing, and 'rithmetic) with the three Rs of Christian education—*rigor, relevance,* and *relationships*. Better yet, add a fourth: *renewal*. Drexler's book helps us dig more deeply into how we might craft *rigorous* and *relevant* programs fueled by the power of *relationships* while we equip students to be instruments of *renewal* in a broken world.

—*David J. Koetje, President*
Christian Schools International

CHRISTIAN SCHOOLING presents us with one of the greatest institutional opportunities of all time to both practice and perpetuate the kingdom of God. The very term *Christian schooling* brings into embrace two crucial aspects of life and living: education and faith in Christ.

No one disputes the value of an education. Its implications have an impact on our livelihood, our service, our culture—indeed, on every part of human society. Reaching a high level of educational effectiveness requires an array of activities—including leadership, governance, organization, understanding of community, classroom management, collaboration, and professional development—and these cross multiple boundaries and disciplines. We educators know that education doesn't happen automatically. It requires our intensive attention. We must sort and prioritize. We must learn and relearn.

Christian schooling brings to the nearly indescribably complex notion of education the element that represents the very core of human existence: the Christian life. In Christian schooling the bonding of spiritual formation to every dimension of intellectual development produces men and women capable of serving God with excellence. As Christian school educators, we face additional challenges in confronting the culture. We must be appropriately engaged, but not overcome. We must risk, yet not be defeated.

This book presents an anthology of challenges and strategies that will invigorate and inspire all of us Christian educators as we pursue an agenda of effectiveness in the development of students who think Christianly.

—Ken Smitherman, President
Association of Christian Schools International

INTRODUCTION

GETTING THE FOCUS RIGHT

by James L. Drexler

SCHOOLS AS COMMUNITIES have a long and rich history.

It can be argued that the original mission statement for Christian schooling is found in Deuteronomy 6:4–9, which (in part) commands believing parents to "impress" the words of God on their children ("teach them diligently," NASB) in all contexts and in all places. This "schooling" became more formalized centuries later during the Exile with the development of synagogues, which had become commonplace by the time of Jesus. During the early centuries of the church, Christian education was often accomplished in secret, perhaps even in the catacombs. Paul Kienel (1998) chronicles this history along with other stories of Christian schooling.

Later, the sixteenth-century Protestant Reformation breathed new life into the urgency for Christian schooling through the work of Martin Luther, John Calvin, John Knox, and others. W.S. Reid (1982) elucidates the varied ways that this Reformation faith has shaped Western civilization, particularly in education. For example, Calvin argued that knowledge of Christian theology was critical for the success of the Reformation, so schooling was a top priority in Geneva. Inspired by the model of Martin Bucer's academy in Strasbourg, Germany, Calvin returned to Switzerland determined to establish his own school. In 1559 the Academy of Geneva was opened to provide instruction for all children, especially poor children, who were taught free of charge. The academy proved to be a model for many early American schools.

The linkage is striking. God's people have consistently and persistently joined together to nurture and train the next generation for faithful service to the Lord. This generational transfer of the knowledge of God through teaching and relationships is done so that students will "put their trust in God and [will] not forget his deeds but [will] keep his commands" (Psalm 78:7).

Major Themes of This Book

This book touches on a variety of subjects and issues related to educational leadership, but in particular stresses several key themes.

1. *Community*

Richard Mouw writes of a New Jersey man traveling in the South for the first time. After considering the menu options for breakfast, and noting that several combination meals featured grits, he asked the waitress, " 'Miss, what is a grit?' She replied, 'Honey, they don't come by *themselves*!' " Mouw concludes, "Like grits, 'Christian' is a plural thing. To follow Jesus is to be part of a community" (2004, 65–66).

The apostle Peter makes a remarkable and descriptive claim when he states that Christians are "a chosen people, a royal priesthood, a holy nation ... the people of God" (1 Peter 2:9–10). It is instructive that Peter does not refer to a chosen person, a single priest, or an individual citizen. When people are saved by grace, Jesus calls them into a spiritual family, a church, a kingdom. As Stanley Grenz writes, "Community—or more fully stated, persons-in-relationship—is the central, organizing concept of theological construction, the theme around which a systematic theology is structured" (2000, 214–15).

Some of God's first recorded words in Scripture—as readers eavesdrop on a heavenly conversation—express a relationship: "Let *us* make man in *our* image, in *our* likeness" (Genesis 1:26, emphasis added). The triune God—Father, Son, and Holy Spirit—exists eternally in community; and humans, created in God's image, reflect that relational, social quality.

As the story of salvation unfolds, God deals first with the families of Abraham, Isaac, and Jacob. He later creates the nation of Israel. Eventually the church is established, the community of God's people (Ephesians 2:11–22). John envisions the culmination of this theme as a new heaven and a new earth in which a redeemed body of believers live together for all eternity, reconciled with God, with one another, and with creation. In a very real sense, then, one cannot fully understand redemption, the church, and the kingdom of God without understanding, appreciating, and living in community.

Schools are communities, and Thomas Sergiovanni, among others, has written extensively about the importance of building community within schools. "*Communities* are collections of individuals who are bonded together by natural will and who are together bound to a set of shared ideas and ideals" (1996, 48; emphasis in original).

"We will tell the next generation the praiseworthy deeds of the Lord, his power, and the wonders he has done. He decreed statutes for Jacob and established the law in Israel, which he commanded our forefathers to teach their children, so the next generation would know them, even the children yet to be born, and they in turn would tell their children. Then they would put their trust in God and would not forget his deeds but would keep his commands" (Psalm 78:4–7). This generation-to-generation telling of the gospel is the foundation for Christian schooling and community.

As the reader will soon discover (and hopefully appreciate), this book was written by a variety of authors who offer a diversity of opinions and perspectives, features that reflect the reality of the community of believers in God's kingdom. By necessity, certain chapters focus on the particulars of educational leadership that guide the day-to-day activities and decision making within a school; others are more general and global in scope. Some chapters speak directly of community concerns within that global scope; others address the more detailed specialization and professionalism of school administration.

In looking closely at a multicolored mosaic, one might see only blue triangles, green shapes, or red circles; however, when viewed as a whole, the mosaic is a beautiful and unified work of art. So, too, for the chapters in this volume. When it may appear that the specific functions of administration are discussed apart from specific concerns about community, the reader must step back and see the organic reality of the whole, remembering that everything an educational leader does and says is either supportive of or counter to community building in the school.

2. Grace-based perspective

Related closely to the theme of community and relationships is the acknowledgment that Christians are saved by grace alone and must live new lives in Christ by grace alone. Titus 2:11–14 is one of many passages that make these truths clear: "For the grace of God that brings salvation has appeared to all men [redemption accomplished]. It teaches us to say 'No' to ungodliness and worldly passions, and to live self-controlled, upright and godly lives in this present age [redemption applied], while we wait for the blessed hope—the glorious appearing of our great God and Savior, Jesus Christ [redemption consummated], who gave himself for us to redeem us from all wickedness and to purify for himself a people that are his very own, eager to do what is good."

For example, in classroom management and schoolwide discipline, the maxim "rules without relationships lead to rebellion" must be emphasized as teachers and administrators deal daily with their own sinful actions and attitudes, sinful students, broken and decaying buildings and equipment, and other realities of a fallen world. Sin is very real, but God's grace is sufficient; so an effort is made in each chapter to lay hold of grace rather than human efforts or solutions.

Galatians teaches that Christians should no longer live and function as slaves because Jesus has redeemed them and they are now heirs to the kingdom (4:1–7). The tendency, Paul argues, is for Christians to revert to the law, bondage, and slavery. Instead, "You are all sons of God through faith in Christ Jesus.... If you belong to Christ, then you are Abraham's seed, and heirs according to the promise.... So you are no longer a slave, but a son; and since you are a son, God has made you also an heir (3:26, 29; 4:7). The implications of this reality will be explored in each chapter.

3. "The weightier issues of the Law"

In Matthew 23:23, Jesus rebuked the Pharisees and religious leaders: "Woe to you, teachers of the law and Pharisees, you hypocrites! You give a tenth of your spices—mint, dill and cummin. But you have neglected the more important ["weightier," KJV] matters of the law—justice, mercy and faithfulness. You should have practiced the latter, without neglecting the former." Jesus is not discouraging tithing in this reprimand but instead is encouraging higher callings for Christians.

Jesus' words are consistent with passages in both the Old and New Testaments. In Micah 6:8, for example, the prophet reveals what God's will is for His people: to act justly, love mercy, and walk humbly with God. Isaiah 58:6–7 declared that the nation of Judah was being judged in part for forsaking these commands of God. God's people are called to loosen the chains of injustice, set the oppressed free, clothe the naked, and spend themselves on behalf of the hungry. (See also Job 31:16–23; Ezekiel 18:7, 16; Matthew 25:31–46; James 1:27.) In the New Testament, the early Christians shared what they had, and as a result, "There were no needy persons among them" (Acts 4:34), a remarkably similar situation to the one predicted in Deuteronomy 15:4–6.

How can Christian schools teach, model, and promote these weightier issues of the Law? How can teachers lay before students the need for righteousness, justice, and mercy and encourage them to live out these truths? How can leaders encourage the "look" and practice of the kingdom of God, which consists of a diverse combination of folks from every tribe, language, people, and nation (Revelation 5:9)?

4. Culturally relevant and engaged

Christians are saved by faith in Jesus Christ alone, but for what purpose? Does redemption have implications only for eternal life—"fire insurance"—or are there implications for right now?

One of the important themes for Christian schooling is for faculty and students to know that God has saved *and* called his new ambassadors and representatives to bring the gospel into all areas of life. If Christianity is not relevant to life today, it will not be relevant at all. This is true for the Christian school and for its students, teachers, board members, and families.

Christian education must be more than simply adding Bible classes and chapels to an otherwise secular curriculum. Christian education is not complete until head knowledge changes the heart and directs the hands and feet into service to God and others (Graham 2003). Students and teachers must be taught, led, and exhorted to weave the truths of Scripture into everything they do, which includes the formal curriculum and all cocurricular endeavors. To have "the mind of Christ"

(1 Corinthians 2:16), to learn how to think and live Christianly, and to take what is learned and experienced into the marketplace—these are all worthy goals for a culturally engaged Christian education.

Educational Leadership

The historical development of administration and educational leadership is fascinating and varied. In the nineteenth century, Horace Mann's common school featured the "head teacher," one who fulfilled a variety of tasks, including teaching, administering school discipline, and carrying out administrative duties ranging from janitorial to supervisory. These head teachers soon evolved into building principals.

In the twentieth century, school administration moved through several significant historical phases. Frederick Taylor, the father of "scientific management," emphasized efficiency, control, centralization, and standardization in what Raymond Callahan later called "the cult of efficiency" (1962). This bureaucratic, top-down, routinized practice of administration was challenged in various ways in subsequent years through the human-relations approach advocated by Mary Parker Follett and the discovery of the Hawthorne effect in the 1930s, both of which emphasized people, psychology, and relationships (English 2005). School administration, then, was built on two main pillars: "concepts from management, especially from the private sector, and theories and constructs borrowed from the behavioral sciences" (Murphy, Hawley, and Young 2005, 48). The second half of the twentieth century produced numerous new approaches to school leadership, many of which are discussed in this book (particularly in chapter 5, "Weighing Leadership Models").

As an academic discipline, then, educational leadership is centuries old, although the formal discipline is a recent development. In fact, some have argued that educational leadership has roots in the 1990s with the formation of the National Policy Board for Education Administration and the publication of the Interstate School Leaders Licensure Consortium (ISLLC) in 1994, which shifted "the focus of school administration from management to educational leadership" (Murphy, Hawley, and Young 2005, 49). This volume adds to the developing knowledge base for the new field of educational leadership.

The Purposes of This Book

This volume has at least the following uses in mind:
- a textbook for undergraduate students preparing for teaching and administrative service in Christian schools
- a textbook for graduate programs in educational leadership
- an on-the-job sourcebook for Christian school administrators and other educational leaders in schools
- a resource for ACSI and CSI professional-development programs

In addition, this book contains the following features:
- It provides references to current research and writing on various educational leadership topics. Its authors are conversant with current theories and models, while adding new information to the growing knowledge base for effective educational leadership.
- It suggests practical and useful application of the material presented. Each chapter concludes with a "Now What? Application to Practice" section, with suggestions for further study, questions to prompt further thought, or useful tips for applying the material in the chapter.
- It models an enthusiastic commitment to biblical, grace-based Christian schooling.

The Drama of Servant Leadership

Finally, educational leadership for the Christian school is an *acknowledgment*, an *attitude*, and an *ambition*:

1. Christian education is an *acknowledgment* about God's world. He created it, He holds it together, He rules it, and His children have an obligation to learn all they can about it. Students are not simply learning about math, science, and history; they are learning about God's world. Christian education seeks to produce competent graduates who know the world—and the one who created it.

2. Christian education is an *attitude* toward God's Word. Studying God's world from the perspective of the Word is critical. Life can be understood only as it is viewed through the "spectacles" of Scripture.

"For with you is the fountain of life; in your light we see light" (Psalm 36:9). Seeking to bring all thought and activity under the lordship of Christ, Christian school students must be passionate about their God, their lives, and their call to service.

3. Christian education is an *ambition* to do God's will. Because it is a lifelong process of transforming minds, Christian education spans "the cradle to the grave." Students must not be satisfied with this world but instead must be instructed to see the sin in themselves and in the world, and to commit their lives to the pursuit of justice, compassion, and integrity.

"We want to serve our culture," writes Harry Blamires in *The Secularist Heresy*, "we want our civilization to work—not because it is the only good we can conceive, and not because we are finally and securely at home in it—but because it is a great drama that we have been staged in, and it is good that we should play our parts well" (1956, 155).

The drama of educational leadership that unfolds in the following pages is at once provocative, frustrating, daunting—yes, even impossible for one to do alone—yet a thrilling and immensely rewarding call from God.

References

Blamires, Harry. 1956. *The secularist heresy: The erosion of the gospel in the twentieth century.* Ann Arbor, MI: Servant Books.

Callahan, Raymond E. 1962. *Education and the cult of efficiency: A study of the social forces that have shaped the administration of the public schools.* Chicago: University of Chicago Press.

English, Fenwick W., ed. 2005. *The SAGE handbook of educational leadership: Advances in theory, research, and practice.* Thousand Oaks, CA: Sage Publications.

Graham, Donovan L. 2003. *Teaching redemptively: Bringing grace and truth into your classroom.* Colorado Springs, CO: Purposeful Design Publications.

Grenz, Stanley J. 2000. *Renewing the center: Evangelical theology in a post-theological era.* Grand Rapids, MI: BridgePoint Books.

Kienel, Paul A. 1998. *A History of Christian school education.* Vol. 1. Colorado Springs, CO: Association of Christian Schools International.

Mouw, Richard J. 2004. *Calvinism in the Las Vegas airport: Making connections in today's world.* Grand Rapids, MI: Zondervan.

Murphy, Joseph, Willis D. Hawley, and Michael F. Young. 2005. Redefining the education of school leaders: Scaffolding a learning-anchored program on the ISLLC standards. *NCPEA Education Leadership Review* 6 (Fall), no. 2:48–57.

Reid, W. Stanford, ed. 1982. *John Calvin: His influence in the Western world.* Grand Rapids, MI: Zondervan.

Sergiovanni, Thomas J. 1996. *Leadership for the schoolhouse: How is it different? Why is it important?* San Francisco: Jossey-Bass.

PART ONE

Building Community:
Foundational Principles

CHAPTER 1

SCHOOLS AS COMMUNITIES OF GRACE

Flourishing as Living Water and Living Stones

 و

By Bruce Hekman

Bruce Hekman, PhD, is a retired Christian school administrator who is currently an adjunct professor of education at Calvin College, teaching graduate courses in educational leadership. He is an author and a workshop speaker for teachers and administrators.

CHAPTER 1

SCHOOLS AS COMMUNITIES OF GRACE

By Bruce Hekman

CHRISTIAN SCHOOLS IN North America are too often vulnerable to the charge that they look just like public schools—with a frosting of spirituality. In their marketing materials, schools like to proclaim their success at meeting public-school standards of excellence: high test scores, scholastic awards, and athletic championships. In the desire to measure up to the best in their communities, they sometimes unwittingly fall into the pit of competition.

The thesis of this chapter is that Christian schools should be known as communities of grace—places where visitors clearly see God at work in the way relationships are conducted. This is not to slight the value of a distinctive Christian worldview, or efforts to help students to become all God intends for them to be. Rather, the intent is to point to the *context* of schooling as an important and often overlooked part of the *content* of education.

The wisdom and strength found in biblical communities is both countercultural and desperately needed in Christian schools. Several recent books have highlighted the serious downside of the cultural worship of individualism. As the evidence clearly shows, loss of genuine community produces a litany of social pathologies. These pathologies have drawn the increasing interest of influential people in medicine, social psychology, education, and government.

The Best of Times, the Worst of Times

"We are witnessing high and rising rates of depression, anxiety, attention deficit, conduct disorders, thoughts of suicide, and other serious mental, emotional, and behavioral problems among U.S. children and adolescents" (Institute for American Values 2003, 5). The report, titled *Hardwired to Connect*, continues:

> Scholars at the National Research Council in 2002 estimated that at least one of every four adolescents in the U.S. is currently at serious risk of not achieving productive adulthood. According to another recent study, about 21 percent of U.S. children ages nine to 17 have a diagnosable mental or addictive disorder associated with at least minimum impairment....
>
> Several studies have found that an estimated eight percent of U.S. high school students suffer from clinical depression....
>
> About 20 percent of students report having seriously considered suicide in the past year....
>
> [In spite of] broad recent improvements in our *material* well-being, ... U.S. young people not only appear to be experiencing sharp increases in mental illness and stress and emotional problems, but also continue to suffer from high ... rates of related behavioral problems such [as] substance abuse, school dropout, interpersonal violence, premature sexual intercourse, and teenage pregnancy. (8–9; emphasis in original)

Most experienced educators can provide ample anecdotal evidence of these trends among North American children. One reason is that Christian and public schools see more and more children from fractured families. David G. Myers has documented the effects of a toxic family environment on children. He reports that the number of children reported neglected and abused has nearly quintupled since 1976, and that "from 1960 to 1993, arrests for juvenile violent crime increased *seven*fold, from 16,000 arrests to 120,000.... During that time, all types of juvenile arrests soared from 475,000 to 1.74 million" (2000, 66; emphasis in original). "Living in a culture enjoying unprecedented material abundance and unrivaled freedom to pursue one's personal bliss, America's children are plagued by social pathology.... America is creating a self-perpetuating, intergenerational cycle of nonmarital births, divorce, school dropout, poverty, and associated pathologies" (67–68).

Nomads or Pilgrims?

Robert D. Putnam, in his book *Bowling Alone*, has documented the increasing individualism of American culture. "For the first two-thirds of the twentieth century a powerful tide bore Americans into ever deeper engagement in the life of their communities, but a few decades ago— silently, without warning—that tide reversed and we were overtaken by a treacherous rip current. Without at first noticing, we have been pulled apart from one another and from our communities over the last third of the century" (2000, 27). He argues that people who have active and trusting connections to others—whether family members, friends, or fellow bowlers—develop and maintain characteristics that are good for the rest of society. "Joiners become more tolerant, less cynical, and more empathetic to the misfortunes of others.... Without such an opportunity, people are more likely to be swayed by their worst impulses" (288–89).

One of the reasons for "bowling alone" is the increasing number of global nomads in our society. "According to the U.S. Census Bureau about 43 million Americans move in an average year. That accounts for 16 percent of the population.... The typical American is now expected to move fourteen times over the course of his or her life" (Barnes 2003, 15). Corporate and government policies and practices and the globalization of business send workers all over the world to live and work. A growing number of children brought up in this environment become "third-culture kids," born in one culture but growing up in another and at home in neither. The result, Barnes says, resembles "what John Barth called 'the floating opera of friends.' They come onto the stage of our lives for a while but all too soon float away. We resolve to keep in touch and stay close, but close is exactly what we are not" (33).

It is an important task of the church and the Christian school to turn nomads into pilgrims. A nomad's restless spirit calls him or her to leave and move on to a new adventure; a pilgrim's restlessness is for the paradise that was lost and can be regained only in heaven. Pilgrims have a destination and a passion for getting there. In their wandering, nomads turn to others for moments of pleasure and fellowship, but only for a time and a season. The nomadic life is a life alone, with all the attendant pathologies. Pilgrims are on the road together, supported in their struggles and challenges by other pilgrims, rejoicing together in their common goal and sustained by their fellowship around the table of grace.

Belonging

The picture is painfully clear: we are discovering that there are serious spiritual and social consequences to life alone. Social scientists and school theorists are looking more and more often to relationship needs as a way to address the current crisis. *Hardwired to Connect* concludes its analysis of the crisis by saying, "In large measure, what's causing this crisis of American childhood is a lack of connectedness … close connections to other people, and deep connections to moral and spiritual meaning" (Institute for American Values 2003, 5).

Thomas Sergiovanni has extensively explored the idea of schools as communities. In *Building Community in Schools* he writes, "When students experience a loss of community they have two options: to create substitutes for this loss, and to live without community, with negative psychological consequences" (1994, 11). He quotes from the work of Larry K. Brendtro, Martin Brokenleg, and Steve Van Bockern (*Reclaiming Youth at Risk: Our Hope for the Future*), who observe that "today's children are desperately pursuing 'artificial belongings' because this need is not being fulfilled by families, schools, and neighborhoods" (38, cited in Sergiovanni 1994, 11).

Brendtro, Brokenleg, and Van Bockern (47, cited in Sergiovanni 1994, 11) summarize some of the consequences of this loss of community:

Belonging		
Normal	*Distorted*	*Absent*
Attached	Gang loyalty	Unattached
Loving	Craves affection	Guarded
Friendly	Craves acceptance	Rejected
Intimate	Promiscuous	Lonely
Gregarious	Clinging	Aloof
Cooperative	Cult vulnerable	Isolated
Trusting	Overly dependent	Distrustful

Christian Community

Caring relationships within a confessional community provide an important key to effective schooling. A school as a community provides students with the moral, intellectual, social, and spiritual resources to live and serve fully wherever God directs their pilgrim paths. The *context* of schooling is an important part of the *content* of schooling. Furthermore, Christian school communities should be characterized by grace so that the world sees that God is at work within them.

It is a biblical norm for human beings to live in community. From the beginning when God made Eve as a partner with Adam, through God's covenant with Abram to make Israel His people, into the second covenant between God and the people of His kingdom, the Bible's constant emphasis is on relationships as the key to faithful living. The immediate result of the gift of the Holy Spirit was a community of Christians in which "they committed themselves to the teaching of the apostles, *the life together*, the common meal, and the prayers" (Acts 2:42, *The Message*, emphasis added). Jesus used the image of the vine and branches; Paul used the picture of community as a body in 1 Corinthians 12. The Bible says that Christians are *put together, joined together, built together, members together, heirs together, fitted together, held together*, and *will be caught up together*. "Each part gets its meaning from the body as a whole, not the other way around. The body we're talking about is Christ's body of chosen people. Each of us finds our meaning and function as a part of his body. But as a chopped-off finger or a cut-off toe we wouldn't amount to much, would we?" (Romans 12:4–5, *The Message*).

As Dallas Willard puts it, "The aim of God in history is the creation of an all-inclusive community of loving persons, with Himself included in that community as its prime sustainer and most glorious inhabitant" (cited in Foster 1978, 162).

A community that is nothing more than a group of individuals, all with dreams for what they need it to be, isn't community at all. As Dietrich Bonhoeffer warned, there is nothing more dangerous to authentic community than our dreams for it because we love those dreams more than the people around us. Community is not a human ideal, he says, but a divine reality (1954, 30).

Stanley Hauerwas and William Willimon put it this way: "Christian community, life in the colony, is not primarily about togetherness. It is about the way of Jesus Christ with those whom he calls to himself. It is about disciplining our wants and needs in congruence with a true story, which gives us the resources to live truthful lives. In living out the story together, togetherness happens, but only as a by-product of the main project of trying to be faithful to Jesus" (1989, 78).

The Christian school community can become a community by being clear about its center, about what Thomas Sergiovanni calls a "community of the mind" (1994, 7). He writes, "Communities are defined by their centers of values, sentiments, and beliefs that provide the needed conditions for creating a sense of 'we' from 'I' " (4).

The *center* of the Christian school begins with a passionate commitment to live as disciples of Jesus Christ and to develop a worldview based on the lordship of Christ over all creation. A Christian "community of the mind" will have a clearly understood theology and philosophy that becomes the touchstone for all the activities of the school. Further, a community of the mind requires that the members work together to define a mission, vision, and belief about the nature of mankind, of teaching and learning, and of all members as God's image bearers. A Christian school that is a community of the mind will know what it is trying to accomplish and how to use a diversity of gifts to reach those goals. A community of the mind in a Christian school will devote its resources to developing its members into a learning community that practices teamwork, collegiality, cooperation, and the development and use of all gifts.

Boundary issues can draw any Christian school into divisive discussions. But where the core set of beliefs and values is clearly communicated and understood, these discussions can deepen understanding and commitment to the school's mission and vision.

No formula or twelve-step plan for achieving this community of the mind exists. It requires the hard, patient, and persistent work of a community with wise leadership committed to achieving the goal.

Christian communities have Christ at the center as the members collectively work out their discipleship commitment to be prophets, priests, and kings to their culture. Grace is the hallmark characteristic of Christian communities.

Communities of Grace

Scott Hoezee describes God's grace in this way:

> We could define grace as being first of all that power of God, rooted in his abiding love, by which God forgives the sinful, accepts the unacceptable, revives the spiritually dead, and so enables a reunion between the Creator and his wayward creatures....
>
> Beyond forgiveness, grace also aims to transform our way of life. Encountering God's grace is a formative, creative moment as a result of which a person is not only graced by God's love but also becomes *gracious* because of God's love." (1996, 4; emphasis in original)

Lewis Smedes writes,

> Grace ... is shorthand for everything that God is and does for us in our tired and sinful broken lives....
>
> Grace is the one word for all that God is for us in the form of Jesus Christ. (1982, 3)

Sloppy grace replaces the grace of the Bible with mercy, letting people off the hook for their sins. Some want to see people get what is coming to them for breaking the rules, unless they themselves have broken the rules. People want others to pay for their violations while they themselves escape the consequences. Others want to change other people by making examples of them. But Jesus shows a better way in the story of the woman caught in adultery. Jesus turns the tables on her accusers by replacing the two categories of sinners (the woman) and the righteous (the men) with two different categories: sinners who admit and sinners who deny. But He does not stop when He declines to condemn her. He says, "Go, and sin no more" (John 8:11, KJV). Accepting other people does not mean refusing to confront or challenge that sin in them which could harm others and damage their own souls. Failure to confront, to speak the truth in love, can ultimately be as fatal to the growth of community as judgmentalism.

Christian educators need to remember that they are sinners saved by grace. When people become disciples of Jesus, they join the community of all those who have been called to serve the kingdom. Christians are not better than other people; they need to remember that they are beggars telling other beggars where to find food. The school community in which Christians live and nurture their children must reflect the redeemed character of their lives. Christian schools, families, and churches must be communities of grace—places where every member will feel the hands of God.

What might characterize a school that is striving to become a Christian community of grace?

Grateful

A persistent sin in all faith communities is the sin of ingratitude. Faith communities always want more, better, different. They never to seem to have enough money or enough stuff, even though they live incredibly well by most of the world's standards. They tend to complain about anything that causes discomfort, forgetting, in Bonhoeffer's words, "When Christ calls a man, he bids him come and die" (1954, 8). On the other hand, in a community of grace, the members are constantly remembering and celebrating God's blessings: the gift of salvation and the power of the Holy Spirit, enabling them to overcome their sinful nature and at least occasionally be the kinds of people that God wants them to be. Will those who overhear the conversations of faculty and staff—at home, in the staff lounge, at school events, in the local coffee shop, or in the fellowship hall at church—hear the constant refrain of a grateful people, or a litany of woes? A community of grace is grateful, even in the face of the most challenging circumstances.

Mission-driven

A community of grace is focused on its work, defined by its mission. The Lord's Prayer captures the essence of the Christian's mission in the phrase "your kingdom come, your will be done on earth as it is in heaven" (Matthew 6:10). Jesus' essential work was preaching and modeling "the good news of the kingdom" (Matthew 4:23), a phrase that is found repeatedly in the first three Gospels. The mission of Christians, as disciples following in the dust of Jesus the rabbi, is to make it down here as it is up there. They are called to the work of restoring what sin and the Fall have corrupted, including their life together in school. A mission-driven school sees its work in relationship to the ongoing vision of the coming to fullness of the kingdom of God on the earth, completed by Christ's return. A mission-driven school looks outward at the world's need for healing and redemption. A mission-driven school knows that it has God's work to do and is constantly reminding its members, in its service projects and prayers, that even the very young can be a blessing to hurting people.

Mission, rightly understood, can unify a diverse community. Unity in community also flows from the understanding that all people have been created by God with His fingerprints all over them. Unity in community is found in the desire and commitment to be Christ followers. Unity in community is also found in traditions, which take the nonnegotiable truths of Scripture and attempt to apply them to life together. But because no one person and no one tradition can fully capture God's image or Christ's teaching, Christians tend to allow the negotiable elements of their traditions to divide them. A community of grace focuses attention on what binds them together and shows grace in inviting dialogue and discussion about the issues on the margins.

Inviting

A community of grace is persistently inviting. Adults are rarely deliberately disinviting (with the possible exception of when the fourth telemarketing call interrupts dinner). Christian theology is invitational and hospitable by nature; and homes, churches, and schools should be open, inviting, hospitable places where new students, parents, and guests are gladly welcomed and made to feel at home.

Unfortunately, students do not always feel very welcome, because all too often schools are unintentionally disinviting. A teacher introducing ratios to a fifth-grade class selects the largest and smallest boys to illustrate the concept, highlighting the painfully obvious differences between the two and causing an anguish of embarrassment for both boys.

When teachers and staff and students live in a building all day, they don't always realize how hard it can be for a guest to find the way to the restroom or the appropriate office. The physical environments of schools likewise send multiple messages of invitation or disinvitation to people who visit. Dark corridors, bad smells, dingy or institutional colors, overflowing trash containers, bare walls, dead or dusty plants, peeling paint, rust, sticky floors, lack of handicap access, and no designated parking for visitors are a kind of institutional bad breath.

Nonverbal behavior can be equally disinviting. Ignoring people in the halls, continuing to work at a task without looking up when someone enters the office, frowning, breaking a promise to call back "today," looking at a watch during a serious conversation, ignoring a student's question, interrupting someone who is trying to explain something, doodling or shuffling papers when someone is speaking, and being late are all what William Purkey (1984) calls examples of disinviting messages that communicate to the recipients that they are irresponsible, incapable, insignificant, not worth our time, and therefore not expected to make a useful contribution to the community.

On the other hand, an inviting message (Purkey 1984) tells people they are valuable, able, responsible, and invited to use their gifts and talents to take part in the worthwhile activities of the community. Inviting messages include verbal comments such as these: "Good morning." "Thank you." "We missed you." "We've been thinking about you and praying for you." "How are you doing?" "I am impressed!" "Of course I have the time!" "Let's do it together." "I like what you did." "How can I help?"

Inviting nonverbal messages include shaking hands, offering hugs (when appropriate), giving pats on the back, arriving on time, sending a thoughtful note, returning phone and email messages promptly, learning names and using them correctly, smiling, picking up trash, showing someone how to find the way instead of just pointing. All these behaviors express a warm, caring, accepting, and hospitable attitude. Common civility is another often overlooked, very simple, deliberately inviting behavior.

All Christians believe that human beings are created in the image of God and have intrinsic worth, as well as gifts and talents to be used in partnership with other members of the communities in which God has placed them. For that reason, schools that are committed to the vision of becoming communities of grace will make a constant effort to be deliberately and consistently inviting, to make all members and guests feel welcomed, affirmed, valuable, and able.

A deliberately inviting community can have a major impact on the behavior of its members. Such a climate encourages respect for individuals, a cooperative spirit, and a sense of belonging, hope, and high expectations.

Accepting

Members of a community of grace should feel the hands of God through one another. Martin Buber describes such a relationship as an "I-You" relationship, in contrast to an "I-It" relationship (1970, 53). Lewis Smedes writes about the grace of seeing others with "the magic eyes"—eyes that see past the surface behavior into a person's heart to see the soul that God is calling (1984, xiii–xv). One of the practical consequences of this concept is that no Christian school should tolerate any kind of bullying, harassment, or put-downs. No person in our school communities should ever treat any other person as an "it," and those who do should be quickly and strictly held to account. A community of grace always protects its weakest members.

However, communities that think love can be practiced without discipline will quickly disintegrate. Learning and teaching how to nudge others when it's needed by being direct but kind and without ascribing motives or giving labels to those who have strayed are skills all Christians need to learn and practice. Kind but direct discipline is a channel, not a stainless steel wall with no handholds.

A community of grace is the context in which sin should be confronted. Dallas Willard writes, "We do not have to—we *cannot*—surrender the valid practice of distinguishing and discerning how things are in order to avoid condemning others. We *can*, however, train ourselves to hold people responsible and discuss their failures with them—and even assign them penalties, if we are, for example, in some position over them—without attacking their worth as human beings or marking them as rejects" (1997, 225; emphasis in original).

A community of grace is patient and persistent with its members. The Bible tells the story of the master who forgave a servant's large debt, only to have the servant throw one of his customers into jail over a much smaller debt. Members of a community of grace remember how much they need to be forgiven, and they are in turn willing to forgive others again and again. One can argue that the grace of forgiveness is the most powerful of all gifts from God's love, and that experiencing and practicing forgiveness is one of the most powerful gifts that must be given in a community of faith. Jesus powerfully links forgiveness and love in the Gospel account of a "woman who had lived a sinful life" when she anointed Jesus with a jar of perfume. Jesus said, "She loved much. But he who has been forgiven little loves little" (Luke 7:37, 47).

A community of grace always seeks repentance and restoration of relationships as a result of its discipline. People in a community of grace practice the biblical model of admonition, confession, repentance, and restoration with one another. The world—torn as it is with divisions, differences, quarrels, disappointments, losses, and sin—desperately needs to learn and practice these acts of grace.

Loving

Bonhoeffer (1954) writes that a caring community based on a human wish or social ideal is bound to fail. Human love cannot tolerate the absence of love in return. Only spiritual love (*agape*) can enable us to maintain fellowship with an enemy, someone who seriously and stubbornly resists our human love. Human love tends to produce hothouse flowers; spiritual love nurtures the free-flowering of the fruits of the Spirit. This spiritual love is summarized in 1 Corinthians 13:4–7. Eugene Peterson has paraphrased this passage in *The Message*:

> Love never gives up.
> Love cares more for others than for self.
> Love doesn't want what it doesn't have.
> Love doesn't strut,
> Doesn't have a swelled head,
> Doesn't force itself on others,
> Isn't always "me first,"
> Doesn't fly off the handle,
> Doesn't keep score of the sins of others,
> Doesn't revel when others grovel,
> Takes pleasure in the flowering of truth,
> Puts up with anything,
> Trusts God always,
> Always looks for the best,
> Never looks back,
> But keeps going to the end.

Some things are loved because they are worthy; some things are worthy because they are loved. God so loved the world that He gave His one and only Son. By going to the Cross, Jesus showed that His love was fierce in its intensity—almost a battle cry. Every major part of God's plan—the Creation, the Exodus, the return from exile, the coming of Christ our Savior, the gift of the Holy Spirit—has God's love behind it. The good news of the gospel is that God will not leave people just as they are. The bad news is that God will not leave people just as they are. God's love is a refining fire; it is always out to render people new, beautiful, and lovely, to remake them into God's original design—and even beyond that original design to something altogether new and transcendent.

A community of grace is characterized by God's love flowing through the speech and behavior of all the members.

Living Stones

Peter describes Christ's followers as "living stones," who are "being built into a spiritual house to be a holy priesthood" (1 Peter 2:5). It was a common practice among Jewish people to erect "standing stones" to tell important stories of God's faithfulness. When the Israelites crossed the Jordan River into the Promised Land, God commanded that each tribe select a stone to place on the riverbank to serve as a sign: "When your children ask you, 'What do these stones mean?' tell them ..." (Joshua 4:6–7). Adults in school are the living stones—models and examples of God's faithfulness in the lives of His people from generation to generation. One of the implications of this understanding is that adults in a school community should be prepared to share their faith storeis, the stories of God's grace in their own lives. But it also means that the adults in school are models for one another and for children and parents.

Research on modeling clearly shows that the decisive determinant of how children act is always the action of the model. Nicholas Wolterstorff says, "Overwhelmingly, it was the model's practice that influenced the practice of the subject.... Preaching induced *preaching* rather than practice" (1980, 57; emphasis in original). Adult behavior—especially by adults who are high in a child's affection and esteem because of their prestige, power, intelligence, and competence—has a profound influence on the behavior of children. Teachers are almost inevitably prime candidates for decisive modeling influence. How teachers behave themselves is even more important than what they say when it comes to affecting student behaviors. Teachers or administrators who are mean-spirited will thereby increase the incidence of mean-spirited acts in their students. No amount of noble or pious talk will counteract a mean spirit.

One of the keys to earning respect and trust is consistency between deeds and words. People respect others who do what they say they will do—who are covenant keepers, people of integrity. When students turn in their homework, take tests, or write essays, teachers need to keep their word about when that work will be returned with grades and comments. Teachers need to use classroom time wisely and well, starting class on time and ending with a bang, not a whimper. Teachers need to come to class prepared, no matter how skilled they are at winging it. Teachers need to model diligence and responsibility, and not just preach about them to students.

Adults in a community of grace also need to model confession of sin as an example for one another and for students. When teachers and administrators recognize that they have been unfair, that they have rushed to judgment before listening carefully, or that they haven't kept their promises, they need to practice the spiritual disciplines of confessing, asking forgiveness, and seeking reconciliation.

Trustworthy people are confidence keepers. Gossip is a persistent sin in Christian school communities, even when it is sanctified by referring to the "grapevine." Students have frequently testified that they hate the talk about them that goes on in faculty rooms and staff lounges, which they rightly discern is too often not complimentary.

Dietrich Bonhoeffer recommends that members of a Christian community diligently practice the "ministry of holding one's tongue" (1954, 91). Referring to James 3:2 ("He who holds his tongue in check controls both mind and body"), Bonhoeffer goes on to say, "Thus it must be a decisive rule of every Christian fellowship that each individual is prohibited from saying much that occurs to him" (92). Proverbs 10:19 says, "When words are many, sin is not absent, but he who holds his tongue is wise." Following such a rule would transform most Christian schools into much quieter places.

Living Water

The prominence of water as a biblical image fits the cultural and geographical context of the land in which God's people lived. As those who travel there today quickly discover, water is scarce—so scarce that there is some speculation that the Middle East will someday become a bloody battleground, not over oil reserves, but water. God's people spent their first forty years of freedom from Egypt in the desert south of the Promised Land. In addition to providing manna and quail, God supplied them with water.

Over the centuries of life in that region, water held the key to life. The snows on Mount Hermon melted in summer to fill the Galilee and the Jordan rivers. At certain times of the year, the dew descended at night, even in very dry areas, to nourish sprigs of grass, the green pastures for the flocks and herds of goats and sheep. Shepherds and farmers dug wells and cisterns to capture what water was available.

Cisterns served as prisons (Jeremiah 38:6–13) and as hiding places (2 Samuel 17:18). Herod built a four-story plastered cistern in the side of his fortress at Masada. He designed it to contain a ten-year supply of water.

In this context God used the picture of cisterns to describe human plans: "My people have committed two sins: They have forsaken me, the spring of living water, and have dug their own cisterns, broken cisterns that cannot hold water" (Jeremiah 2:13).

Water running from a spring or river came to be known as "living water," in contrast to the stagnant water of wells and cisterns. In the Old Testament, God is associated with springs of living water (Psalm 107:35, Isaiah 35:6–7, Jeremiah 2:13). Jesus described Himself as living water in John 4:13–14 and 7:37–38. Jesus used this image at the end of the Jewish feast of Sukkot, which took place at the end of the dry season. Included in the ceremonies was a priestly procession to the Pool of Siloam, which is fed by the Spring of Gihon. It was a ritual asking God for life-giving rain.

"On the last and greatest day of the Feast [in the midst of the water ceremony], Jesus stood and said in a loud voice, 'If anyone is thirsty, let him come to me and drink. Whoever believes in me, as the Scripture has said, streams of living water will flow from within him' " (John 7:37–38).

Christian teachers and administrators continue to find their strength in a relationship with Jesus Christ, renewed daily through their personal devotions and corporate worship. As Spirit-filled, redeemed people, they in turn can be "streams of living water" to their students, especially when those students find themselves struggling in a wilderness of doubt, low self-esteem, ill health, conflict, or other trouble. As these students come to believe in Jesus, they in turn can become living water to their classmates, their parents, and other family members.

In a community of grace, living water flows every day, and hope is born and nurtured in the soul of every member.

Now What? Application to Practice

WHILE IT IS not possible to force the people in a school to become a community, there are things a leader can do to help establish an environment in which community can develop and flourish. Here are some suggested activities:

A. Schools striving to be communities need to address several questions. Effective answers to these questions require that faculty and staff meet in small groups to discuss and share their thoughts. Teachers can lead discussions about these questions in their classes as well.

- What can we do to increase the sense of connection, caring, neighborliness, and collegiality in our school?
- What is disinviting about our school, and what can I do to be more intentionally inviting?

B. Schools that want to become communities of grace are learning to use the language of grace. School leaders might consider a small-group study of a book on this topic, such as Donovan Graham's *Teaching Redemptively*, Dietrich Bonhoeffer's *Life Together*, or John Ortberg's *Everybody's Normal Till You Get to Know Them*.

C. Ideas bind people together into what Thomas Sergiovanni calls a "community of the mind." One practical way to become a like-minded community is for the faculty and staff to develop "lists of five"—promises and commitments that are widely displayed and published and that reflect the beliefs, values, mission, and vision of the school. These lists might include the following:

- Five promises we make to students
- Five promises we make to one another
- Five characteristics you will see in our teaching
- Five things we expect from parents
- Five things that parents can expect from us
- Five examples of great assignments that teachers give
- Five examples of great student work

Discussion of these lists has great value in itself, but when the lists are posted and published, they invite students and parents to hold the school accountable for keeping its promises.

D. Henri Nouwen observes, "Community is the place where the person you least want to live with always lives" (cited in Ortberg 2003, 13). School leaders can sensitively explore conflict in the community in order to develop biblical models for dealing with conflict and to develop plans for teaching these biblical values and skills to students.

E. A community of grace is rich in relationships. Relationships depend on our careful use of the gift of language. In a faculty-staff retreat or in a workshop setting, participants can read and reflect on Colossians 3:1–17 for a few days before meeting. Faculty and staff can focus on Colossians 3:12 and answer these questions:

- How can we learn to express the truth in love?
- How can we learn to be kind but direct as we hold each other accountable for what we say and do?
- How do we respond with grace to relationship issues?
- How will our language reflect "compassion, kindness, humility, gentleness and patience"?

Then, small groups can role-play and discuss the following case studies:

1. Jack is a high school senior who is chronically late for his first-period class. As his first-period teacher, how will you address this concern in ways that reflect the instruction in Colossians 3:12?

2. A teacher is chronically late for playground duty, leaving her colleague alone to keep an eye on all the children. The conscientious teacher on duty grows increasingly frustrated by her colleague's tardiness. What should she say to her colleague in the spirit of Colossians 3:12?

3. A student often arrives at school looking unkempt, wearing clothing that is dirty, wrinkled, and sometimes torn. The student often has no lunch, or a lunch consisting of a bag of chips and a juice box. The parent is a single working mother of three children. As the child's teacher, you want to call the mother about this situation, which the other children have noticed. How will your conversation be infused with grace?

References

Barnes, M. Craig. 2003. *Searching for home: Spirituality for restless souls*. Grand Rapids, MI: Brazos Press.

Bonhoeffer, Dietrich. 1954. *Life together*. Trans. John W. Doberstein. New York: Harper and Row.

Buber, Martin. 1970. *I and thou*. Trans. Walter Kaufmann. New York: Touchstone.

Foster, Richard J. 1978. *Celebration of discipline*. San Francisco: Harper and Row.

Graham, Donovan L. 2003. *Teaching redemptively: Bringing grace and truth into your classroom*. Colorado Springs, CO: Purposeful Design Publications.

Hauerwas, Stanley, and William H. Willimon. 1989. *Resident aliens: Life in the Christian colony*. Nashville, TN: Abingdon Press.

Hoezee, Scott. 1996. *The riddle of grace: Applying grace to the Christian life.* Grand Rapids, MI: Eerdmans.

Institute for American Values. 2003. *Hardwired to connect: The new scientific case for authoritative communities.* New York: Institute for American Values.

Myers, David G. 2000. *The American paradox: Spiritual hunger in an age of plenty.* New Haven, CT: Yale University Press.

Ortberg, John. 2003. *Everybody's normal till you get to know them.* Grand Rapids, MI: Zondervan.

Purkey, William Watson. 1984. *Inviting school success: A self-concept approach to teaching and learning.* 2nd ed. Belmont, CA: Wadsworth.

Putnam, Robert D. 2000. *Bowling alone: The collapse and revival of American community.* New York: Simon and Schuster.

Sergiovanni, Thomas J. 1994. *Building community in schools.* San Francisco: Jossey-Bass.

Smedes, Lewis B. 1982. *How can it be all right when everything is all wrong?* New York: Harper and Row.

_____. 1984. *Forgive and forget: Healing the hurts we don't deserve.* New York: Harper and Row.

Willard, Dallas. 1997. *The divine conspiracy: Rediscovering our hidden life in God.* New York: HarperCollins.

Wolterstorff, Nicholas P. 1980. *Educating for responsible action.* Grand Rapids, MI: Eerdmans.

CHAPTER 2

THE GOSPEL OF MERCY AND JUSTICE

Schools as Agents of Societal Change

❧

Vernard T. Gant

Vernard T. Gant, DMin, is the director of urban school services for ACSI. He graduated from Columbia International University, Birmingham Theological Seminary, and Trinity Evangelical Divinity School. Along with his wife, Cynthia, he helped develop two urban Christian schools in Birmingham and has been involved in urban ministry for thirty years.

CHAPTER 2

THE GOSPEL OF MERCY AND JUSTICE

Vernard T. Gant

MANY CHRISTIAN SCHOOL leaders consider it part of their mission to encourage students to become engaged in ministry and to prepare them for that ministry. While some students will devote themselves to full-time or vocational ministry, the ultimate desire is that all Christian school graduates practice lifestyle ministry—that is, wherever they go or in whatever vocation they engage, they will "do" ministry. This desired or expected student outcome is evident in the mission and vision statements of many Christian schools. Often there is some mention of the Great Commission, the impact that the graduates of a particular school will make on society, or both. In whatever position or capacity, the goal is that Christian school students will minister the love of God to a broken world.

A Broader Mission

All the ills of society are rooted in two basic violations: a failure to love God and a failure to love others. When an expert in the law of Moses asked Jesus what was required to "inherit eternal life," Jesus asked what the Law said. The expert quoted, " 'Love the Lord your God with all your heart and with all your soul and with all your strength and with all your mind'; and 'Love your neighbor as yourself' " (Luke 10:25–27). Jesus commended him for his answer. Christians affirm the lawyer's statements as the two great commandments.

Implicit in these commandments is that the fundamental governing principle of salvation and eternal life is love. To love God is to keep His commandments; to love others is to seek their highest good. Every failure to love God is idolatry because it involves putting something or someone before Him. Every failure to love others is injustice because it either actively harms them or passively withholds from them what they need. The apostle Paul, under the inspiration of the Holy Spirit, states it succinctly: "Love does no harm to its neighbor. Therefore love is the fulfillment of the law" (Romans 13:10).

Some Christian educators have a simplistic view of what it takes to fulfill these two commandments. Their emphasis is on getting people saved. The assumption is that when a person fulfills the first command-ment (love God), the second commandment (love the neighbor) will automatically follow. This chapter maintains that school leaders must intentionally address both commandments in order for students to fulfill both of them. This world shows the wounds of millennia of sin. Individ-uals and groups and whole societies are broken and needy. If we expect Christian school students to love their neighbors in God's name, they must be taught how to do so. They must internalize the truth that when they committed their lives to follow Christ they enlisted in a broader mission than simply evangelizing the lost. They are called to be God's agents of love and reconciliation and restoration; they have a role in repairing what sin has broken.

Justice and mercy

The concept of this broader mission can be found throughout the Old Testament. For example, God revealed to the prophet Micah His requirements of people and His assessment of ultimate good: "He has showed you, O man, what is good. And what does the Lord require of you? To act justly and to love mercy and to walk humbly with your God" (Micah 6:8).

Jesus describes these issues as the "weightier" matters of the law (Mat-thew 23:23, NKJV). Upon reproving the religious leaders of His day, Jesus pointed out that they had meticulously engaged in their religious activities but had "neglected the more important matters of the law—justice, mercy and faithfulness" (Matthew 23:23). Justice simply means to do what is right. It means aligning with God's law—His requirements. Mercy goes a step further by not only doing what is right toward others but acting toward others as we would have them act toward us. Mercy is illustrated in the parable of the good Samaritan. There was no law that required the Samaritan to assist the victim on the Jericho road—other than God's command to "love your neighbor as yourself" (Luke 10:27). After identifying the two great commandments, the expert in the Law asked, "And who is my neighbor?" (10:29). Jesus told the parable in response to his question. After telling the parable, Jesus asked the questioner, "Which ... was a neighbor to the man who fell into the hands of robbers?" The correct and telling response followed: "The one who had mercy on him" (Luke 10:36–37).

Mercy is love in action. Not only does love do no harm, but it also seeks the best interests of one's neighbor, as Jesus indicated in the parable. This parable teaches that one who loves seeks to remedy the ills of society—first by no longer contributing to its ills (doing justly), and second by endeavoring to correct existing ills (showing mercy). Furthermore, the parable clearly establishes that the definition of *neighbor* crosses societal lines. In other words, one's neighbors are *all* the members of society; and in loving their neighbors, the members of God's kingdom serve as agents of healing. In doing so, they both represent and promote the kingdom among those who have not yet embraced it.

Harvie Conn summarizes this truth: "What will be the instrument of the church in effecting this change? Not simply charity but also justice. Charity is episodic, justice is ongoing. One brings consolation, the other correction. One aims at symptoms, the other at causes. The one changes individuals, the other societies. One cries out in the name of Jesus, 'I love you.' The other adds, 'Because I love you, I do for you what is right'" (1987, 147).

The broader mission of the church is applied in four instances in Scripture where it is recorded that Jesus sent His disciples to bear witness to Him. The passages below contain a common theme:

> He called his twelve disciples to him and gave them authority to
> drive out evil spirits and to heal every disease and sickness.... "As you
> go, preach this message: 'The kingdom of heaven is near.' Heal the
> sick, raise the dead, cleanse those who have leprosy, drive out demons."
> (Matthew 10:1, 7–8)

He appointed twelve ... that they might be with him and that he might send them out to preach and to have authority to drive out demons.... They went out and preached that people should repent. They drove out many demons and anointed many sick people with oil and healed them. (Mark 3:14–15, 6:12–13)

When Jesus had called the Twelve together, he gave them power and authority to drive out all demons and to cure diseases, and he sent them out to preach the kingdom of God and to heal the sick. (Luke 9:1–2)

"When you enter a town and are welcomed ... Heal the sick who are there and tell them, 'The kingdom of God is near you.' " (Luke 10:8–9)

The kingdom of God

When Christ sent His disciples into the world, their primary task was to declare that the kingdom of God was at hand. Along with this proclamation, however, was a demonstration of the power of the kingdom. The power of the kingdom is its ability to effect change where it is present. In every instance, when Jesus dispatched His disciples, they addressed people at their point of brokenness. The Greek word for *heal* is *therapeuo*. The kingdom of God carries with it the therapeutic power to address the sick, the leprous, the demonized, and the diseased.

Speaking through the prophet Ezekiel, God reproved the shepherds who had been entrusted with the care of His people for their failure to properly care for them. He expressed consternation and pronounced condemnation upon them: "You have not strengthened the weak or healed the sick or bound up the injured. You have not brought back the strays or searched for the lost" (Ezekiel 34:4). Because of the great love that God has for His sheep, He committed Himself to addressing their plight, saying, "I will search for the lost and bring back the strays. I will bind up the injured and strengthen the weak.... I will shepherd the flock with justice" (Ezekiel 34:16).

God promised through the prophet Jeremiah that He would raise up shepherds who were according to His own heart. These shepherds would feed His people with knowledge and understanding (Jeremiah 3:15). Of course, the ultimate fulfillment of this promise is His Son, Jesus Christ, who came as the Good Shepherd and gave His life for the sheep (John 10:11). He is the Shepherd who is so concerned for His lost sheep that He leaves ninety-nine sheep in the fold to search for the lost one (Luke 15:3–7). Or, as He put it on another occasion, "Those who are well have no need of a physician" (Matthew 9:12, NKJV). He comes to address the plight of the sick.

This theme of the kingdom as an instrument of healing and deliverance is embodied by Christ at His first public address. Upon launching His earthly ministry, Jesus stated, "The Spirit of the Lord is on me, because he has anointed me to preach good news to the poor. He has sent me to proclaim freedom for the prisoners and recovery of sight for the blind, to release the oppressed, to proclaim the year of the Lord's favor" (Luke 4:18–19).

These activities both accompany and manifest the operation of His kingdom. The kingdom is seen most clearly by the way it addresses broken people. Such manifestation is as obvious as light in the midst of darkness and salt on savorless food. It has such an impact that it causes the casual observer to sit up and take notice. It provokes inquiry that calls for some type of explanation. The explanation, of course, is that the kingdom of God is present. What is observed is the power of the kingdom to make an impact and to effect change where it is present.

How do Christian schools and educators prepare and engage their students in the work of ministry by promoting the gospel and addressing the ills of society?

Primary vs. Secondary Beliefs

The Christian school must confront the natural human tendency to grade, rate, or classify external, observable differences among people groups. Racial differences are classified as superior or inferior. Social differences are classified as upper or lower. Cultural differences are graded as advanced or primitive. These biased value judgments are passed on from generation to generation, either formally or informally, via various modes of communication. Categories such as these establish in the individual a primary belief structure or frame of reference that determines that person's social cognition. As a result, the behavior of the observed group is often interpreted in light of the primary beliefs, and the behavior also has the effect of reinforcing those beliefs. Such primary beliefs are often behind such statements as "Why do black people …?" or "Poor people don't …" Such broad biases can apply to everything from the way people talk to the way they worship.

Primary beliefs tend to be very resistant to change. While it is possible

29

to layer them with other beliefs, it is rarely possible to eradicate them. That is why, typically, people adamantly state that they are not prejudiced, even though all individuals have prejudices. For example, many teachers working in Christian schools are there because they want to make a difference in the lives of children and in society. Although their intentions are usually noble and well-meaning, the fact remains that these same teachers approach their classrooms with a latent belief structure about different people groups, including their students. These beliefs form early in the teacher's life and inform the primary sentiments that the teacher has toward other people. These sentiments can lie dormant for years. The teacher can even attempt to suppress them or overcome them by a commitment to make a positive contribution to the lives of others, including those who are different. This positive attitude and the ensuing behaviors form the basis of the teacher's secondary beliefs. The problem arises, however, when the teacher's primary beliefs are triggered and reinforced by observed performances or behaviors that conflict with the secondary beliefs.

For example, teachers in a Christian school might object to taking in students from a lower socioeconomic class because of the belief that low-income parents do not value education and therefore do not provide adequate parental support. The teacher, however, has been taught to establish a secondary belief structure that "all children can learn." The teacher works sincerely and diligently to make learning happen for all the students. If, however, the child from the low-income home does poorly in the classroom, there is a natural tendency—based on a primary belief—to equate the child's inferior performance with the child's socioeconomic class. In other words, the teacher observes how the child is performing academically and draws a conclusion—or has an assumption reinforced—about the child. The applied secondary belief gives way to the acquired primary belief.

The teacher's beliefs establish and fuel the expectations concerning the students. Jeff Howard and Ray Hammond summarize such self-fulfilling expectations:

> Years of research have clearly demonstrated the powerful impact of expectancies on performance. The expectations of teachers for their students have a large effect on their academic achievement. Psychological studies under a variety of circumstances demonstrate that communicated expectations induce people to believe that they will do well or

poorly at a task, and that such beliefs very often trigger responses that result in performance consistent with the expectation. There is also evidence that "reference group expectancies"—directed at an entire category of people rather than a particular individual—have a similar impact on the performance of members of the group. (1985, 19–20)

The Christian school must educate its students to help them recognize their biases and address them in such a way that they do not act on and transmit those biases in society. Such education must begin with the Christian school staff. Development of racial, cultural, and social sensitivity and awareness is one step in the process. Another critical step—and perhaps the most difficult—is bias cognition. That is, people need assistance in recognizing their latent biases, or primary beliefs, which are based on the natural prejudices born of their affinity toward people with whom they relate. Primary beliefs are also based on an individual's introduction to and orientation toward people of another race, class, or culture. This introduction shapes the primary beliefs a person has toward other people. The primary beliefs form the basis for expectancy beliefs and expectancy communications. In other words, the initial beliefs about another person's race, culture, or class form the basis of what is expected behaviorally from that person and what expectations are communicated to that person.

Secular vs. Sacred Ministry

In addition to helping people recognize and confront their biases, the Christian school must pay attention to how it categorizes and teaches ministry. Historically, the church and its education arm, the Christian school, have classified ministry into two basic categories.

The first category can best be described as spiritual ministry. This type of ministry focuses primarily on the internal spiritual dimension of a person's life. The desire is for all individuals to hear the gospel in the hope that they will dedicate their lives to Jesus Christ as their Lord and Savior. Those individuals who accept Christ then begin observing the spiritual disciplines while following spiritual codes or ethics. Even when believers participate in externally based activities such as feeding and clothing those in need, the objective is to win the right to preach the gospel in order to save souls.

The second category of ministry is largely external in nature and

31

usually includes assistance to address physical and emotional needs. This type of ministry has been described as social or mercy ministry. Soup kitchens, homeless shelters, and food pantries are just a few of the efforts that fall into this category of ministry. Even in this type of ministry, however, the first objective is usually present. People are given the things needed for their physical well-being, but for the purpose of evangelism. Once the people have been clothed, fed, counseled, or entertained, then the gospel will be presented to them in the hope that they will accept Christ into their lives.

A Christian education that focuses exclusively on an invisible, spiritual view of ministry can inadvertently promote an unbiblical dichotomy between the sacred, which is seen as inward and personal, and the secular, which is considered merely outward and public. This dichotomy can foster the belief that God values one above the other. It misses the fact that, in the end, there will be "a new heaven and a new earth" (Revelation 21:1). It misses the fact that God never negated, suspended, or corrected the original mandate to take care of the earth. This truth is often missed as Christian schools and educators endeavor to equip their students to engage in ministry. The emphasis is too often on personal faith and piety, with a secondary or minor emphasis on public service. For fear of promoting a social gospel, the tendency is to shy away from social responsibility while emphasizing only personal responsibility. The result can be faith without works. (See James 2:14–18.)

This dichotomy between sacred and secular partially explains why, in the past, godly men could practice and promote a system of brutal slavery and deny certain human beings—people created in God's image—the basic civil rights of life, liberty, and the pursuit of happiness. This also explains how devout Christians could be devoted Klansmen. Michael Emerson and Christian Smith (2000, 132) describe a consequence of such a dichotomy:

> White evangelicals, without any necessary intent, help to buttress
> the racialized society. Like their forebears during Jim Crow segregation,
> who prescribed kindness toward people of other races and getting to
> know people across races, but did not challenge the Jim Crow system,
> present-day white evangelicals attempt to solve the race problem with-
> out shaking the foundations on which racialization is built. As long
> as they do not see or acknowledge the structures of racialization, they
> inadvertently contribute to them. And, insofar as they continue to give

solutions that do not challenge racialization, they allow racial inequality and division to continue unabated.

The Christian school must equip its students to understand and apply the essence of the gospel along with all its implications for the individual and for society. This education must include as its goal that the student learn to contextualize the gospel through personal example and proclamation. Thus, the products of Christian school education must become part of the solution to the ills of society and no longer contributors to those ills. They must embrace what Charles Colson and Nancy Pearcey (1999, 295–96) describe as the cultural mandate:

> It is our contention in this book that the Lord's cultural commission is inseparable from the great commission. That may be a jarring statement for many conservative Christians, who, through much of the twentieth century, have shunned the notion of reforming culture, associating that concept with the liberal social gospel. The only task of the church, many fundamentalists and evangelicals have believed, is to save as many lost souls as possible from a world literally going to hell. But this implicit denial of a Christian worldview is unbiblical and is the reason we have lost so much of our influence in the world. Salvation does not consist simply of freedom from sin; salvation also means being restored to the task we were given in the beginning—the job of creating culture.

Mercy vs. Pity Service

Groups and individuals who engage in charitable services toward the needy often seek the highest good of the giver rather than the highest good of the recipient. These efforts tend to be largely external and limited to targeting immediate needs. However, when these same individuals and groups are asked to support efforts that are more foundational and empowering in nature, they are often reluctant, and sometimes they refuse to do so. The rationale is either that there is not a perceived need, or that they have not felt led to do so. Moreover, they fail to distinguish between feeling pity and showing mercy.

Generally, *pity* focuses on the *giver* and is designed to make the giver feel better as a result of the act of giving. *Mercy*, on the other hand, focuses on the *recipient* and is designed to enable the recipient to do better. When a gift is given out of pity, the recipient is usually left in the same basic condition that prompted the gift; however, when the motivation is mercy, the recipient is usually better enabled to help himself so that the gift eventually is no longer needed. When the Samaritan of Jesus' parable helped the man who had become a victim, the goal was to give the man what was needed so that he would be made whole. The intention was to care for him in such a way that the services offered would one day no longer be necessary.

This principle of service is often missed because of a failure to understand and apply the Golden Rule of Matthew 7:12: "So in everything, do to others what you would have them do to you." We can apply this principle by using our own desires and interests as the standard: "What would I want done for and to me?" At the end of the day, we can gauge the outcome of our actions by asking, "Is this what I would have wanted?" This principle can also be applied to children. In settings such as the Christian school, when services to children are being discussed, those engaged in the discussions should ask, "Are the services and outcomes what we would want for our own children?" In working with a challenging or difficult child, Christian educators should approach the situation as if the child were their own. This principle is often missed since it applies to "other folk."

For example, there was a large white evangelical church that had sponsored an annual one-week children's camp for urban black children for well over a decade. The cost of sponsoring the camp had reached several thousand dollars. All efforts at year-round follow-up had proven futile, so what the camp staff accomplished in the lives of the children was limited to whatever transpired during that one week of the year. The camp sponsors were approached about using those same funds and efforts to establish a Christian school in the targeted poor community. The school could potentially make an impact on the lives of those same children nine months a year and could lay a foundation in their lives upon which they could build successful futures. That is, they could be educated to the point at which they no longer needed the benevolence of charitable camp sponsors. The sponsors of the camp expressed strong resistance to the proposal, saying, "Our people like doing things for the children." Apparently, they did not have the highest good of the children in mind, but rather the good feeling they experienced from temporarily helping the children. Had the discussion related to their own children—"What would we want for our children?"—there would not have been a discussion. Ultimately, they were driven by how they felt as opposed to what the children needed.

While a weeklong camp for children who otherwise could not afford it (although during the last few years of the camp, most of the children who attended were from well-to-do families) is a nice thing, it is nevertheless an assistance program; therefore, it will always need external support. On the other hand, an education is foundational in nature, and it will eventually enable the individual to be in a position in which support is no longer needed. It will also enable the individual to be a resourceful contributor one day. The response of the camp sponsors, however, fits the description of what Paulo Freire calls "assistencialism." Freire uses this term to describe "policies of financial or social assistance which attack symptoms, but not causes, of social ills" (1973, 15). The camp sponsors did not have the highest good of the children in mind, but rather the good feeling they derived from doing things for the children. In rejecting the counsel about the school, the camp sponsors violated what Freire calls "the important thing, [which] is to help men (and nations) help themselves, to place them in consciously critical confrontation with their problems, to make them the agents of their own recuperation" (16).

It is an insult and a major hindrance to progress for any individual or group to think that it can have a higher interest and can better provide for the long-term physical, social, and spiritual development of another group—especially when the members of that group are able to provide for their own needs when given the opportunity and the correct type of assistance. It is unnatural to continually export efforts to a people group to accomplish a task when those people possess the potential to do it themselves naturally and more effectively. This principle holds true whether that effort is "having a ministry" among a people group or revitalizing a community. Any other attitude hinges on paternalism, and paternalism hinders the development of those it "helps." Instead of fostering wholesome independence, it breeds a condition that destroys dignity and perpetuates dependency. Such behavior does not have the highest good of the target group at heart, but rather the highest good feeling of the giving group. When the goal is the highest good of the target group, the objective is to give the members of the target group the means to work toward their own development and self-sufficiency. *Empowerment* is a term often used to describe efforts of this nature.

Educating in the Weightier Matters

It is important to teach Christian school students their responsibility to act justly and love mercy while walking humbly with their God. As they do so, they make the crooked places straight, whether it is the crookedness in their own lives or in society. Ultimately, this approach involves holistic biblical reconciliation in one's relationship to God, self, and others.

One of the great hindrances and stumbling blocks in properly relating to God, self, and others is a faulty assessment of the worth of each. It is practically impossible to divorce one's assessments of self and others from the intrinsic estimation one has of God and His values. This assessment will inevitably determine both the giver's attitude and actions in addressing others and the receptivity of others to the giver. Thus, if there is a flaw in the estimation of the worth of the individuals who are receiving help, then the efforts of the givers are marred by that attitude. For example, if the givers feel that they are "better" than the recipients, their actions toward that group both stem from and reinforce the attitude of superiority. By the same token, if the recipients believe that they are in the condition they find themselves in because they are somehow inferior, the actions directed toward them will also reinforce this attitude, thereby perpetuating that misguided assumption. Both giver and recipient are further damaged because not only is their faulty, unbiblical thinking not corrected, but they are also more solidified in that thinking.

Lamentably, in a relativistic, secularized society, neither worth nor values are rooted in absolute truth. On the contrary, society teaches that worth is based on skin color, gender, genealogy, income, geography, and other extrinsic factors. Society, however, is not in a position to determine worth. Establishing worth is a right of the owner. God, who reveals Himself in the Holy Bible as the creator and owner of the universe, is alone in a position to confer value and worth to His creation; society does not have the right to determine the worth of that which belongs to another. Therefore, the ultimate question before every individual should be, "What is *God's* estimation of my worth?" God leaves absolutely no doubt concerning the answer to this question. In the sight of the God of Scripture, every individual has inestimable worth because every individual is made in God's image.

God has also demonstrated how valuable His creatures are to Him by providing a means by which they may know Him in an intimate manner and spend eternity with Him. God has demonstrated His love for people by sending His Son to make atonement for their sin (1 John 4:9–10). Sin alienates people from God and from one another. Jesus Christ removed this alienation by His death on the Cross. His death paid the full penalty for sin. As a result of Christ's atoning death, God invites those who are His enemies to enter into a new relationship with Him. All who respond to His gracious invitation become His children and heirs of His divine kingdom—ranking as princes and princesses of the King of kings—while living, serving, and ruling in the most powerful domain in existence.

All of God's children are equally near and dear to His heart. God is no respecter of persons. Therefore, He cannot be the author of attitudes of superiority or inferiority; these are rooted in sin—and promote sin. These attitudes both establish and promote racism, classism, elitism, sexism, and the like. They are hindrances to acting justly, loving mercy, and walking humbly with God. They foster a false sense of personal piety while failing to serve the public good.

The Christian school must educate its students in a more excellent way. Christian school students must be taught with the weightier matters of the Father's heart in view. This education should include the following:

- a more gospel-centric presentation of missions and ministry
- exercises designed to identify primary beliefs fueling unbiblical attitudes of superiority and inferiority
- more biblically balanced instruction on the nature of and relationship between the secular and the sacred, the physical and the spiritual, and the earthly and the heavenly
- students equipped to relate to others in the same way as they themselves wish to be treated

At its core, educating this way means teaching students how to love as God has first loved them—and how to love others in the same way. A rather simple formula, the ACID test of love, helps in this process. It is a way to test both the actions directed toward others and the attitude or motivation behind those actions.

Acceptance. Does the giver accept people on the basis of Christ's acceptance of the giver? In other words, what is moving the giver to act? How does God feel about the people being acted upon?

Commitment. Is there a commitment to the other person as an act of the will? An emotional commitment, including pity, ebbs and flows. It is the reason many marriages dissolve. It is the reason many commitments are broken. A volitional commitment, on the other hand, remains firm even when the feelings are no longer present.

Identification. Students should answer this question: "If I were this person, what would I want done for me?" This question applies the Golden Rule of Matthew 7:12 and Luke 6:31 to the motivation behind the actions. It allows the actors to put themselves in the place of those being acted upon. It is the stuff of empathy.

Dedication. Is the giver dedicated and determined to make the other person successful? Sometimes this dedication is at the expense of the giver.

Christ embodied and practiced these actions and attitudes. They demonstrate the Father's love, for God is love (1 John 4:7–8). As God's love is instilled in students, they will engage and practice the requirements He has revealed as good and important to Him: justice, mercy, and faithfulness.

Now What? Application to Practice

WHAT CAN THE Christian school administrator do to lead faculty, staff, and students to a more biblically based social, cultural, and racial awareness in the Christian school? Here are a few suggestions:

1. Set aside professional development time to engage the staff in diversity-assessment exercises. These would include the following:
   A. Examine the racial, cultural, and social makeup of the staff, board, and students.
   B. Critically evaluate the textbooks to determine any cultural, national, social, and racial biases or insensitivities.

2. Survey staff and students to ascertain their perception of socio-economic, class, cultural, and racial differences. This survey can be in the form of an anonymous questionnaire used to reveal primary beliefs. For example, the survey can ask such questions as these:
   A. Why do you believe that most poor people are poor?
   B. What did you hear about [a particular racial group or groups] as you were growing up?

3. Examine the missions emphasis of the school to determine if it does the following:

A. Does it promote a sense of cultural, social, national, or racial superiority?

B. Does it give the impression that "missions" is an overseas or distant activity?

C. Does it emphasize pity versus mercy?

4. With the help of outside consultants (whether paid or unpaid), examine the school culture.

A. Outsiders can bring a degree of objectivity, particularly if they come from different backgrounds than most of the school's students and faculty.

B. These individuals should engage the school in much the same way that an accreditation self-study would engage it.

5. Consider a course of study on kingdom theology and kingdom living.

A. What does it mean to live for and advance God's kingdom on earth?

B. How can we apply love as the ruling principle of God's kingdom?

References

Colson, Charles, and Nancy Pearcey. 1999. *How now shall we live?* Wheaton, IL: Tyndale House Publishers.

Conn, Harvie M. 1987. *A clarified vision for urban mission.* Grand Rapids, MI: Zondervan.

Emerson, Michael O., and Christian Smith. 2000. *Divided by faith: Evangelical religion and the problems of race in America.* New York: Oxford University Press.

Freire, Paulo. 1973. *Education for critical consciousness.* New York: Continuum.

Howard, Jeff, and Ray Hammond. 1985. Rumors of inferiority. *The New Republic* 9 (September): 17–21.

THE LIFE OF THE LEADER

Leading with Grace

ها

By Jeff Hall

Jeff Hall is the vice president for academic affairs at Covenant College. He is a graduate of Grove City College, and he earned his EdD at the University of Tennessee. He served for sixteen years as a teacher and an administrator in Christian day schools before working at Covenant College as a professor and an administrator.

CHAPTER 3

THE LIFE OF THE LEADER

By Jeff Hall

THE CHARACTER OF Leadership is a course at Covenant College offered to students who receive a leadership scholarship. The study includes a series of biographies of a wide variety of people who have been leaders or who have at least been influential. At the end of the course, students are required to write a reflective essay on the nature of leadership. Even the best student papers never fully capture the nature of leadership. In a similar way, many theorists continue to provide reflective, descriptive, and prescriptive theoretical work on the nature of leadership. And year after year more books on leadership are published. It is an elusive topic. Why is this so difficult? Why does the true definition of leadership continually escape definitive analysis?

The Importance of Persons

Leadership is a personal matter. It is not personal in the confidential sense, but it is personal in the sense that is rich with persons. The person of the leader and the persons of those being led are central to the shepherding of schools and other organizations. Although a comprehensive theory of leadership must include a consideration of authority structures and organizational contexts, much of the influence of leaders resides in who they are and how they embody vision, values, and character.

The personal nature of leadership should not be a surprise because people are very important in the created order. For example, truth in its most fundamental sense is a person. Jesus claims, "I am the way and the truth and the life" (John 14:6). Nonetheless, people are not accustomed to thinking of truth as a person. People tend to think of truth propositionally (Palmer 1998). Although there certainly are true propositions and there is a propositional aspect to truth, propositions do not embody truth. True truth is embodied only in the person of Jesus Christ. In order to apprehend true knowledge—biblical heart knowledge—we must realize that truth is a holistic complexity embodied in a person.

Michael Polanyi, in his book *Personal Knowledge: Towards a Post-Critical Philosophy*, captures some of the challenges of describing the complex nature of knowing and practicing skills. He states, "*The aim of a skilful performance is achieved by the observance of a set of rules which are not known as such to the person following them*" (1974, 49; emphasis in original). He illustrates this point with reflections on the rudimentary physics involved in swimming and bike riding, claiming that the children who practice these skills have little ability to articulate the laws involved in successful practice. For example, relative to the weaving back and forth of a bicyclist once the training wheels are removed, he states, "A simple analysis shows that for a given angle of unbalance the curvature of each winding is inversely proportional to the square of the speed at which the cyclist is proceeding" (50). Obviously, the young bicycle rider could not state such a principle. The cyclist may have a sense that the faster the speed, the less the winding. However, successful bike riding is more a matter of *feeling* the laws of physics than *articulating* them. If this is true for bike riding and physics, how much more is it true for the complex skills practiced in the psychological and sociological spheres of effective leadership.

Leadership is understood only in relation to its embodiment in a person. The wholeness and complexity of humanity and human action provide the venue for leadership. Of course, propositions can be derived from this human enterprise; however, theories that reify leadership to a list of traits, explanations of contexts, charts of authority, or the like have sorely underestimated the rich landscape of the life of a leader. Similarly, the written words of this chapter will fall short of truly conveying the personal nature of leadership. The purpose of these reflections on the life of the leader is to point to a comprehensive life that is embodied in real people. Some if not much of that reality is ineffable, simply beyond words. The experience of being in the presence of a truly great leader is both informative and influential. Growing to be like an effective leader is likely to involve more imitation than description. When it comes to providing a sufficiently textured landscape for instruction and growth, apprenticeship is preferred to didactic lecture.

Given this foundation of the personal nature of leadership, reflection on some basic principles may prove helpful.

Biblical Anthropology

Considering the person-rich reflection of the nature of leadership, a biblical reflection on the nature of people is a fitting starting point. First, people are created in the image of God. People reflect the image of God in terms of their characteristics and their common office (Berkhof 1938). Donovan Graham (2003), in his book *Teaching Redemptively*, describes a series of characteristics or attributes that reflect the image of God in people. His list of attributes includes active and purposeful, rational, creative, moral, free and responsible, faithful, exercising dominion, social, loving, merciful, and dependent. Although this list is not exhaustive, it is illustrative of the complexity of human beings.

The extent to which these dimensions of the image of God are honored, idolized, or minimized by a particular theory of leadership will determine the faithfulness and truth of leadership so practiced. For example, if a leadership theory idolizes the active and purposeful nature of human beings, it may allow the leader to reign without restraint. Minimizing the same dimension would result in an overly restrictive, robotic theory. A balanced view of the active and purposeful nature will result in prescriptions that allow for creativity within appropriate boundaries of authority and restraint.

In addition to these characteristics, people have an office as stewards of creation. In Genesis 1:28, God gives this command to Adam and Eve: "Be fruitful and increase in number; fill the earth and subdue it. Rule over the fish of the sea and the birds of the air and over every living creature that moves on the ground."

Second, despite their lofty beginning as image bearers who were caretakers of God's good creation, Adam and Eve fell into sin. This was no mere mischief or simple disobedience. Rather, it was treasonous rebel-

45

lion; they attempted to supplant God's rule in creation by being "like God." At the heart of sin are pride and unbelief. Sin removes people from communion with God, and without His help no reconciliation is possible. The sin of Adam and Eve placed all their descendants under the curse of the Fall. The remedy for this rebellion did not reside with humanity; rather, it had to come from God.

Third, the remedy came in the form of a person. "For as in Adam all die, so in Christ all will be made alive" (1 Corinthians 15:22). John the Baptist referred to Jesus as the Lamb of God (John 1:29). Scripture further states that Jesus "made himself nothing, taking the very nature of a servant" (Philippians 2:7). This concept of emptying Himself (kenosis) is central to the redemptive act, allowing Jesus to fully identify with Adam's race. It is this sacrificial act of atonement that forms a model for the inner life of the leader. Faithful leading requires an imitation of Jesus, who gives Himself to the Church. Leaders are forgiven by the redemptive work of Jesus, and they should imitate His self-sacrificial humility in daily life.

This brief threefold biblical anthropology forms a biblical foundation for a consideration of the life of a leader. Faithful leaders bear God's image, have rebellious hearts (desiring to take God's place), and find their redemption in the sacrificial Lamb of God. These realities form the basis for kenotic, or self-sacrificial, leadership.

Called to Lead

The paths to leadership in Christian education are varied, but all of them constitute a call. Some leaders find themselves at the head of a small school because no one else is available. Simply being a responsible person with a reasonable interest in the school is sufficient. Others have followed a more traditional path, receiving education, credentialing, and mentoring. No matter how one arrives as a leader in Christian education, simply being in the station provides the call to a faithful response.

The narrative of the Old Testament has wonderful stories of God calling His people to service in various ways. Two of these stories are particularly instructive. Even children enjoy hearing and reading about the calls of Moses and Isaiah.

Life as a professor and an administrator at a college has afforded me many opportunities to speak with students who are struggling with life callings in many dimensions, from career to marriage, and from majors to roommates. At times a student may say, "I just wish God would give me a burning bush so I would know what to do." This type of wish seems to be a bit naive in light of Moses' response to the burning bush. When God clearly revealed His call to Moses in Exodus 3, Moses did not feel any relief. In fact the biblical narrative records a rather lengthy discussion, in which Moses attempted to convince God that He would be better off sending someone else. Moses claimed that no one would believe him and that he was not an eloquent speaker, and he pleaded with God simply to send someone else. So a student's wish for a burning-bush experience is ironic because when it comes to God's call in a life, it is much less about knowing what God wants one to do and much more about an obedient response.

The call of Isaiah is a bit different. As described in Isaiah 6, the prophet was in the temple when God appeared to him. Unlike Moses, who needed to be told he was on holy ground and to remove his sandals, Isaiah recognized that he was in the presence of the Lord God, and he felt undone. When God sent an angel to him with a coal from the altar to remove the sin from his lips, Isaiah was ready to serve God in any way He asked. Isaiah responded to God's search for a messenger by saying, "Here am I. Send me!" (Isaiah 6:8). Moses was called to be a hero, to lead God's people out from the bonds of slavery, but Isaiah was called to declare God's displeasure and judgment "until the cities lie ruined and without inhabitant" (6:11).

In these passages we have two calls: one to be a hero of deliverance, one to be a prophet of judgment; one unwilling, one willing; both used by God by His grace to further His plan of redemption for the sake of His Son and His kingdom. Similarly, all believers are called. Sometimes they are called to stations and works of honor, and sometimes they are called to tasks that are repugnant. People are at times willing and at times unwilling. Sometimes they seem gifted and equipped for the work before them, and at other times the task is utterly beyond all human limits. Yet God is faithful, and He patiently continues telling His story of redemption with everyday people in everyday places. He continues to use this life to shape His people—including those who are in leadership positions in Christian schools—for the next.

Sometimes people are confused about how God extends His kingdom, particularly in education. The good news is that God is extending His kingdom through His redeemed people. Louis Berkhof, in his *Systematic Theology*, says of the kingdom of God:

> In connection with the present day tendency to regard the king-
> dom of God simply as a new social condition, an ethical kingdom of
> ends, to be established by human endeavors, such as education, legal
> enactments, and social reforms, it is well to bear in mind that the term
> "kingdom of God" is not always used in the same sense.... In fact, if
> all those who are now citizens of the Kingdom would actually obey its
> laws [call] in every domain of life, the world would be so different that
> it would hardly be recognized. (1938, 408)

Berkhof is reminding his readers that it is sufficient simply to respond
to God's call. If people wait to respond until they are fully gifted for
the challenges ahead, they will never respond. The good news is that
the Lord will see fit to use His people as they find their delight in Him.
Leaders in Christian schools rarely feel equal to the tasks before them,
but God is faithful.

Stresses of Leadership

Leading a Christian school is a demanding calling for which there is
no comprehensive training other than the job itself. Some say that being
the administrative leader of a Christian school these days is similar to
being the president of a small college. There are educational challenges
related to students, teachers, and curriculum. There are disciplinary
challenges with students and employees. There are logistical responsibilities of operational budgets, capital concerns, facility management,
technology services, marketing, and development. At the same time, all
the expectations that fall to the educational leader of a school must be
balanced with life at home and church.

Hans Selye (1984) describes the general adaptation syndrome and
the three stages of response to stress: alarm, resistance, and exhaustion.
He writes extensively on the physiological effects of encountering stress.
Tasks involved in school leadership are rife with opportunities for stress.
Obviously, coping with stress is a must for each leader. There are many
coping strategies, and general remedies are idiosyncratic (Hall 1992).
Each school leader must find stress reduction in a way that is congruent
with his or her situation and personality.

Robert M. Sapolsky (1998) suggests a number of coping strategies that a school leader might try. The following are in his list: finding an outlet for frustration; temporarily denying reality in the face of great tragedy; relinquishing the hope of controlling the past while focusing on the future; seeking predictable, accurate information; and finding sources of affiliation.

A 2006 survey of 1,151 ACSI administrators showed that administrators experienced statistically significantly more stress from school finances, job scope, school facilities, interruptions, receiving complaints, mediating conflicts, and teacher recruitment than in other areas of responsibility. There is a sense that the stress associated with leadership in schools is a constant. Little can be done to reduce the stress aside from attention to defining one's job description (Hall 1992). Simply put, once the job is well defined, a school leader must find ways to cope with a life of stress.

Gospel Leading in a Covenantal Context

Leadership is primarily a matter of incarnation. Effective leaders embody the life they advocate. The recognition of the personhood of all members of the learning community is essential to understanding the nature of effective leadership. The calling and tasks of the learning community are complex. Leaders need to lead in a way that moves beyond verbal propositions to a covenantal, personal relationship with all the other members of the community. This type of relational leadership puts an emphasis on the administrator's living an educated and transparent life. It need not be a perfect life, but it needs to be an authentic life of integrity. It is a life that embodies the truth of the gospel, valuing all people as created in God's image, confessing sin quickly and plainly, being self-sacrificial and forgiving in reconciliation—thus providing a living picture of leadership.

This type of leadership creates a covenantal community that finds its definition in a relational context. It allows each member to experience a continual sense of dignity and a chance for reconciliation when difficulties result from sin or differences of opinion. This is the type of leadership that is advocated by Wayne Alderson and his daughter Nancy Alderson McDonnell in *Theory R Management* (1994). They emphasize five Rs: doing what is *right*, building *relationships*, *reconciling*, owning *responsibility*, and striving for positive *results*.

Of course, leadership of this nature is beyond the scope of human effort. It is essential that leaders not look to themselves for the resources to live a life that shapes a community. Looking to one's own gifts, even if they are considerable, only creates occasions for idolatry and rebellion, even if those who are following want the leader to do this. Godly leaders must lead in humble reliance on the Holy Spirit, with repentant hearts and with a sense of piety. There are many tools of leadership that should be used in budgeting, planning, curricular design, and the like. However, these are all meaningless if the educational leader is not a person after the heart of God.

Agency of the Holy Spirit

Since Christian leadership involves a relationship with God, the Holy Spirit must be involved. Perhaps the most difficult person of the Trinity to understand is the Holy Spirit. Whereas the Father and the Son are presented in language that is more metaphorically apprehendable, the Holy Spirit is much more elusive. In the Scriptures the Holy Spirit does many different things. Perhaps the most noticeable task of the Holy Spirit is to bring an individual to a place of repentance and salvation. The Holy Spirit's works of conversion and regeneration are evident and clearly documented in Scripture, especially in the Gospel of John. The Holy Spirit is also involved in the continuation of the Christian life by empowering believers in their work (Erickson 1998).

The Holy Spirit is intimately involved in the processes of teaching, learning, and leading. Though most Christians have been willing to admit the Holy Spirit's agency in the school community, they may have been somewhat at a loss to explain the details of that agency. In the school, the work of the Holy Spirit is the difference between experiencing simple common-grace insights (unrealized revelation) and apprehending the revelation of God. Simply put, revelation is God telling about Himself. He tells His people about Himself in the Bible (special revelation) and in the created order (general revelation). His word calls into existence and sustains the created order. God the Son became flesh and dwelt among us. His Word reveals Him to us. The special involvement of the Holy Spirit in the processes of teaching, learning, and leading ensures that believers consciously encounter the person of God (Dooyeweerd 1953). The Holy Spirit ensures that Christians encounter the Creator when they encounter the creation and the Bible.

Revelation and repentance

When believers encounter the Creator, they have an experience similar to Isaiah's in the temple. He saw God revealed, and he was undone. He repented of being a person of unclean lips living among a people of unclean lips. When God reveals something of Himself, believers cannot help perceiving their sin and their distance from Him. Revelation is linked to repentance. In this way, repentance is an indicator of the apprehending of revelation. Although there are many indicators that a person has experienced revelation—such as awe, wonder, worship, or dread—repentance is helpful in that it seems to be particularly unusual in the current cultural experience. Further, without repentance, transformation of souls and cultures is not possible.

"Repentance is a pure gospel grace" (Watson 1987, 13). In Scripture, four terms are translated as "repentance." One Hebrew term is an onomatopoeic word meaning "to pant," "to sigh," or "to groan" and is often associated with a heart filled with pain. The other Hebrew word for repentance is used in the prophets' calls to Israel to repent and return to the Lord. In the New Testament, the Greek word *metamelomai* means to have a feeling of care, concern, or regret, and it is like the first Old Testament term. The second Greek term, *metanoeo*, means "to think differently about something" or "to have a change of mind." This term is characteristic of John the Baptist's call to repentance (Berkhof 1938). Few Christians would doubt the necessity of repentance in the process of salvation. However, in addition to a salvific response, repentance is a part of the daily life of the believer. In the first of his Ninety-Five Theses, Martin Luther states, "When our Lord and Master Jesus Christ said 'Repent,' he intended that the entire life of believers should be repentance" (Nichols 2002, 23). Again in the fourth thesis, "The penalty of sin, therefore, continues so long as hatred of self, or true inward repentance, continues, and it continues until our entrance into the kingdom of heaven" (25). The process of sanctification involves continual exposure of sin and repentance thereof. It is this process that intertwines the mortification of the flesh and the vivification of the Spirit.

The life of the leader, then, must be one of repentance. As members of the school community witness the leader's life of humble repentance, a culture of forgiveness and healing can be initiated. In short, a repentant leader becomes a human gateway for the gospel. Without this personal model, the community is more likely to be a venue for a life of pride and unbelief.

Personal piety

Perhaps the most sobering aspect of leadership is the area of personal piety. The very heart of the leader has a deep effect on the community. There is some mystery to this, but it is true. Techniques and methods of leadership are deeply influenced by the person of the leader, especially in relationship to personal piety. Care must be taken on this account. In a sense it is always true that the community and the leader are mutually influenced. "People tend to aggrandize the role of leaders. They tend to exaggerate the capacity of leaders to influence events" (Gardner 2000, 9). Nonetheless, the influence is present.

The life of Saul provides one of the most frightening narratives in the Bible regarding leadership. Saul had many leadership traits. His stature and appearance physically fit the image of a king. He seems to have had a personality that fit well with leadership. And of course, he was anointed by Samuel to be king. Despite these advantages, Saul made critical errors that showed his heart was not "after the heart of God" as was the heart of his successor, David (1 Samuel 13:14). Saul trusted himself rather than God. He trusted his gifts rather than the Giver. On two specific occasions, Saul took matters into his own hands. In 1 Samuel 13, Saul decided to rush ahead to sacrifice before the arrival of Samuel. He was previously instructed to wait for Samuel to offer the sacrifice. But as Saul assessed the situation, he believed that he needed to move faster than the circumstances allowed. He disobeyed and offered the sacrifice. Of course, just as he finished, Samuel came to confront him. Later in a battle against the Amalekites (1 Samuel 15), Saul decided to disobey the Lord by not killing all the people and livestock. At the request of his people, he saved some of the animals for a sacrifice after the battle. He sought to please people rather than God. For this disobedience, God took the kingdom from Saul.

These are frightening stories for any leader who is attempting to be faithful. The lure of expediency and popularity is powerful. Temptations to idolatry of many sorts abound, and mistakes can have dire consequences. Leaders of school communities must have a heart after the heart of God. Faithful leaders must be quick to pray and careful in their actions. An ardent prayer life is not optional. In fact, the degree to which leaders see prayer as a necessity is a good indicator of their personal piety and the condition of their hearts.

In this matter perhaps more than in all the rest, the person of the leader affects the life of the community. In the same way, the leader needs to be a person of prayer—specific prayer. Faithful leaders pray for their schools, the teachers, the staff workers, the students, the parents, and the board members by name. A prayerful life is the only way to lead in authentic dependence on the grace of God.

A Theology of Interruptions and Meetings

According to Max De Pree, "The first responsibility of a leader is to define reality. The last is to say thank you. In between the two, the leader must become a servant and a debtor" (1989, 9). School administrators must lead expectantly. God cares deeply about His people, and He is eager to have His participation acknowledged and appreciated. This truth is illustrated in two realities of the administrator's life: interruptions and meetings.

C. S. Lewis (1979) expressed a wonderful insight concerning interruptions in his letter to Arthur Greeves. He reminded Greeves that interruptions in this life are not really interruptions. Rather, they are simply the real life that God intends for His people. The real life that seems to be getting interrupted is simply a product of personal imagination. If God is sovereign and truly cares about the number of hairs on heads and the birds of the air (Luke 12:7), He must care about the interruptions that occur in the stream of daily work. Interruptions take the form of everything from weather events to parent complaints, from medical emergencies to fights on the playground. To be a school administrator is to live an interrupted life. Of course, one needs to manage time and set priorities in order to minimize interruptions, thus stewarding time and resources. Nonetheless, interruptions will occur. The question is not whether one will be interrupted, but how one will respond to the interruptions when they occur.

Leaders must give consideration to what is important. When circumstances call for action not previously planned, leaders need to make sure that they give priority to the important things. When people are involved, setting aside the work on the desk to give full attention to the people in the office is imperative.

People are not victims of their circumstances. God has plans for His people, and He is in sovereign control of all events. Leaders must be careful to present hope in all situations, but not a Pollyanna-type hope; rather, faithful leaders narrate and anticipate God's faithfulness in current challenges. Consider this statement by Paul: "Therefore we do not lose heart. Though outwardly we are wasting away, yet inwardly we are being renewed day by day. For our light and momentary troubles are achieving for us an eternal glory that far outweighs them all. So we fix our eyes not on what is seen, but on what is unseen. For what is seen is temporary, but what is unseen is eternal" (2 Corinthians 4:16–18).

Measured and gracious responses will communicate the values of the community. Thomas J. Sergiovanni talks about the importance of this aspect of schools in his book *Building Community in Schools*. He states, "Participants feel the crisis inside schools is directly linked to human relationships.... Where positive things about the schools were noted, they usually involve reports of individuals who care, listen, understand, respect others and are honest, open and sensitive" (1994, 18–19).

Meetings are an opportunity to celebrate the various gifts of the Body of Christ. Meetings are not to create buy-in; they are to provide a venue for the full expression of the gifts for the community. If all people have gifts and the local school is one body with many members, as is the Church, then there is a certain complementarity to collective gatherings. Although all meetings should have agendas, agendas should not presuppose outcomes. Real meetings are exciting because they anticipate a result that is greater than the insights of any individual. Effective leaders should create a sense of expectation that good things are about to happen and that God will be faithful as His people prayerfully work together, even in very difficult situations. There is a sense in which meetings help to narrate God's providence. They can also be hothouses for sanctification. Leaders should help their school communities perceive these realities as they unfold.

Summary

The life of the leader is an exciting life, full of challenge and opportunity. The leader is called by God and equipped for God's purposes. An effective leader appreciates the complexity and wonder of human beings and knows that all people are God's image bearers, are utterly sinful, and are in need of the redeeming work of Christ. Leaders also know that Christ's redemption through His suffering sacrifice provides a model to be imitated in servant leadership. Effective leaders are people who hunger for piety, narrate God's faithfulness, and anticipate His providence through authentic, loving relationships with all members of the school community.

Now What? Application to Practice

CHRISTIAN SCHOOL leaders, like all other Christians, are people in development. Here are some specific suggestions, based on the content of this chapter, that can contribute to the process of becoming effective leaders.

The importance of persons

A comprehensive appreciation of the nature of persons in the school community is necessary for effective leadership. School leaders must both embody and narrate the importance of the personal, idiosyncratic nature of the members of the community. To highlight this dimension of the school community, leaders can do the following:

1. They can regularly acknowledge the unique gifts of teachers, staff members, and students in formal and informal ways at school gatherings. Leaders can do so through teacher-of-the-week awards and student-in-the-spotlight displays. Care should be given to honor all the members of the community in one way or another so that the rich diversity of the body will be evident to all.

2. They can resolve conflict by owning the blame. When conflicts arise, leaders first attempt to find their part in the conflict and own the blame. This type of kenotic leadership will honor the personhood of the others and may lead to surprisingly positive reactions.

Stress management

School leadership entails a great deal of stress. Long-term leaders must cope with and manage the stress of their worlds. These implementation ideas will help address this area.

1. Effective leaders limit the scope of their jobs. By making a list of all the tasks involved in daily work and deciding which ones can be eliminated and which ones can be delegated, leaders can adjust their span of control. Managing the scope of the job is the most effective stress-management tool.

2. Listing coping strategies will form the foundation of a stress-management system. A good diet and regular exercise are necessary as a

part of a disciplined life. Effective leaders schedule stress-reducing activities as a regular part of the workweek.

Testimonies of providence

School leadership is a matter of faith and providence. God surprises His people with His goodness and provision. School leaders would do well to keep a record of the blessings of God in the school community. A school journal could be a helpful tool to narrate testimonies of providence.

1. Leaders should maintain a record of significant learning experiences that give evidence to apprehended revelation and to responses of humility and repentance.

2. A record of how meetings exceed the expectations of agendas would provide a narration of God's grace in community gatherings.

3. A list of helpful interruptions in the life and work of the school could be humorous and instructive. It may teach members of the school community to embrace the uncertainty of interruptions as a part of God's providential care.

Attention to personal piety

Faithful school leaders live lives rooted in a personal relationship with God. A life of personal piety sustains the public work of school leaders.

1. An effective leader often chooses a mentor who can provide a listening ear and a level of faithful accountability regarding matters of personal piety. A mentor can provide reminders that a relationship with God is not a checklist of daily activities. Rather, personal piety is based on a living relationship that extends throughout each day.

2. Many faithful leaders make a prayer list of specific people in the school and use it regularly.

3. Effective leaders should pray for the activity of the Holy Spirit in all dimensions of the life of the school.

References

Alderson, Wayne T., and Nancy Alderson McDonnell. 1994. *Theory R management: How to utilize value of the person leadership principles of love, dignity and respect.* Nashville, TN: Thomas Nelson.

Berkhof, Louis. 1938. *Systematic theology.* Grand Rapids, MI: Eerdmans.

De Pree, Max. 1989. *Leadership is an art.* New York: Doubleday.

Dooyeweerd, Herman. 1953. *A new critique of theoretical thought.* Vol. 1. Trans. David H. Freeman and William S. Young. Philadelphia, PA: Presbyterian and Reformed Publishing.

Erickson, Millard J. 1998. *Christian theology.* 2nd ed. Grand Rapids, MI: Baker.

Gardner, John W. 2000. The nature of leadership. In *The Jossey-Bass reader on educational leadership.* San Francisco: Jossey-Bass.

Graham, Donovan L. 2003. *Teaching redemptively: Bringing grace and truth into your classroom.* Colorado Springs, CO: Purposeful Design Publications.

Hall, Jeffrey B. 1992. An investigation of the sources of stress among chief administrative officers in Christian Schools International member institutions. Dissertation, University of Tennessee, Knoxville.

Lewis, C. S. 1979. *They stand together.* New York: Macmillan.

Mason, Charlotte M. 1954. *A philosophy of education.* London: J. M. Dent and Sons.

Nichols, Stephen J. 2002. *Martin Luther's ninety-five theses.* Phillipsburg, NJ: P&R Publishing.

Palmer, Parker J. 1998. *The courage to teach: Exploring the inner landscape of a teacher's life.* San Francisco: Jossey-Bass.

Polanyi, Michael. 1974. *Personal knowledge: Towards a post-critical philosophy.* Chicago: University of Chicago Press.

Sapolsky, Robert M. 1998. *Why zebras don't get ulcers: An updated guide to stress, stress-related disease, and coping.* New York: W. H. Freeman and Company.

Sergiovanni, Thomas J. 1994. *Building community in schools.* San Francisco: Jossey-Bass.

Selye, Hans. 1984. *The stress of life.* Rev. ed. New York: McGraw-Hill.

Terry, Robert W. 1993. *Authentic leadership: Courage in action.* San Francisco: Jossey-Bass.

Watson, Thomas. 1987. *The doctrine of repentance.* Carlisle, PA: Banner of Truth Trust.

THE LEADER AS RISK TAKER

Equipping Students to Engage the Culture

ᴏᴄ

*By Stephen R. Kaufmann
and Kevin J. Eames*

Stephen R. Kaufmann, PhD, is a professor of education at Covenant College, where he has taught since 1982. Before teaching at Covenant he was a high school teacher and administrator for twelve years. His doctoral studies were in the field of social foundations of education.

Kevin J. Eames, PhD, is the director of institutional research at Covenant College, and he teaches organizational leadership in the MEd program there. Before serving at Covenant, he was an assistant professor of psychology and the director of graduate education at Dordt College. His doctorate is in counseling psychology.

CHAPTER 4

THE LEADER
AS RISK
TAKER

*By Stephen R. Kaufmann
and Kevin J. Eames*

SEVERAL YEARS AGO, a local Christian high school began a pro-life club on its campus. The purpose of the club was to raise awareness of the perils of abortion and to discuss the importance of programs designed to help young mothers and the newly born. The club's faculty sponsor effectively presented important issues for discussion at club meetings. One of the topics concerned the city's abortion clinic. Club members debated strategies for closing the clinic, such as holding prayer vigils at the abortion site, as well as petitioning the city government to rezone the area to make it off-limits for the practice of abortion.

Unbeknownst to the club's sponsor, several of the club's members decided that the pro-life adults of the city were too slow and indecisive in taking action against the abortion clinic. So, they decided to take the initiative to chain themselves to the front door of the clinic. They expected to be arrested, and thus bring unwelcome publicity to the local abortionist and his clinic.

Soon the word spread of their plan, and parents in the school began to call the high school principal to protest. The following comment was typical: "I thought I was sending my child to a safe place. What are you teaching our students that would make them want to do such a thing?" In the face of mounting pressure, club members decided against going ahead with their plan, and soon the routine of ordinary school life resumed.

At the end of the year, one of the members of the school board was talking with the high school principal about the events of the year. The principal said, "Do you remember that week last winter when several students were planning to chain themselves to the abortion clinic? That was easily the roughest week of the year for me. Board members were upset, parents were upset, and students were distracted. It seemed that we were consumed as a community by that one issue, and no one was happy about it."

The board member agreed, but also said to him, "I know it was a rough time for us at school, but we have to consider that it also might have been the most important week of the year as well. We often lament the self-absorption and pleasure-seeking habits of our youth, but these students were other-directed. They put the welfare of the at-risk fetus ahead of their own welfare. Perhaps we should be praising them for their good intentions rather than rebuking them."

The abortion clinic episode and its meaning for Christian high schools offer much to consider. The question of the irate parent—"What are you teaching our students that would make them want to do such a thing?"—is a key one. The plan of the students, though ill advised, does suggest that the school was fostering an environment in which student thinking and valuing went beyond the pursuit of personal fulfillment. The conversation of the principal and the board member also suggests that the other-directed student attitudes were consistent with school goals. Equally true, however, is the unsettling effect of the students' plan on the school community. The students' proposed civil disobedience was contrary to parents' expectations of the school as a place that was free from the turbulence of society. Caught in between was the school's principal, who affirmed both the value of the school as a safe place and the value of the school as a place to discuss and even challenge societal evil.

Preparing Students for a Fallen World

Clearly, the pressures put upon contemporary administrators go beyond merely managing the school's calendar, curriculum, and personnel. How are Christian-high-school administrators supposed to lead their schools in an unsettled, values-questioning age? If they opt for creating an idealized "safe place," they risk a kind of head-in-the-sand irrelevance for the school. Such schools tend to identify themselves as places to escape the world rather than places of judicious engagement with it. On the other hand, if administrators opt for creating communities that lead students to question and challenge the issues and ideas of the day, they risk the possibility that students will hatch plans similar to the one of the pro-life club.

In response to changing societal conditions, educational theorists are calling for the job description of educational leaders to be redefined. David Marsh says that tomorrow's educational leaders will need a new form of expertise other than as managers of personnel and academic programs. The new leaders will need to acquire expertise that is "more a matter of culture and reflection rather than of technical skills ... and includes norms of experimentation, risk taking, common technical language, and collaboration" (2000, 131).

Robert J. Marzano, Timothy Waters, and Brian A. McNulty include the job of change agent in the leader's responsibilities. They say that a key concern for the leader as change agent is to "assess the magnitude of a change and identify levels of comfort and discomfort" for the community (2005, 109). Jerry Patterson identifies a shift from today's values to what he designates as tomorrow's values. One of those values is openness to conflict. He notes that traditional school communities value "group harmony and happiness." Tomorrow's schools, however, will seek to resolve conflict in a way that "leads to stronger solutions for complex issues" (1993, 8).

There are similar calls for rethinking leaders' roles within Christian-high-school communities. In a report to administrators based on a study of selected schools of the Association of Christian Schools International (ACSI) and Christian Schools International (CSI), Stephen Kaufmann urges them to adopt risk-based and conflict-resolving paradigms for their schools:

> I would have you consider that instead of producing competent, well adjusted students, maybe our schools should be producing competent, maladjusted students. By maladjusted students, I don't mean those who are psychologically unhinged, but rather those who have developed a keen sense of the discrepancy between the world as it is and the world as it ought to be. You see, maladjusted kids would find the hedonism, relativism, and racism of our day to be profoundly

unsettling. Maladjusted kids would dream about and begin to work for a world characterized by justice, compassion, and moral integrity (2005, 31).

The report concludes that for the Christian high school to meet its mission, it must incorporate "systematic, regular, and purposeful student action" that has social relevance (Kaufmann 2005, 44). Merely communicating right ideas, though vitally important, is inadequate. Student ownership of the values and purpose of the school is directly related to student involvement in meeting that purpose.

In a similar way, Stefan Ulstein comments that the great danger for Christian schools today is not the perils of a hedonistic culture but the creation of a "G-rated education for a *Leave It to Beaver* world." He argues that in order to take the calling of Christian education seriously, schools must not "teach for an idealized future based on a nostalgic longing for a simpler time" (1988, 11).

Educational philosopher Nicholas Wolterstorff exhorts Christian schools to teach, among other things, for lament. He notes that "the struggle for the healing of broken and distorted relationships can be genuine only if it emerges from a heartfelt lament.... [Even though] to teach our students to love the earth, to love God, to love culture, to love each other, to love oneself, is ... to court the possibility, indeed, the certainty, of grief and sorrow" (2002, 263).

These conclusions by educational theorists are consistent with that dimension of a Christian worldview that explores the implications of humanity's fall into sin. The writer of Ecclesiastes reflects this human condition in these words: "I saw the tears of the oppressed—and they have no comforter; power was on the side of their oppressors—and they have no comforter" (4:1).

Perhaps it could be argued, therefore, that Christian education in a fallen world will often include some controversy as the classroom investigation of society inevitably points to injustice in the political arena, dysfunction in the home, or corruption in the business community. Should Christian schools take the risk of discussing the brokenness that besets the culture? Most, no doubt, would favor such discussions. But what if ideas taught in school lead to students taking action to address the problems discussed? The thesis of this chapter is that educational leaders must be engaged occasionally in educationally warranted, though risky, activity in order to meet their purpose as culturally relevant Christian high schools.

Of course, much of Christian school education properly focuses on the positive investigation of God's truth and God's world. There is much to arouse curiosity, there is much to delight in, and there is much to learn in order for students to be influencers of culture and society in the name of Christ. But if classroom teaching ignores the problems of the world, then schools may well be reduced to offering the G-rated education against which Ulstein warns. Could it be that some degree of risk taking, in terms of what is discussed and modeled in school, ought to be welcomed rather than avoided? Should constructive risk taking be a part of the job description of educational leaders?

Analyzing Risk Taking

The time is ripe for an analysis of the issue of risk taking for several reasons. First, the Christian school movement has matured significantly. In the past twenty-eight years the number of Christian schools affiliated with ACSI has grown to more than 5,300 schools and nearly 1.2 million students. These schools typically are not operating out of the church basement; they have a competent and growing teacher corps and an expanding student base. This historical moment is good for reviewing school programs and assessing their Christian distinctiveness.

Second, the conception of the school principal has changed over time. Now the principal is regarded as an educational leader who balances the need for continuity and change within the school, with both as essential factors leading to the fulfillment of the school's mission.

Third, students are no longer regarded as empty vessels merely to be filled with information, no matter how important the information. Christian schools see students as active learners, made in God's image, called to be responsible agents within the learning community. When students are given freedom to exercise choice as responsible agents, the possibility exists that they may make immature choices.

How can the school leader create the conditions for responsible (though not always fully mature) choices, and yet avoid unsafe or reckless behavior? How is the principal to lead in a way that promotes continuity yet provides for growth and change? What is the difference between foolhardy change and necessary change? When is risk taking an appropriate step, and when is it a reckless step?

These are not easy questions to answer, nor is it likely that appropriate risk taking will be the same in all schools. A critical assumption, however, is that effective leaders will embrace risk taking in some form as an essential component in a healthy learning community. The embrace of risk taking also entails the willingness to deal with controversy and disagreement within the community of board members, parents, teachers, and students. The leader will need great skill in guiding the discussion and demonstrating that meeting the school's mission and taking legitimate risks are not incompatible.

A Major Study

In order to determine current risk-taking practices among administrators, surveys containing items related to risk taking and stress were sent to 4,319 administrators whose schools belonged to ASCI. A total of 1,129 responded. Of the total respondents, 609 were in some way responsible for the administration of high school students. These school administrators labeled themselves as high school administrators (166), superintendents (136), or K–12 administrators (307). Other demographic information collected included school size based on number of students, age of the school, administrators' years of experience, and administrators' ratings of their administrative competence.

Schools were categorized into three groups: small (100 or fewer students), medium (101–500 students), and large (more than 500 students). Of the respondents, 123 led schools categorized as small, 354 led schools categorized as medium, and 132 led schools categorized as large. Additionally, respondents were asked to indicate the age of the school, selecting from 0–1 years (7 schools), 2–5 years (36 schools), 6–10 years (79 schools), 11–15 years (72 schools), and over 15 years (415 schools, constituting 68 percent of the sample).

The survey categorized administrators' years of experience similarly to how it categorized the age of the schools: 23 respondents indicated they had 0–1 years of experience, 121 indicated 2–5 years, 117 indicated 6–10 years, 84 indicated 11–15 years, and 264 (43.3 percent of the respondents) had over 15 years of experience. Respondents were also asked to rate their leadership effectiveness on a Likert scale from low (1) to high (5). Of the respondents, 6 rated themselves as moderately low, 140 rated themselves as average, 359 rated themselves as above average, and 104 rated themselves as high. None of the respondents rated themselves at the lowest anchor of the scale.

Respondents received a survey asking them to respond to twenty-three items related to admission policies, assembly speakers, curriculum, cocurricular programs, service learning, and student discipline—all of which were designed to assess risk taking. The items contained references to specific cases (for example, inviting a qualified non-Christian to speak at a school's assembly), and respondents were asked to indicate on a five-point Likert scale how likely they would be to take the specified risk, using a scale anchored by 1 (not likely) to 5 (likely). In addition, respondents were asked to respond to fourteen items for their stress-inducing potential, from 1 (no stress) to 4 (high stress).

The questions were intended to raise difficult issues or policies (some more difficult than others) that schools typically face. It was also assumed that each decision to discuss an issue or adopt a policy would entail some degree of risk (again, the amount of risk varies with the issue). For example, would a policy of open enrollment adversely affect the school's ability to meet its mission as a Christian school? Would a school-sponsored dance introduce unwelcome behaviors to the school? Would community-service projects introduce an element of danger to the students? Would a pregnant student in the school be an inappropriate role model? These are not easy questions to answer in the abstract, but what they all have in common is that they are issues of relevance to society today.

The items on the questionnaire included the following:

How likely is it that you would

1. Invite a qualified non-Christian to speak at your school's assembly?
2. Have a school assembly on the following topics:
   a. Should American forces be in Iraq?
   b. Should married women work outside the home?
   c. Is there racism at our school? (Assembly led by a panel of minority students.)
3. Support a policy of not requiring a profession of faith by applicants to your school?
4. Support the following supervised student-learning projects:
   a. Visiting residents in a nursing home
   b. Tutoring youth in an urban setting

c. Clean-up, paint-up, fix-up projects in an urban setting

d. Collecting canned goods for the poor

e. Clean-up, paint-up, fix-up projects on schools grounds

f. Tutoring elementary youth at your school

5. Include the following topics in your school's academic program:

a. AIDS and STD awareness

b. Drug awareness

6. Have a school-sponsored cocurricular dance.

7. Decide on expulsion in response to the following student behaviors:

a. A student becomes pregnant and is repentant.

b. A student becomes pregnant and is not repentant.

c. A student engages in theft and is repentant.

d. A student engages in theft and is not repentant.

A factor analysis of the risk-related items revealed a three-factor model with several items tending to cluster around the three factors. The first factor, labeled the *service-learning scale*, contained items related to service-learning, such as collecting canned goods and tutoring children in an urban environment, and it included cocurricular activities, such as having a debate time and allowing students to lead chapel. The second factor, labeled the *academic-program scale*, contained items related to assembly topics and topics for the academic program. Items included assemblies on Iraq, the role of women, and academic topics such as AIDS and drug awareness. The third factor, labeled the *discipline factor*, contained all items related to discipline. The questions involved two discipline cases (theft and pregnancy) with the variable of repentance or lack of repentance. There were several items that did not load on any factor, and they were treated as individual variables. These three factors constituted scales; means were calculated for each scale and were used in making comparisons among groups. In addition, means from the fourteen stress-related items were also calculated and used in the analysis.

A comparison of high school principals, superintendents, and K–12 administrators showed significant differences on the academic-program scale. High school administrators were more likely than K–12 administrators to permit controversial assembly topics and topics related to AIDS and drug awareness. This difference is probably related to the K–12 administrators' responsibilities for elementary and middle grades. High school principals and K–12 administrators were also significantly different in their overall mean responses on the risk-related items; high school principals scored higher than K–12 administrators. (See chart 1.) Whereas high school principals tended toward more risk taking, they also reported significantly more stress than their colleagues.

School size appears to be a significant factor in risk taking. Means on overall risk taking, the service-learning scale, and the academic-program scale were all significantly different; the small schools were the most averse to risk, and the large schools the least averse to risk. (See chart 2.) Conversely, school age did not appear to be a significant factor in risk taking, with the exception of the items reported in chart 3.

Principal experience and self-ratings did not have a significant impact overall on risk taking. (See chart 4.) However, self-ratings were inversely correlated with stress. The higher the administrators rated their own leadership effectiveness, the lower their overall mean on stress. Those who rated themselves as high or above average on leadership effectiveness were significantly lower on stress than their average and moderately low colleagues. Three risk items and administrators' self-ratings indicated significant differences; those reporting a low self-rating were the most averse to risk. (See chart 5.)

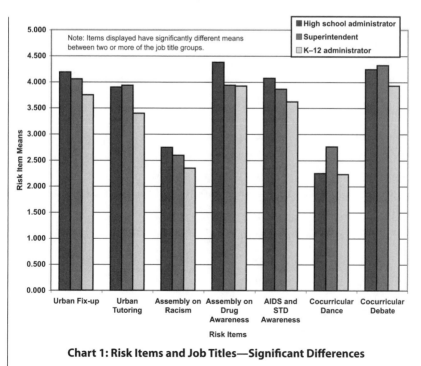

Chart 1: Risk Items and Job Titles—Significant Differences

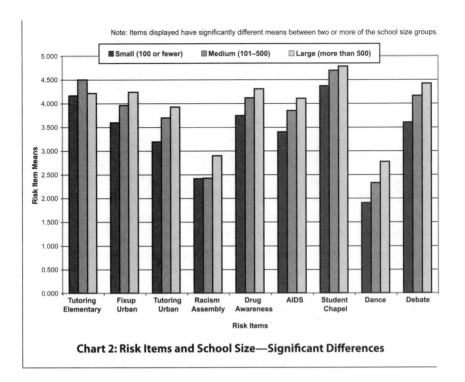

Note: Items displayed have significantly different means between two or more of the school size groups.

Chart 2: Risk Items and School Size—Significant Differences

Summary of scores on selected items

Mean scores of 3.5 or higher per item are regarded as pro-risk scores. Scores of 2.5 or lower are regarded as risk-averse scores. Items with scores between 2.5 and 3.5 are not included. No attempt has been made to prioritize items as being more risk worthy or less risk worthy.

Pro-risk policies sorted by the type of administrator (scores above 3.5)

Administrator responses are sorted by job title: high school administrator, superintendent, and K–12 administrator. What follows are items that were categorized as pro-risk responses. Administrators were asked the following:

How likely is it that you would

1. Support the following supervised student-learning projects:

    a. Visiting residents in a nursing home

High school administrator	4.38
Superintendent	4.25
K–12 administrator	4.33

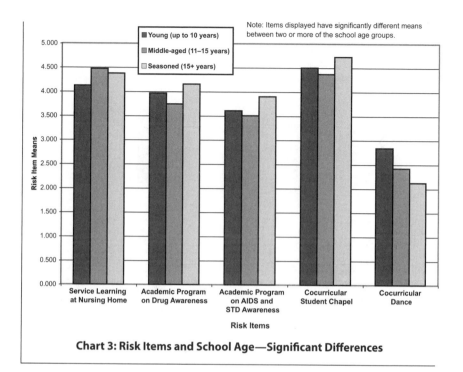

Chart 3: Risk Items and School Age—Significant Differences

b. Tutoring youth in an urban setting

High school administrator	3.89
Superintendent	3.93
K–12 administrator	3.39

c. Clean-up, paint-up, fix-up projects in an urban setting

High school administrator	4.18
Superintendent	4.05
K–12 administrator	3.74

d. Collecting canned goods for the poor

High school administrator	4.52
Superintendent	4.38
K–12 administrator	4.47

e. Clean-up, paint-up, fix-up projects on schools grounds

High school administrator	4.22
Superintendent	4.14
K–12 administrator	4.32

f. Tutoring elementary youth at your school

High school administrator	4.41
Superintendent	4.26
K–12 administrator	4.37

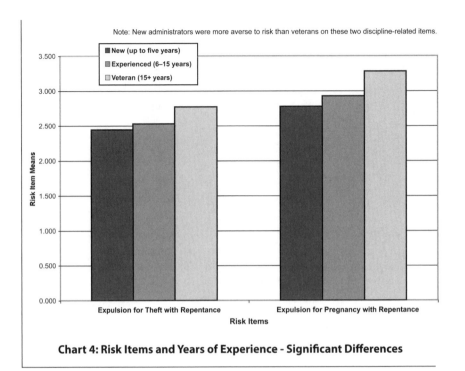

Note: New administrators were more averse to risk than veterans on these two discipline-related items.

Chart 4: Risk Items and Years of Experience - Significant Differences

5. Include the following topics in your school's academic program:

   a. AIDS and STD awareness

High school administrator	4.07
Superintendent	3.86
K–12 administrator	3.61

   b. Drug awareness

High school administrator	4.37
Superintendent	3.93
K–12 administrator	3.92

Risk-averse policies sorted by the type of administrator (scores below 2.5)

How likely is it that you would

1. Invite a qualified non-Christian to speak at your school's assembly?

High school administrator	2.31
Superintendent	2.32
K–12 administrator	2.04

2. Have a school assembly on the following topics:

   a. Should American forces be in Iraq?

High school administrator	2.25

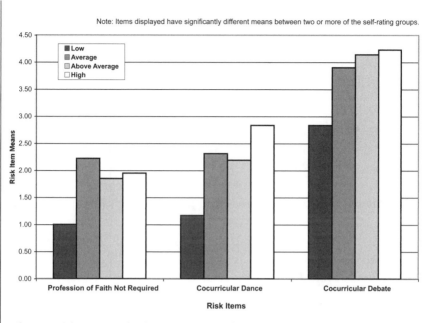

Chart 5: Risk Items and Administrators' Self-Ratings—Significant Differences

Superintendent	2.20
K–12 administrator	2.01

b. Should married women work outside the home?

High school administrator	2.06
Superintendent	1.88
K–12 administrator	1.79

c. Is there racism at our school? (Assembly led by a panel of minority students.)

High school administrator	2.74
Superintendent	2.59
K–12 administrator	2.34

3. Support a policy of not requiring a profession of faith by applicants to your school?

High school administrator	1.92
Superintendent	2.03
K–12 administrator	1.93

4. Have a school-sponsored cocurricular dance?

High school administrator	2.24
Superintendent	2.75
K–12 administrator	2.22

5. Decide on expulsion in response to the following student behaviors:

[Note: In this set of questions, risk-averse scores are 3.5 and higher]

a. A student becomes pregnant and is not repentant.

High school administrator	4.43
Superintendent	4.24
K–12 administrator	4.46

b. A student engages in theft and is not repentant.

High school administrator	4.26
Superintendent	4.21
K–12 administrator	4.41

Pro-risk policies sorted by school size (scores above 3.5)

Administrator responses were sorted by school size: small (100 students or fewer), medium (101–500 students), and large (more than 500 students). What follows are items that were categorized as pro-risk responses. Administrators were asked the following:

How likely is it that you would

1. Support the following supervised student-learning projects:

a. Visiting residents in a nursing home

Small (100 or fewer)	4.17
Medium (101–500)	4.38
Large (more than 500)	4.35

b. Tutoring youth in an urban setting

Small (100 or fewer)	3.18
Medium (101–500)	3.69
Large (more than 500)	3.92

c. Clean-up, paint-up, fix-up projects in an urban setting

Small (100 or fewer)	3.59
Medium (101–500)	3.95
Large (more than 500)	4.23

d. Collecting canned goods for the poor

Small (100 or fewer)	4.35
Medium (101–500)	4.50
Large (more than 500)	4.52

e. Clean-up, paint-up, fix-up projects on schools grounds

Small (100 or fewer)	4.34
Medium (101–500)	4.28
Large (more than 500)	4.12

f. Tutoring elementary youth at your school

Small (100 or fewer)	4.16

Medium (101–500)	4.49
Large (more than 500)	4.21

2. Include the following topics in your school's academic program:

a. Drug awareness

Small (100 or fewer)	3.73
Medium (101–500)	4.11
Large (more than 500)	4.30

b. AIDS and STD awareness

Small (100 or fewer)	3.39
Medium (101–-00)	3.84
Large (more than 500)	4.10

Risk-averse policies sorted by school size (scores below 2.5)

How likely is it that you would

1. Invite a qualified non-Christian to speak at your school's assembly?

Small (100 or fewer)	2.18
Medium (101–500)	2.10
Large (more than 500)	2.32

2. Have a school assembly on the following topics:

a. Should American forces be in Iraq?

Small (100 or fewer)	2.13
Medium (101–500)	2.04
Large (more than 500)	2.32

b. Should married women work outside the home?

Small (100 or fewer)	1.93
Medium (101–500)	1.81
Large (more than 500)	2.07

c. Is there racism at our school? (Assembly led by a panel of minority students.)

Small (100 or fewer)	2.41
Medium (101–500)	2.42
Large (more than 500)	2.89

3. Support a policy of not requiring a profession of faith by applicants to your school?

Small (100 or fewer)	1.85
Medium (101–500)	1.96
Large (more than 500)	2.00

4. Have a school-sponsored cocurricular dance?

Small (100 or fewer)	1.90
Medium (101–500)	2.32
Large (more than 500)	2.76

5. Decide on expulsion in response to the following student behaviors:

[Note: In this set of questions, risk-averse scores are 3.5 and higher]

a. A student becomes pregnant and is not repentant.

Small (100 or fewer)	4.27
Medium (101–500)	4.45
Large (more than 500)	4.49

b. A student engages in theft and is not repentant.

Small (100 or fewer)	4.23
Medium (101–500)	4.35
Large (more than 500)	4.30

Now What? Application to Practice

THE THESIS OF THIS chapter is that leaders of Christian high schools should seek ways to engage students in culturally relevant ideas and activities, even when such ideas and activities entail the risk of bringing a degree of unsettledness and controversy to the school. Educational leaders should look for educationally warranted and mission-driven ways to incorporate such activities into the life of their high school communities, endeavoring to steer between an uncritical acceptance of the values of the larger culture on the one hand and a world-flight separatism on the other. Schools should seek to develop strategies to present their students with culturally engaged Christian academic and social perspectives, thus developing in their students a "salt and light" approach to the world in which they live.

There is cause for encouragement in the results of the study of ACSI administrators.

An analysis of the survey results can give an educational leader a sense of the way other leaders would act in some potentially risky situations, and it might help a leader identify options to consider when facing similar situations.

There was general support of service-learning programs, even when those programs take place off campus in nursing homes and in urban settings. There was also support for addressing awareness of drugs, AIDS, and STDs in school programs. Clearly, these responses are indicative of schools that attempt a connection between quality Christian education and engagement with social problems, even when such engagement may entail some risk.

The study also found that large schools were more likely to incorporate risk-taking activities into their programs than either medium or small schools. One explanation for this difference may be the stability of large schools. Large schools have more resources, more personnel, and more policies in place to address the needs of large numbers of students, along with more structural buffers to absorb any negative consequences from risk taking. Smaller schools are not as likely to have such buffers in place. One solution for smaller schools is for boards of trustees to assume the buffer role to support risk-taking decisions by the administrator. The education committee of the board, in particular, could act as a sounding board for the community, thus helping to take pressure off the educational leader.

The survey finding that high school administrators were more likely to engage in risky school activities than K–12 administrators or K–12 superintendents is not surprising. Both the K–12 superintendents and the K–12 administrators have a broader age range of students in their charge, a fact that affects their decision making. Where possible, it is desirable for K–12 or 7–12 schools to have at least a part-time high school administrator. Short of that, smaller schools may opt for a steering committee of high school teachers to recommend activities and programs to the educational leader.

Risk-averse practices in the study centered on school assembly policies, admissions policies, and selected discipline situations. Whether sorted by administrator type or by school size, policies governing school assemblies were uniformly averse to risk. Schools as an aggregate would not choose to invite qualified non-Christians to speak in school assemblies, nor would they choose assembly topics such as exploring whether American forces should be in Iraq, whether married women should work outside the home, or whether there is racism in the school. These topics are the kinds that stir controversy in the school community; therefore, many administrators choose not to take the risk of discussing them.

With respect to the qualified non-Christian speaker, the issue can be further broken down into two categories: controversial and noncontroversial topics. An instance of the latter case is an elected official who comes to address a civic topic. Had the questionnaire specified this kind of example, it is very likely that support for hosting the qualified non-Christian speaker would have increased. A more difficult case would be a scientist speaking in favor of evolutionary theory. Is this kind of risk taking warranted or reckless? It may be reckless if the speaker presents the position without a response from a scientist in support of intelligent design. In the latter case, the result may be an educationally valuable exchange of ideas that positions students to understand how the intelligent-design position differs from the evolutionary one. An additional benefit is that students may come to see that their school prizes truth and does not fear challenges to it. Let students see the challenges firsthand, say such schools, and let them come to perceive that Christianity rightly understood and science rightly understood are not incompatible.

As mentioned previously, schools of all sizes were disinclined to address any of the following issues in their school assemblies: whether American forces should be in Iraq, whether married women should work outside the home, and whether there is racism in the school. It is likely that some schools decided that such complicated topics as these are not easily resolved in a school-assembly-type meeting. Others may think that these topics should be addressed at home or in the church. The argument for addressing them at school stresses the value of students' forming opinions on these matters in a setting where all the sides of the topics can be carefully considered. What better place, according to this argument, than schools to take up issues that all Americans are concerned about? It may be true as well that schools have chapel times designated for worship but don't have school assembly times for discussion of general topics. Those schools should consider modifying their schedules to include regular times for nonchapel assemblies.

With respect to the theft and pregnancy cases, it is not surprising that schools would opt to expel those students who were unrepentant (though, interestingly, small schools were slightly more open to keeping those students than were the larger schools). Schools were less averse to risk when dealing with repentant students, but not to the point of having scores in the pro-risk category. Those scores suggest that repentance is the key factor for some schools, and for others the deed itself is the key factor. The argument for letting repentance be the key factor is that it allows the school to model grace and forgiveness before the students. Such a position is riskier than expulsion, but it also sends the message to the school community that expulsion is not the only way to treat students caught up in increasingly common social problems.

The survey indicates that schools were slightly less averse to risk in formulating school policies on sponsoring cocurricular dances. The pro-risk position assumes the possibility of respectful, modest dances without music that includes suggestive language. In other words, this position is that it is possible to "redeem" the dance from immoral influences. Schools that attempt to do this are undertaking a difficult project, but one that may well communicate to students that it is possible to engage in current practices in popular culture without condoning immoral aspects of these practices.

Respondents did not support a policy of open enrollment with respect to faith profession. This may be the most risky of all options for schools to consider. The case for close ties linking school, family, and church as ideal for students is a well-accepted one. The pro-risk perspective raises the possibility of open-enrollment schools arising alongside profession-of-faith schools as a way to meet the needs of children from non-Christian backgrounds. Increasingly, Christian schools in urban settings opt for open enrollment in order to provide a stable educational setting for those whose home and church backgrounds are unstable. In the face of increasing social turbulence, schools may choose to better position themselves to help by modifying the profession-of-faith requirement to a parent-and-student contractual agreement that includes the moral and religious position of the school.

In a 1992 study of selected Christian high schools (all affiliated with either ACSI or CSI), Stephen Kaufmann noted a disconnect between what schools say they are about in their brochures and the actual understanding and implementation of their mission by teachers and students. He concludes by advocating programmatic changes that build in opportunities (such as service learning) for students to act upon what they are learning in their schools. The study found that students who had a hand in achieving the mission of the school were more likely to personally embrace that mission than students who did not (45).

Typically, Christian school expressions of mission entail effecting change in students and, through the students, a change in society. A school mission such as equipping students to affect culture and society for Christ suggests a difference between the goals and values of the Christian school and the goals and values of the larger society. Today's students in Christian high schools have a foot in each world, and schools face the challenge of preparing students to be in the world as change agents without being defined by it. When schools have programs that implement change of some sort, they are engaging in an inherently risky business, and this engagement calls for the type of leaders who are ready to embrace change and the risks that it entails.

Why take risks? The answer ultimately is to equip Christian-high-school students with the knowledge, skills, and values to live in and interact with a secular culture without losing their moorings as Christians. Christian schools fervently desire that their students live for Christ in every aspect of their lives. Ironically, risk-averse policies by schools may well run the risk of an unintended consequence: rebellion by students against or indifference to an education that they see as irrelevant to their lives. Equally troubling is the possibility of producing graduates who unreflectively embrace some of the values of the secular culture, and then baptize those values with religious language. These students often wind up as "yuppies for Jesus," equally at home in the self-absorption of the secular culture and in the church.

What about the example of the pro-life club members? Their school was not averse to risk, and it was willing to deal with the sometimes painful consequences of students who wanted to act decisively on what they believed to be true. Perhaps the day will come when those students as adults will champion the cause of the fetus, the widow, the orphan, and the stranger within their gates. Christian high schools could wish for no greater outcome for their students.

References

Kaufmann, Stephen. 1992. Sabbatical study report to schools in study. Faculty forum paper. Covenant College.

_____. 2005. *History and philosophy of American education*. Lookout Mountain, GA: privately printed.

Marsh, David D. 2000. Educational leadership for the twenty-first century: Integrating three essential perspectives. In *The Jossey-Bass reader on educational leadership*, 126–45. San Francisco: Jossey-Bass.

Marzano, Robert J., Timothy Waters, and Brian A. McNulty. 2005. *School leadership that works: From research to results*. Alexandria, VA: Association for Supervision and Curriculum Development.

Patterson, Jerry L. 1993. *Leadership for tomorrow's schools*. Alexandria, VA: Association for Supervision and Curriculum Development.

Ulstein, Stefan. 1988. G-rated education for a *Leave it to Beaver* world. *Christian Home and School* 66, no. 5 (May/June): 8–11.

Wolterstorff, Nicholas P. 2002. *Educating for life: Reflections on Christian teaching and learning*. Ed. Gloria Goris Stronks and Clarence W. Joldersma. Grand Rapids, MI: Baker.

PART TWO

Building Community
Among Faculty and Staff

CHAPTER **5**

WEIGHING LEADERSHIP MODELS

Biblical Foundations for Educational Leadership

By Gordon Brown

Gordon Brown, EdD, directs the doctor of education program at Columbia International University. He is the author of Guiding Faculty to Excellence *and several articles and chapters on Christian school education. His experience includes nineteen years as a Christian school administrator and seventeen years as a Christian-college teacher and administrator.*

CHAPTER 5

WEIGHING LEADERSHIP MODELS

By Gordon Brown

CHRISTIAN SCHOOL ADMINISTRATORS encounter a wide range of decisions every day: "Where should we put the new coffeemaker in the teachers' lounge?" "Which of the four applicants for the English position should we hire?" "How can we develop a clear vision of what our school wants to be?"

Faced with such an array of decisions, Christian school leaders respond from several perspectives. Some show concern for the feelings and well-being of faculty and students. Some give precedence to accomplishing the school's goals and objectives. Others base decisions on reasoned conclusions, or they emulate respected leaders. Some select options they imagine will work best, while others act within structured models of leadership. The real question facing all of them is, "By what rationale does one evaluate which courses of action are best?"

Decision making by Christian school leaders should be *by design* and not *by accident*. In order to decide purposefully, leaders must make choices rooted in understandings of the truth about the nature of human beings, the function of order in human society, and the role of authority and leadership in human groups.

To clarify the *design* and eliminate the *accident* of leadership, researchers have observed the behavior of leaders and organizations in attempts to postulate explanations for success and failure. Such investigations have led to the creation of multiple leadership models. Though helpful, these models have been misappropriated at times as guides for administrative decision making. So, a further question arises: "By what criteria should leadership theories and models be evaluated?"

Biblical Foundations for Evaluating Leadership Models

To answer this question, Christian educational leaders turn to the Bible, which describes truths about human relationships, community, and leadership. Biblical principles provide the foundation for relationships within the Church, a community of people pursuing common goals. These same principles speak to other Christian communities—such as Christian schools—that pursue kingdom goals.

These principles are important for educational leaders because they (1) form the evaluative framework by which leaders can assess the validity of theories and models, (2) suggest an organizing template for the discussion of research-based leadership, and (3) provide a foundation for educational decision making and leadership behavior.

Leadership as the Incarnation of Values

During interviews for a teaching position, an applicant asked interviewers for advice they would give a new faculty member. One response was so profound the applicant never forgot it: "Be who you want your students to be." This observation highlights a foundational scriptural principle for leadership. Leaders must be who they want their community members to be. The embodiment of values and purpose within leaders is the basic biblical criterion for leading others.

Biblical examples

In a recent study of Jesus' teaching methods, Gordon Brown (2005) identified 111 individual teaching-learning episodes in Jesus' ministry. For each episode, several variables—including objectives, types of learners, questions asked, outcomes, and types of teaching methods—were tracked.

The compiled results on teaching methods revealed that, among the seven types of methods cataloged, Jesus most frequently used *demonstration*. By His own words and actions, He demonstrated the truth He was teaching to students, or He modeled the learning He wanted them to acquire. John 10:37 reflects Jesus' readiness to be who He wanted His students to be when He said, "Do not believe me unless I do what my Father does."

In his apostolic role, Paul calls upon believers to imitate him. "Therefore I urge you to imitate me," he writes in 1 Corinthians 4:16. He repeats this concept in other epistles. "Whatever you have learned or received or heard from me, or seen in me—put it into practice" (Philippians 4:9). "You became imitators of us and of the Lord" (1 Thessalonians 1:6). "We did this ... in order to make ourselves a model for you to follow" (2 Thessalonians 3:9).

Scripture also includes general categories of leaders whom believers should imitate. Hebrews 6:12 commands Christians "to imitate those who through faith and patience inherit what has been promised." This command is followed by a similar one in Hebrews 13:7: "Remember your leaders.... Consider the outcome of their way of life and imitate their faith."

The heart as the locus of values

Scripture consistently emphasizes the importance of the heart as the repository of values and the generator of behavior. The prophet Samuel said of David, "the Lord has sought out a man after his own heart and appointed him leader of his people" (1 Samuel 13:14). David was a sharp contrast to Saul, who tried to lead while having a disobedient heart. In another example, the Lord told Israel in Jeremiah 3:15, "Then I will give you shepherds after my own heart, who will lead you with knowledge and understanding."

The heart reflects the person. Jesus affirmed this truth with these words: "For out of the overflow of the heart the mouth speaks" (Matthew 12:34), a statement that is similar in meaning to "as he thinks in his heart, so is he" (Proverbs 23:7, NKJV).

Leadership as a Service Function

The modeling role of leaders sets the stage for this second biblical principle: leadership is a service performed for the good of the community. Leaders lead their communities by serving and serve their communities by leading. Paul instructed masters to render service to servants (Ephesians 6:5–9), a paradigm antithetical to societal expectations in Paul's day for the master-servant relationship. By setting an example of service, leaders influence organizational members to relate similarly to one another.

The New Testament admonished church elders to serve the congregation with humility: "Be shepherds of God's flock that is under your care ... not greedy for money, but eager to serve; not lording it over those entrusted to you, but being examples to the flock" (1 Peter 5:2–3).

The premier example of service is Jesus. After washing the disciples' feet, He said, "Now that I, your Lord and Teacher, have washed your feet, you also should wash one another's feet. I have set you an example" (John 13:14–15). He also reminded the disciples, "The Son of Man did not come to be served, but to serve, and to give his life as a ransom for many" (Matthew 20:28), and "I am among you as one who serves" (Luke 22:27).

Leaders serve well when they recognize their authority as a God-ordained tool to assist in accomplishing His work. Authority has less to do with the individual possessing it and more to do with God's plan for the functioning of human groups (Romans 13:1–5).

Administration is one of many personnel functions that God has given to the Body. Paul reminds the Church that the Body is a unit made up of many parts, including apostles, prophets, teachers, and administrators (1 Corinthians 12:28). The absence of any one of these roles leaves a gap in the smooth functioning of the group. If administrators, with their accompanying leadership influence, were to vacate their vital role of providing order within the group, Corinthian-like chaos (1 Corinthians 11, 14) may result. In other words, leaders serve by viewing their responsibilities not as hierarchical, but as laterally interdependent with other roles.

Biblical leadership calls for leaders to possess sincere care for others. Timothy exemplified this concern. Speaking about him, Paul told the Philippians, "I have no one else of kindred spirit who will genuinely be concerned for your welfare" (2:20, NASB). This care surfaces when leaders "submit to one another" (Ephesians 5:21) by forgoing personal agendas to attend to the needs of subordinates. Leaders also embody this concern when they pray regularly for subordinates, as Christ did for His disciples (John 17).

Leadership as Community Transformation

A third major leadership principle found in Scripture focuses on the involvement of all community members in influencing one another toward continuous improvement in achieving the mission.

Every part of the Body influences other parts (1 Corinthians 12). When one person influences another, leadership happens. Therefore, every group member should be equipped to lead and influence in a positive manner because the accomplishment of the Church's mission requires the participation of all. God gave the Church a diversity of members "to prepare God's people for works of service, so that the body of Christ may be built up" (Ephesians 4:12). When many participate, the full community grows and changes, and transformation takes place.

When the full community embraces the mission and when all levels of individuals are equipped to influence and lead, then the community presses for continuous improvement in pursuit of organizational goals. Freedom to create and innovate permeates the community.

Scripture advocates the full involvement of all members. In 1 Corinthians 12:7 we read, "Now to each one the manifestation of the Spirit is given for the common good"—a clear reference to the interdependence of community members in achieving goals. Paul further supports this interdependent relationship in verses 25–26: "There should be no division in the body.... Its parts should have equal concern for each other.... if one part is honored, every part rejoices with it."

A transformed community is never satisfied with current levels of accomplishment; it perpetually reaches toward improvement. Paul emulates this principle in Philippians 3:12–14: "Not that I have already obtained all this, or have already been made perfect ... I press on toward the goal...." He also told the Corinthians to "try to excel in gifts that build up the church" (1 Corinthians 14:12).

Models Focusing on the Leader

Moral leadership

The moral-leadership model, most notably espoused by Thomas Sergiovanni (1992), focuses on two dimensions of leadership. On the one hand, leaders must embody the values, beliefs, purposes, and goals desired for the school. In doing so, leaders' moral leadership emanates from substantive qualities. According to Kenneth Leithwood, Doris Jantzi, and Roseanne Steinbach (1999), if leaders are going to enjoy legitimate authority and influence, they themselves must personify conceptions of what is right and good, and these conceptions must make sense to community members. Sergiovanni elaborates further on the leader's role of exemplifying substance: "Within communities leadership is defined by its source of authority—an authority that is embedded in ideas that connect us and encourage us to respond from within. Instead of following *someone*, the emphasis is on following commitments, promises, obligations, validated research, sound principles, agreed-upon standards, and other ideas" (2005, 56; emphasis in original)

The second dimension of moral leadership is exercised through the leader's processes. The leader believes strongly in processes that engage the entire followership in forming a community of shared ideas, principles, and purposes (Sergiovanni 1999). According to Sergiovanni (1984), schools may be thought of as having a "religion" that gives meaning and guides actions. Moral leadership, he posits, should give attention to the processes of developing and nurturing this religion so that it permeates the school community and becomes the normative basis for behavior.

Moral Leadership: A Comparison with Biblical Principles		
Leadership as the incarnation of values	**Leadership as a service function**	**Leadership as community transformation**
Moral leadership requires leaders to possess the values that the community believes are sound and good.	Moral leaders serve the community by initiating processes that allow the community to develop and nurture central cultural values.	As moral leaders embody values in themselves and in processes, they work to transform community members into committed participants who possess common beliefs, principles, and values.

Adaptive leadership

Schools today face complex and ever-changing problems. The variables affecting educational achievement are so multifaceted that the outcomes of any particular course of action are unpredictable (Heifetz 1994). Educational leaders have to deal not only with organizational issues but also with societal forces such as poverty, changing family structures, and increasing diversity.

Robert Owens takes the position that "problems confronting schools today, particularly problems of school reform, are clearly adaptive problems and require adaptive leadership concepts and techniques" (2004, 259). He believes that leaders must find innovative ways to lead under such unstable conditions. Such adaptation calls for utilizing the knowledge and cooperation of people at multiple levels in the organization in the leadership process. Collaboration among many individuals in an iterative process over time best equips the organization to focus its full personnel resources on development of solutions (2004).

Adaptive Leadership: A Comparison with Biblical Principles		
Leadership as the incarnation of values	**Leadership as a service function**	**Leadership as community transformation**
Adaptive leadership requires leaders to value the involvement of people at multiple levels within the organization as the best means of problem solving.	Adaptive leaders serve their schools by welcoming the input of many individuals while the school seeks innovative solutions to changing problems.	As adaptive leaders involve multiple community members in problem solving, they foster broad ownership of the results of the iterative leadership process.

Servant leadership

In 1970, Robert Greenleaf published an essay that elevated the concept of "servant leadership" into the public discussion of leadership and management (1991). His premise was that a leader is a servant first, having a natural disposition to serve rather than to be served. While Greenleaf did not espouse biblical underpinnings for his theory, some Christian leaders saw connections to the servant leadership of Jesus.

Ken Blanchard and Phil Hodges' description of Jesus' leadership style portrayed the core of leadership as first a matter of the heart's being other-centered. "Whenever we have an opportunity or responsibility to influence the thinking and the behavior of others, the first choice we are called to make is whether to see the moment through the eyes of self-interest or for the benefit of those we are leading" (2003, 15).

Blanchard and Hodges (2003) offered their previously developed situational-leadership model as a vehicle for putting servant leadership into practice. In this model, servant leaders take their behavior cues from the needs of those they lead. In one example, people with high levels of commitment but low levels of competence need leaders who not only provide specific directions about roles and goals but also closely track performance in order to provide specific feedback on results. Leaders who respond appropriately to the commitment and competence levels of their subordinates are truly serving them.

Blanchard and Hodges (2003) further connected the results of servant leadership to its focus on people. By encouraging the long-range growth of people involved in producing the desired end product, the servant-leadership model culminates in the effective accomplishment of the product itself.

The true success of servant leadership rests on the values embedded within the leader. Blanchard and Hodges postulated that such success "depends on how clearly values are defined, ordered, and lived by the leader" (51). In this proposition, Blanchard and Hodges connected to the biblical principle of leadership as the incarnation of values.

Servant Leadership: A Comparison with Biblical Principles		
Leadership as the incarnation of values	Leadership as a service function	Leadership as community transformation
A precondition of servant leadership is the personal ownership and living out of the values desired in the community.	Servant leadership calls for leaders to view leadership as meeting the needs of others rather than as satisfying personal ambitions.	When servant leaders respond suitably to the varied commitment and competence levels of people, they create a community of growing, developing, and productive people.

Principle-centered leadership

Principle-centered leadership, a term popularized by Stephen Covey (1991), rests on principles more than on behaviors or strategies. Covey identified four levels of principle-centered leadership, each accompanied by key principles. The center, or core level, is personal and is based on the principle of trustworthiness. The second level is interpersonal, and it requires trust between leaders and followers in the community. Third, the managerial level has as its driving force the empowerment principle. And fourth, the organizational level calls for engagement of the alignment principle.

At the center of Covey's model are the characteristics of principle-centered leaders themselves. Because of the principles on which they consistently operate, such leaders possess the following characteristics:

- become trustworthy persons
- are continually learning new principles, skills, and ideas
- are service oriented, seeing life as a mission rather than a career
- radiate positive energy by being cheerful, pleasant, optimistic, helpful, and enthusiastic
- believe in other people, realizing that current inadequate performance is different from unseen potential
- lead balanced lives emotionally, intellectually, spiritually, physically, and relationally
- see life as an adventure, rediscovering people each time they meet them
- are synergistic change-catalysts who improve almost any situation in which they find themselves
- engage in self-renewal by intentionally exercising the physical, mental, emotional, and spiritual dimensions of their personalities

Principle-Centered Leadership: A Comparison with Biblical Principles		
Leadership as the incarnation of values	**Leadership as a service function**	**Leadership as community transformation**
Principle-centered leaders consistently live and act in concert with deeply held principles. In doing so, they become trustworthy persons.	Principle-centered leaders operate out of service, contribution, and mission.	Principle-centered leadership creates a climate for growth among community members, transforming them into principle-centered people themselves.

Models Focusing on the Instructional Enterprise

Principals and student achievement

In recent years the national call for accountability in education has become more insistent. From the Goals 2000 statement prepared in 1994 to the No Child Left Behind Act of 2001, the focus on ensuring student learning has intensified. The important question is, "How can schools improve student learning?" For educational leaders, this question translates into "How can principals influence student learning in their schools?"

These questions have triggered numerous research studies and reviews of previously conducted explorations in attempts to discover causal relationships between behaviors of educational leaders and the learning achievement of students. To synthesize a diversity of findings, Kathleen Cotton (2003) conducted a meta-analysis of eighty-one research reports on principal effectiveness. Her study identified five broad categories of principals' behaviors that relate positively to enhanced student learning in schools:

1. Establishing a clear focus on student learning (vision, clear learning goals, high expectations for all students)
2. Relating and interacting in supportive and accessible ways
3. Establishing a school culture of shared leadership, collaboration, risk taking, and continuous improvement
4. Supporting and promoting instruction through classroom observation and feedback, protection of instructional time, and discussion of instructional issues
5. Establishing accountability for student learning through monitoring progress and using student data for program improvement

Principals and Student Achievement Meta-analysis: A Comparison with Biblical Principles		
Leadership as the incarnation of values	**Leadership as a service function**	**Leadership as community transformation**
Meta-analysis research shows that educational leaders should possess vision, clear goals, and high expectations for student learning.	Meta-analysis research shows that educational leaders should share leadership and decision making and should support teacher development and autonomy.	Meta-analysis research shows that educational leaders should seek to build community involvement in the vision and goals for high student achievement.

School leadership that works

Robert J. Marzano, Timothy Waters, and Brian A. McNulty (2005) collaborated to produce a meta-analysis of effective school leadership. They isolated sixty-nine studies since 1970 that directly examined the quantitative relationship between building individual-school leadership and the academic achievement of students. The studies involved 2,802 schools at various levels: elementary (1,319 schools), middle/junior high (323 schools), high school (371 schools), K–8 (290 schools), and K–12 (499 schools). The total estimated number of teachers involved was 14,000, and the estimated number of students was 1,400,000.

From analyzing the studies, Marzano, Waters, and McNulty found twenty-one principals' responsibilities that correlate with student achievement. Of those twenty-one, nine are necessarily the purview of the principal as the foundation for establishing a purposeful school community (2005).

Responsibilities Necessarily the Purview of the Principal (Marzano, Waters, and McNulty 2005)	
Responsibility	*The extent to which the principal ...*
Affirmation	recognizes and celebrates accomplishments and acknowledges failures
Communication	establishes strong lines of communication with and among teachers and students
Culture	fosters shared beliefs and a sense of community and cooperation
Ideals/beliefs	communicates and operates from strong ideals and beliefs about schooling
Input	involves teachers in the design and implementation of important decisions and policies
Optimizer	inspires and leads challenging innovations
Relationships	demonstrates an awareness of the personal aspects of teachers and staff
Situational awareness	is aware of the details and undercurrents in the running of the school and uses this information to address current and potential problems
Visibility	has quality contact and interactions with teachers and students

The additional twelve responsibilities identified through the meta-analysis were those that could be distributed among members of a leadership team. Certainly the principal should be part of the team and thus should participate in these responsibilities, but they could be shared with, or distributed among, other leaders.

Responsibilities That Can Be Shared (Marzano, Waters, and McNulty 2005)	
Responsibility	**The extent to which the leaders ...**
Change agent	are willing to change and actively challenge the status quo
Contingent rewards	recognize and reward individual accomplishments
Discipline	protect teachers from issues and influences that would detract from their teaching time or focus
Flexibility	adapt their leadership behavior to the needs of the current situation and are comfortable with dissent
Focus	establish clear goals and keep those goals in the forefront of the school's attention
Intellectual stimulation	ensure that faculty and staff are aware of the most current theories and practices and make the discussion of these a regular aspect of the school's culture
Involvement in curriculum, instruction, and assessment	are directly involved in the design and implementation of curriculum, instruction, and assessment practices
Knowledge of curriculum, instruction, and assessment	are knowledgeable about current curriculum, instruction, and assessment practices
Monitoring/evaluating	monitor the effectiveness of school practices and their impact on student learning
Order	establish a set of standard operating procedures and routines
Outreach	are advocates and spokespersons for the school to all stakeholders
Resources	provide teachers with materials and professional development necessary for the successful execution of their jobs

Marzano, Waters, and McNulty (2005) provide school leaders with research-based behaviors that relate positively to the instructional enterprise. The meta-analysis also generated suggestions to help principals orchestrate two levels of change: (1) incremental change that fine-tunes a system and (2) decisive, quick action that generates dramatic departures from the expected.

In addition, the meta-analysis reminded principals that simply exercising good leadership is not enough to improve student achievement. Good leaders must also make good decisions regarding the work that needs focused attention. Examples of "right work" include guaranteed and viable curriculum, a safe and orderly environment, instructional strategies, classroom management, and motivation (2005).

School Leadership That Works: A Comparison with Biblical Principles		
Leadership as the incarnation of values	**Leadership as a service function**	**Leadership as community transformation**
Effective school leaders operate out of a set of strongly held beliefs and values about schooling.	Effective school leaders serve the school community by working to make all community members effective and productive contributors to the school's success.	Effective school leaders work to foster a transformed culture in which all members share common beliefs while developing a sense of community and cooperation.

Supportive supervision

Supportive supervision is a philosophy, an approach, and a specific program or process, all at one time. As a philosophy, it affirms that leaders develop effective schools by emphasizing strong instructional leadership programs. As an approach, it focuses on developing and communicating expectations for professional performance at all stages of teacher performance and evaluation. As a specific program or process, it follows a cycle consisting of six elements: goal setting, lesson planning, observation, professional development, extensive professional commitment, and end-of-year evaluation (Coppola, Scricca, and Connors 2004).

Supportive supervision endorses core values that are integral to the smooth functioning of any organization. The words and actions of leaders widely promulgate these values throughout the school, and eventually, faculty, staff, students, and parents share them.

The six elements of the supportive-supervision process are designed to develop teachers who skillfully affect student learning. The process begins with goal setting by teachers in which they identify the broad, general educational changes they want to bring about. Step two, lesson planning, follows the established curricular and instructional goals for the year. The third component is observation of classroom dynamics. Observation is foundational because school administrators use it to engage themselves in teaching teachers. The fourth component, professional development of faculty, is integral to the other supportive-supervision components. The fifth feature is extensive professional commitment, which develops teachers' dedication to the school, its shared values and culture, its philosophy of education, and its students. Through the final component, end-of-year evaluation, leaders provide an insightful, comprehensive, and goal-oriented summary of teachers' professional performances for a full school year (Coppola, Scricca, and Connors 2004).

Supportive Supervision: A Comparison with Biblical Principles		
Leadership as the incarnation of values	**Leadership as a service function**	**Leadership as community transformation**
Supportive-supervision leaders believe in and communicate a strongly held set of core values and beliefs about schooling.	Supportive-supervision leaders contribute to developing the instructional expertise of faculty and, as such, see themselves as rendering service to faculty and the school's entire community.	Supportive-supervision leaders seek to create a school community that supports teacher development and student learning

Models Focusing on Community Transformation

Transformational-leadership model

Though his best-selling book dealt with political leadership, James MacGregor Burns (1978) strongly influenced many of the current theories of transformational leadership, which have found application in business, education, and other venues. Burns distinguished transformational leadership from transactional leadership. Transformational leadership appeals to the moral values of followers, attempting to raise their commitment to ethical issues and energizing them to reform institutions by using their energy and resources. By contrast, transactional leadership motivates followers by appealing to their self-interest (Yukl 2002). Followers simply conduct transactions with leaders, exchanging services and productivity for benefits and rewards.

Several years later, Bernard Bass (1985) extended the understanding of transformational leadership. His ideas are summarized by Gary Yukl:

> With transformational leadership, the followers feel trust, admiration, loyalty, and respect toward the leader, and they are motivated to do more than they originally expected to do.... The leader transforms and motivates followers by (1) making them more aware of the importance of task outcomes, (2) inducing them to transcend their own self-interest for the sake of the organization or team, and (3) activating their higher-order needs. (2002, 253)

Many writers use the terms *transformational* and *charismatic* interchangeably when referring to certain leaders. Followers of charismatic leaders perceive their leaders as endowed with exceptional qualities. The influence of charismatic leaders is based on this perception, not on tradition or formal authority. Because of their charisma, they attract followers who believe in the vision they espouse, thus *transforming* the organization.

Transformational Leadership: A Comparison with Biblical Principles		
Leadership as the incarnation of values	**Leadership as a service function**	**Leadership as community transformation**
Transformational leaders believe passionately in a vision or values.	Transformational leaders believe they serve great causes, the organization, and its individual members well when they motivate followers to endorse and pursue a vision or values.	Transformational leadership results in a remaking of the community of followers who wholeheartedly espouse and endorse a new vision or values.

Leadership in a culture of change

The dynamics of society today require that educational leaders be equipped to guide schools successfully despite new demands and challenges. Michael Fullan (2001) addresses this issue while calling on leaders to give patient, reasoned attention to the change process rather than pursue rapid, reactionary innovation.

Fullan espouses five themes for successful leadership. The first is *moral purpose*, a quality that leaders possess when they hold strong personal ownership of the school's core mission. The second theme is *understanding change*. Fullan asserts that leaders who truly understand the change process take into account the organization's system and all stakeholders. The third theme centers on *relationships*. Leaders who focus on building relationships during times of change position their schools to focus on systemic improvements that will generate the long-lasting change they are seeking. The fourth theme is *knowledge building*. By this, Fullan means that developing knowledge, as opposed to merely collecting information, produces a usable base that will support and enhance lasting change. Fullan's final theme is *coherence building*. During change and disruption of the status quo, leaders allow people's differences to surface, thereby generating creative ideas and novel solutions for the institution. Out of this practice, coherence develops (2001).

Leadership in a Culture of Change: A Comparison with Biblical Principles		
Leadership as the incarnation of values	**Leadership as a service function**	**Leadership as community transformation**
Leaders facing change remain firmly committed to the deepest purposes of the school.	Leaders facing change, while guiding the process of dealing with change, do so in a manner that serves the good of the entire community.	Leaders facing change engage in building relationships within the community, thereby involving the full community in facing and solving its problems.

Leadership capacity for lasting improvement

What happens to a school's momentum when an energetic and innovative leader departs? That is the question addressed in Linda Lambert's (2003) case for building leadership capacity throughout the school. Lambert defines *leadership capacity* as broad-based, skillful participation in the work of leadership by the principal, a vast majority of teachers, and large numbers of parents and students. When this participation occurs, the school will probably possess a strong leadership capacity that results in high student performance.

Since principals, teachers, students, and parents are the key players in the work of schooling, they must collaborate to form a partnership of leadership that becomes a powerful force in the school. If effective principal leadership is present, teachers will often form professional teams that invite students and parents to participate in the work of leadership. Under these conditions, individuals working together maximize their combination of talents for the betterment of student learning.

Lambert identifies five additional features characteristic of high leadership capacity in schools. First, participants share a vision or purpose for the school that is based on their core values and hopes. This shared vision provides coherence to programs and activities. Second, decisions and practice are informed by collective inquiry-based use of information. "Questions are posed, evidence is collected and reflected upon, and decisions and actions are shaped around the collected findings" (2003, 6). Third, the broad involvement of staff and school families creates a collective responsibility for all students in the school. Fourth, when all stakeholders regularly reflect on practice, they generate new and better approaches to their work. Parents improve their parenting, students improve their learning, teachers improve their teaching, and so on. Fifth, schools with strong leadership capacity experience high or steadily improving student achievement. Achievement includes not only academic growth but personal and civic development as well (2003).

Leadership Capacity for Lasting Improvement: A Comparison with Biblical Principles		
Leadership as the incarnation of values	**Leadership as a service function**	**Leadership as community transformation**
Leaders who build leadership capacity in schools involve multiple stakeholders in the creation of a shared vision based on commonly held core values.	Leaders who build leadership capacity in schools serve by skillfully involving teachers, students, and parents in the leadership enterprise.	Leaders who build leadership capacity transform the school into a purposeful, self-renewing community of people who continuously pursue new and better ways to achieve the school's mission.

Now What? Application to Practice

Developing Leaders' Capacity as Values Carriers

As biblical principle, leadership theory, and current research all suggest, the starting point for leadership development is the person of the leader. Christian educational leaders who envision purpose-driven schools must lead the way and set the example by who they are and what they deeply believe. The *objective* is to develop the leader's personal investment in and ownership of the mission and values desired in the school and its community. The starting point is to answer this *evaluative question*: "How strongly are the desired values incarnated in the leader?" The following are implementation ideas for pursuing this objective and answering the evaluative question.

■ *Leader accountability relationship.*

Leaders secure one or more mature people who agree to ask accountability questions of the leader regularly. Areas for accountability may include the leader's personal walk with God, personal purity, family and spousal relationships, professional development, faculty relationships, student relationships, and servant attitude.

■ *Leader renewal days.*

Leaders schedule and implement time for spiritual, intellectual, and emotional restoration and renewal. They schedule personal vision days for communing with God, setting annual performance goals, or evaluating progress.

■ *Reflections on practice.*

How closely do the leaders' day-to-day activities align with the school's mission? Leaders should journal their activities for a sample week, then analyze the extent to which each activity (or time block of activities) contributes to the school's stated mission. Do the leaders' behaviors focus on essential mission elements? Are there elements of the leaders' behaviors that are peripheral and should be replaced with more strategic activities?

Developing Leaders' Service Mentality

The alignment is clear: biblical principle, leadership theory, and current research agree that truly effective leaders view themselves as serving the organizational community in pursuit of its mission. The organizational community does not serve the leader. The actual focus and nature of the leader's service will vary in different organizational environments. The *objective* is to deepen the leader's capacity for and participation in servant leadership within the context of the school community. The starting point is to answer this *evaluative question*: "How is the leader serving the organization?" The following are implementation ideas for pursuing this objective and answering the evaluative question.

■ *Development of human resources.*

Leaders serve their schools when they increase the capacity of teachers, students, and parents to contribute to the school's mission and ministry. Leaders do so by scheduling and budgeting for training and development activities. Leaders may mentor one or more people who have leadership potential.

■ *Self-evaluation of tasks.*

Leaders evaluate their catalog of personal tasks, asking, "Which tasks, if delegated, would help grow the capacity of others to contribute to the school's mission?"

■ *Evaluation of decision hierarchy.*

Leaders examine the decisions made within the organization and the levels (such as board, principal, department, and teacher) at which they are made. Are decisions made by people whose quality of work is affected? Are they made by people who are in a position to implement solutions most directly? Leaders serve schools when they communicate decisions to people who have the power in their work to influence the quality of solution implementation.

Enhancing Leaders' Impact on Community Transformation

A leader has truly transformed a school community when that community perpetuates cherished values well after the leader's departure.

In such a scenario, one would find a high percentage of administrators, teachers, students, and parents exercising influence, or leadership, that maintains and even extends those values. The incarnation of values in many individuals matures into transformation of the full community. Another evidence of community transformation is the pervasive presence of innovation and the pursuit of excellence throughout the organization. The *objective* is to develop mission passion, commitment, and leadership among individuals and groups that make up the school community. The starting point is to answer this *evaluative question*: "To what extent do the various constituencies in the community espouse the mission and core values while possessing the capacity to pursue innovative improvement?" The following are implementation ideas for pursuing this objective and answering the evaluative question.

■ *Annual "vision day" retreat.*

Once a year, leaders conduct an all-day retreat for faculty, staff, and representatives of parents and students to revisit the school's mission and vision. The day could include presentations of examples of mission-focused activities, evaluation of the school's current "mission temperature," and the brainstorming of new ways to enhance pursuit of the mission throughout the school.

■ *Annual state-of-the-school address.*

Principals prepare and deliver annual state-of-the-school addresses or documents. Such a project requires principals to assess the community's cohesiveness around the mission and goals of the school. Principals can set the bar high while challenging and encouraging the entire school community to press on.

■ *Committee to monitor "mission heartbeat."*

Leaders form a committee of selected people to monitor the pulse of mission buy-in and the pursuit of excellence in all sections of the school community. As a result of its meetings, which take place every other month, the committee makes recommendations for action steps to enhance community transformation.

■ *Mentoring of immediate subordinates.*

In regular conferences with immediate subordinates (such as assistant principals and department heads), principals intentionally model the desired values for all persons in the school community. Principals ask assistants to evaluate how deeply other people they supervise believe in the school's mission and values.

■ *Review of existing committee structure and performance.*

Leaders conduct an administrative review of committee work over the past year. Have committees been making decisions that contribute to mission enhancement? Are the school's mission and goals the foundation for their discussions, recommendations, and action plans? Do committees need infusions of mission alignment?

Summary

Educational leadership aligns itself best with biblical principles when (1) leaders model the values desired in the school community, (2) leaders exercise leadership as a service to the community, and (3) leaders equip members of the school community to be carriers of the school's mission and values as the members interact with and influence others in the organization.

Multiple theorists, researchers, and practitioners espouse some or all of these principles. Though they may not perceive the God of the Bible to be the source of these truths, they nevertheless acknowledge that empirical research and practice bear witness to the efficacy of these truths in human relationships. Such theorists and researchers have studied leadership that focuses on (1) leaders' personal values, (2) the school's instructional enterprise, and (3) the transformation of most or all community members.

On the basis of analyses of biblical principles and research findings, Christian educational leaders can have confidence that they are tapping into God's truth as they pursue the development of organizations. As they do so, leaders should ask themselves three basic questions:

1. Am I the person I expect teachers, students, and parents to be?
2. Do I understand how my leadership role is a service to the entire school community?
3. If I were to leave the school, would the community I leave behind carry on the mission and core values with continued passion and commitment?

References

Bass, Bernard M. 1985. *Leadership and performance beyond expectations.* New York: Free Press.

Blanchard, Ken, and Phil Hodges. 2003. *The servant leader: Transforming your heart, head, hands, and habits.* Nashville, TN: J. Countryman.

Brown, Gordon. 2005. The ultimate in differentiated instruction: A new look at Jesus' pedagogy. Presentation given at Grace Christian School Convention, Manila, Philippines.

Burns, James MacGregor. 1978. *Leadership.* New York: Harper and Row.

Coppola, Albert J., Diane B. Scricca, and Gerald E. Connors. 2004. *Supportive supervision: Becoming a teacher of teachers.* Thousand Oaks, CA: Corwin Press.

Cotton, Kathleen. 2003. *Principals and student achievement: What the research says.* Alexandria, VA: Association for Supervision and Curriculum Development.

Covey, Stephen R. 1991. *Principle-centered leadership.* New York: Simon and Schuster.

Fullan, Michael. 2001. *Leading in a culture of change.* San Francisco: Jossey-Bass.

Greenleaf, Robert K. 1991. *The servant as leader.* Westfield, IN: Robert K. Greenleaf Center.

Heifetz, Ronald A. 1994. *Leadership without easy answers.* Cambridge, MA: Belknap Press.

Lambert, Linda. 2003. *Leadership capacity for lasting school improvement.* Alexandria, VA: Association for Supervision and Curriculum Development.

Leithwood, Kenneth A., Doris Jantzi, and Roseanne Steinbach. 1999. *Changing leadership for changing times.* Buckingham, UK: Open University Press.

Marzano, Robert J., Timothy Waters, and Brian A. McNulty. 2005. *School leadership that works: From research to results.* Alexandria, VA: Association for Supervision and Curriculum Development.

Owens, Robert G. 2004. *Organizational behavior in education: Adaptive leadership and school reform.* 8th ed. Boston, MA: Allyn and Bacon.

Sergiovanni, Thomas J. 1984. Leadership and excellence in schooling. *Educational Leadership* 41, no. 5 (February): 4–13.

_____. 1992. *Moral leadership: Getting to the heart of school improvement.* San Francisco, CA: Jossey-Bass.

_____. 1999. *The lifeworld of leadership: Creating culture, community, and personal meaning in our schools.* San Francisco, CA: Jossey-Bass.

_____. 2005. *Strengthening the heartbeat: Leading and learning together in schools.* San Francisco, CA: Jossey-Bass.

Yukl, Gary A. 2002. *Leadership in organizations.* 5th ed. Upper Saddle River, NJ: Prentice-Hall.

CHAPTER 6

ORGANIZATIONAL THEORY

*Understanding
Schools as Systems*

✍

By Kevin J. Eames

*Kevin J. Eames, PhD, is the director of institutional research at Covenant College,
and he teaches organizational leadership in the MEd program there. Before serving at Covenant, he was an assistant professor of psychology and the director of
graduate education at Dordt College. His doctorate is in counseling psychology.*

CHAPTER 6

ORGANIZATIONAL THEORY

By Kevin J. Eames

KELLY CHADWICK IS confronted with a problem. As a Christian school superintendent, Kelly has overseen a significant increase in enrollment over the past four years. In fact, enrollment has increased so rapidly that finding qualified teachers to meet the demand is difficult, and the school has had to make do with a series of one-year appointments. Accompanying this increased enrollment is a discouraging decline in standardized test scores on mathematics and reading comprehension. Since academic excellence is one of the school's hallmarks, the school board has expressed alarm over the trend of declining test scores, and it is pressuring Chadwick to reverse the trend. Faculty members claim that the curriculum needs to be enhanced, but the elementary principal believes that it is a personnel problem and can be remedied by hiring experienced teachers. Of course, hiring more experienced teachers also means higher salaries, which will stress the budget despite the increase in enrollment. Chadwick has been struggling to reduce full-time equivalency (FTE) numbers as costs have grown along with enrollment. Another emerging problem is the reception new students receive from those who have been with the school since kindergarten. There are clearly two cliques developing: the "olds" and the "news." Some of the new students complain that even the faculty treat them differently from their "old" classmates.

Kelly Chadwick's problem is not unique. Christian school leaders are frequently confronted with competing demands from multiple constituencies. Moreover, they find that accommodating one constituency can have unintended and unanticipated consequences for other parts of the school. Even compromise can have unintended consequences. These less-than-satisfying outcomes are not necessarily the result of inexperienced leadership. Educational organizations are dynamic and complex, and in order for leaders to be effective, they must recognize the reality of these characteristics and learn how to accommodate them.

Organizing Organizations

Despite its unique educational mission, a school functions like any other organization. Traditional definitions of an organization tend to emphasize goal-directedness and cooperation for mutual benefit. W. Richard Scott defines organizations as *"social structures created by individuals to support the collaborative pursuit of specified goals"* (2003, 11; emphasis in original). Edgar H. Schein defines an organization as *"the planned coordination of the activities of a number of people for the achievement of some common, explicit purpose or goal, through division of labor and function, and through a hierarchy of authority and responsibility"* (1994, 15; emphasis in original). In an exposition of the thought of philosopher Herman Dooyeweerd, L. Kalsbeek differentiates between institutional communities and noninstitutional communities. Institutional communities are part of God's structural creation; they include marriage, the family, the state, and the church. Noninstitutional communities are defined as *"goal-oriented voluntary associations"* (1975, 251; emphasis in original) that members are free to join or leave (in contrast to institutional communities, where a separation such as divorce or excommunication constitutes a significant rupture of the community).

Christian schools are organized for the purpose of providing a Christian education. The task of providing that education requires the involvement of a faculty, support staff, and administrators who divide the labor involved and (presumably) cooperate with one another to accomplish their goal. Moreover, the Christian school contains an authority structure that provides accountability for achieving its goals: administrators are accountable to governing boards, faculty members are accountable to administrators, and so forth. While the Christian school certainly conforms to the traditional definition of an organization, that definition is incomplete. The traditional definition reflects a rational paradigm for organizations that emerged from the industrial revolution and is characterized by a linear, cause-and-effect perspective on behavior.

This rational paradigm for organizations translates to a bureaucratic structure that promotes the optimal use of time, materials, resources, and personnel toward the organization's goals (Hanson 2003). Additionally, management concepts such as hierarchical reporting structures, span of control, job and task specialization, and quantification of outcomes are also part of the bureaucratic structure. E. Mark Hanson demonstrates a number of ways in which the rational approach has been applied to schools. This application includes a hierarchical reporting structure involving superintendents, principals, and teachers; a span of control that involves a specific number of assistant principals reporting to one principal; job or task specialization reflected by teacher subject area and grade level; and quantification of outcomes through achievement and aptitude testing. Many of these bureaucratic principles are so thoroughly embedded in educational administration that managing a school without them would be hard to imagine. The rational, bureaucratic approach has its limitations, however, including a resistance to change and the perspective that comes with the narrow focus of a bureaucracy. Moreover, the rational paradigm with its emphasis on fixed structures and repetitive processes is insufficient to accommodate the dynamics of organizational behavior. A more complex paradigm is necessary.

Introduction to Systems Theory

In 1968, biologist Ludwig von Bertalanffy published the seminal *General System Theory: Foundations, Development, Applications*. This work introduces general systems theory and applies the basic concepts to multiple disciplines, including engineering, social problems, biology, and psychiatry. Systems theory applies unsurprisingly to the natural and technical sciences, but researchers in the social sciences have also expanded on von Bertalanffy's work, making significant contributions to their respective fields. Notable examples include family-systems theory (Bowen 1986; Minuchin 1974), organizational learning (Senge 1990), and organizational design (Hanna 1988).

There are an ample number of definitions of a system in the literature (Beer 1980; Hanna 1988; Schein 1994; Scott 2003; Senge 1990), but

111

certain characteristics remain consistent in most. These characteristics include the following:

- boundaries of various degrees of permeability
- subsystems that are delineated by boundaries within the system and are demarcated by functions, goals, roles, physical location, or a combination of these
- interaction with the surrounding environment, including input from and output to that environment, where the output results from processes that constitute the core purpose of the system
- feedback from the environment concerning the system's output, allowing the system to self-regulate and self-correct
- homeostatic mechanisms that maintain the equilibrium of the system, resist change, and seek to preserve the system from disintegration
- organizational complexity

A systems definition applies to a Christian school in that its boundaries are both physical and psychological. The physical boundaries are perhaps most obvious, and they best illustrate the application of permeability. A Christian school bordered by a high fence or wall with one entrance that is closely monitored would have a much less permeable boundary than one with an open field surrounding the physical plant and multiple entrances. Similarly, a Christian school with strict admissions policies (for example, requiring both parents to be Christians with active church membership) would be less permeable than a school with an open admissions policy. Subsystems within a school may be conceptualized by group membership (teachers, students, staff), by academic department, by job function, or by ages. Additional constituencies would also be considered subsystems, including parents, alumni, and board of trustees.

Interaction with the environment highlights the purpose of the Christian school. Input in the form of tuition dollars and other revenue, as well as the students themselves, enter the school-as-system. Revenue is applied toward instruction and all ancillary functions. Students are instructed with the goal of transforming them toward some institutional definition of what a student should look like at the end of a school year. The core processes that occur between input and output involve the educational processes, including curriculum, instruction, discipline, athletics, and cocurricular activities. Feedback from the environment comes in multiple forms: standardized test results, increasing or decreasing enrollment, donations, and feedback from parents and other concerned constituents. This feedback enables the school-as-system to self-correct. For example, if standardized test results consistently reveal a deficit in mathematics, remedial action can rectify the deficit.

Homeostatic mechanisms are employed by the system to maintain its stability. Systems resist change in order to maintain their current level of integration. When a significant change occurs in an organizational system, individuals and groups react consciously or unconsciously as if threatened with the disintegration of the organization as they know it. In a Christian school, this homeostatic mechanism is experienced when there is a major change in policy, administration, or curriculum. A new principal or superintendent must often cope with the mistrust and superstition of faculty members who have an obvious preference for the previous administrator. For the first year at least, grumbling and references to how things used to be drift from the faculty lounge. Other sources of homeostasis include students, parents, staff, and board members. Anyone with a stake in the outcome of the school-as-system will respond to change with some level of caution and mistrust. This response is one reason that educational institutions are conservative by nature, are not nimble, and are not able to respond quickly to changes in the market.

Systems Theory and Organizational Complexity

Organizational complexity is a characteristic that is represented by two key concepts: (1) nonlinear causality and (2) levels, or layers, of complexity. Nonlinear causality rejects a simple cause-and-effect explanation for outcomes; instead, it recognizes the dynamic and unpredictable interaction among subsystems. These interactions can yield unanticipated outcomes, even as the system strives to maintain equilibrium. Richard Scott notes that complex social systems maintain three types of equilibrium: (1) environmental feedback that corrects overly volatile changes and returns the system to its initial state (also referred to as *negative feedback*); (2) environmental feedback that amplifies the initial disturbances so that small changes over time lead to explosive outcomes (also referred to as *positive feedback*); and (3) a combination of both positive and negative feedback, yielding unpredictable outcomes (2003, 93).

It is important to understand the application of the terms *positive feedback* and *negative feedback* in systems theory. In common usage, *positive feedback* refers to receiving flattering or encouraging responses from others, and *negative feedback* refers to receiving critical or discouraging responses from others. In systems theory, however, *positive feedback* refers to feedback that moves the system away from its current homeostatic state; conversely, *negative feedback* returns the system back to its homeostatic state.

A simple example taken from Christian school administration demonstrates the uses of these terms. Assume that the board of trustees approves the implementation of a football program at the high school level. However, such an implementation requires an increase in tuition of 12.5 percent to offset expenses such as the cost of personnel, equipment, and insurance associated with a high-risk athletic program. When the tuition increase is announced and linked with the football program, a majority of families respond with strong objections to the increase, complain that the school is deviating from its tradition of strong academics for the sake of athletics, and threaten to go elsewhere for their children's education. In the face of a significant reduction in enrollment and the overall ill will generated by the move, the board rescinds the tuition increase and decides against implementing the football program. The figure below demonstrates how this school-based drama illustrates both positive and negative feedback.

Systems theorists have also recognized the importance of acknowledging levels of complexity in systems. Systems may range from the simple to the highly complex, from the deterministic to the highly variable and

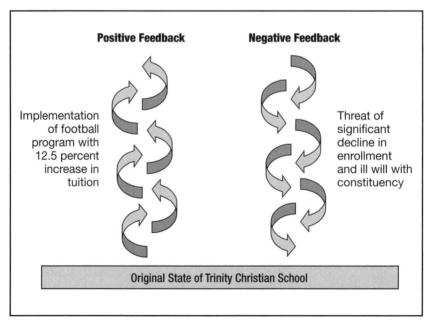

Positive Feedback   **Negative Feedback**

Implementation of football program with 12.5 percent increase in tuition

Threat of significant decline in enrollment and ill will with constituency

Original State of Trinity Christian School

probabilistic (Scott 2003). In addition to such one-dimensional continua that describe the character of systems, there have also been taxonomies proposed to encapsulate all systems. Kenneth Boulding proposed such a taxonomy by conceptualizing an "arrangement of theoretical systems and constructs in a hierarchy of complexity, roughly corresponding to the complexity of the 'individuals' of the various empirical fields … leading towards a 'system of systems' " (1956, 202).

Boulding's system of systems contains nine levels. The first three levels, the simplest levels, refer to nonorganic properties, including descriptions of static structures; the mechanical movement of natural and constructed systems such as the movement of astronomical bodies; and feedback systems that take in external information and regulate or control the system. These three levels constitute the necessary components of more complex biological and social systems. Levels four through seven constitute individual biological levels. The fourth is the "level of the cell" (203). Levels five and six refer to the plant and animal worlds, respectively, while level seven refers to the individual human being as a system. Level eight refers to social systems—systems constituted by individuals with an emphasis on the particular roles they assume within a given social system. The final level is the transcendental level. According to Boulding, components of the transcendental level are "the ultimates and absolutes and the inescapable unknowables" (205).

The value of Boulding's approach is its introduction of a hierarchical structure of systems (Hatch 1997). Although the last level refers to a metaphysical level, the focus of the taxonomy is on the empirical sciences. Moreover, Boulding's taxonomy is largely positivistic. In contrast, Dooyeweerd provides an explicit Christian taxonomy that is rooted in biblical truth that may be applied to the school-as-system.

A Christian Approach to Systems Theory in Schools

Herman Dooyeweerd (1894–1977) was a Christian philosopher and legal scholar who taught at the Free University of Amsterdam. His writings include the four-volume *A New Critique of Theoretical Thought* and an introduction to his philosophical thought entitled *In the Twilight of Western Thought*. C. T. McIntire notes that Dooyeweerd's writings were not theology so much as "philosophy informed by Christian insights. As such, he wrote not about God but about the general structure of the world and human existence" (1997, 160). One of his more salient philosophical ideas is modal theory as a conceptualization of reality. According to Dooyeweerd, reality consists of levels of modes, or modal aspects, that reflect the creational structure. The modal aspects consist of fifteen aspects of reality: (1) the quantitative; (2) the spatial; (3) the kinematic, or properties related to movement in space; (4) the physical, or properties related to energy of objects; (5) the biotic, or properties related to life; (6) the sensory, or properties related to sensation and feeling; (7) the logical; (8) the cultural/historical, or properties related to the formation of cultural influence; (9) the linguistic, including properties related to symbolic communication; (10) the social; (11) the economic; (12) the aesthetic; (13) the judicial; (14) the ethical; and (15) the pistic, or properties related to faith and transcendent belief.

Cultural/historical modal aspect

In reference to the school-as-system, the last eight of Dooyeweerd's modal aspects are most applicable. These modal aspects are what Stephen Monsma refers to as normative principles because they "all involve human choice, and all thereby involve valuing and human responsibility" (1986, 70). Inasmuch as they involve human choice, the normative nature of the modal aspects may be compromised. In his description of culture, Henry van Til notes that all humans still retain their cultural character despite the Fall, but their cultural striving may be considered apostate because such striving does not seek to glorify God. Despite the distortion of God's image because of sin, "man has not lost his cultural urge, his instinct to rule, his love of power, his ability to form and to mould matter after his will" (2001, 58). While culture will not be fully restored until the return of Christ, cultural norms and values may be more closely aligned with what God intended, hence the normative/nonnormative distinction. Educational leaders should have as a goal to lead the school in accordance with these normative structures, employing the uniquely Christian gifts of spiritual wisdom and Christ-centered love, as well as exercising the skills and knowledge of competent leaders.

The cultural/historical aspect of a school has two critical parts: (1) the salient events of the school's past that inform the school's current mission and practices and (2) the current shaping of the institutional culture of the school. School culture includes institutional norms and attitudes, social interaction, use of technology, and any other activity that fulfills the *cultural mandate* to subdue the earth and have dominion over it (Genesis 1:28). The past and the present provide a continuity that shapes the school's culture. Deviations from this continuity through policy changes, implementation of new technology, or significant changes in management styles will invariably provoke the system to react to maintain its equilibrium.

The wise school administrator will recognize the importance of the past-present continuity in the culture formation of the school and will make changes with deliberation and caution. Monsma (1986) offers the guiding principle of cultural appropriateness specifically for technological activity, but it may be applied to all cultural activity. Cultural appropriateness involves the importance of continuity in implementing change. Victor Papanek describes an incident that illustrates an application of this principle. During the harvest, Tanzanian women and young boys engage in grueling manual labor to thresh grain. During the eight to nine hours of daily labor, the young boys are acculturated through interaction with one another and with the adults involved in the harvest. A group of consultants from a more industrialized nation suggested the use of electric grinders that would complete the harvest in a drastically reduced amount of time. Although implementing the idea would have alleviated the strenuous and tedious work of manual grinding, it would also have eliminated a critical element of cultural transmission. An approach more consistent with the principle of cultural appropriateness would be the use of hand grinders. While this change would reduce the level of strenuous labor, it would also preserve the social and cultural aspects of the work. Since progress is by its very nature discontinuous, continuity and progress may seem to have competing goals; but progress can occur incrementally, thereby providing a more harmonious integration of progress with other cultural phenomena (1983, cited in Monsma 1986).

A second example of cultural appropriateness is found in the work of social scientists from the Tavistock Institute of London (Trist and Bamforth 1978, cited in Hanna 1988). Traditional methods of work structure focus strictly on the mechanical-technical aspects. However, these social scientists believe that productivity and efficiency are as dependent upon social factors as technical factors. They refer to the interaction of the social and technical as the sociotechnical systems method. The traditional method requires coal miners to work on one task without social interaction, whereas the sociotechnical systems method increases the variety of tasks, and during the tasks the coal miners engage in cooperative work with other members of a work group. Results demonstrate that the sociotechnical systems method of work structure is superior to the traditional method; overtime hours, turnover, and stress indicators were lower for the sociotechnical method (Emery and Trist 1960, cited in Hanna 1988). The Tavistock Institute scientists, either wittingly or unwittingly, uncovered a normative principle that aligns the work culture of the South Yorkshire coal mine more closely with God's normative creational structure by acknowledging the social nature of human beings.

Linguistic modal aspect

Inasmuch as education is a type of cultural formation, much of the content of this cultural transmission involves the linguistic modal aspect. The linguistic modal aspect involves not only the acquisition and use of language but all types of symbolic communication. For the school-as-system, two applications emerge. First, the teaching of the linguistic aspect—namely, the basic skills of reading, writing, and mathematics—provides the necessary foundation for understanding all academic content. Therefore, pedagogy and curriculum should involve effective outcomes and should have external empirical support from educational research supporting such methods. There is also value in standardized testing for demonstrating the school's effectiveness in achieving these goals. A second application of the linguistic aspect involves educational jargon. Every professional "guild" has a set of terms that are specific to that profession. Terms such as *rubric, learning styles, scaffolding,* and any number of acronyms (ESEA, IEP, NCLB) that populate the educator's speech may communicate at the professional level, but they can serve to alienate those who have not been acculturated into the educator's "guild." Students, parents, community members, and all others with whom leaders want to communicate will require translation. The unnecessary use of educational jargon breaks the continuity between the communicator and the listener, and thus this use is ultimately culturally inappropriate.

Social modal aspect

With respect to the social modal aspect, the school occupies a unique position. In describing social communities, Roy Clouser (1991) differentiates between institutions and organizations. Institutions are characterized by the intent of lifelong, often involuntary, and close-knit membership. Examples include marriage, the family, and membership in civil government. Conversely, organizations are characterized by voluntary membership, nonpermanent tenure, and a more informal bond among their members. Schools would largely qualify as organizations, though some overlap occurs as the school assumes the role of in loco parentis, particularly when academic content contains reference to character and morality. While schools may vary in terms of their level of commitment to in loco parentis, activities that belong primarily to the sphere of the family also occur in schools. Examples of such activities include implementing discipline, providing nutrition, and giving minor medical care. Anthony Conte notes, "Schools continue to be institutions to which parents look for help in their efforts to best serve their children. Schools are doing more because other elements of society (home, church, community) seem to be unable or unwilling to continue their historic roles. Teachers, parents, and community members need to recognize certain domains belong to parents and others to educators. With in loco parentis, both students and teachers benefit" (2000).

In his or her leadership role, the school administrator establishes how the school chooses to exercise in loco parentis—how it will communicate its "parental" values to parents and students and what boundaries separate the school in this role from the parents themselves.

Aside from assuming the role of in loco parentis, the school-as-system invariably contains informal social subsystems that form naturally, both among students and among employees. Social support among coworkers is important, as the Tavistock coal-mining research indicated. The natural propensity for social support reflects the God's-image-bearing desire for relationship. An environment that encourages appropriate social relations is beneficial to all concerned.

Economic modal aspect

The economic modal aspect is certainly familiar to school administrators. In research conducted by Jeff Hall (see chapter 3), educational leaders rated school finances as their highest stressor. In his introduction to Dooyeweerd's philosophy, Kalsbeek describes the central concept of the economic modal aspect as "frugality in managing scarce goods" (1975, 100). Most Christians are familiar with the concept of stewardship, and the Christian school leader is called to steward both human and material resources wisely and well. However, despite the obvious relationship between a school's operation and its economic status, Sarah Daignault (2003) notes that schools and money have historically had an awkward relationship and that private schools are apt to be less willing to discuss finances than programs or policies. Nevertheless, providing an education requires resources. From a systems perspective, the management of scarce resources takes place in the input-throughput-output process that yields the "product" of the school's core mission: Christian education. The environment, consisting primarily of those who pay tuition or make charitable contributions, provides feedback to the school-as-system explicitly through enrollment and ongoing gifts. Feedback may also come from standardized test results, college placements, or community involvement. Although it is tempting to view the economic modal aspect as strictly the balance of revenues and expenses, the nonlinear nature of systems suggests that economic activities may have unintended consequences.

One example emerging from the school finance literature is the debate over whether money makes a difference in the public sector when it comes to educational outcomes. Anthony Rolle notes that the research literature is populated with two diametrically opposed premises: "There is no economically efficient relation between educational expenditures and outcomes," and "There is an economically efficient relation between educational expenditures and outcomes" (2004, 32). Moreover, other researchers in school finance admit that it is difficult to quantify a link between educational expenditures and student outcomes.

Aesthetic modal aspect

The aesthetic modal aspect refers to the properties of beauty and harmony. Some obvious applications refer to the school landscaping and physical-plant maintenance, as well as aesthetic curricular content such as art and music. Monsma uses the term *"delightful harmony"* (1986, 73; emphasis in original) to describe the desired relationship between beauty and function. Work tasks that rely on the use of tools or technology may be assessed to determine how well beauty and function are integrated. Monsma quotes Wolterstorff's example of the shovel: "A good spade is one that serves its purpose well. And that in turn consists of two things: being effective for digging holes, and proving generally good and satisfying to use for this purpose" (Wolterstorff 1980, 156, quoted in Monsma 1986, 73–74).

Judicial and ethical modal aspects

The judicial and ethical modal aspects may be considered together. The former refers to properties related to fairness, whereas the latter refers to properties related to love (Clouser 1991). At the student level, the judicial aspect informs the school's philosophy and practice of discipline. At the employee level, the judicial aspect informs the school's exercise of organizational justice. Dail Fields notes that there are two perceptions of organizational justice: distributive justice and procedural justice. The first is derived from employees "comparing the equity of the ratio of their inputs to their outcomes in comparison to those of their coworkers" (2002, 163). The second is derived from employees' perception of the fairness of management decision-making processes. Perceptions of injustice in either of these categories are certainly problematic, and the perceptions may indicate a violation of judicial norms. Conversely, perceptions are not always reality; and even though decisions may indeed be made fairly, the information involved in the decision-making process may not be available to everyone because of legal or privacy reasons. In instances such as these, it is imperative that the educational leader has already established an environment of trust.

The judicial aspect introduces the next modal aspect, the ethical, which Clouser claims may also be called the "love ethic." But, he says, "We do not merely mean that it is better to be loving than not, we mean that love is what ethics is *about*" (1991, 207; emphasis in original).

The ethical modal aspect reflects the taxonomic nature of the modal aspects. As Clouser notes, "We may be just to someone without also being loving, but we cannot be loving to that person without being just. Love often bids us go beyond what someone strictly deserves, but we would have to be at least as just to someone as circumstances permit before we could succeed in being loving to that person" (207). The ethical modal aspect acknowledges the universal human attribute of love, but the quality of the love shown in the Christian school should highlight the school's commitment to the ethic of love embodied in the Bible's repeated admonitions to love one another. Love is at the very heart of the gospel, as seen in 1 Corinthians 13:4–7:

> Love is patient, love is kind. It does not envy, it does not boast, it is not proud. It is not rude, it is not self-seeking, it is not easily angered, it keeps no record of wrongs. Love does not delight in evil but rejoices with the truth. It always protects, always trusts, always hopes, always perseveres.

These attributes were first commended to the Corinthian church in order to preserve the church's unity (Calvin 2005). Such expressions of

Christian love are as applicable to the harmony of any other Christian organization, including the Christian school. The apostle encourages the positive expressions of patience and kindness that lack any hint of jealousy. An administrator's dealings with employees, students, parents, and other constituents should be characterized by these attributes. The lack of jealousy, bragging, and arrogance to which Paul refers in the latter half of verse 4 may be addressed when the school recognizes all members as playing equally important roles. The temptation is to privilege the faculty, but the accounting office, custodial crew, and administrative assistants are as vital to the school's operation as the faculty. In the previous chapter of 1 Corinthians, Paul tells the Corinthians, "There are different kinds of gifts, but the same Spirit. There are different kinds of service, but the same Lord. There are different kinds of working, but the same God works all of them in all men. Now to each one the manifestation of the Spirit is given for the common good" (12:4–7).

Paul's admonition against seeking one's own interest in 1 Corinthians 13:4–7 may at first blush be applied to the administrator's ambition for enrollment growth, greater responsibility, or prestige in the community. Calvin, however, notes that self-seeking gets at the very heart of all sinfulness. Because of our inclination to care exclusively for ourselves, "we rush headlong into it" (2005, 423).

The ethic of love to which the ethical modality refers must be reflected in the ethos of the Christian school community. Love should be the motivation for tuition rates, financial aid, dress codes, curriculum decisions, personnel decisions, student discipline, and fund-raising. Francis Schaeffer, in the essay "The Mark of a Christian," notes that Jesus' high priestly prayer for Christian unity in John 17:21 is "the final apologetic" (1982, 189). According to Jesus' prayer, the purpose of this exhibition of unity among His followers is "that the world may believe" that God has sent Him (John 17:21). To those who do not know Christ despite their profession for school admission, the Christian school should demonstrate this final apologetic.

Pistic modal aspect

The pistic modal aspect is so named for *pistis*, the Greek New Testament word for "faith." This is the last of Dooyeweerd's modal aspects, and it reflects the anthropological tendency of all humans to engage in some expression of faith. In his exploration of faith development, James

W. Fowler (1981) notes that belief in the supernatural is unnecessary for this developmental phenomenon; expressions of faith may be directed toward the state, a philosophy, or even oneself. Certainly, an expression of faith that is not directed wholly toward Christ is faith sinfully expressed, reflecting a nonnormative response to this modal aspect. While it is unlikely that any educational leader would overtly place faith in idols or false deities, it is possible for the educational leader to trust inadvertently in technology or curricula or fund drives for the fulfillment of the school's mission. To do so is to engage in idolatry. Therefore, the wise educational leader will frequently ask, "Where is our faith affixed?" Faith that does not emerge out of the normative expression of the other modalities is irresponsible. Faith expressed without proper stewardship, without concern for justice, or without love is false faith. For example, submitting a budget that depends on a miraculous provision of God for solvency violates the normative properties reflected in the economic modal aspect.

Although it is at the top of the modal structure, the belief system of the pistic modality provides the epistemological framework that governs decision making in organizations. When expressed normatively as a biblically based decision-making framework, the modal structure provides the necessary counterbalance to the intricacy—even chaos—of complex organizations. The more complex an organization, the greater the likelihood of probabilistic outcomes; the more probabilistic, the less predictable and certain these outcomes are (Scott 2003). In the face of such uncertainty, faith in a sovereign, omniscient, and loving God is comforting compensation.

In addition to providing a counterweight to the uncertainty of complex organizations, the pistic modality also provides a check and balance against the tendency for open systems to seek self-preservation. It is a natural tendency for all open systems to seek self-preservation, but seeking self-preservation can lead members of the organization to make decisions that promote self-preservation while compromising the mission of the organization. Similarly, subsystems in an organization (for example, departments or programs) will naturally compete for scarce resources. Therefore, the values derived from the belief system of the pistic modality provide the decision-making framework for allocating those scarce resources.

Now What? Application to Practice

BY VIRTUE OF THE creational structure, organizations have specific characteristics that have been uncovered by social scientists, and many of these characteristics explicitly reflect the God's-image-bearing nature of human beings. The school-as-system consists not only of boundaries that separate it from its environment but also of subsystems that interact dynamically within the school-as-system and contain boundaries. These boundaries have varying degrees of permeability: some explicit, such as admissions criteria, and some implicit, such as acceptance of new students or faculty members. The dynamic processes of the school-as-system involve human and material resources that produce an outcome we recognize as Christian education. Feedback from the environment provides the school-as-system with information necessary to gauge the quality of its input and with opportunities for self-regulation and error correction. The complexity of the school-as-system may be reflected in the multiple perspectives provided by Dooyeweerd's modal aspects. Each of the modal aspects is represented in all facets of the school-as-system, some more prominently than others. Because of the nonlinear and dynamic nature of a system, maintenance of normative expressions of these modal aspects—including responsible culture formation, stewardship, harmony, justice, love, and faith—requires ongoing diligence and leadership.

Superintendent Kelly Chadwick's situation, introduced at the beginning of this chapter, is representative. Chadwick's school is experiencing significant growing pains. Rapidly increasing enrollment has been accompanied by falling standardized test scores, budget challenges, and social problems among students. A systems interpretation of the school's case may be insightful. While the boundaries of the overall system of the school are diffuse enough to allow a rapid increase in enrollment, the student subsystem is becoming less permeable, excluding new students and forcing them into a subsystem of their own. Standardized test scores serve as environmental feedback requiring error correction. This requirement is reflected by the board's increasing insistence on a remedy to the problem. Budget challenges and student resistance to rapid growth, coupled with problems associated with maintaining academic excellence, reflect the system's tendency toward homeostasis. The rapid increase in enrollment may be stressing the system significantly, and the resulting problems suggest the wisdom of an incremental approach to growth with a cap on enrollment.

A review of the modal aspects of Chadwick's school underscores the stresses on the system. The rapid growth in enrollment has exceeded the system's tolerance for discontinuity, violating the norms associated with the school's history and culture. The decline in basic academic skills reflected in the standardized test scores suggests stress at the linguistic modality as well. The social stressors are appearing in the growing tension between the two student groups and in the overlap among the faculty. Economic challenges are evident in the difficulty in managing the FTE numbers associated with the rapid growth. Such challenges may threaten the institution's ability to maintain the physical plant or to offer nonessential courses such as art and music (the aesthetic modality). The social stressors leading to unhealthy student cliques appear to be influencing the faculty members, who have been accused of being unjust by showing favoritism (the judicial modality). An argument may be made that permitting unchecked enrollment growth is not loving (the ethical modality), inasmuch as it creates conditions in the system that promote partiality and discord. Unchecked growth also can reduce the exercise of good stewardship in the academic outcomes the school produces. Finally, does the unchecked enrollment reflect a systemic faith in numbers of students (the pistic modality)? Both the superintendent and the board appear to be seeking alternatives to managing the enrollment crisis that don't involve limiting enrollment. How does the enrollment crisis affect the institution's ability to meet its core mission, the foundation of which is found in the belief system of the pistic modality? While there may not be easy answers to these questions, a careful analysis of the issues associated with these modal aspects can provide leaders with a taxonomy for a comprehensive review of their institutions. If nothing else, such an analysis is a curative to the tendency to focus on one aspect to the exclusion of all others.

Key questions an administrator must keep in mind include the following:

- Do contemplated changes take into account continuity with the school's historic mission and traditions?
- Are changes in curriculum, technology, policy, or cocurricular activities incremental enough to maintain continuity?
- How would you describe the faculty's use of educational jargon and acronyms with the school's constituencies?
- How are students performing on standardized tests of basic educational skills?

- How well does the school steward its financial, material, and human resources?
- Does the curriculum contain opportunities for music, art, and other forms of aesthetic experiences?
- How would you describe the landscaping and general maintenance of the school and its environs?
- Do faculty members administer discipline fairly without regard to student status?
- Do administrators treat their staff fairly?
- Are all members of the school community treated as image bearers of God, with respect for their contributions, abilities, and persons?
- Where is the school community's faith affixed?
- What are the potential idols that may tempt the school community?

Perhaps the most discouraging aspect of this application of organizational systems to schools is the reality of complexity. Organizations do not change in a linear fashion; they change unpredictably while simultaneously resisting change. An educational leader must recognize that schools, as organizational systems, will respond accordingly, despite the leader's best efforts at top-down command and control. Becoming equipped with the knowledge of systems characteristics will reduce the frustration associated with trying to manage something as unpredictable as a whirlwind. Most important, however, is the need for the educational leader to know the God who is sovereign over the chaos and to have faith in His leading and direction, even when the way is not clear. Without this foundational belief, all the effort at taming the whirlwind is for naught.

References

Beer, Michael. 1980. *Organization change and development: A systems view.* Santa Monica, CA: Goodyear Publishing.

Boulding, Kenneth E. 1956. General systems theory—the skeleton of a science. *Management Science* 2, no. 3 (April): 197–208.

Bowen, Murray. 1986. *Family therapy in clinical practice.* Northvale, NJ: Jason Aronson.

Calvin, John. 2005. *Commentary on the epistles of Paul the apostle to the Corinthians.* Vol 1. *Calvin's Commentaries.* Grand Rapids, MI: Baker Books.

Clouser, Roy A. 1991. *The myth of religious neutrality: An essay on the hidden role of religious belief in theories.* Notre Dame, IN: University of Notre Dame Press.

Conte, Anthony E. 2000. In loco parentis: Alive and well. *Education* 121, no. 1 (Fall). http://www.findarticles.com/p/articles/mi_qa3673/is_200010/ai_n8908773.

Daignault, Sarah. 2003. Facing money, facing ourselves: How to think about money and schools. *Independent School* 63, no. 1 (Fall): 12–20. http://search.epnet.com/login. aspx?direct=true&db=aph&an=12634087.

Emery, F. E., and Eric L. Trist. 1960. Socio-technical systems. In *Management sciences, models and techniques.* Vol. 2, ed. C. W. Churchman and M. Verhulst. London: Pergamon Press.

Fields, Dail L. 2002. *Taking the measure of work: A guide to validated scales for organizational research and diagnosis.* Thousand Oaks, CA: Sage Publications.

Fowler, James W. 1981. *Stages of faith: The Psychology of human development and the quest for meaning.* San Francisco: HarperCollins.

Hanna, David P. 1988. *Designing organizations for high performance.* Reading, MA: Addison-Wesley Publishing.

Hanson, E. Mark. 2003. *Educational administration and organizational behavior.* 5th ed. Boston, MA: Allyn and Bacon.

Hatch, Mary Jo. 1997. *Organizational theory: Modern, symbolic, and postmodern perspectives.* Oxford, UK: Oxford University Press.

Kalsbeek, L. 1975. *Contours of a Christian philosophy.* Toronto, Canada: Wedge Publishing Foundation.

McIntire, C. T. 1997. Herman Dooyeweerd in North America. In *Reformed theology in America: A history of its modern development,* ed. David F. Wells, 157–72. Grand Rapids, MI: Baker.

Minuchin, Salvador. 1974. *Families and family therapy.* Cambridge, MA: Harvard University Press.

Monsma, Stephen V., ed. 1986. *Responsible technology.* Grand Rapids, MI: Eerdmans.

Papanek, Victor J. 1983. *Design for human scale.* New York: Van Nostrand Reinhold.

Rolle, Anthony. 2004. Out with the old, in with the new: Thoughts on the future of educational productivity research. *Peabody Journal of Education* 79, no. 3:31-56.

Schaeffer, Francis A. 1982. *The complete works of Francis A. Schaeffer: A Christian worldview, volume 4, A Christian view of the church.* Westchester, IL: Crossway Books.

Schein, Edgar H. 1994. *Organizational psychology.* 3rd ed. Upper Saddle River, NJ: Prentice-Hall.

Scott, W. Richard. 2003. *Organizations: Rational, natural, and open systems.* 5th ed. Upper Saddle River, NJ: Prentice-Hall.

Senge, Peter M. 1990. *The fifth discipline: The art and practice of the learning organization.* New York: Currency.

Trist, Eric L., and Ken W. Bamforth. 1978. Some social and psychological consequences of the long wall method of coal-getting. *Human Relations* 39, no. 12.

Van Til, Henry R. 2001. *The Calvinistic concept of culture.* Grand Rapids, MI: Baker Academic.

Von Bertalanffy, Ludwig. 1968. *General system theory: Foundations, development, applications.* New York: George Braziller.

Wolterstorff, Nicholas P. 1980. *Art in action: Toward a Christian aesthetic.* Grand Rapids, MI: Eerdmans.

CHAPTER 7

LIBERATING DICHOTOMIES

Appreciating the Complexities
of Educational Leadership

By Niel B. Nielson

Niel B. Nielson, PhD, is the president of Covenant College. He has taught college philosophy, traded options at the Chicago Board of Trade, managed an American-Russian joint venture, pastored in a large church, and currently serves as a director of several for-profit and not-for-profit organizations.

CHAPTER 7

LIBERATING DICHOTOMIES

By Niel B. Nielson

CHRISTIAN EDUCATIONAL leaders deal with a daunting array of constituencies: students, parents, faculty, staff, board members, donors, and church and community leaders. Navigating the crosscurrents of competing values, needs, and demands of these stakeholders can make education seem like an impossible task.

How do school leaders balance and appropriately respond to the often contradictory expectations of their diverse constituencies? How do they honor and perpetuate their educational mission in an age of "customer satisfaction" and "money talks"? How should decisions be made when everyone has not only a view but a principled view, and when people's careers are at stake? How can people be held appropriately accountable for their performance? How do school leaders know how much to say, when, and to whom?

Challenges of Christian Community

While these questions characterize educational communities in general, for those in explicitly Christian educational contexts the Scripture provides a "higher standard" for how to treat one another. Amid the complexities and layers and multiple constituencies that all school leadership presents, Christian leaders must follow the calling of godliness: biblical care, compassion, truthfulness, justice, and eternal perspective.

Of course, a first response to these questions could be, "Stop your whining!" These challenges are really no different from those faced by Christians in any complex organization. Businesses, dentists' offices, government agencies, churches, even families can be described in many of the same terms, and schools are in no privileged, or rather underprivileged, position.

This response is certainly right to a great degree. Human organizations have much in common, both in their assets and in their liabilities. Communication is key, and breakdown in communication means trouble. Various priorities among various members of the organization vie for attention. Availability of resources does in an important sense determine the path ahead. Living and working together biblically while staying competitive in the wider marketplace can be challenging. Yet, every enterprise led by Christians for the glory of God must wrestle with this historic calling to be in the world but not of the world, to demonstrate their kingdom calling without making excuses for incompetence or poor performance.

Living with Tensions

If these complexities and tensions are present under ordinary circumstances, they become acutely challenging during periods of change, testing, and difficulty. Community is fragile in the best of times, and weaknesses are often masked by "success." During times of plenty and abundance, it is likely that Christian schools, like God's people when they settled in the land flowing with milk and honey, can tolerate or even overlook a lack of understanding and coherence in handling the complexities noted above. However, testing and trial force school leaders to ask such questions as these:

- Do we all mean the same thing when we state our mission?
- Do we agree about what we want to happen in the minds and hearts and lives of our students, and about what it takes to make it happen?
- Are we sure we understand the values and norms that guide the school?

- Do current marketing strategies cohere with what we are actually doing?
- Are we sure we understand our various constituencies as well as we think we do?
- Are we pulling together?

These are questions that must be asked, for they are crucial, and they often bubble to the troubled surface when things go awry. How, in the midst of both the best of times and the worst of times, do school leaders sustain and grow coherent educational communities?

Testing and trial are considered good for any institution. Stresses and strains are often God's instruments to arrest straying attention and to refocus vision. Such times are not easy, and casualties and hurt feelings often result. Contrary to many idealistic expectations, human communities are messy things, reflecting the realities of living in a fallen world and experiencing the tension between the "already" of the life, death, resurrection, and present reign of Jesus Christ and the "not yet" of His imminent return with the accompanying consummation of God's redemptive purpose for His creation. The writer to the Hebrews declares, "Yet at present we do not see everything subject to him" (Hebrews 2:8), and the present reality includes sin, suffering, and the painful lack of perfect resolution. But the writer also calls his readers to look ahead, not only to seeing Jesus, now "crowned with glory and honor because he suffered death" (Hebrews 2:9), but also to the certain hope of His "bringing many sons to glory" (Hebrews 2:10) with Him.

The consistent call of Scripture is to live in the midst of this tension between the already and the not yet. We do so by looking back to the finished work of Christ on the Cross, looking forward to His glorious return, and living faithfully in the present by the faithful witness of the Bible and the enabling ministry of the Holy Spirit.

It comes as no surprise that this tension between the already and the not yet involves a host of other tensions. The purpose of this chapter is to call attention to tensions that characterize human communities in general and that are particularly relevant to Christian educational communities. These tensions arise between opposing poles in areas of ethical, spiritual, and organizational concern, and they are often the source of great frustration for those who would prefer neat resolutions and nice syntheses of dialectical contraries.

While we anticipate that these tensions will be resolved in the life to come, they are with us now. More than that, they are not all bad: The tensions actually reflect good purposes in both opposing poles, and communities that strive to resolve the tensions by embracing one pole and avoiding the other will suffer. Further, communities that strive to find the golden mean between the poles will also miss the mark. Instead, the dichotomies that Christian school leaders face often bring liberating vitality and blessing to educational communities.

Dichotomy #1: Effective Leadership vs. Shared Governance

Educational communities historically have wrestled intensely with the issue of governance. Educational leadership has often been understood very differently from leadership in business or government, or even in other not-for-profit enterprises. While administrators have the executive titles, these titles traditionally represent less hierarchically defined roles that carry less top-down authority. Because the core work of education is teaching, teachers have rightly assumed significant authority over the curriculum.

The tensions that can arise over governance are well known, and adversarial relationships between faculty and administration are not uncommon. An article in *The Chronicle of Higher Education: Chronicle Careers* offered advice to college faculty members who would choose to assume administrative roles. The article, titled "Crossing Over to the Dark Side," signals the deeply rooted suspicion and enmity that exist, particularly in higher-education contexts (Dowdall and Dowdall 2005). Governance issues in elementary and secondary schools may differ from those in higher education, but the "we-they" tensions persist there, too.

In many cases, the constitutions and by-laws of institutions spell out specifically and clearly the respective roles of administration and faculty, and these documents provide a more definitive role for the administrator than emerges in practice. The tradition of faculty governance often competes directly with language about an administrator's role in directing all the affairs of the institution, including hiring faculty, determining budgets, developing campuses, and leading strategic planning. The result is that governance becomes a murky matter and can create an environment of distrust and controversy, even in Christian educational settings.

Effective leadership authority grasps the gracious truth that our institutions are filled with thoughtful and talented people who have real stakes in the present and the future and that the challenge is to create an environment in which these gifted people can put their varied gifts to work most fruitfully and joyfully to further the institutional mission. In fact, this is the key issue of authority and governance in any organization, Christian or not. Effective leadership in business is a function not of how imperial the leader can be but of how well the leader can unite the organization's people and resources toward the common goal. Leaders who try to succeed by asserting their authority will most likely fail, not because they don't have the "right" to exercise such authority, but because, even if they do have it, it is how that authority is exercised in real time and situations that will determine success.

Here are questions for leaders of educational communities—particularly Christian educational communities, where gifts and talents are understood to be God given, where the school's mission is explicitly grounded in God's revelation, and where the goal must always be to glorify and exalt Jesus Christ in every dimension and aspect of the work.

1. How can space be created and protected for the vitality and creativity of individuals in positions of responsibility so that they are set free to do their best work without criticism and second-guessing?

Faculty members must have space so that they can "swing from the heels" in their teaching and scholarship within the context of institutional mission, values, and norms. Administrators must have space so that within the same context they can develop programs that further the mission and enable faculty members to do their academic work effectively. The concept of "shared governance" does not mean that all responsibilities are shared equally, a situation that would be foolish at best and destructive at worst. It means that different aspects of the organization are the responsibilities of different people, uniquely gifted for just those responsibilities, and thus the organization moves forward in an ethos of respect for others' respective roles and with a gracious sharing of leadership. In biblical terms, sharing in the institutional governance is less about one person's demand that others share with him or her, and more about that person's eagerness to share with others the space to exercise their gifts fully to the glory of God.

2. How can respect be shown for those who feel threatened when exuberant leaders are moving quickly down a path that may lead to dramatic change?

Educational institutions are often characterized as suspicious of change and liable to bog down new initiatives with endless process. Yet opportunities abound for effective, mission-driven change that will enable the institution to serve its constituencies in new and God-honoring ways. Communication is key, and effective leaders in healthy communities bring together key people from across the organization to gather input, test ideas, and anticipate consequences. Honoring respective responsibilities is also key, and the principle of giving "full say but not final say" must be followed. Others in the organization must grant "final say" to those with ultimate responsibility, even as those with ultimate responsibility must provide opportunity for "full say" from all those affected.

3. How can biblical leading and following be encouraged in Christian educational communities?

Both Jesus and Paul remind us that biblical leadership is servant leadership, and yet it does not cease to be leadership. Godly leadership always seeks the best good of the led, even when there is disagreement with the led about the direction of the leading. In other words, servant leadership is not the same as egalitarian leadership, in which everyone has equal say on every matter. It is thoughtful, caring leadership that honors the led even as difficult decisions are made. It is leadership that recognizes, as did the Roman officer in Luke 7, that leaders are under authority also (Luke 7:8). Conversely, biblical following is servant following, gratefully respecting God's call on and gifting of leaders to exercise their leadership authority and accountability. Common wisdom is that those who resist authority most aggressively when they do not have it become the most tyrannical when they do. Identifying those with leadership potential includes measuring how well a person follows.

In healthy Christian educational communities, leaders lead biblically—with servant hearts, open and effective communication, and the willingness to be accountable for outcomes. Also in these communities, responsible and gifted people are given space to exercise their responsibilities with zeal and creativity; "shared governance" is understood, not as the absence of leading and following, but as honoring respective roles and primary responsibilities; and the long-term good of the entire community is always held in mind and heart.

The risky business of leadership and governance will not be finally addressed simply by pointing to an organizational chart. This dichotomy will not be effectively resolved by announcing that leaders have autocratic authority or that everyone has an equal vote. A beneficial chart will identify, however, respective roles and responsibilities that, if honored and carried out with biblical guidance and the ministry of the Holy Spirit, will enable all to exercise their God-given gifts with liberating exuberance and mission-fulfilling effect.

Dichotomy #2: Communication vs. Confidentiality

Educational leaders often regard communication as the "no-win" area of their responsibility, for no matter how determined the effort to communicate, someone somewhere feels left out of the loop on something about which he or she ought to be informed. Leaders are sometimes tempted simply to give up, despairing over the impossibility of satisfying everyone's communication expectations.

Yet healthy communities are in fact characterized by healthy and vibrant communication—contexts in which information flows in and around the institution continuously and speedily, at all levels and in all directions. Such communication cannot be the responsibility of one person or one department, and neglect of this principle is often the source of the trouble. When people criticize communication dynamics in an institution, they are often thinking, "They have not communicated well with us," or "Why didn't I know about that?" Much less frequently do people criticize their own communication: "I should have come to you," or "I didn't think to tell you that."

So there is always room for improvement in communication in educational institutions, and this must be a continual area of attention and exhortation. But healthy communication is often pitted against the requirement of confidentiality. The tension is especially real in difficult situations that have personal consequences; for example, when an employee is terminated, when difficult financial decisions are in process, or when job performance or compensation is discussed. Where is the balance between healthy and open communication and proper care for sensitive information?

Leaders often tend toward one pole of the tension or the other. Some are likely to say too much, believing that there is safety in making sure that everyone has all the information. At times this tendency flows from defensiveness or the self-protection instinct: for example, wanting to make sure that everyone knows why a particular employee was terminated— "If only they knew what this person is really like, or how poor his or her job performance really was, they would understand the decision."

Other leaders are likely to keep control of virtually all information, believing that others in the institution cannot handle the heavy weight that knowing brings. Paternalism is alive and well, not only in educational but also in business settings. This keeping of information can be used manipulatively, as when someone says (with rolling of eyes), "If only you knew what I know …," raising speculation and suspicion beyond where they would be if nothing had been said.

The tension between communication and confidentiality extends not just to what is said, but also to how it is said. People often feel that they have not fully communicated without adding the emotional intensity of all the feelings in their hearts, adding such prefatory remarks as "I'm appalled that …" or "I'm shocked that …" Healthy communication often involves giving input and offering opinions without the emotional manipulation of how one feels about it. Administrators are often shocked by what happens in their institutions, but the situation is rarely improved when they share their deepest feelings of disgust or offense at others' behavior.

Further, there is a huge difference between healthy communication and gossip or backbiting. Even in Christian communities, the tendency to talk behind people's backs, to avoid going directly to the person criticized, and to perpetuate what can be called "orbital conversations" is alive and well. Godly self-restraint and the courage to speak in the open are sadly lacking in many contexts—sometimes out of fear of retribution, but more often out of sinful failure to live up to biblical expectations.

Every leader knows the struggle of keeping one's mouth shut when it seems that it would feel so much better to tell it as it is, or at least to tell it as he or she sees it. Healthy communication in healthy Christian communities is open and continuous, but it is also characterized by a godly and sometimes frustrating restraint in the interests of the individuals involved and the mission of the institution. Leaders must be prepared to take the brunt of criticism for not answering certain questions, even as those affected by the decisions may be energetically and critically telling only one side of the story. This asymmetry, while sometimes irritating, is part of the burden of leadership.

The flip side of this situation is that others in the community must accept this responsibility of leaders to balance carefully the calls of communication and confidentiality. Ironically, those who demand information most vociferously when they do not have it are often those who become most protective of it when they do. Healthy educational communities are those in which all members acknowledge that there are just some things they will never know and probably should never know.

There is no simple formula for resolving this tension between communication and confidentiality. Leaders will frequently fail to get it exactly right: they will say too much or too little, and they will often need to apologize for this failing. But it would be a wrong response to gravitate to one pole rather than the other. Healthy communities are not those in which all the people say everything they think in any way they choose. They are those in which, by God's grace and the prayers and daily interactions of God's people, members of the community wrestle with what to say, when and how to say it, and when to keep their mouths shut—always seeking to serve the mission of the school, to care for one another with godly compassion, and to honor Jesus Christ with their words.

Dichotomy #3: Conflict vs. Peace

Christian school leaders face a particularly difficult challenge in addressing people issues involving such matters as performance appraisal and interpersonal conflict. The challenge stems from the tension between the biblical call to demonstrate grace, compassion, and care in all situations and the mandate to address problems directly and effectively for the good of the institution.

Christian organizations often suffer from the "spiritualization syndrome"—the tendency to see organizational and personnel issues solely in terms of Christian compassion and community. Here are a few examples of this tendency:

- "How could the principal fire that teacher? I thought this was a Christian school!"
- "I don't understand why the headmaster didn't give me a raise. Don't these people understand what it means to care for their employees?"
- "How could they get rid of that program? They don't understand how God has used it to bless many students."

Biblical teaching does call Christians to attitudes and behavior that honor Christ. Yet this teaching sometimes becomes the basis for avoiding conflict and confrontation, and even for criticizing those who must address difficult situations directly.

Scripture provides numerous examples of both sides of this dichotomy. Some passages strongly encourage believers to bear with one another for the sake of the unity of the Body of Christ, to graciously consider others in their weaknesses, to sacrifice for the sake of others, and to recognize the varying gifts and abilities that community members have. Other passages exhort believers to address problems of laziness, dishonesty, gossip, divisiveness, and theological error in aggressive, even abrupt, ways.

Everyone longs for a peaceable educational community. Such a community is a wonderful place to work, and students and families are the beneficiaries of an environment in which people "get along" and there are no glaring conflicts. But leaders must assess whether this peace has been purchased at the cost of tolerating poor performance, putting up with poor attitudes, or maintaining a status quo that will hurt the institution in the long run.

Leaders must recognize that appropriate conflict and confrontation often constitute the path to peace. Those who call out bad attitudes, who address performance issues, and who challenge the comfortable ruts into which people and institutions sometimes fall, most often find that their willingness to face up to these confrontational situations leads to a new and more enduring peace.

On the other hand, not every issue is worth attacking, and certainly not with the same passion. Leaders who itch for fights often create conflicts where none are necessary, and the result is that the community is left more troubled than before, even if a problem is addressed. Wise leaders pick their issues carefully, confronting when biblical principle and organizational risk are involved, but perpetuating calm when the cost of "resolving" the conflict would clearly outweigh the reward.

Strong, vision-minded leadership will create conflict as it charts a course that some in the institution will accept and some will not. A school in which there is never the need for confrontation is a school that is not going anywhere in particular and where people problems are not being addressed. Leaders must avoid the spiritualizing "stopper"—that confrontation is not Christian. Poor performance, bad attitudes, and institutional weakness must be addressed for the sake of serving students and their families well and in order to honor Jesus Christ.

At the same time, biblical leadership will seek the peace of the institution and its people. Even in conflict, the leader must follow the scriptural instruction to speak the truth in love, to show compassion, and to seek the best good of those he or she is confronting. Such a leader will let some issues go, trusting that God will honor the one who puts up with human weakness. Such a leader will never relish conflict for its own sake, but will pursue it with energy, focus, and resolve when necessary.

Healthy communities address problems readily and courageously; they do not avoid conflict and confrontation when mission, values, and norms are at stake. But they also seek genuine peace through the conflict by how they honor the community's members through the conflict and how they delight in the resolution.

Dichotomy #4: Patience vs. Decisiveness

Educational leaders know the burden of decision making very well. Situations arise that demand immediate attention and immediate action, often without complete information available. Even with time to gather data and input and to consider a matter carefully, decisions carry the risk of unknown or unknowable consequences, especially in a rapidly changing culture and an evolving educational marketplace. Decisions that seem good at the time can turn out badly, and decisions that seem overly risky can end up as godsends.

How do educational leaders manage the tension between patience and decisiveness, between the inevitable fact that there is always more relevant information to gather and always one more factor to consider and the need to move ahead with courage and vision? How do they know when to act and when to wait?

This tension becomes more and more challenging in an environment of continual change. Educational choices are proliferating rapidly, such as for-profit education, distance learning, homeschooling, and competing versions of Christian education. Market expectations create pressure to add programs, facilities, staff, and experiences to stay competitive. The perceived need to move quickly is keenly felt at all educational levels, yet schools and colleges are traditionally resistant to change.

The tension is felt internally as well. If there is a problem with a teacher or a staff member, how long does an administrator wait before taking decisive action? When should someone be reprimanded or let go? Such decisions can be especially difficult to sort out in Christian settings, where termination is sometimes seen as unchristian. Often the leader will grasp the reality of a situation long before it is appropriate to engage in resolving action, and the leader will face both the painful reality of waiting until the appropriate time to act and the equally painful consequences of the decision.

For some, the "let's get this over with" attitude rules the day. Often the heightened emotion of a given situation will prompt the leader to follow the path of least resistance in the short run in order to achieve some sort of resolution. The leader may act to preserve the status quo, hoping that somehow the situation will get better. In some cases it does, but only if additional effort is focused toward behavior change and greater accountability. In many cases, maintaining the status quo, while easier in the short term, carries problems forward, and before long the leader will face the same decision again.

Christian educational institutions tend in this direction, often with good motives. They tolerate dysfunction in the name of Christian love, and the dysfunction becomes virtually institutionalized. Once that institutionalization happens, addressing the dysfunction is perceived as tantamount to attacking the very values of the community, when in fact the leader is addressing attitudes and behaviors that should never have gained a foothold.

There are some leaders whose "let's get this over with" approach involves knee-jerk decisions uninformed by available data and by the shared wisdom of the educational community. Claiming the right of leadership and the talent of knowing how to get things done does not justify precipitous decision making. For other leaders, the real need is courage. No important decision will please everyone, no matter how long or comprehensive the process leading up to it. The leader who is such a pleaser that he or she fails to face and make tough decisions when they are called for will undermine the long-term effectiveness of the institution.

Effective leaders make tough decisions when the situation calls for it, after they have done what they can to collect information, to seek input from relevant internal and external stakeholders, and to weigh carefully the consequences of a particular course of action against other possible courses of action or no action at all.

Knowing when to move and when to wait presents one of the dichotomies of educational leadership. Again, there is no simple formula for determining precisely how much information is needed or how long a decision-making process should take. Situations vary, and it can be assumed that decisions of larger scope and consequence demand greater due diligence and broader input. Nevertheless, healthy communities are characterized by, and in fact liberated by, this abiding tension between patience and decisiveness, and by the encouraging support of the community toward those charged with the responsibility to make difficult decisions in a timely way.

Dichotomy #5: Predictability vs. Surprise

Healthy organizations are rightly described as orderly and predictable. They and the people in them behave in regular patterns and follow standard procedures that can be communicated to all and are discernible to the careful observer. Administrators need to be trusted to behave in similar ways in similar situations, faculty need to fulfill expectations for their teaching and mentoring of students, and students are expected to follow rules and policies regarding their learning and life within the school setting.

Chaos will ensue in a setting where the rules change from day to day, where administrators arbitrarily or randomly assign responsibilities and manage compensation, where teachers give tests that have nothing to do with the content of their teaching, and where students are permitted to establish their own idiosyncratic criteria for effective learning. Stability in any community depends on consistent and predictable standards and mutual expectations so that when people show up each day, there is at least some clarity about what they should do, how they should do it, and how their work will be evaluated.

At the same time, as Ralph Waldo Emerson said, "A foolish consistency is the hobgoblin of little minds!" Stability can in fact be an excuse for inertia and stubborn resistance to change; healthy organizations always leave room for, and even promote, the element of surprise. Often the time to introduce change is precisely when things seem most comfortable and settled and when change seems most counterintuitive. Companies that continue to grow and become better will introduce new thinking and new developments in the midst of success rather than waiting until the business has taken a downturn. A much-discussed topic in the financial markets is the value of contrarian behavior: when the rest of the world is buying, it is probably a good time to start selling, and vice versa.

Although the usual course will be the predictable one, at critical times the right decision will often be the one that most people do not expect because they are used to doing things the same way over and over again. The solutions to current challenges that most readily present themselves are incremental, that is, doing more (or less) of the same kind of thing that has been done (for example, more quizzes, fewer writing assignments, more money spent on recruiting). Incremental change is good, and it will cover a good majority of the situations that schools face. But there are times when genuine breakthrough thinking is needed: "What if we look at this situation in a new light? What if we approach it in ways that we have not thought of before?"

The radical moves that sometimes result from blue-sky thinking may bring disorientation and sometimes may leave people feeling as if their feet are not firmly touching hard ground. Therefore, it is important to reassure the community that the new approach is not a departure from the core mission of the organization.

Healthy communities are those that tolerate and even court surprise from every level of the organization. These surprises are the stuff of God's gracious providence and guidance, and they are the fruit of gifted people who are encouraged to think in fresh ways about what they are called to do. Educational leaders who learn to delight in communities that produce and embrace surprises will discover dynamism and liberating creativity in the people they lead. Those communities will be vibrant places even in the regular and predictable patterns that characterize most of their activity.

Dichotomy #6: Realism vs. Hope

Healthy communities refuse to commit either of two opposite errors: pie-in-the-sky optimism or down-in-the-mouth pessimism. They live in the tension between the often brutal realities of their situations and an irrepressible hope for the future of the mission.

Leaders often cluster in two groups on this issue. There are those who almost pathologically refuse to acknowledge that anything is wrong. They may believe that those they lead will lose hope if they are told the truth about difficult circumstances. They may not want to accept responsibility for their own roles in getting the school into those circumstances. They may think that acknowledging problems will reflect badly on their leadership. Whatever the reason, these leaders act and speak as if nothing were amiss. They are doing a great disservice to their organizations and the people in them, creating cynicism about their leadership among those who know better and creating false security among those who do not. A naive optimism that refuses to face the facts is not the trait of a strong leader.

Then there are those who seem to see only what is wrong. They are only too ready to face the brutal facts, to remind everyone every day of the difficulties, and perhaps to use this overbearing pessimism to retain control or to position themselves as the saviors. This one-sided "honesty" does indeed create tremors in any organization as people wonder if the place will still be there tomorrow. Further, as the organization continues to survive in the midst of this pessimism, people learn to discount the negativity, and the leader loses a crucial capability to direct the organization to the severest struggles when necessary.

In his well-known book *Good to Great*, Jim Collins recalls the effective leadership of Admiral Stockdale, the highest-ranking U.S. military officer to be a prisoner of war in Vietnam (2001, 65–89). Prisoners of war tended toward optimism or pessimism. The optimists kept telling one another and themselves that they would be free by Christmas, then by Easter, then by Labor Day. As each month passed, they began to despair of release, to fail to care for themselves—and many in fact died, their deaths attributable in large part to this loss of hope and the resulting inattention to patterns and practices that would have enabled them to survive. On the other hand, the pessimists gave up hope almost immediately upon entering the camps, and many died in much the same manner.

In contrast, Admiral Stockdale led by means of paradox: to face the brutal realities of the camp and the possibility of many years of imprisonment, yet at the same time to nurture and sustain an irrepressible hope that somehow the U. S. prisoners would triumph in the end. Psalm 112 describes the godly man not as one who hopes that he will not receive bad news, but as one who has "no fear of bad news" (Psalm 112:7), for he has learned that, in the providence of God, he can face the worst the world can bring and still come through by God's grace and mercy.

In this sense, educational leaders have to give the straight scoop without patronizing stakeholders, but they also need to articulate a vibrant hope that the institution continues to have a unique role to play and a blessed future to enjoy. Healthy communities are sustained by the liberating dichotomy of realism and hope.

Now What? Application to Practice

HERE ARE QUESTIONS for leaders to use to evaluate where they are indeed embracing the liberating dichotomies.

1. Effective Leadership vs. Shared Governance
   A. Does the leader seek the input and involvement of others in the organization for decisions at all levels? Is his or her leadership style viewed as inclusive or exclusive?
   B. Do others in the organization accept the leadership responsibility of the leader and allow him or her truly to lead?
   C. Do all the members of the organization have clearly defined responsibilities and the authority and accountability that those responsibilities entail?
   D. Where is the current balance between effective leadership and shared governance?

2. Communication vs. Confidentiality
   A. Are the leader and the organization characterized by openness in communication or by holding information tightly?
   B. Do people feel safe in sharing information or opinions?
   C. Is openness used as an excuse for harsh talk or gossip? Is confidentiality used as an excuse for keeping secrets?
   D. Where is the current balance between open communication and appropriate confidentiality?

3. Conflict vs. Peace
   A. Does the institution tend to avoid conflict even when it may be necessary? Are "Christian" reasons given for this?
   B. What are the reasons for most of the conflicts in the institution? (Some possible reasons are budgets, job performance, attitudes, and decision processes.) Are conflicts resolved through a discernible process, or are they mostly ignored? Are the parties to the conflict honored biblically?
   C. Does overall institutional direction or the leader's vision cause conflict? How would the community react to the possibility that resolution may require some to leave the institution?
   D. Where is the current balance between conflict and peace?

4. Patience vs. Decisiveness
   A. Does the leader tend toward either precipitous decision making or procrastination?
   B. Is the failure to act sometimes rationalized spiritually? Are the consequences of inaction tolerated more than the consequences of action?
   C. Is the leader known for spur-of-the-moment decisions? Do others feel that decisions "come down from above" without adequate process and thought?
   D. Where is the current balance between patience and decisiveness?

5. Predictability vs. Surprise
   A. Is the organization characterized as orderly and stable, or creative and innovative?
   B. How are new ideas received? Are these ideas viewed with suspicion, or are they heard with interest?
   C. Do members of the organization come to work wondering what will happen next?
   D. Where is the current balance between predictability and surprise?

6. Realism vs. Hope
   A. Is the organization characterized by optimism or pessimism? If optimism, is it embraced at the cost of ignoring hard facts or situations? If pessimism, is it held despite clear evidence of God's blessing?
   B. Does the leader tend to communicate good news or bad news? In which direction—more positive or more negative—do the members of the organization tend to interpret what the leader says about the state of the organization?
   C. Where is the current balance between realism and hope?

Conclusion: Thriving in the Dichotomies

The six dichotomies discussed in this chapter are genuine features of all communities. Healthy communities recognize the good that exists in both poles, and seek to embrace the tensions. Weaker communities tend toward one pole or the other, and they fail to experience the vitality of holding on dynamically to both poles.

Nevertheless, it must be recognized that living in the tensions is not the easy path. People who prefer everything perfectly clear and defined will gravitate toward one side of the dichotomy, where navigating the churning waters of real people in real situations is replaced by rigid application of established formulas. While the tensions are energizing and vitalizing, they are also dynamics that elicit many of the problems faced by educational communities. What leadership and spiritual traits will enable the Christian educational leader to navigate the dichotomies in liberating fashion?

- There must be a clear vision, a picture of the future, that everyone can see. It is critical that leaders articulate a compelling picture of where the institution is going. The tensions, then, become the raw materials in God's hands for this future to unfold.
- There must be humility and repentance. The very same tensions that will rip apart pride-filled communities will promote fellowship and partnership in the educational venture when people repent of sin and forgive one another.
- There must be a keen sense of stewardship, an understanding that the educational communities to which we belong do not belong to us. The larger the sense of God's ownership, the less severe will be defensiveness and imperial urges, and the sweeter will be the offering up of gifts and energies for the larger kingdom work to which God has called us.
- There must a relentless pursuit of Christlikeness, a Spirit-enabled putting away of the sins of anger, jealousy, gossip, bitterness, and harsh words, and a Spirit-empowered putting on of the fruit of the Spirit.

With vision, humility, repentance, stewardship, and pursuit of Christlikeness, the dichotomies of educational leadership can be liberating and lifegiving. What a future there is for Christian educational communities that have leaders who grasp this truth!

References

Collins, Jim. 2001. *Good to great: Why some companies make the leap ... and others don't.* New York: HarperCollins.

Dowdall, George, and Jean Dowdall. 2005. Crossing over to the dark side. *The Chronicle of Higher Education: Chronicle Careers* 52, no. 5:C1, 4.

CHAPTER 8

PROFESSIONAL DEVELOPMENT

*Gathering the Scattered in
School Communities*

✥

By Jack Beckman

Jack Beckman is an associate professor of education at Covenant College. He received his PhD from the University of Cambridge, UK, and has thirty years of experience as a teacher and an educational leader in the Christian school movement. He is a coauthor of When Children Love to Learn.

CHAPTER 8

PROFESSIONAL DEVELOPMENT

By Jack Beckman

THE REACTION OF the teachers was a mixture of shock, tears, acceptance, and consternation at the behavior of their principal. The veterans wondered if he had finally succumbed to the pressure, and the new teachers pondered whether they had made a mistake in signing a contract at Ridgemont Christian School.

John Richards had completed his seventh year as principal of Ridgemont. These years had not been easy ones: economic issues and budget restraints, lowering student population, teacher turnover, an unruly schedule, and a feeling that the school was stagnant. So the board had granted him some extra time for a vision retreat over the summer. Richards had slept, prayed, read, written, and spent time with his wife and children. They attended a quaint white clapboard church near the retreat site; the pastor preached simply and with conviction from the Gospel of John. Slowly, Richards began to sense his former optimism reawaken. Upon his return to the office several weeks before the teachers arrived, he had his new plan in place.

On the day the teachers arrived, they noticed a large half circle of chairs facing the stage of the cafeteria, where meetings usually occurred. Quietly playing in the background was Michael Card's song "The Basin

151

and the Towel." As Richards greeted the teachers, they nervously noticed on the front table a bucket and a number of hand towels neatly folded beside it. After everyone was seated, he took his place at the apex of the half circle. With great zeal and passion, he related his retreat experiences to the faculty. He repented for not having served them and their needs and confessed that as educational shepherd he had led his flock astray in their practice as teachers. He wanted to accomplish two goals for this first meeting: to establish a servant leadership model as exemplified by washing their feet and to introduce a new instructional model that would revitalize their instructional practice.

Hours later, an outside observer would have wondered what was more astonishing to the faculty: the washing of their feet or the introduction of a multipage lesson-planning model based on Howard Gardner's multiple intelligences (MI).

Six months into the school year, the board intervened in a tense situation: teachers were refusing to complete the time-consuming and cumbersome MI lesson plans, parents were questioning the direction of the school toward "humanistic" methods, and the principal was asking where it all had gone wrong.

Sorting Out Professional Development

The landscape of professional development in schools is littered with stories such as this. The scope and the nature of the term *professional development* are contested issues, and the term is defined by an array of possibilities according to the framework of the person using the phrase. A foray through the current literature and research in such scholarly periodicals as *Educational Administration Quarterly, Journal of Teacher Education, Journal of Curriculum and Supervision,* or *Phi Delta Kappan* reveals the various understructures—critical theory, constructivism, positivism, behaviorism, and pragmatism—that drive the plurality of applications of the subject. At the level of the school, we can see a similar diversity. Teachers—representing a wide range of experience, varying in expertise from novice to expert, exemplifying a variety of instructional strengths and weaknesses, and possessing multiple understandings of the school's mission and values—can become for the educational leader the scattered flock that must be gathered into a cohesive whole.

This chapter explores a number of sticky issues in the field of professional development. Numerous books address the craft aspects of this subject: mentoring, peer coaching, action research, workshops and symposia, supervision-by-observation cycles, collegial inquiry, and collaborative problem solving. This chapter focuses on the bigger issues that often elude scrutiny: issues of disposition, practice, and philosophy that subtly influence instructional leaders to think the way they do and so influence the world they create in the school where teachers live and work.

The term *professional development* is synonymous with another: *supervision* (in which the emphasis is upon assessment, growth, and development) as opposed to *evaluation* (which seeks to make judgments for the purposes of employment decision making). This chapter will focus on the growth aspects of teachers and teaching. Therefore, within the frame of this chapter, the working definition of *professional development* is "that aspect of transformational and shared instructional leadership within a learning community that leads to organizational learning and change and to the developmental growth of teacher practitioners from novice to expert."

This chapter addresses the following issues: the endemic problems of professional development as conventionally envisioned, the nature of the principal as a servant-equipper who engenders both transformational and shared leadership, the work of professional development in a community of learners, and alternative routes to the care and growth of teachers under the principal's instructional and pastoral leadership.

Clinical Singularity vs. Communities of Collaboration

The way it was—and still is

Old paradigms are hard to shift. They stubbornly persist, even with the arrival of new evidence and more accurate portrayals of reality. Thomas Kuhn's book *The Structure of Scientific Revolutions* (1996) offers a number of intriguing instances of this phenomenon. Two examples of this pattern are electricity as a liquid and phlogiston as the vehicle of combustion. Both of these ideas endured despite subsequent contrary data and in both cases lasted years before being overthrown in favor of what has become our contemporary understanding of these phenomena.

On the leading edge of the twenty-first century, this same disposition resides within the profession of educational leadership. Leaders shaped by the thinking of the past—where school is portrayed as a machine to be maintained (Frase 2005) or as a place where information is merely transmitted and reproduced (Haas and Poyner 2005)—may have a tendency to hold on to models and practices of professional development that conflict with our theological understandings of pedagogy or with what we know to be true about developmentally appropriate teaching and learning. This tendency in turn affects the many complex choices that leaders make as they undertake the professional care and oversight of teachers in their individually diverse growth from novice to master teacher. Professional development of a teaching staff may carry with it archetypal baggage that has gathered and overflowed in its contested definitions, unsure relationships, unclear objectives, and ill-advised models of evaluation of what teachers believe, think, and do in their work (Guskey 2003).

Robert Goldhammer developed the model of professional development most often used and lauded in educational circles. His 1993 book *Clinical Supervision* is the classic text from which this model arises. Reviewing Goldhammer's book, Carl Glickman, Stephen Gordon, and Jovita Ross-Gordon (2004) enumerate the technical and clinical aspects of the supervisor-teacher relationship in which it is assumed that the educational leader is adept at capturing and analyzing in a scientific manner the many complexities of the classroom. This systematic structure unfolds as a sequence of five interactions with the teacher: preconference, observation, analyzing and interpreting the data of the observation, postconference, and critique of the process.

Don Beach and Judy Reinhartz (2000) summarize a sequence of supervisory and evaluative models that have evolved over the years to capture and assess the work of teachers in the classroom environment. They illustrate a movement from the clinical and analytical (as in Goldhammer's book) during the 1970s and '80s, through the management era of reform in the late 1980s and '90s, to the present age of differentiation and collaboration. The movement from modernity (which represents the hope of a unified science of teaching) toward the postmodern turn (which celebrates both diversity and community) is remarkable.

Goldhammer's method of clinical supervision remains the gold standard to which educational leaders aspire. It is organized, dispassionate, systematic, seemingly objective, and singular. A perusal of much of the extant literature on the subjects of supervision and evaluation leads the community of instructional practice down this path (Brown 2002; Glickman, Gordon, and Ross-Gordon 2004; Nolan and Hoover 2004; Sergiovanni and Starratt 2002). And the path has generally led us true, although the hard data regarding how effective clinical supervision has been in teacher growth is marginal at best (Duffy 2000). Thomas Sergiovanni and Robert Starratt (2002) note that the use of clinical supervision for teacher growth works best when it is done as a collegial activity between expert teachers and novices and when the principal works in this capacity with only a limited number of faculty members. They recommend that teachers take on the major burden of clinical supervision and that the principal "stay involved by helping them, finding time for them to help each other, arranging schedules to allow them to work together, and participating in conversations about 'what is going on, how effective is it, and what do we do now?' " (229).

If *supervision* is defined as developmental interactions that teachers encounter as they move toward expert status (Reiman and Thies-Sprinthall 1998)—interactions such as the initiation rites of induction into the school culture; the assignment of mentors to the care and growth of novice teachers; or normative workshops on instructional methods, behavioral management, or the latest curriculum component—organized teacher watching takes a pivotal role both for instructional growth and in employment decisions. Indeed, as teachers evolve through experience, reflection, professional relationships, trial and error, and feedback in order to become master practitioners, supervision opens up into a fruitful grove of possibilities. Mentoring novices, peer coaching, curriculum design, action research, collaborative study groups, and further advancement within the school leadership track follow this kind of thinking and practice in many schools (Gordon 2004). Master teachers, who bypass the yearly employment evaluation of novices, are instead formally observed by the principal every two or three years.

Singular approaches to complex issues

Do educational leaders truly understand what effective instructional practices look like in the classroom, much less what kinds of efforts are necessary to encourage these practices in the instructional staff? Often, busy principals are distanced from the classroom experience, and so they lose the vital instructional interactions with students—interactions that enable teachers to be on the front lines of organization and management, planning and implementation of lessons, assessment, and collegiality. As a result, these leaders may be tempted to delegate professional development to others; to design and implement programs that are out of touch with the classroom; or to provide diluted, simplistic, or uninformed feedback to the teachers under their care. Moreover, upon what foundation or authority do educational leaders have permission to engage the lives of teaching staff? What responsibilities do educational leaders have for the supervision, evaluation, advice, and counsel of teachers? Finally, are educational leaders, in the midst of so many levels of daily complexity, able to be on the leading edge of these activities?

These questions lead to an associated issue—that of the one-dimensional managerial perspective to which principals might default in terms of their supervisory and professional-development responsibilities and the narrowness of that perspective in light of the complexities of the classroom. According to Alfie Kohn (1993), the behavioral model of teaching and learning continues to dominate the teaching and learning scene. The reigning educational paradigm—which has affected teacher-education programs, school curriculum and methods, and classroom organization and management—is Skinnerian behaviorism. Leaders trained to function within this paradigm bring significant baggage that may hamper the adoption of new teaching and learning paradigms that use alternative models such as inquiry, collaboration and cooperative learning, and differentiated instructional and assessment models. Most principals have been trained to evaluate the singular direct instructional method espoused by Madeline Hunter and the instructional decision-making approach that typifies much of the teaching in today's schools (Bryant and Currin 1995). This systematic lesson-planning methodology (anticipatory set, behavioral objectives, checking for understanding, guided practice, and closure) is well aligned with conventional clinical supervision and its own affiliated systematics (260). Although this model easily captures instruction in a checklist that contains little narrative, it does not fully reflect the actual complexity of how teachers teach and students learn. As Christians, don't we need to critically analyze the effects such paradigms have on our schools?

Thomas Sergiovanni decries the managerial model of school leadership as a rational, linear "clockworks mindscape" that often backfires. The clearly delineated aspects of planning for change in the school culture that holds allegiance to this model are as follows (1996, 160):

1. Decide what it is you want to accomplish, and if possible, state it as a measurable outcome.
2. Provide clear behavioral expectations to people by deciding and communicating who will do what and how it will be done.
3. Train people to function in the new way.
4. Once the change is introduced, monitor by comparing what you

expected with what you observed.

5. Make any corrections in the system that may be necessary (160).

This kind of detailed planning, when applied to school change, professional development, or classroom supervision, assumes a stable environment in which all variables have been controlled, as in a clinical and scientific experiment. The model also assumes a behavioral worldview in which a teacher's motivation is purely extrinsic and oriented toward rewards rather than intrinsic and motivated by a moral obligation to something worthy and meaningful. Sergiovanni states that "what counts most to people is what they believe, how they feel, and the shared norms and cultural messages that emerge from the groups and communities with which they identify" (1996, 164). In this thinking, rules of engagement are replaced by norms reflective of shared moral values.

In a managerial system, the novel, the unexpected, the unintended consequence, or the alternative idea is discouraged. Indeed, the principal as manager occupies an almost surreal position outside the machine in order to make objective and accurate judgments of what is going on inside (Guba and Lincoln 1989). Moreover, the principal as manager "disempowers those being evaluated by affording them no voice in the analysis of their own practice," does not extend "editorial rights" over gathered or observed data, and may prompt the one evaluated to "collude with the evaluator ... in order to stay on the evaluator's good side" (Bryant and Curran 1995, 251).

Where is the community of collaboration? A personal perspective

Having spent twenty-five years either as a teacher or as a principal, I now find myself on the other side of the desk. Rather than working with and observing teachers fresh out of college and new to the classroom, I now mentor preservice teachers as an associate professor of education. The stark reality is that I still know little about what effective teaching and learning look like, much less how to encourage effective practices in my young preservice teachers. As I make the school rounds, both announced and unannounced, am I seeing snapshots that represent the reality of what teachers do, or is the portrait skewed into something unrealistic? Though I make numerous observations that I analyze with great vigor, often I sense that my feedback is weak and unproductive.

In college courses I emphasize the school as a community of practice, where expert practitioners collaborate on meaningful activities of instructional expertise—team planning, problem solving, mentoring and peer coaching, and action research. The student work for these courses includes collaborative and cooperative-learning activities that apply new learning in ways that teachers in the field should attend to—working in teams to develop a management plan or a thematic unit, assess a new textbook, or solve a realistic problem. Our teacher-education program also provides preservice teachers real-time experiences in schools before student teaching. These experiences, though not unproblematic, serve to connect content and pedagogical course work with active classrooms. I want students to do what real teachers do in their everyday work. Yet, when they talk about their student-teaching experiences in real schools, they at times do not observe or participate in this kind of professional activity (Moore 2003). For those who graduate to the classroom, this disconnect from higher educational ideals to the real-time world of the classroom continues for some of them. There are those, however, who rise above the theory-practice dilemma to enact change locally in their own classrooms and then among their grade peers.

The issue of school as community is also problematic in its meaning and application. Often what masquerades as community and collaboration between instructional leaders and teachers is at heart a traditional management model redolent of business metaphors and applications for bureaucratic agendas in schools. On the one hand we celebrate the profession of teaching, while on the other we distrust, monitor, and inspect it for fear that its products might spoil (Frase 2005, 432–35). Patricia Holland and Noreen Garman (2001) expose this spurious kind of thinking, in which collaboration and community in schools is viewed as empty rhetoric and teachers are left as isolated technicians under the disciplinary gaze of the supervisor.

These numerous and disturbing problems put the instructional leader in the center of troubled waters. The models, the efficacy, the work, and the very focal points of educational ministry—school, teachers, and students—are called into question. Like Ezekiel, the principal has willingly been placed in the gap. In some ways, John Richards' story is not unlike our own. In the next section, these issues will be addressed from a biblical and theological framework to set us on a proper path of understanding. We will attempt to follow advice from the writer of the book of Hebrews—"Let us fix our eyes on Jesus, the author and perfecter of our faith" (12:2)—to see if there is a model to imitate that will fulfill both our vertical responsibilities to God as well as those on the horizontal plane in our vocation as transformational and shared instructional leaders who are also servant-equippers.

The Educational Leader as Servant-Equipper

John 13 as a theological starting point

Principal Richards' actions appear shocking, and yet he was merely trying to imitate what Jesus did for the disciples before the Passover Feast. Jesus' behavior in John 13 was emblematic of the countercultural and salvific work given Him by His Father. Jesus was, in fact, subverting the disciples' conventions of what the Messiah was really like. On the Mount of Transfiguration, they sought to anchor Him to the world; as Jesus entered Jerusalem, they entertained thoughts of a Warrior-King and deliverance from oppression; overall, they could not fathom the foolishness of a sacrificial Savior who would willingly give Himself up for them. This is certainly not the kind of leadership to which anyone in his or her right mind would aspire.

Thus we have at the feet of the disciples the Good Shepherd who gives up His life for His sheep—with a towel and bowl in hand, on His knees, washing the filthy, well-traveled feet of His misfit band of brothers. John 13 presents a protest, a rebuke, and then, obedience and a lesson for them all: "That you should do as I have done for you" (verse 15). And embedded in that lot was one who would betray Him to the authorities—a traitor, thief, and liar, and indeed soon to be filled with Satan (John 13:27). Yet, the betrayer's feet ended up as clean as Peter's.

There are a number of critical things to notice from John 13. First, the disposition of Jesus as a servant was an engine that motivated His life and work. Just as Jesus recognized that the heart is the starting point of all external behavior (Matthew 12:34), the attitudes and dispositions that shape the relationships of life and work must be considered—both in and out of school. The Messiah is keenly interested in transforming the heart in order to transform the world. Second, Jesus was not operating from a distance or in a vacuum. He was in close proximity to those He served, and He desired that they continue His work, thus sharing ministry with them—a teaching method seen over and over as Jesus prepared the disciples for the work ahead. The servant example of Jesus was part of His plan for equipping His followers to continue faithfully in His ministry (John 13:15).

Jesus as the Servant-Equipper models a leadership that is both *trans-*

formational (from the inside out and with humility and courage as one faces or enacts change) and *shared* (empowering others to share in the work of transformation). This type of leadership is essentially theological work on a grand scale; it is the origin of the type of mind that Paul wrote about in Philippians 2:1–5—the mind of Christ and His unexpected tactic of leading by serving. This leadership has a subversive nature: when the world seeks powerful, evocative, and dominant persons to lead, Jesus washes feet. Unless educational leaders understand this paradox, how will they ever wish to encourage professional development in their scattered flock of teachers? When John wrote that "the Word became flesh" (John 1:14), he was referring to Jesus, and by extension he was making a promise—that as believers are indwelt by the Holy Spirit and sanctified in Christ and as they live the principles of Scripture, they will also be the Word becoming flesh.

Parker Palmer's *The Courage to Teach* (1998) elucidates the centrality of the inner life of the teacher along with the inherent risks of transparency in teaching. Eugene Peterson's *Subversive Spirituality* (1997) has nothing to do with educational leadership or professional development, but has everything to do with the life of a pastor, a life that is instructive for the Christian school principal. Indeed, in the frontispiece of his book, Peterson quotes Matthew 10:16 from his paraphrase *The Message* to illustrate the perilous waters of leadership:

> Stay alert. This is hazardous work I'm assigning you. You're going to be like sheep running through a wolf pack, so don't call attention to yourselves. Be as cunning as a snake, inoffensive as a dove.

Finally, two books by Henri Nouwen, *In the Name of Jesus* (1999) and *Creative Ministry* (1991), take very familiar themes—such as Jesus' desert experience and the lifework of the pastor—and apply them in profound ways. Books written from outside the profession of educational leadership often contain insights that can lead educators to greater self-understanding.

Common-grace insights on transformational and shared instructional leadership

Ontologically, the idea of transformational and shared instructional leadership through service and equipping resonates in both the Christian and secular worlds. N. A. Yoder describes five dimensions of effective educational leadership and how each applies to the school culture. The fourth dimension is servant leadership and is characterized by a "leader's beliefs regarding the potential of others, the significance of relationships and personal development, shared leadership" (Keyes, Hanley-Maxwell, and Capper 1999, 234). The leader is committed to enhancing and creating relationships of trust, openness, self-examination, and reflection. Stephen Gordon invokes a model of professional development founded on the empowerment of the learning community: "It involves enabling teachers for life-long learning, teaching, and leadership" (2004, 13).

The dual leadership dimensions—transformational and shared—must be mutually informed and integrated in order to facilitate a culture of professional growth in school communities. Vision without shared praxis becomes empty and meaningless. Helen Marks and Susan Printy posit that transformational leadership with its lifeworld of vision and purpose must be balanced by instructional elements that accentuate teaching and learning. Instructional leadership demonstrates this balance, "emphasizing the technical core of instruction, curriculum, and assessment, provides direction and affects the day-to-day activities of teachers and students in the school" (2003, 377). In this context, "Transformational leaders motivate followers by raising their consciousness about the importance of organizational goals and by inspiring them to transcend their own self-interest for the sake of the organization" (Marks and Printy 2003, 375).

Kenneth Leithwood, Lawrence Leonard, and Lyn Sharratt describe several dimensions of transformational leadership, including these (1998, 264–266):

- "Identifies and articulates a vision"—builds consensus about school goals and priorities (mission centered)
- "Conveys high performance expectations"—provides individualized support, supplies intellectual stimulation (performance centered)
- "Builds a productive school culture"—models organizational values, strengthens productive school culture, builds collaborative cultures, creates structures for participation in school decisions (culture centered)

Risk-taking behaviors are endemic to the transformational leader. They require the skill to forage through ambiguity in order to reach clarity. They encourage openness, transparency, and willingness to learn by trial and error. There is a brazen challenge in this stance to the bureaucratic tendencies of schools that import a businesslike structure to the institution of the school.

The mirror image to this, of course, is shared instructional leadership, which presents another challenge, described as follows by Marks and Printy (2003, 371):

> Shared instructional leadership involves the active collaboration of principal and teachers on curriculum, instruction, and assessment. Within this model, the principal seeks out the ideas, insights, and expertise of teachers in these areas and works with teachers for school improvement. The principal and teachers share responsibility for staff development, curricular development, and supervision of instructional tasks. Thus, the principal is not the sole instructional leader but the "leader of instructional leaders." (2003, 371; Glickman 1989, 6)

In this paradigm, teachers assume a major responsibility for their own professional growth, and they become active instruments of instructional improvement in the lives of other teachers. The principal exchanges the traditional role of inspector for one of facilitator and co-learner for the improvement of the wider school community.

Getting it right by getting it wrong

Six months after principal John Richards washed his teachers' feet and communicated to them his vision for instructional improvement, he was sitting alone in his office, head in hands, anxious (and a bit angry) at how Ridgemont Christian School was in a state of turmoil. He reviewed the carefully detailed action plan developed during his summer retreat and noted its organizational structure: regular weekly training for teachers on the philosophy and application of the multiple-intelligences theory, the reading together and discussion of several of Howard Gardner's books, a progressive model of change from traditional lesson planning to the multipage document for each content area, and scheduled checkpoints for Richards to observe and evaluate teacher instructional change as well as to scrutinize the new lesson plans. Part of the problem had been the teachers' resistance to the new approach. It wasn't so much the new teachers, but the ones who had been there the longest, who had set up siege works of opposition. Angry words from both sides were exchanged. Richards was accused of being a tyrant and of not considering the feelings of his teachers by overwhelming them with the new imposed workload. When several veteran teachers came to him with ideas for compromise, Richards had shut them down.

In his deepest heart, Richards felt like what he thought Jesus must have felt as He washed the feet of Judas.

No one can revile John Richards for his zeal and desire to serve and challenge his learning community. However, it is excruciatingly clear that his well-planned moment of change was doomed to failure on a number of levels. First, instructional leadership that is both transformational and shared must include both cultural and instructional components of the school. But he was attempting to initiate a managerial, top-down approach to critical professional development and school change. His approach was indicative of an outside-in progression in which an objective external observer makes judgments about what needs changing, creates a plan for that change, and then trains and inspects for that change in conformity to the plan's objectives. Real change, however, happens from the inside out, when the transformational leader operates within the community of practice to collaborate with those constituents most likely to encounter the disequilibrium of broken or ineffective practice. Second, rather than taking the risk of being inclusive and collaborative in effecting change or cocreating change, Richards also failed the test of shared instructional leadership. His faculty members were left out of the process, and they discovered the direction of professional development as it was projected to them. The result was that Richards found himself with a fragmented and alienated staff and very little in the way of real change or professional development. Although his heart was in the right place, he did not show the wisdom necessary to apply the servant-equipper paradigm in a way that unified and empowered his scattered flock of teachers.

This approach runs counter to the ways that teachers learn and the motivations that persuade them to seek professional development (Scribner 1999). On an informal and daily basis, teachers collaborate on crucial aspects of instructional practice—they identify problems and issues, dialogue around those issues, find and develop resources, apply what they have learned, and then assess effectiveness—yet this same critical approach is not consistently used in formalized professional development (248). Principals should use the informal knowledge-development domain natural to teachers, and turn its collective energies toward the broader concerns of the school community.

For example, educational leaders can gather teachers to discuss an agenda for teacher learning based upon the concerns, interests, and experiences that teachers have, and these can be negotiated and modified as they collegially work toward the shared mission and goals of the school and the need for instructional growth and development on all levels of teacher experience. Multiple-grade-level, subject-level, and school-level collaborative studies can be envisioned and fulfilled—studies that place educational leaders and teachers in close professional proximity. Then, the very practical aspects of mentoring new teachers—who themselves have much to offer in the way of shared learning—peer coaching, collaborative action research and study groups, and workshops can focus on the shared work of the community of learners. These become engines in the implementation of a vibrant professional development model.

Building Collegial Communities

John Richards and his scattered and alienated faculty were on the verge of an all-out civil war. Because of his choices in leadership style, a series of potentially destructive fault lines had appeared. But for Richards and his faculty—Christians filled with the Holy Spirit—there is a real possibility of *metanoia*, which can lead to healing and a reforging of the covenants that they share in the school community. *Transformational* and *shared leadershi*p (along with *servant equipping*) are terms that have little meaning unless they are planted in a school context. Appropriate leadership attracts a community of followers, a collegial community in which the leadership is shared.

A school must have a mission statement, which is a covenantal confession of educational purpose and values that its constituency agrees on and that binds the school and its constituency into a unified body moving together toward shared goals. Thomas Sergiovanni writes of this ideal organism when he reviews the work of Ferdinand Tönnies and the sociological theory of *gemeinschaft*, which represents "a vision of life as sacred community" (1996, 49) in which the "ties that bind ... come from sharing with others a common commitment to a set of ideas and ideals" (50). *Gemeinschaft* is set over against another construct, that of *gesellschaft*, analogous to the modern corporation, in which "relationships are formal and distant, having been prescribed by roles and expectations. Circumstances are evaluated by universal criteria as embodied in policies, rules and protocols. Acceptance is conditional. The more a person cooperates with the corporation and achieves for the corporation, the more likely he or she will be accepted.... Subjectivity is frowned upon. Rationality is prized" (49–50).

According to Sergiovanni, the challenge is that we must decide whether schooling is to be a corporate organization or a collaborative community. This challenge, in essence, is the crux of the leadership crisis in schools: whether the transformational leader who stands on the cutting edge of teacher learning in the school can wed these ideals to an affiliated collegial community of shared leadership, decision making, problem solving, curriculum and instructional change, and the care and growth of teachers from novice to expert. The radical and subversive nature of the leadership of Jesus, and His pattern to shape our understanding of what it means to be a servant-equipper, can directly affect how educational leaders lead and transform the community of professional learners.

Leadership and community are not at odds with each other, and indeed are created to complement each other. This collegial community then becomes what Peter Senge calls the *learning organization*, "where people continually expand their capacity to create the results they truly desire, where new and expansive patterns of thinking are nurtured, where collective aspiration is set free, and where people are continually learning how to learn together" (1990, cited in Duffy 2000, 140). The learning organization has also been described as "skilled at creating, acquiring, and transferring knowledge, and at modifying its behavior to reflect new knowledge and insights" (Garvin 1993, 80; cited in Duffy 2000, 140).

The current research on best practices in the local classroom demonstrates that collaborative communities of practice are the source of powerful learning in the vital relationships between teachers and students (Brophy 1996). This same disposition can be applied to the professional community of practice as teachers, empowered through shared instructional leadership, work with instructional leaders to create compelling learning experiences for teachers in the field; in other words, professional development (Leithwood, Leonard, and Sharratt 1998, 264–65). Anita Hoy and Wayne Hoy (2005) and Donald Cruickshank, Deborah Jenkins, and Kim Metcalf (2006), who have written two other texts that represent the best-practices movement, also emphasize the cultural and communal aspects of teaching and learning.

In fact, if the care and growth of teachers leads to better learning for students—a key objective of any professional development cycle—then the community of learners is involved in a reciprocal relationship between what teachers do and what occurs in the classroom.

> Few axioms are more fundamental than the one that acknowledges the link between what happens to teachers and what happens to students. Inquiring classrooms, for example, are not likely to flourish in schools where inquiry among teachers is discouraged. A commitment to problem solving is difficult to instill in students who are taught by teachers for whom problem solving is not allowed. Where there is little discourse among teachers, discourse among students will be harder to promote and maintain. And the idea of making classrooms into learning communities for students will remain more rhetoric than real unless schools become learning communities for teachers too. (Sergiovanni 1996, 139)

What Sergiovanni exhorts here is that the disposition encouraged among *students* to become lifelong learners who use tools of inquiry and who have the desire and capacity to do so ought to be the same kind of disposition that instructional leaders encourage in *teachers*, regardless of the teachers' experience or status in the school community. Gathering the scattered is the risky business of relationship building. The transformational leader must know the flock, communicate on an ongoing basis the shared educational and spiritual values that make for a collegial community, and then make space for teachers to share in the work of professional instructional development as empowered peers.

Taking Up the Basin and the Towel

Revising the image of what principals do is hard work, particularly if paradigms—like old wardrobes in the attic—are to be moved. The leader must challenge the thinking that reduces professional development to a series of activities on the principal's full calendar. As discussed previously, John 13 confronts educational leaders by providing a subversive model for educational leaders—that of the servant-equipper—modeled by the Savior as He humbly washes the feet of His disciples.

Solving the Puzzle: The End of the Story

John Richards came to the realization that his repentance was in order. His hurt, anger, and feelings of betrayal finally let him know that sin had gotten the best of his new plan to restructure instructional practice at Ridgemont Christian School. His plan had ignored what his teachers might have to offer as professionals. He had acted as if they would quietly submit to his wonderful idea, and with a little training, all would be well. But he did not count on his teachers having ideas of their own, and possibly good ones at that. In the midst of the worst part of the storm, several older teachers had come to him in private to propose some solutions and to offer a compromise, but he had rejected them out of hand, deeply resenting what he thought was insubordinate behavior. Later, when he showed their ideas to his wife, she surprised him by asking him to look them over one more time. He did, and with tears he saw his sin. The next day, with the board and his wife there as support, he met first with the faculty as a whole and then individually with a few teachers for whom he had harbored particularly hard feelings. He asked their forgiveness and made a commitment to try with God's help to serve his teachers and include them in the lifework of the school. There is much yet to be done at Ridgemont Christian School, but the principal and teachers are now working as a team.

The principal is the author of this chapter.

Now What? Application to Practice

THIS CHAPTER HAS been designed to create a sense of dissonance in the lifework of educational leaders. It has been unashamedly dispositional in nature, as the author firmly believes that change in leadership equates with a change in heart. Certain aspects of critical knowledge and skills, however, were embedded explicitly and implicitly within the text. The purpose of this final section is to draw out those principles and practices, which illustrate the heart of the chapter. These are written as propositions to help answer the questions "What should I know?" and "What should I do?"

Critical knowledge: What should I know?	Critical skills: What should I do?
1. Transformational and shared leadership is first of all theological in nature, and it follows the life of Christ	A. Leaders should schedule weekly and monthly blocks of time for reading and reflection. They should choose books and articles that will challenge their thinking and help them make connections outside the instructional profession. B. A yearly personal retreat for prayer and reflection upon the shepherding aspects of instructional leadership should be a top priority. C. If possible, leaders should teach students regularly, not merely observe others' teaching.
2. The values of mutual trust, empowerment, and reflection are essential paths of knowledge, along with a disposition for teachers and leaders to build relationships for their mutual development.	A. Leaders should ask for the Holy Spirit's wisdom and guidance to become aware of their blind spots, especially in the areas of trust and empowerment of others. Leaders should go to those with whom they openly struggle and ask forgiveness, and in this way recommit themselves to a servant model of educational leadership. B. Each leader should find a spiritual mentor who will keep the leader accountable and ask the more difficult questions pertaining to the leader's personal walk and public vocation.

Critical knowledge: What should I know?	Critical skills: What should I do?
3. A collegial community has shared values, but not everyone in the community understands or applies these values evenly across the community. Thus, a key role of educational leaders is to build and maintain relationships with teachers to create an atmosphere of common communication, care, and concern.	A. Educational leaders should reflect on the last two or three times significant pedagogical changes took place in the school context. What was the change process? What were some unanticipated leadership challenges? What did the leaders learn about the teachers? Questions like these will help leaders be more effective at implementing change. B. To foster a sense of community among teachers and between teachers and principals, leaders should schedule an annual faculty retreat for the purposes of prayer, fellowship, and recommitment to shared school values. C. Leaders should regularly emphasize shared values and principles that undergird the school community and pedagogy. Leaders should write about them, discuss them, challenge them, and make them visible to all stakeholders.
4. Everyone in the collegial community, regardless of status or experience, can participate in ongoing professional development activities such as mentoring, peer coaching, collegial inquiry and study groups, shared decision making, and action research.	A. Leaders and teachers should cocreate a plan of professional growth that meets the unique needs of teachers. Novices and veterans alike should be involved in this process. B. Leaders should ask teachers to create a list of pedagogical issues, such as management or guided reading, and then facilitate a professional study group to develop a plan to address those issues. C. Key teacher-leaders—both novice and veteran teachers— must be identified and empowered to colead.

Critical knowledge: What should I know?	Critical skills: What should I do?
5. Life in the collegial community does not mean lessened accountability. Rather, it affirms the commitments made by teachers as they fulfill the shared values of the school mission.	A. Leaders should design a clear and cohesive model of instructional accountability that includes attributes and characteristics of professional growth along a continuum from novice to master teacher. Leaders should involve a number of small groups in the process. B. Leaders and faculty members should develop a model of accountability that includes the most current effective practices of action research, mentoring, peer coaching, and shared inquiry.

References

Beach, Don M., and Judy Reinhartz. 2000. *Supervisory leadership: Focus on instruction.* Needham Heights, MA: Allyn and Bacon.

Brophy, Jere. 1996. *Teaching.* Educational practices series 1. Geneva, Switzerland: International Bureau of Education, UNESCO.

Brown, Gordon B. 2002. *Guiding faculty to excellence: Instructional supervision in the Christian school.* 2nd ed. Colorado Springs, CO: Purposeful Design Publications.

Bryant, Miles, and DeAnn Currin. 1995. Views of teacher evaluation from novice and expert evaluators. *Journal of Curriculum and Supervision* 10, no. 3 (Spring): 1995, 250–61.

Cruickshank, Donald R., Deborah Bainer Jenkins, and Kim K. Metcalf. 2006. *The act of teaching.* 4th ed. New York: McGraw-Hill.

Duffy, Francis M. 2000. Reconceptualizing instructional supervision for 3rd millennium school systems. *Journal of Curriculum and Supervision* 15, no. 2 (Winter): 123–45.

Frase, Larry E. 2005. Refocusing the purposes of teacher supervision. In *The SAGE handbook of educational leadership: Advances in theory, research, and practice,* ed. Fenwick W. English, 430–62. Thousand Oaks, CA: Sage Publications.

Garvin, David A. 1993. Building a learning organization. *Harvard Business Review* 71 (July–August): 80. Quoted in Francis M. Duffy, Reconceptualizing instructional supervision for 3rd millennium school systems. *Journal of Curriculum and Supervision* (15, no. 2 Winter, 2000), 140.

Glickman, Carl. 1989. Has Sam and Samantha's time come at last? *Educational Leadership* 46 (8): 6. Quoted in Helen M. Marks and Susan M. Printy, Principal leadership and school performance: An integration of transformational and instructional leadership. *Educational Administration Quarterly* 35, no. 2 (August): 370–97.

Glickman, Carl D., Stephen P. Gordon, and Jovita M. Ross-Gordon. 2004. *The basic guide to supervision and instructional leadership.* Boston: Allyn and Bacon.

Goldhammer, Robert. 1993. *Clinical supervision: Special methods for the supervision of teachers.* 3rd ed. San Diego: Harcourt Brace Jovanovich.

Gordon, Stephen P. 2004. *Professional development for school improvement: Empowering learning communities.* Boston: Allyn and Bacon.

Guba, Egon G., and Yvonna S. Lincoln. 1989. *Fourth generation evaluation.* Newbury Park, CA: Sage Publications. In Miles Bryant and DeAnn Currin. 1995. Views of teacher evaluation from novice and expert evaluators. *Journal of Curriculum and Supervision* (10, no. 3 Spring), 251–52.

Guskey, Thomas R. 2003. Professional development that works: What makes professional development effective? *Phi Delta Kappan* 84, no. 10 (June): 748–50.

Haas, Eric, and Leslie Poynor. 2005. Issues of teaching and learning. *The SAGE handbook of educational leadership: Advances in theory, research, and practice,* ed. Fenwick W. English, 483–505. Thousand Oaks, CA: Sage Publications.

Holland, Patricia E., and Noreen Garman. 2001. Toward a resolution of the crisis of legitimacy in the field of supervision. *Journal of Curriculum and Supervision* 16, no. 2 (Winter): 95–111.

Hoy, Anita Woolfolk, and Wayne Kolter Hoy. 2003. *Instructional leadership: A learning-centered guide.* Boston: Allyn and Bacon.

Keyes, Maureen W., Cheryl Hanley-Maxwell, and Colleen A. Capper. 1999. "Spirituality? It's the core of my leadership": Empowering leadership in an inclusive elementary school. *Education Administration Quarterly* 35, no. 2 (April): 203–37.

Kohn, Alfie. 1993. *Punished by rewards: The trouble with gold stars, incentive plans, A's, praise, and other bribes.* New York: Houghton Mifflin.

Kuhn, Thomas S. 1996. *The structure of scientific revolutions.* 3rd ed. Chicago: University of Chicago Press.

Leithwood, Kenneth, Lawrence Leonard, and Lyn Sharratt. 1998. Conditions fostering organizational learning in schools. *Educational Administration Quarterly* 34, no. 2 (April): 243–76.

Marks, Helen M., and Susan M. Printy. 2003. Principal leadership and school performance: An integration of transformational and instructional leadership. *Educational Administration Quarterly* 39, no. 3 (August): 370–97.

Moore, Rita. 2003. Reexamining the field experiences of preservice teachers. *Journal of Teacher Education* 54, no. 1 (January/February): 31–42.

Nolan, James, Jr., and Linda A. Hoover. 2004. *Teacher supervision and evaluation: Theory into practice.* 2nd ed. Hoboken, NJ: John Wiley and Sons.

Nouwen, Henri J. M. 1991. *Creative ministry.* New York: Image Books.

———. 1999. *In the name of Jesus: Reflections on Christian leadership.* New York: Crossroad Publishing.

Palmer, Parker J. 1998. *The courage to teach: Exploring the inner landscape of a teacher's life.* San Francisco, CA: Jossey-Bass.

Peterson, Eugene H. 1997. *Subversive spirituality.* Grand Rapids, MI: Eerdmans.

Reiman, Alan J., and Lois Thies-Sprinthall. 1998. *Mentoring and supervision for teacher development.* Boston: Addison Wesley Longman.

Scribner, Jay Paredes. 1999. Professional development: Untangling the influence of work context on teacher learning. *Educational Administration Quarterly* 35, no. 2 (April): 238–66.

Senge, Peter M. 1990. *The fifth discipline: The art and practice of the learning organization.* New York: Currency, 1990. Quoted in Francis M. Duffy. 2000. Reconceptualizing instructional supervision for 3rd millennium school systems. *Journal of Curriculum and Supervision* (15, no. 2, Winter, 2000), 140.

Sergiovanni, Thomas J. 1996. *Leadership for the schoolhouse: How is it different? Why is it important?* San Francisco: Jossey-Bass.

Sergiovanni, Thomas J., and Robert J. Starratt. 2002. *Supervision—A redefinition.* 7th ed. New York: McGraw-Hill.

Yoder, N. 1997. The spiritually centered leader: How personal spirituality influences professional practice. In Maureen W. Keyes, Cheryl Hanley-Maxwell, and Colleen A. Capper. 1999. "Spirituality? It's the core of my leadership": Empowering leadership in an inclusive elementary school. *Educational Administration Quarterly* (39, no. 3, April, 1999), 234.

PART THREE

Building Community
for Students

CHAPTER 9

STRATEGIC STEWARDSHIP

*Resource Management for the
Educational Leader*

❧

By Barrett Mosbacker

Barrett Mosbacker, EdD, serves as the superintendent of Briarwood Christian School, which enrolls nearly 1,900 students in Birmingham, Alabama. He received his doctorate in educational leadership from the University of North Carolina, Charlotte, and has worked for several U.S. corporations and as a management consultant to the Legal Services Corporation, Washington.

CHAPTER 9

STRATEGIC STEWARDSHIP

By Barrett Mosbacker

THE HUMAN HEART beats with a yearning to be significant. People want to matter. People want to believe that, in the end, the value of their lives transcends the routines of daily existence. Getting married, bearing children, earning a degree, climbing the ladder of success, or joining a volunteer organization are efforts driven in large measure by a desire to satisfy the longing for significance.

What does this search for significance have to do with resource management? For most people, managing budgets, creating policies, and managing personnel don't exactly get the blood pumping and the adrenaline flowing. Resource management is typically seen as something that merely must be done, not something of eternal worth or significance. And herein lies the problem: leaders often fail to understand the value of managing a school's resources because they do not view resource management within the awe-inspiring framework of serving as God's agents in creation.

Foundations of Resource Management

Men and women are rulers and stewards of the cosmos, created a little lower than the angels. God created human beings to be fruitful and to multiply, to rule over His creation. In describing the call to be fruitful and to multiply, Nancy Pearcey notes, "Martin Luther liked to say that our occupations are God's 'masks'—His way of caring for creation in a hidden manner through human means. In our work, we are God's hands, God's eyes, God's feet" (2005, 50).

God's hands, God's eyes, God's feet—what a beautiful way to view work! God uses us to preserve and maintain His creation and to accomplish His will on the earth. Resource management is not merely about managing personnel, planning, and budgeting; it is nothing less than the means by which leaders reflect the image of God in the skillful stewardship of the people, ministry, and resources entrusted to their care for the glory of God and for the good of others.

Stewardship of self, others, and culture

As redeemed image bearers, men and women have been endowed by God with both natural and spiritual gifts. God gives natural gifts to all so that humankind is equipped to fulfill the creation mandate to multiply and to subdue the earth (Genesis 1:28). Artistic, mechanical, intellectual, and physical gifts are not the sole possession of believers—they are universal.

Spiritual gifts, however, are peculiar to believers. God bestows spiritual gifts for the purpose of spreading the gospel and strengthening His Church. When natural and spiritual gifts unite in an individual, they produce a powerful force capable of personal and cultural transformation.

School leaders must marshal school resources for the development of the natural and spiritual gifts of employees and students. In this context, resource management is about nurturing the potential of every student and staff member in the school. School leaders fill vital roles in culture because they stand at its headwaters. Few careers allow individuals to contribute more directly to the shaping of lives and the welfare of a nation than education. Like falling raindrops, educators shape lives and "drop" them into the tributaries of culture—homes, churches, and communities. Each life creates ripples—some small, some large—that radiate out into the community, affecting it for good or bad. Like a steady rain, the drops fall year after year, all contributing to the national pool of talent and character that shapes the nation's culture and determines its destiny.

Resource management reflects the outworking of God's image in the stewardship of the ministry and resources entrusted to a person's care for the present and the future. Management, in the final analysis, should be informed, thoughtful, and skillful stewardship under the eye of God: stewardship of self, of others, and of culture.

Strategic stewardship for the twenty-first century

Twenty-first-century school leaders face profound environmental shifts that exert external pressure on their schools. Significant advances in technology have accelerated globalization and have given rise to the information worker. In addition to experiencing technological and economic shifts, schools are also being buffeted by systemic cultural changes in the family and in cultural mores.

Globalization

The International Monetary Fund (IMF) defines *globalization* as "a historical process, the result of human innovation and technological progress. It refers to the increasing integration of economies around the world, particularly through trade and financial flows. The term sometimes also refers to the movement of people (labor) and knowledge (technology) across international borders" (IMF Staff 2002).

The IMF identifies four components of economic globalization, referring to four different flows across boundaries: flow of goods and services (trade), flow of people (migration), flow of capital, and flow of technology (2000). The author has added the flow of information because it reflects the newest form of globalization made possible by new digital technologies. For example, access to research is now global, and it increasingly involves collaborative research across international boundaries. A consequence of economic globalization is the increasing relations among members of an industry in different parts of the world (globalization of an industry), along with a corresponding erosion of national sovereignty in the economic sphere.

Globalization is not new; what is new is the magnitude and focus of twenty-first-century globalization. In his award winning book *The World Is Flat*, Thomas L. Friedman (2005) sketches the outlines of globalization in three eras. Globalization 1.0 centers on countries and power, Globalization 2.0 orients around multinational corporations, and Globalization 3.0 shifts from multinational corporations to individuals.

Globalization will have a profound impact on the futures of our students. Twenty-first-century school leaders must have an understanding of the three trends of globalization that directly affect students' futures:

outsourcing, the rise of the knowledge worker, and ever-rising international standards of academic excellence.

1. *Outsourcing*. Students will increasingly experience the impact of outsourcing. Outsourcing is the practice of subcontracting internal institutional functions and local work to skilled workers in other cities or countries.

Blue-collar manufacturing jobs were among the first to be outsourced to markets that offered cheaper labor. To put this phenomenon into perspective, consider the following advice given by Ohio State University business professor Oded Shenkar: " 'If you still make anything labor intensive, get out now rather than bleed to death. Shaving 5% here and there will not work.' Chinese producers can make the same adjustments. 'You need an entirely new business model to compete' " (Friedman 2005, 117). In other words, if a significant percentage of a business's costs is labor, it can be off-shored to other countries such as China or India.

The danger for leaders of Christian schools, most of which are billed as college preparatory, is to assume that outsourcing and off-shoring are issues primarily facing students not headed for college or students attending low-performing public schools. This illusion is quickly dispelled when one considers that even highly skilled professional and white-collar jobs are now being outsourced overseas.

2. *The information worker: Brains vs. brawn.* To compete economically in the twenty-first century, students will have to become lifelong learners and will need increasingly sophisticated skills. Increased globalization and the rapid expansion of low-cost telecommunications technologies have combined to internationalize economies, resulting in the erosion of national economic boundaries. The result is that the economic boats of what Robert Reich (1997) calls redundant and in-person service workers have sprung leaks and are sinking. By contrast, symbolic analysts are prospering. Possessing the knowledge and skills most needed in the information-based, technologically driven economies of the West and in parts of Asia, symbolic analysts are able to auction their knowledge and skills to the highest bidder.

Most schools are preparing students to compete for jobs on a local, regional, or national scale when they should be preparing them to compete globally. "Skilled people are needed to discover new knowledge," asserts Lester Thurow. "It is ... education that lies behind the continuous improvement in standards of living.... New skills are going to become even more dominant relative to old skills, and globalization is becoming ever more of a reality" (1999, 131–45).

3. *International standards of academic excellence.* Given the increasing expectations and demands of a globalized and information-based economy, it is essential that students have a solid grounding in math and science. Frighteningly, the trends indicate a backward slide in math and science performance in the United States (Barton 2002; Willms 1999). The figures are even more troubling in the most recent international comparison of mathematics literacy. In 2003, U.S. performance in mathematics literacy and problem solving as measured by the Program for International Student Assessment (PISA) was lower than the average performance for most member countries of the Organisation for Economic Co-operation and Development (OECD), an intergovernmental organization of industrialized countries (Lemke et al. 2004).

Even when students in Christian schools score above the national average on standardized tests, they are probably performing significantly below international standards. In other words, parents, teachers, and administrators are comparing student performance to a low standard of achievement. As indicated above, the highest-performing U.S. students were outperformed on the PISA.

What many Americans, including Christian school administrators, fail to understand is that Peter is not just competing with Susan for college admission or for a good job; Peter is also competing with Shivaji from India and with Li from China. Lester Thurow warns about an era of man-made brainpower industries: "With the ability to make anything anywhere in the world and sell it anywhere else in the world, business firms can 'cherry pick' the skilled ... wherever they exist in the world" (quoted in Neef 1997, 208).

Increased globalization, then, requires that Christian school leaders position their schools to provide an education that will equip students to meet these new challenges and opportunities. As rapid external changes exert pressure on schools, the necessity of effective resource management increases. As a function of resource management, planning is a vital tool for focusing the school's programs, finances, and staff on preparing its students for the opportunities and challenges of a globalized, information-rich world.

The Focus of Resource Management

Biblical perspective on planning

Knowing that God is in control of life and work gives birth to humility, peace, and boldness. Leaders are humbled in recognizing that "unless the Lord builds the house, its builders labor in vain" (Psalm 127:1). Leaders can have peace because they know that a loving God superintends the details of their lives and work. Boldness characterizes their leadership because confidence in the sovereignty of God removes paralyzing fear and anxiety.

The recognition that God lovingly directs the steps of His people should lead to faithful and earnest prayer as the starting point for any endeavor or decision. Prayer as authentic recognition of dependence upon God should pervade the leader's daily activities: "Be joyful always; pray continually; give thanks in all circumstances, for this is God's will for you in Christ Jesus" (1 Thessalonians 5:16–18).

Strategic planning

Prayer is indispensable but is not sufficient. Prayer and good intentions are no substitutes for thoughtful and decisive action. Undergirded by prayer, strategic planning is an essential component of effective leadership. Strategic plans are based on the school's overall objectives. Plans typically span five or ten years, and they use goals-based or other planning methods that identify assumptions, risks, and environmental factors that may affect the school (McNamee 1999).

Benefits of planning. Strategic planning offers at least eight compelling reasons for its use:

1. Forces a look into the future and thereby provides an opportunity to influence that future by assuming a proactive posture
2. Sharpens awareness of existing and projected needs
3. Helps define the overall mission of the school and focuses on specific objectives
4. Gives direction and continuity to the school community
5. Establishes a framework for the strategic staffing of the school
6. Integrates stakeholders into the school
7. Establishes standards of accountability
8. Creates a framework and direction for the strategic allocation of school resources

Elements of the plan. Carter McNamara (1999) identifies goals-based, issues-based, organic, and scenario planning models. Goals-based planning is the most common and most appropriate model for most Christian schools. Goals-based planning typically includes the following elements: creation or revision of the school's mission and vision statements, review of core organizational values, identification of organizational strengths and weaknesses (including an assessment of external variables that are making an impact on or may have an impact on the school), specific goals to accomplish, and an action plan that outlines the specific strategies and tasks to be accomplished—by whom and when.

Mission and vision. The mission statement is a succinct statement of the school's primary goals or objectives. It is not a statement of philosophy or doctrine. It should be concise and easily memorized by all school staff and easily understood by parents.

Vision statements declare and define an institution's aspirations. Jack Welch, former CEO of General Electric and widely recognized as one of the world's most effective business leaders, once said that "good business leaders create a vision, articulate the vision, passionately own the vision, and relentlessly drive it to completion" (Tichy and Charan 1989). The vision is the beacon on the hill, shining a light on the distant horizon and illuminating an image of the school's future.

The distinction between mission and vision statements is important. The difference may be illustrated by a family trip. The vision may be "to be a deeply bonded family that shares lifelong memories of significant experiences." The mission may be "to take a family trip to Walt Disney World." Typically, a vision statement is strategic and future oriented, and it may begin with the words "to be." The typical mission statement is goal oriented and often begins with "is to."

Values. Whether implicit or explicit, values undergird a school's mission and vision statements. Values are statements of the school's most fundamental beliefs concerning education in general and Christian education in particular. Such beliefs include the instructional philosophy, financial parameters, admissions standards, qualifications for faculty and staff, compensation philosophy, and the ideal graduate "profile" created by the school.

SWOT analysis. A SWOT analysis (strengths, weaknesses, opportunities, and threats) is an extremely effective and vital tool in strategic planning. By creating a systematic method for examining the school within a larger context, a SWOT analysis provides critical information and insights for building a plan that will maximize the school's strengths and eliminate or ameliorate existing weaknesses.

Strengths are unique characteristics that enhance the effectiveness of the school, areas in which the school excels relative to other educational options available to parents in the community. For example, if all area schools provide high-quality reading instruction, then a high-quality reading program is not a unique strength. The purpose and focus of this analysis is to identify the unique strengths that the school possesses and that distinguish it from others in the community.

It is helpful to write down a realistic list of the school's characteristics, some of which will be strengths. Strengths should be considered from an internal perspective and from the point of view of present and prospective parents in the community.

Weaknesses are variables that limit a school's effectiveness. It is best to face the reality of any unpleasant truths as soon as possible. It is here that thoroughness and brutal honesty must characterize the assessment. The temptation is to gloss over the harsher realities.

Examining weaknesses is accomplished in a two-step process. First is a brainstorming session in which participants identify what they perceive to be institutional weaknesses. This "free" exchange has no boundaries. Second, weaknesses may be grouped by academic discipline, grade level, campus/division, or department (for example, business office, admissions, athletics, or fine arts).

Opportunities are untapped resources that often go unrecognized in daily activity and work. Opportunities can come from such things as changes in technology, in social patterns, in population profiles, in lifestyle, or in local educational, civic, and business institutions. All these changes open new opportunities for the school to grow and to enhance and expand its programs.

Opportunities are best identified by examining weaknesses and strengths through brainstorming exercises that encourage creative thinking. What are the possibilities for the school? What programs can be added? How can technology expand and enhance the educational experience for students?

Threats are events, people, or circumstances that may hinder the school's mission, vision, and goals. Threats may be internal or external. Examples of threats are the opening of a new private school down the road, declining enrollments, changing community demographics, rising unemployment or underemployment, increased levels of parent complaints, or rapidly rising costs and tuition rates.

Comprehensive assessment. An effective strategic plan will enhance the SWOT analysis with a broad and penetrating assessment of the school's effectiveness. This assessment should include both institution-wide surveys and an analysis of hard data.

Stakeholders—including parents, board members, staff, alumni, major donors, and students (usually juniors and seniors)—should be invited to participate in the survey. Administrator effectiveness, the quality of the support staff, the quality of academic programs and instruction by division, student growth and learning, activities and cocurricular programs, school communication, curriculum, school technology, facilities, and perceived value are examples of areas to include.

An analysis of critical institutional data should supplement survey data. Institutional data is important because it provides objective insight into trends and the overall health of the school. Enrollment trends, student and personnel retention rates, test scores, college matriculation and scholarship data, cost and revenue information (for example, costs per student, tuition increases compared with the consumer price index, salary assessments, program net revenue, divisional cost data), and fundraising results are a few examples of data to be collected and analyzed.

Defining goals. Establishing concrete, measurable, and achievable goals breathes life into the strategic plan. Without specific goals, a strategic plan is akin to dressing up in a tuxedo but having no place to go. Goals put flesh on the bones of the plan. After the assessment is complete, goals give specific direction by outlining what is supposed to be accomplished.

Too often, goals are soft or fuzzy. Action plans and accountabilities cannot be attached to ill-defined goals. Effective goals are those that can be measured. Here are some examples: "Raise average SAT scores by five points in two years." "Add Spanish instruction to the fifth grade next year." "Before current seventh-grade students reach the ninth grade, develop an assessment instrument to measure the worldview of entering freshmen and graduating seniors."

The action plan. The action plan specifies the concrete tasks and resources deployed in accomplishing the stated goals. The action plan contains the "next steps" and includes specific accountabilities. Details of the action plan can be checked off as they are accomplished.

The importance of creating and implementing the action plan cannot be overstated. The strategic plan is effective when accompanied by the rigorous implementation of the action plan. If the strategic plan is the mind and eyes of the school, the action plan is its hands and feet.

Institutional intelligence: Data-based decision making

Data-based decision making is the process of collecting, organizing, analyzing, and interpreting data for use in assessing current conditions, spotting trends, and guiding and monitoring planning and decision making. While some researchers advocate replacing "hunches" and "gut feelings" with facts, a more balanced view recognizes that leadership is both a science and an art. Objective data provide the "scientific" foundation or context for the exercise of the art of leadership, an art that includes using the insights gleaned from experience and supplemental anecdotal evidence to frame and to interpret the data.

Accountability. "What gets measured gets done!" One may argue the merits of extrinsic versus intrinsic motivation, but the fact is that most people need accountability to perform. To be just and credible, however, accountability must be to a clearly understood and measurable standard.

The success of the strategic plan hinges on holding specific individuals accountable for the accomplishment of specific and measurable tasks. It will be obvious to all whether the individual responsible for a task has completed it.

A simple and effective way to monitor progress is to develop and review a goal-and-task summary sheet at each administrative meeting. For example, the chief administrator of the school may hold monthly management meetings with all division and department heads, including principals. During these meetings, one of the first agenda items is to review progress on all goals and associated tasks. This method serves a threefold purpose: (1) it creates accountability and a heightened level of concern about the seriousness of the goals, (2) it reinforces the credibility of the strategic planning process and of the administrator, and (3) it provides a forum for adjusting the timelines and tasks on the basis of changing circumstances.

To position Christian schools to equip students for the postmodern, global, and information-rich world of the twenty-first century, school leaders must learn to mine and use data that reflect current conditions, identify trends, and monitor progress on short-term and long-term goals. Data collection and interpretation is a form of "institutional intelligence." School leaders are conducting reconnaissance that answers the questions "Where have we been?" "Where are we now?" and "Where are we headed?"

Management reports. The management report is an extremely useful leadership tool for building institutional intelligence on the basis of key indicators, which are discrete pieces of information that give a quick, easy-to-understand, and accurate snapshot of the school's effectiveness, health, and progress on the strategic plan. To be useful, the data must be timely, accurate, and meaningful. It must provide knowledge and facilitate understanding, not merely catalog information.

School finance: Economics 101

If there is one unalterable truth about school resource management, it is this: the laws of economics do not discriminate. The laws of economics apply equally to both religious and nonreligious institutions, regardless of their mission. Assuming that God will suspend the laws of economics because the school is a ministry, too many Christian school leaders believe they can violate those laws with impunity. With the best of intentions, usually with the goal of making Christian education affordable for everyone, many administrators and boards establish financial policies that violate basic economic principles, good business practices, and common sense.

The cost of excellence. A basic law of economics is that for an organization to survive, let alone thrive, its revenue must equal or exceed its costs. Motivated by the laudable desire to provide a Christian education to as many children as possible, many school leaders abandon common sense. Sadly, such well-meaning intentions threaten the survival of the very ministry to which they have devoted their professional lives.

Artificially low tuition is one example of violating basic economic law. Yet many administrators and boards routinely establish tuition rates below the actual cost to educate, and they compound the problem by providing multichild and vocationally based tuition discounts regardless of parents' ability to pay. With inadequate revenue, programs are often underfunded, limited, and mediocre. Shallow fine-arts programs, outdated or underutilized technology, limited foreign-language offerings, and limited or nonexistent programs for gifted and special-needs students are common. Providing an excellent Christian education cannot be done cheaply.

Many Christian school teachers bear the burden of subsidizing below-cost tuition rates through low salaries and poor benefits. In ACSI member schools, 68 percent of teachers with at least ten years of experience earn less than $30,000 per year (Association of Christian Schools International 2005). By contrast, a survey by the National Center for Education Statistics (2002, 22) shows that the average starting salary for teachers with no experience in public *charter* schools that used a salary schedule was $26,977, compared with $25,888 for *public* school districts.

Low salaries and poor benefits often produce high staff turnover, creating discontinuity in the academic program. The applicant pool is small, forcing the administrator to hire the "best available" from a pool of relatively mediocre teachers. The result is poor to average instructional and academic quality, the loss of parental confidence, low student-retention rates (especially at the upper-school level), and a reputation for mediocre quality.

Many Christian leaders find themselves caught in a vicious and self-defeating cycle. Underfunding produces poor quality, which in turn restricts enrollment levels and school revenue. To increase revenue, the school leadership must raise tuition rates, but many current and prospective parents do not believe that the school's quality justifies the higher cost. Parents choose to leave or not to enroll their children in the school in the first place. In a desperate attempt to stem the loss of students or to stimulate enrollment, tuition continues to be set below actual cost, thus perpetuating the cycle.

Supply and demand. The theory of supply and demand is one of the most basic in economics. Simply stated, supply is the amount of product or service that a business or an organization is willing or able to provide at a specified price. Demand is the amount of product or service that a consumer is willing to buy at a specified price (International Society for Complexity, Information, and Design 2005.). The modification of this definition for the Christian school market may read as follows: supply is the quality of education that a Christian school can provide at a specified tuition level, while demand is the amount of tuition that parents are willing to pay for the perceived value of the education provided. Everything else being equal, demand (enrollment) will be strong when the market (parents) believe that the school provides an education that has a value at least equal to the tuition charged. Stagnant or declining enrollment is a sign that the market does not perceive the value offered to be equal to the tuition charged.

Price elasticity. Elasticity refers to market sensitivity to price changes. Demand for price-elastic products or services will vary significantly on the basis of price, assuming that the quality of the service in relation to competitive offers remains constant. Relatively small increases or decreases in price will have a significant impact on demand. On the other hand, demand for products and services that are price inelastic is relatively stable, even with relatively wide swings in price. For example, farmers face a relatively inelastic market: modest increases or decreases in groceries have only a modest effect on consumer demand for staples. However, airfares are elastic: even slight price increases or decreases in airfare can dramatically affect ticket sales.

The availability of substitutes affects elasticity: the more possible substitutes, the greater the elasticity. For the Christian school this fact means that, other factors being constant, the availability of schooling options in the community will affect the administration's ability to increase enrollments and tuition. The more options, the more probable that tuition rates will be elastic. Likewise, the fewer alternatives that parents have, the less probable that tuition will be elastic.

Marginal value. A concept closely related to elasticity is marginal value: the amount of benefit perceived by purchasing an additional "unit" of a product or service in comparison with purchasing other goods or services. Several factors influence marginal value; price and perceived value are among the most important. Vern Brimley and Rulon Garfield (2002) define the marginal dollar (a way of understanding marginal value) as the dollar that would be better spent for some other good or service. As applied to the Christian school, marginal value can be understood as the following calculation that parents make: that an incremental increase in tuition is worth more than a nicer home, a nicer car, or a vacation. That is, as tuition increases, parents make a calculation that the added cost is or is not producing an incremental value equal to or greater than the increase in cost relative to other educational options and other purchases. If parents do not perceive the quality of education provided to be of more value than other options, parents will choose those options.

The reflex response by many school leaders is to assume that the way to increase the marginal value of their schools is to keep tuition low. Controlling tuition costs is certainly an important element in maintaining value. Another approach, however, is to increase the incremental value of the education provided relative to the tuition charged by improving quality, expanding programs, hiring better teachers, and enhancing facilities. In other words, value can be increased by giving parents more for their tuition dollars.

Strategic budgeting for marginal value. There are many ways to increase a Christian school's marginal value. Three of the most important are to hire superior teachers, to integrate technology effectively, and to practice careful stewardship of existing funds. To accomplish these goals, school leadership should engage in strategic budgeting instead of default budgeting, which is budgeting based on current realities, existing exigencies, and existing allocations. By contrast, strategic budgeting aligns planned expenditures to strategic initiatives designed to enhance marginal value. Leaders allocate funds on the basis of the school's strategic plan, not merely the existing spending patterns.

1. *Personnel.* Since a school is only as good as its teachers, one of the most powerful ways to increase marginal value is to establish a long-term plan to enhance the school's ability to recruit, hire, and retain superior teachers by offering competitive salaries and benefits. To accomplish this goal, prayerful, strategic, and sometimes hard decisions must be made concerning the existing allocation of resources. Are there personnel who should be let go? Are there curriculum offerings that should be dropped? Are there programs that should be eliminated or reduced?

Reevaluating the standard salary scale is another example of strategic budgeting. The basic idea is to create salary ranges designed to differentiate pay on the basis of market supply and demand. Under such a plan there may be a range for elementary teachers, a range for junior-high and senior-high teachers, and a separate range for scarce specialty teachers and personnel such as advanced math and science teachers or technology specialists.

The idea of creating differentiated salary ranges, whereby teachers in certain classifications are paid more than those in others, is a foreign concept for many educators. Ingrained in the psychology of school leadership is the assumption that teacher salaries must be based on experience and credentials, regardless of competence and market conditions.

When assessing teacher compensation, leaders must keep in mind that money is not the primary motivator for teachers. If it were, many would have chosen a different profession. Hiring teachers who are intrinsically and passionately committed to the ministry of Christian education is critically important to ensuring that teachers are kingdom focused rather than self-focused.

Nevertheless, "the worker deserves his wages" (Luke 10:7). Creating differentiated pay ranges has the benefit of positioning the school to recruit and retain the finest faculty available, without requiring the uniform and universal raising of all salaries. The result is that the school is able to attract advanced science and math teachers while simultaneously avoiding the large tuition increases that would result from adjusting the entire salary scale upward. And the marginal value of the school is enhanced by increasing quality and minimizing tuition increases.

2. *Technology integration.* Leaders can also enhance marginal value by enriching the academic program through integrated instructional technology. The key concept is "integrated." The vast majority of both ACSI and CSI member schools offer computer classes, but very few integrate the technology into daily instruction (Mosbacker 2005).

Technology integration means that technology is an instructional tool, not merely a subject of instruction. Integrated technology is the seamless infusion of technology in both instruction and learning so that technology becomes a ubiquitous tool used by students and teachers alike. Integration goes beyond the creation of computer labs to the natural incorporation of technology into teaching and learning as naturally as that of a whiteboard and a notebook. Using technology for the sake of using technology is not the objective. The objective is to use technology to enhance teaching and learning when it provides the most effective way to teach and to learn. Technology is not the end; it is the means.

Many parents will immediately perceive an increase in marginal value through the addition of integrated technologies. For this integration to become a reality, leaders will need to develop strategic budgets that fund the necessary hardware, software, and—of particular importance—staff training. Realizing increases in marginal value will require reassessing current budget allocations and may require eliminating or reducing other expenditures in order to fund technology development without adding significantly to tuition.

3. *Strategic allocations.* An important way to increase marginal value is to control costs by the prayerful and careful use of the resources entrusted to the school's care—in other words, by practicing wise stewardship. Being cheap is not equivalent to practicing wise stewardship. Increased value and marginal return on investment are the marks of wise stewardship. Being cheap does not promote excellence, nor does it add marginal value. The wise use of resources through the strategic allocation of scarce resources does both. Excellence is promoted by allocating funds

to strategic initiatives designed to enhance value and expand programs.

Strategic allocation is the practice of seeking the "biggest bang for the buck." The concept of marginal return complements the concepts of marginal utility and marginal value. Although a financial concept, marginal return can be thought of as the return or the impact on the school that is realized from the dollars invested. For example, if a school is given an undesignated gift of $50,000, where will that money produce the greatest results?

It is notoriously difficult to quantify marginal return in the educational context. Nevertheless, carefully aligning expenditures to a strategic plan will increase the impact (return) for every dollar invested. The problem is that pressing short-term needs or pressure from parents may trump the strategic allocation of tuition revenue and financial gifts. Rather than allocating the funds according to a strategic plan or upon a careful assessment of what will add the most marginal value for parents, many leaders spend the funds to cover short-term needs or to placate the loudest constituency.

Now What? Application to Practice

SOME OF THE changes facing our schools are for the worse, some are for the better, and the character of some changes depends on the leader's response. What is certain is that Christian school leaders, serving as the eyes, hands, and feet of God, must be cognizant of these changes and must align their schools and prepare their students for the opportunities and challenges of the twenty-first century. To state the matter simply and bluntly, a 1950s-style education, no matter how well intended, is not adequate for preparing students for the challenges and opportunities of the twenty-first century.

References

Association of Christian Schools International. 2005. *2004–05 annual school survey.* Colorado Springs, CO: Association of Christian Schools International.

Barton, Paul E. 2002. *Meeting the need for scientists, engineers, and an educated citizenry in a technological society.* Princeton, NJ: Educational Testing Service.

Brimley, Vern, Jr., and Rulon R. Garfield. 2002. *Financing education in a climate of change.* 8th ed. Boston: Allyn and Bacon.

Friedman, Thomas L. 2005. *The world is flat: A brief history of the twenty-first century.* New York: Farrar, Straus and Giroux.

IMF Staff. 2002. Globalization: Threat or opportunity? (January). http://www.imf.org/external/np/exr/ib/2000/041200.htm#II.

International Society for Complexity, Information, and Design. 2005. Supply and demand theory. http://www.iscid.org/encyclopedia/Supply_and_Demand_Theory.

Lemke, M., A. Sen, E. Pahlke, L. Partelow, D. Miller, T. Williams, D. Kastberg, and L. Jocelyn. 2004. *International outcomes of learning in mathematics literacy and problem solving: PISA 2003 results from the U.S. perspective.* No. NCES 2005-003. Washington, DC: U.S. Department of Education: Institute of Education Sciences, National Center for Education Statistics.

McNamara, Carter. 1999. Strategic planning (in nonprofit or for-profit organizations). http://www.managementhelp.org/plan_dec/str_plan/str_plan.htm.

McNamee, David. 1999. Risk assessment glossary. http://www.mc2consulting.com/riskdef.htm.

Mosbacker, Barrett. 2005. An investigation of technology and school leadership in Christian schools in the United States. Dissertation, University of North Carolina, Charlotte.

National Center for Education Statistics. 2002. *Schools and staffing survey, 1999-2000: Overview of the data for public, private, public charter, and Bureau of Indian Affairs elementary and secondary schools.* No. NCES 2005-335.Washington, DC: U.S. Department of Public Education.

Neef, Dale, ed. 1997. *The knowledge economy.* Woburn, MA: Butterworth-Heinemann.

Pearcey, Nancy R. 2005. *Total truth: Liberating Christianity from its cultural captivity.* Study guide ed. Wheaton, IL: Crossway Books.

Reich, Robert B. 1997. Why the rich are getting richer and the poor, poorer. In *Education: Culture, economy, and society,* ed. A. H. Halsey, Hugh Lauder, Philip Brown, and Amy Stuart Wells, 163–71. New York: Oxford University Press.

Thurow, Lester C. 1999. *Building wealth: The new rules for individuals, companies, and nations in a knowledge-based economy.* New York: Harper Business.

Tichy, Noel, and Ram Charan. 1989. Speed, simplicity, and self-confidence: An interview with Jack Welch. *Harvard Business Review* (September/October).

Willms, J. Douglas. 1999. *International adult literacy survey: Inequalities in literacy skills among youth in Canada and the United States.* Ottawa, Canada: Statistics Canada.

CHAPTER 10

CURRICULUM LEADERSHIP

Guiding Instructional
Development

∾

By Derek J. Keenan

Derek J. Keenan, EdD, is the vice president for academic affairs of ACSI, a position
he has held since 1996. He is the executive editor of Christian School Education
magazine, and he served as a Christian school leader for more than twenty-five
years. His writing is included in the edited volumes Called to Lead *and* Critical
Issues Facing Christian Schools.

CHAPTER 10

CURRICULUM LEADERSHIP

By Derek J. Keenan

THE CALL TO LEAD a school brings with it a passionate sense of care about the lives of students and what they will be taught by the teachers. This profound responsibility is embodied in curricular leadership—perhaps the most significant part of the job description for any head of a school.

Educational leaders know that it is essential for effective schools to hire a professionally competent staff who know what they are supposed to be doing each day in their classrooms. The curriculum in its simplest form—whether it is listed in guides, maps, or strands—indicates to teachers how much instructional time will be used to deliver content to the students. In the holistic education of the Christian school, teachers are guiding children to become grounded, shaped, molded, and framed as Christian persons. Geraldine Steensma and Harro Van Brummelen write that "the Christian educator uses the curriculum to equip his students to live lives of response to their Creator, Redeemer, and Lord" (1977, 15).

Curriculum Leadership in a Christian School

School leaders need to agree on an institutional definition of *curriculum*. For example, these are four common definitions: (1) curriculum is what is taught, particularly the subject matter contained in a school's course of study; (2) curriculum is an organized set of documented, formal educational plans intended to attain preconceived goals; (3) curriculum is a dynamic series of planned learning experiences; and (4) curriculum is everything learners experience in school (Van Brummelen 2002). A comprehensive definition, then, is as follows: *curriculum is the planned learning program that is delivered to students, developed, documented, reviewed, modified, and evaluated in light of the school's mission, vision, and expected student outcomes.*

These definitions have useful words such as *subject matter, organized, plans, goals, dynamic,* and *learning experiences.* These definitions do not include the word *textbook.* Textbooks are most appropriately viewed as well-chosen tools in the hands of a skilled teacher who utilizes them to add to the effectiveness and efficiency of instructional preparation and curricular delivery. In addition, terms such as *priorities, outcomes, order,* and *instructional sequence* should be considered. Christian schools add terms such as *biblically integrative concepts, worldview orientation,* and *correlative Scriptures.*

Robert Bruinsma notes that the school curriculum is organized around a myriad of pieces regardless of the emphasis on integration or holistic curriculum. There are pieces of knowledge, time periods, courses, and disciplines. The need is to construct the pieces in such a way that they contribute to the wholeness and interconnectedness of life and living. He notes, "When we design school curriculum ... how do we take the seamless whole that is life in all its complexity, and present it to children for their learning? ... We take a piece of God's creation ... and examine it more closely to enrich our experience of the whole" (2003, 114).

Philosophy, Curriculum, and the Leader

The term *instructional leader* is often used to describe the curricular role that is expected from leadership. This is an integral function of the school's philosophical leader. The leader articulates the philosophical foundation of the school throughout the instructional program. Connecting curricular priorities to both the grade-level and the schoolwide learning goals is perhaps the most important part of instructional leadership, and responsible administrators take it seriously.

The involvement of the leader in curricular planning, implementation, assessment, review, and adjustment verifies the importance of this function. Administrators, whose depth of knowledge may be limited to a particular academic discipline, must educate themselves and become aware of how each field of study contributes to the school's desired outcomes for its students. School leaders validate the instructional program by articulately and succinctly expressing the linkage between the school's mission and its curriculum. An example is as follows: "Teaching the subjects of the Christian school in such a way that students develop a biblical world view out of which to think and act" (MacCullough 1999, 11). This kind of professional dialogue assists teachers in being mindful of the school's instructional priorities and its schoolwide learning goals.

Establishing curriculum as a priority is critical to assisting teachers in maintaining focus in the classroom. There is not enough time to teach all the concepts, ideas, and skills that could be addressed in a classroom, and in the absence of guidance, teachers will teach what they estimate ought to be taught in that subject instead of relying on the curriculum plan of the grade level, department, or school.

A useful rubric for the prioritization of content within the instructional program is found in the Understanding by Design model (Wiggins and McTighe 1998), which uses three concentric rings to illustrate three levels of content priorities. Content that is worth being acquainted with is in the outer and largest ring; things that students should know and be able to do are in the middle ring; things worthy of "enduring" (eternal) understanding are in the inner ring (10). Later, the authors use a list of essential questions from each discipline to uncover the most important ideas for each subject. The prioritization of content within the curriculum gives the academic program its focal points and the school its instructional focus and identity.

There are schools that allow instructional priorities to be determined by the textbooks that are being used or by the classroom teacher alone. Both of these prioritizing methods jeopardize the education of the students and set the stage for ineffective education. The textbook model defers curricular decision making to publishers, and the classroom model opens instructional decision making to the biases and whims of the individual teacher. Curricular leadership focuses on the needs of the students and aligns these needs with the philosophy, goals, and expected outcomes of the school.

The curriculum, to the extent that it is designed to produce students whose lives reflect the purposes of the school, necessitates alignment with these intended outcomes. One of the ways that these distinctive elements become evident is that they are logically and naturally pervasive within the activities required of students in the classroom. This pervasiveness should be as true in the academic aspects of the school as in activities such as service experiences, mission trips, and chapel programs. When projects and assignments require Christian thinking, students and parents understand that the school is serious about its mission. The requirement for Christian thinking in schoolwork makes the philosophy of the school visible and deepens the understanding and commitment to it.

Christian schools exist for biblical, divine, and instructionally coherent purposes in the lives of students. One of the major tasks of a Christian school community is to educate its members into a full and deep understanding of why the school exists. Stephen Kaufmann (1992) notes that families enroll their children in Christian schools for a variety of reasons, but some of those reasons are inconsistent with the priorities of the school. He calls this incongruity "disinterested agreement" and defines it as a willingness of parents to tolerate the mission-focused activities of the school, but with no strong interest in seeing those same values inculcated into the lives of their children. It has long been known that one of the biggest educative jobs of the Christian school is with the parents.

One purpose of Christian school education is carried out by the inclusion of biblical-worldview thinking in the academic program. This teaching, if it is credible, is supported by the examined lives of teachers. This is the "living curriculum" principle of Christian schooling that is found in Luke 6:40. The pattern of the teacher's life will be reproduced in significant ways in the lives of the students. Perhaps no other aspect of Christian teaching is as daunting as the reality of this principle. Teachers realize this when a note that expresses appreciation arrives and a former student indicates that the teacher's life has become a template for the life of the student. The Christian school leader must assist the faculty, individually and corporately, to function as living curriculum.

A school leader is an example of the outcomes that the school is seeking to instill in the lives of its students. The life of the leader models the vision of what will result if the school is mission effective. Teachers, students, and parents observe—consciously and subconsciously—the example set by the administration, and this example further reinforces the virtues that are taught and honored by the school.

Curriculum as Path and Direction

Foundational to effective education is clarity about what the school has set out to produce in the lives of students. At one time within the wider Christian community, *outcomes* became a politically charged term, but it is valid for use in setting educational goals that are consistent with Christian faith. It is the function of curriculum and instruction to deliver these intended results. The curriculum designates a path, and that path takes students in a specific direction.

The root of the word *curriculum* implies a course or route for running a race. One can picture an individual sitting high in the stands of a stadium and observing the lanes marked for a track meet below. Each lane represents one grade level of the school, and each time a student crosses the start/finish line, he or she moves over one lane. At the end of the outermost lane stands the head of school with a diploma in hand to present to each student completing the required number of laps. This is a visual model of completing a curriculum or a prescribed course of study.

The diploma signifies the accomplishment of specific and general results. The curricular goals associated with the content areas are specific and focused but are not ultimate ends. The general outcomes, which are life-shaping experiences, include evangelism, nurture, worship, incidental and intentional discipleship, and mentoring. These outcomes are not limited to the arenas of spiritual formation or worldview development; instead, they include assisting students in their intellectual, emotional, social, and physical development. These general outcomes are provided for in the curriculum with the same level of intentionality that is applied to the subject disciplines.

Leadership for Curricular Decision Making

Documentation of curriculum is critical to a faculty's common understanding of what is to be taught. These instructional maps also identify for students what is to be learned and indicate to parents what strands unify the instructional program. A well-documented instructional plan is critical to what Robert Marzano identifies as a "guaranteed and viable curriculum." He further notes, "I rank this as the first factor, having the most impact on student achievement" (2003, 22). The effective school consistently delivers on the instructional promises that it makes to its constituencies.

Fledgling schools at times hand off instructional decision making to individual classroom teachers, textbook publishers, or both. Whether this handoff is done intentionally or by default, neither handoff provides a clear and consistent connection to the intended schoolwide outcomes. Teachers require a scope and sequence that establishes expectations for each grade throughout the school and creates maps that guide instructional planning within the classroom. A curriculum document both prescribes the vertical and horizontal aspects of curriculum and organizes instruction by identifying the width and depth of the content components. Although academically sound and credible textbooks are helpful instructional tools, these are not intended as the primary determinant of the school's planned learning program to be delivered to the students.

The ongoing challenge of managing curriculum is its dynamic nature. It is helpful to reflect on the additions and subtractions that have been made to the consensus curriculum of schools in recent years. What was the place, for example, of computer education, worldviews, or Chinese language twenty years ago? What were the demands for advanced classes or differentiated instruction? These are curriculum questions, and they are answered by classroom teachers every day, either individually or in concert with other teachers. Effective schools have an organized process for defining what the school intends that students be taught. The school leader must put in place a rational and communal method for managing the dynamics of curriculum adjustment and change. Schools with a strong sense of identity and purpose are characterized by professional dialogue about curriculum. If curriculum change and adjustment are primarily managed from a whimsical, intuitive, reactive process, the curriculum becomes disjointed and does not serve the needs of the students, faculty, or greater school community.

Effective instructional leadership requires awareness of the clearly identified and specified results intended from the schooling process. Each school community must tailor the decisions about the intended ends of its own educational program. Even though there are many similarities among learning communities, each school must articulate its own desired goals. These broad outcomes are the bases for the specific priorities within grade levels and content areas. Grade-level-specific objectives and course maps guide the lesson-planning process and form the basis for assessment and accountability. At the institutional meta-assessment level, evaluation crosses from grade levels to school divisions and content fields. When the entire primary mathematics program is evaluated, for example, that review may well point to overlaps or discrepancies in the curriculum plan. This evaluative process provides the data for making necessary adjustments to increase students' mastery of mathematical concepts. The faculty discussion about this data and the evidences of achievement from the faculty are rigorously analyzed before making adjustments in the curriculum plan.

Curriculum for Coherent Christian School Community

The faith aspects of a Christian school education are not relegated to a corner of the school day in activities such as a Bible course, chapel, or devotional times. A prayer to begin class appropriately speaks of faith but in and of itself does not deliver transformed lives. The development of skilled and thoughtful Christians does not occur through disjointed and compartmentalized courses or school activities. Linkages, connections, transfers, and a unified perspective are required for the development of a Christian mind. The popular culture, including most of education, is prone to thinking in boxes; the result is an incoherent "pick and choose" approach to life. The Christian school is teaching for learning that coheres around the biblical metanarrative.

Students learn coherence from teachers who routinely and naturally unify educational content while educating children to become dignified human beings who personally apprehend the reality of a sovereign God. The word *university* literally means "one truth." The late Charles Habib Malik (1987) noted that in most of education, one might more accurately think in terms of "multiversity." He was referring to the issue of coherence in education. The curricular process, rightly understood, is one of unity, consistency, and coherence, and this process has clear theological, anthropological, and pedagogical foundations. The result of this type of schooling is a student who, as Dallas Willard states, "walk[s] routinely and easily in the character and power of Jesus Christ" (Gangel 2005).

The philosophy, vision, and mission of the school indicate why the school exists and what its purposes include. No matter how well developed these written statements might be, they have little influence on the students unless they permeate the instructional program of the school. Curriculum documentation identifies clear links between the expected student outcomes and what occurs when the classroom doors close. Curriculum maps demonstrate how these outcomes are distributed across the content in each grade level while providing guidance for the teachers' instructional planning.

Spiritually Formed Academic Thinkers

Schoolwide outcomes of the instructional program may be thought of in four categories: academic thinking, educational skills, biblical worldview, and spiritual formation. Holistic education is the goal, but categories are useful as descriptors of the elements within the whole. These aspects develop in concert with one another as each is developed within the disciplines and across the curricular and cocurricular activities of the school.

Christian schools are focused on producing spiritually formed academic thinkers—students with well-developed minds who grasp significant ideas and concepts, students who are aware that all ideas are not of equivalent value. These students are comfortable discussing ideas, asking thoughtful questions, and thinking through these matters in light of Scripture. This teaching and learning process is designed for all students, and it begins with the earliest levels of schooling. The school curriculum and classroom instruction either foster intellectual development or inhibit it. The teacher develops thinking in students by enlivening the class with the introduction of ideas and broad concepts and then appropriately stirring the students to think about and discuss them. Teaching children to frame and pose well-developed questions is a critical ingredient in this process.

Effectively Skilled Practitioners

In concert with fostering developed minds in students, the instructional program must equip students with a repertoire of educational and life skills. While most of these skills are taught within the content disciplines, many have broad application to life, calling, and vocation. Teachers need to explain to students the connections between life, content, and skills. Students in geometry class, for example, ask, "When am I ever going to use this stuff?" While the simple answer is that it is needed for trigonometry or for success on an exam, the real answer is about life and vocation. Asking a student about vocation can open the door to explaining the everyday use of logical deduction and analytical processes. Each of the content disciplines brings with it the opportunity to broaden skill sets and to link those skills to living and serving. Skills of all kinds—including computational, manipulative, communicative, and technological—are required for effective living in community. They are needed for living in general as well as for fully applying one's gifts and talents to service and worship.

Logically Framed Worldview

Inherent in developing students who are spiritually formed thinkers is making sure that students' basic assumptions about life are consistent with the teachings of the Bible. As James Sire (1977) indicates, students will use their basic assumptions consistently or inconsistently, depending on whether their assumptions are based on truth, partial truth, or lies. Education that is Christian teaches for a life of worldview consistency that makes sense of the world by looking through the lens of Scripture, what R. C. Sproul (1986) calls "lifeviews." Effective school curriculum and instruction infuse worldview development into and across every content discipline and teach it both intentionally and incidentally. Well-trained Christian teachers, for example, recognize the opportunity to teach worldview when a student returns from attending a family funeral. What happens after death is a worldview question, and a student's return from a funeral is an opportunity to teach the biblical answer. In social studies, which addresses the concepts of relationships, authority, and human dignity, the curriculum guides should prompt intentional worldview development.

Worldview assumptions underlie the choices that human beings make and, consequently, the direction of their lives. These big beliefs are the linchpins of life, and, when consistently understood and applied, they establish a logical framework for thinking, choosing, and behaving. George Barna (2003) makes the case that these core beliefs are quite well established in the elementary and early-adolescent years. Therefore, the curriculum of the school needs to include planned worldview development across the curriculum and at every grade level.

A Developed Faith Walk

Evangelism and nurture are hallmarks of Christian school education. The primary role of parents in this area is recognized by schools, but many parents have the expectation that the school will extend and mature the faith development of students. This expectation is particularly prevalent as young people mature into the middle school and high school years. The development of a walk of faith has been too often viewed as an osmotic function of the ethos and culture of the school, and in other cases schools or parents have equated spiritual formation with a student's knowing the verses and terminology of the Bible and the gospel message.

While Bible memorization and knowledge are important, they do not constitute the complete process of ongoing spiritual formation. Spiritual maturity engages the partnership of the home, the church, and the school. Children and young people require intentional discipleship that combines knowledge of scriptural truth with experience in how to apply that truth. Mentoring students to fuller faith requires both a place in the curriculum and time in the program schedule of the school. Morning devotionals take on a new significance when driven by a planned, age-appropriate curriculum that includes specific results. Discipleship groups that meet with a faculty sponsor to read together and discuss their faith and its application to life are appropriate, beginning in the middle-elementary grades. Intentional spiritual nurture not only grounds students in their faith but also instills in them the pattern of exercising the spiritual disciplines as a way of life.

Curriculum Development as a Community Process

Curriculum planning, documentation, review, and adjustment are primarily functions of the professional staff, but this process also provides opportunities to invigorate members of the school community by involving them. Curriculum planning is communal in that it engages constituents of the school in determining the larger goals and intended results of the instructional program. It is educational on both sides of the table as the staff members become aware of the expectations of the community and as the other participants learn more about the desire of the school to educate children. Engaging the instructional staff, trustees, parents, and members of the community in the curricular goal-setting process has multiple benefits. Involvement strengthens commitment by increasing the awareness of how the instructional program is infused with the school's distinctives. In addition, the faculty members benefit from the interaction with those who entrust their children to the school.

Design and Development

Documentation of instruction prescribes with reasonable accuracy the intended curriculum—what teachers are supposed to be teaching in various content areas during a school year. There are multiple types of curricular documentation, and the school must choose one that corresponds with the maturity of the school as well as the demands it puts on the staff. The experience and expertise of the faculty are critical factors in selecting an appropriate process.

The curriculum map is more useful for classroom teachers than is the scope and sequence, as it typically includes a list of unit or strand objectives and an indication of the time that should be allotted to teaching the material. The scope and sequence covers several grades, but maps give teachers enough specific information so that they can plan for each day of lessons in order to meet the instructional-time targets identified in the map. Curriculum maps identify the objectives, time frame, instructional activities, related textbook or other resources that will be utilized, as well as the types of assessment for evaluating student learning.

There are several electronic mapping systems, such as Rubicon's Atlas or Curriculum Mapper, that provide highly efficient formats into which teachers can place content components, as well as related textbook and other resource information. These mapping tools provide connections to lists of standards that relate to lesson objectives. In addition, most mapping tools include assessment banks of questions that connect to the selected objectives and standards. Mapping connects planned content to academic standards set by professional academic associations or by national, provincial, or state education departments. Although Christian schools are not necessarily under the jurisdiction of some of these agencies, it is important that a school be able to verify that it is teaching to those standards, as they often form the basis for transferring credit and testing for college admissions.

Curriculum documentation, once it is developed past the rudimentary stage, provides teachers with a written basis for thinking about how to bring matters of faith, worldview, Christian history, and spiritual formation into the classroom. At times, educators find a Bible verse that correlates in some way with the unit content and consider their use of it as "integrative." Integration is a far more enriched process than correlation, in that integration infuses content with the ideas, concepts, and principles of Scripture, the Church, and its traditions. Ruth Haycock spent her life connecting the Scripture to the academic disciplines, but she was clear about the distinction between correlation and integration. She writes, "It is not enough that we moralize in Bible classes to teach socially acceptable or even Christian conduct. Neither is it adequate that we use incidents from history, or observations from science, to illustrate spiritual truth. Though history and science furnish many possible object lessons, their use in this fashion is not true integration of truth from Scripture and truth from other sources" (2005). Integration occurs in the mind and heart of the teacher before it occurs in classroom instruction, and the prompts in the curriculum guides remind the teacher of this opportunity.

The scope and sequence indicates to teachers what the school has identified as the priorities in the instructional program. Content and skills may be noted as introduced, reviewed, or mastered at specific age levels. The scope and sequence plots the development of concepts and skills across grade levels and informs teachers about what students should know when entering and leaving each grade or course. It is crucial that teachers identify the content mastery expectations of the school for the subjects and grades for which they are responsible.

Instructional Content Management

Teachers have the responsibility to implement the curriculum that the school has documented and intends for them to follow. It is the function of leadership to ensure that the intended curriculum becomes the implemented curriculum of the classroom. This process is completed in the assessment component of measuring what students have achieved. The discrepancies that become evident between the intended, implemented, and achieved curriculum (Wiggins and McTighe 1998) are the content of serious instructional dialogue that permeates a strong school.

Curricular Implications of Instructional Time Management

One of the most significant measures of the implemented curriculum is the time that the teacher spends on any particular content and skill component (Marzano 2003). Instructional time management is a hallmark of effective schools, and educational leaders teach the faculty to both guard and manage it. The great dilemma of content delivery is that the amount of instructional time is limited and the amount of content is virtually unlimited. In effective schools, instructional time is matched with curricular priorities, and leaders protect that time.

School administrators need to prioritize instructional time within the school and carefully fend off the many intrusions that detract from it. The rigorous management of teaching time within the school indicates to parents, staff, and students the high value of teaching and learning within the school. A common valuing of instructional time across the organization is formative in cultivating an atmosphere of academic focus and seriousness about scholarship within the school.

Challenges to Leading for Dynamic and Holistic Curriculum

An effective Christian teaching and learning community is measured immediately and eternally by what it produces in the lives of its students. Leadership is effective as it consistently holds before the staff the instructional program and what the school desires to develop in the lives of students. This is the educational leader's priority—to see that the focus of the school is on the lives of students who are in the process of becoming. In the Christian school the goal is becoming Christian. Nicholas Wolterstorff expands on this idea when he writes, "Thus, any curriculum founded on a dichotomy and disjunction between Christ and culture, between serving God and having dominion, is not a Christian curriculum" (2002, 30). The leadership imperative is the dismantling of curriculum or cocurricular programs that have goals that are inconsistent with the school's mission, vision, and expected outcomes.

Reflective Practice and Informed Change

The teaching and learning process is at the heart of a school, and administrators must give it priority attention. Managing the operational functions of a school can become consuming for leaders and detract from appropriate focus on the more important activities of teaching and learning. Key to keeping this focus is the leader's participation in the professional dialogue on the curricular and instructional issues. Leaders should have regular meetings that focus on the instructional life of the school. As well as meeting with the entire teaching staff at once, leaders should meet with teachers organized by grade levels and by content disciplines.

Wise administrators focus on the evidence piece of assessment by asking to see the various qualities of student work. This level of specificity from the staff maintains the discussion at a professional level and discourages the tendency for issues to be considered on the basis of jargon or broad generalities. Teachers should prepare for these meetings by reflecting on what the curricular issues, questions, and challenges are in the classrooms. Leaders should compile the common issues, and from that information they should work with the staff in developing action plans for thoughtful change. These instructional changes are incorporated into the curriculum guides in order to ensure that they are implemented. The comprehensive end-of-year curricular assessment of achievement and instructional effectiveness is critical to leading the school to make the necessary curricular adjustments.

Textbooks and Teachers

Fledgling schools at times begin without adequate and thorough preparation in determining what they intend to teach and what they want students to learn. The focus may be on facilities, staffing, or simply survival, and preparatory work on the instructional program is often relegated to a lower priority. A simple but ineffective practice is to choose a textbook publisher offering an array of products that seem generally consistent with the school's mission. However, schools do not develop a distinctive identity, attract a strong staff, and mature into highly credible institutions when textbooks define and control the content of the curriculum. Steensma and Van Brummelen (1977) note that the fixation on textbooks as curriculum is one of the more significant problems Christian school leaders face. Mature schools understand that textbooks are clearly subservient to the curriculum.

At times, textbooks are used as curriculum when teachers are not academically prepared for the classes they are assigned to teach. It is important for school leaders to ensure that every classroom teacher is well qualified for what he or she is assigned to teach. A program of professional development is mandatory for any teacher who is not thoroughly prepared. The integrity and testimony of the school is dependent on employing confident and competent teachers who know what they need to teach and how to teach it. Curriculum documents provide this information, but these guides cannot make up for a teacher who is not prepared for the classroom.

Now What? Application to Practice

Instructional leadership: Connecting philosophy, vision, and mission to results

Authentic and vital Christian school education focuses on a consistent linkage of philosophy, vision, and mission to results. It is the task of leaders to see that these linkages enter the classroom curriculum through the content as well as through the life of the teacher. The measure of the success of a school is what it produces in the lives of its students. The major delivery mechanism for these outcomes is the curriculum. In pursuit of effective instructional leadership, the following practices are suggested.

1. The faculty should be led through an assessment activity to document what it is that drives, controls, and determines how instructional time is utilized in the classroom. In addition, teachers should assess how much their preferences, textbooks, curriculum guides, standards (local, state/provincial, national), or school traditions influence their teaching.

2. The entire staff should discuss how the curriculum reflects, in specific ways, the philosophy, vision, mission, and values of the school. Questions such as these should be asked: How do the various aspects of the work we assign to students reflect our commitment to produce mature people of faith? What would school parents see in the assignments for independent study or homework that are reflective of our Christian school distinctives?

Instructional leadership: Managing curriculum for holistic education

Instructional leaders should provide a coherent view of what the organization expects to occur in the classroom so that the school's desired ends in the lives of students are realized. Educational leaders should provide guidance for the staff in order to clarify directions and then should manage the staff so that they routinely and easily follow that course. A set of schoolwide outcomes for students is one of the most effective means of clarifying vision and giving day-to-day feet to mission-appropriate work.

If the school has not developed a set of schoolwide learning outcomes, they should be pursued as a community-involved activity. There are schools and organizations (such as ACSI and CSI) that have done work in this area, and such work can serve as a starting point. A list of expected student outcomes becomes a criterion, along with the school's vision and mission, to ensure that there is alignment between the curriculum and the expected results.

Addressing the domains of intellectual development, educational skills, worldview orientation, and spiritual formation, a rubric can be developed to assess how effective the school is in each area. The results from various constituent groups can then contribute to a community dialogue regarding strategic improvement.

Instructional leadership: Developing practical tools for efficiency and effectiveness

The work of piecing together a well-documented school-based curriculum is no small task. It begins with mapping out what is, so that the way is clearer in determining what ought to be. This model is called discrepancy thinking. Curriculum—and subsequently teaching and learning—improves as a school defines what should be taught, in what order, to what depth, over what period of time, and with what resources. While there are many acceptable methods of accomplishing this process, leaders should keep in mind that the goal is increased staff efficiency to ensure increased instructional effectiveness.

An assessment of the current curricular documents the school has in place is the starting point. Do they meet the criteria for practicality and usefulness? Are they overly sophisticated or too simplistic? Do they assist new teachers in getting oriented to the school, and do they serve as the basis for curricular adjustment and review? Is there consistency in the way curriculum is documented at all levels of the school?

The curriculum documents provide the template that teachers use for preparing daily lessons. Is technology being used to its fullest to articulate grade-to-grade goals and progress? Are there opportunities to post notes on e-documents to raise questions or identify apparent disparities? Do the curricular documents serve as a content time-management tool, and are there allowances for the variations from one year or one class to another?

Leaders should develop the teachers around them and assist them in becoming curricular leaders in their own classrooms and then for others in the school. Which teachers have a passion for curricular organization, and how is that ability utilized for the benefit of all the staff? Do staff meetings regularly focus on the instructional program and the issues that need to be addressed within it?

Conclusion

Teaching and learning are the essence of schooling. Education is directional in that it begins with students who are at one stage of development and deposits them at new places in their lives. The new places toward which schooling leads students are the intended outcomes that the school has specified. These results are achieved, in great measure, only as they align with the instructional goals of the school and match the curriculum of the classroom. The role of the instructional leader is to ensure that the instructional program and every other activity of the school contribute to the achievement of the school's expected student outcomes.

References

Barna, George. 2003. *Transforming children into spiritual champions.* Ventura, CA: Regal Books.

Bruinsma, Robert W. 2003. *The joy of language.* Colorado Springs, CO: Purposeful Design Publications.

Gangel, Kenn. 2005. "Education for renovation": An executive summary of Dr. Dallas Willard's presentations at the 2004 NAPCE Conference. *Christian Education Journal.* Series 3, vol. 2, no. 1.

Haycock, Ruth C. 2005. *Encyclopedia of Bible truths.* Colorado Springs, CO: Purposeful Design Publications.

Kaufmann, Stephen. 1992. Sabbatical study report to schools in study. Report adapted from a faculty forum paper, Covenant College.

MacCullough, Martha E. 1999. *How to develop a teaching model for world view integration.* Langhorne, PA: Philadelphia Biblical University.

Malik, Charles Habib. 1987. *A Christian critique of the university.* Ontario, Canada: North Waterloo Academic Press.

Marzano, Robert J. 2003. *What works in schools: Translating research into action.* Alexandria, VA: Association for Supervision and Curriculum Development.

Sire, James W. 1997. *The universe next door: A basic worldview catalog.* 3rd ed. Downers Grove, IL: InterVarsity Press.

Sproul, R. C. 1986. *Lifeviews: Understanding the ideas that shape society today.* Old Tappan, NJ: Fleming H. Revell.

Steensma, Geraldine J., and Harro W. Van Brummelen. 1977. *Shaping school curriculum: A biblical view.* Terre Haute, IN: Signal Publishing.

Van Brummelen, Harro. 2002. *Steppingstones to curriculum: A biblical path.* 2nd ed. Colorado Springs, CO: Purposeful Design Publications.

Wiggins, Grant, and Jay McTighe. 1998. *Understanding by design.* Alexandria, VA: Association of Supervision and Curriculum Deveopment.

Wolterstorff, Nicholas P. 2002. *Educating for life: Reflections on Christian teaching and learning.* Ed. Gloria Goris Stronks and Clarence W. Joldersma. Grand Rapids, MI: Baker Academic.

CHAPTER 11

BUILDING CULTURALLY INCLUSIVE COMMUNITIES

From Tolerance to Transformation

๛

By Daphne Wharton Haddad and
Susan Schneider Hasseler

Daphne Wharton Haddad, professor of education at Covenant College, was born in England and lived in Pakistan, Canada, and Mexico before coming to the United States. She taught in elementary and middle schools in New Hampshire, South Carolina, and Georgia before completing her PhD at the University of South Carolina.

Susan Schneider Hasseler is the associate dean for teacher education and a professor at Calvin College. She taught for thirteen years in elementary and middle schools in Michigan, Iowa, and South Dakota before pursuing her PhD at Northwestern University. Her professional interests include antiracist multicultural education, educational leadership, and international education

CHAPTER 11

BUILDING CULTURALLY INCLUSIVE COMMUNITIES

By Daphne Wharton Haddad and
Susan Schneider Hasseler

AT FIRST GLANCE, Western Christian Academy seems like a welcoming place for all children and parents. Posters on the walls depict children from many ethnic backgrounds. Books featuring ethnic minority children and authors are displayed prominently in the library. Signs advertise an upcoming international festival featuring Korean acrobats and Spanish singers. Many children have pen pals in other parts of the world. The social studies curriculum mandates the inclusion of a unit on world cultures at each grade level. The principal, teachers, and parents make a conscious effort to invite families from diverse backgrounds to join their school. Ethnic slurs are discouraged, and children are admonished to accept people even if they look or sound different. Teachers often speak of being "color-blind" and "seeing what's inside a child," not the color of his or her skin. The school offers remedial help to students who come from "disadvantaged backgrounds." There are opportunities for children for whom English is a second language to learn to speak English more fluently.

And yet with all these efforts to welcome and include students and parents from many ethnic backgrounds, when one asks the principal or teachers how things are going, they hesitate. The number of ethnic

217

minority families in the school is not growing at the pace that was initially anticipated. Parents of ethnic minority students are seldom involved in PTO or fund-raising events. When asked, some of these ethnic minority parents report feeling like outsiders or guests at the school, not real participants. There are still reports of name-calling on the playground, and students from similar backgrounds tend to "hang out" with one another, especially in the upper grades. A disproportionate number of ethnic minority students seem to be struggling academically, and complaints have been overheard about lowering academic standards and increasing disciplinary issues now that the school population is "changing." Teachers have begun to ask for more training to address the "challenges of working with diverse learners." In spite of all their good intentions, Western Christian Academy administrators, teachers, parents, and students are beginning to realize that they have a long way to go.

Moving from Tolerance to Transformation

Why is it so difficult to create a genuinely inclusive and Christian multicultural school community? What happens when the emphasis in a school is on welcoming the "other" while staying the same? Why does a focus on tolerance alone inevitably fall short—biblically, philosophically, and practically? How might a Christian school be transformed to become a place where students from all backgrounds flourish and work toward bringing about the flourishing of others?

To begin grappling with these challenging issues, it is helpful to establish four basic principles: (1) the kingdom of God, not a particular political perspective, shapes the agenda for Christian schools; (2) history matters; (3) a heart transplant, not a Band-Aid, is needed; and (4) transformation takes time—the commitment is to a marathon, not a 100-yard dash.

The kingdom of God

A Christian school's commitment to be culturally inclusive, just, and nondiscriminatory is not grounded in any particular political perspective or in a pragmatic desire to reflect the composition of the society in which our graduates will live. Rather, a Christian commitment to diversity is grounded in an understanding of the nature of the kingdom of God, which itself is diverse, encompassing people "from every tribe and language and people and nation" (Revelation 5:9). Men and women and boys and girls from all ethnic, cultural, and socioeconomic backgrounds are brothers and sisters within the Body of Christ, called to live in unity (which is different from uniformity) with one another. A Christian school, therefore, should seek to strengthen bonds of Christian understanding and cooperation across cultures, ethnic heritages, and social classes as a model of God's kingdom on the earth. This is an essential calling of Christian education.

History matters

Institutional, group, and individual histories make an impact on every aspect of schooling. The work of schools is not done on a level playing field in which the participants just need to get to know one another better. Past and current inequities and injustices, as well as resistance to inequity and examples of transformation, all influence the teaching and learning process. A first step toward creating a just and inclusive learning environment, therefore, is to acknowledge both the histories of the majority participants in any school setting and the histories of people who are invited to become a part of that school community.

In one author's class, for example, undergraduate teacher-education students read Ronald Takaki's *A Different Mirror: A History of Multicultural America* (1999)and watch documentary footage about the integration of Little Rock High School from the PBS *Eyes on the Prize* series. All too often, students respond with such comments as, "Why didn't I learn about this in my American history classes?" A celebratory approach to teaching American history that acknowledges only its successes and ignores its failures is dishonest and theologically in error. (Remember, the Bible depicts both the failures and the successes of godly men such as Abraham and David.) The grandparents of today's schoolchildren were themselves schoolchildren during the tumultuous decade of school integration, and those memories live on. Ethnic minority families approach historically white schools with the realities of our shared history in mind.

If the school leaders at Western Christian Academy want to move toward creating a culturally inclusive school community, they will need to confront these difficult questions:

- What has been the history of Christian schooling in North America with respect to including people from diverse ethnic backgrounds? What has been the history of Western Christian Academy? Many Christian schools were established to serve a particular ethnic group or a specific religious tradition, and the history of that ethnic group or religious tradition will influence relationship building with people from other ethnic groups or religious traditions. Other Christian schools were established after desegregation laws came into effect and may be associated, rightly or wrongly, with resistance to racial integration. The prevalence of Christian schools in predominantly white suburbs and rural areas versus core city areas raises questions about historic commitments to justice and inclusiveness. These historic realities may affect the perceptions about a particular school by the ethnic minority members of a community. Thus, these issues need to be acknowledged and addressed.

• What are the histories of the people invited to join as partners in schooling? Are they relatively new to the United States, or are they long-term residents? Did their ancestors come to America willingly or involuntarily? Has their ethnic group as a whole been welcomed and included, or have they experienced a history of discrimination and exclusion? What kinds of real-life experiences have they had with people who represent the majority of the participants at Western Christian Academy?

In order to get honest answers to these questions, school leaders need to establish trusting relationships with adults in diverse ethnic communities. Together, they can identify not only barriers to unity but also examples of unity accomplished, as all the participants seek to understand how their perceptions and expectations of one another have been shaped by the past and the present. School leaders, of course, need to approach these conversations primarily as learners who seek to understand the histories, experiences, and perspectives of people different from themselves, not as critics who measure every difference they encounter against the assumed superior norms of their own cultural heritage.

The leaders of Western Christian Academy may discover that ethnic minority families experience the school as welcoming them into a community that demands considerable cultural adaptation from them, but only from them. Even multicultural posters, festivals, and foods may have the unintended effect of reinforcing stereotypes by romanticizing and trivializing cultures while the rest of the school experience requires significant accommodation and assimilation on the part of the ethnic minority participants.

A heart transplant, not a Band-Aid

The establishment of a Christian multicultural school community that reflects the diversity of the kingdom of God requires deep systemic changes. Western Christian Academy's inclusive visual images, written materials, and occasional world-culture units do not go far enough. The "heroes and holidays" approach (Banks 2002; Nieto 2002) is, at best, superficial in that it fails to address deeper issues such as societal racism (both structural and personal), school organization, policies and practices, curriculum, teacher expectations, perspectives on the learner, instructional models, tracking, testing, and the quality of personal relationships and interactions among all stakeholders in the school and in the community.

At this point, Western Christian Academy might "count the cost" and turn back, preferring the comfort and security of serving one population fairly well to the discomfort and multiple adjustments of building a more culturally inclusive school community. Administrators might calculate that their posters, international festivals, minor curriculum changes, and remedial support are all they can safely undertake without alienating their core clientele. They might opt, therefore, for the status quo, continue to extend an invitation to ethnic minority families to "come and be just like us," and thus settle for a compromised witness within their local communities. But not only does that approach ignore the unique calling of Christian education, but the school will suffer real losses in the long run. The heart will grow weaker and weaker without a transplant that can enrich the experiences of all the learners and prepare the school community for greater service.

A marathon, not a sprint

The commitment to model a more authentic Christian community in a divided and fragmented world is not a one-semester initiative that can be accomplished by a short-term task force. Rather, a long-term process is needed—one that requires strategic planning, time, resources, and a multilevel commitment to ongoing transformation. Administrators, staff, teachers, students, and their families will have to work through all the experiences and emotions associated with improvement and growth—not only joy, renewed energy, clarified vision, measured optimism, healthy growth, enriched learning for all students, and solid accomplishment, but also frustration, misunderstanding, disappointment, burnout, and fatigue. The costs are high, but the rewards are rich.

A Strategic Plan

How, then, might Western Christian Academy advance along the challenging pathway toward the goal of a Christian multicultural school community? There are multiple entry points onto that pathway, and educational leaders should analyze the current conditions at their school and determine appropriate and feasible starting points. However, a strategic plan needs to include the following four areas: the content of the curriculum, the processes of instruction, perspectives on the nature of the learner, and the quality of personal relationships and interactions among administrators, staff, teachers, students, parents, and community members.

Curriculum: Reflective of the experiences of all participants

The curriculum is the sum of all the learning experiences that children encounter in school. In addition to the stated curriculum, children also experience what Harro Van Brummelen (2002) and others have called the implicit or hidden curriculum (the unplanned curriculum) and the null curriculum (what is left out). Ethnic slurs or jokes and teachers' responses to them are examples of the hidden curriculum. Omission of Native American perspectives on westward expansion in U.S. history is an example of the null curriculum.

James A. Banks (2002; 2006) has identified four ways in which ethnic minority perspectives are addressed in the stated curriculum in most North American schools today: the contributions approach, the ethnic-additive approach, the transformative approach, and the social-action approach. He ranks these approaches along a continuum that moves from tolerance to transformation, and his taxonomy provides a helpful model that Western Christian Academy can use to structure a critique and revision of its curriculum.

1. Contributions approach. Many schools add ethnic heroes and ethnic holidays to the curriculum. Western Christian Academy already displays posters that include men and women from a variety of ethnic backgrounds, includes biographies of "famous" ethnic minority people in the library, and plans special activities for Martin Luther King Day, *Cinco de Mayo*, and other holidays. However, the criteria for selecting "heroes" are based on mainstream definitions of appropriate role models (for example, professionals such as doctors and inventors, Martin Luther

222

King Jr. but not Malcolm X, Sacagawea but not Geronimo), and the same heroes are often highlighted every year, prompting one student to say to his fifth-grade teacher, "Wow, that Martin Luther King sure did a lot of things all by himself!" Another student told one of the authors of this chapter, "When we studied Booker T. Washington in grade school, the other kids called him Booger T. Washington, and the teacher never said anything about it." She said nothing, but she taught something. The complex history surrounding such heroes is rarely addressed, and except for these added lessons, the curriculum stays the same as it was before. Here, then, is an example of "tolerance" that, at best, widens horizons a bit, and, at worst, patronizes, disrespects, and stereotypes.

2. Ethnic-additive approach. Western Christian Academy, to its credit, went one step further along the pathway toward a culturally inclusive Christian school community by adding a unit to the curriculum that focused on "world cultures." Such units, however, are often flawed, and teachers often find them difficult to teach because they lack knowledge and background in the materials being presented. Their own attitudes toward other cultures may be as ethnocentric as those of their students. They may display the traditions and practices of particular groups without careful reference to whether what is portrayed is historical rather than contemporary (for example, Inuit people with dogsleds, not snowmobiles), or occasional rather than actual everyday practice (for example, Lakota Sioux people dancing in their traditional dress). They may highlight a particular aspect of a country (for example, rice paddies and rickshaws in Southeast Asia) without showing the bigger picture (for example, large cities full of cars and people in Western as well as traditional dress). Themes and perspectives may be added to a unit without changing its basic structure, purposes, or characteristics (for example, adding a few Native American narratives to a unit on "western expansion" while maintaining an exclusive focus on those who "discovered and developed" the West). Materials may be chosen for their visual appeal and instructional value, but with little research to determine whether they were based on input from the people being represented and whether they represent a balanced picture of that group of people (for example, African Americans may be encountered only as slaves or in the persons of a few exceptional individuals). If the cultural group being addressed is connected to the United States in some way, the focus is usually on the group's contributions to "American" culture (for example, jazz, pizza) rather than on the ways North American culture has been shaped by multiple ethnic groups over time. The same dangers of reinforcing stereotypes and creating superficial understandings apply to this approach as well.

3. Transformative approach. A transformative approach to schooling goes beyond the addition of artifacts and special units to an otherwise unchanged curriculum. A transformative approach to curriculum design involves a thorough analysis and transformation of the current curriculum, including careful scrutiny of goals and objectives, and questions such as, "Whose voices are represented in each unit of study?" Slowly, carefully, and over time, the curriculum is reshaped so that concepts, issues, and themes are viewed, at developmentally appropriate levels, from a variety of ethnic, cultural, socioeconomic, and gender perspectives and points of view—all (including mainstream perspectives) subject to biblically informed critique and scrutiny.

This kind of curriculum redesign may require going to primary sources and challenging commonly held beliefs about what students need to know in order to be both good citizens and faithful followers of Christ. For example, a unit on the American Revolution would include the perspectives of the "American" revolutionaries, English loyalists, African slaves and freepersons, Native peoples, and people in Great Britain, as well as a conversation about the moral implications of revolution. (By way of comparison, the English author of this chapter grew up learning about "the rebellion in the colonies"—an example of monocultural curriculum from the other side). Rather than a catalog of campaigns, dates, battles, and victories, the primary conceptual focus of the unit might be "conflict" or "change," and students might explore the ways in which the revolution had a positive impact on some participants and a negative impact on others.

In a transformed curriculum, therefore, the emphasis is on understanding how multiple groups have shaped American and other national societies over time, and how some voices continue to be heard more than others. Choosing themes that naturally include multiple perspectives such as coming of age, community change over time, conflict, progress, and immigration can help shape a curriculum that genuinely represents the multiple voices that have shaped and continue to shape the world today.

Conversations about what should be included in the curriculum will not be easy, particularly in relation to social studies/history and literature. A Western European perspective has dominated the curriculum for a long time, and it is difficult for administrators, teachers, and parents to envision a more multiple-perspective curriculum without a sense of fear and loss. Little consensus exists, and much angry rhetoric has been produced on all sides. Christian school boards, administrators, and teachers, working together with people in their communities, have the opportunity to play a leadership role by developing curriculum that authentically reflects the biblical themes of justice and inclusion, while challenging students to develop the knowledge, skills, and attitudes they need to be God's agents of renewal in the world. Students whose perspectives were not represented in the past will see themselves in the curriculum and be affirmed. Other students' perspectives will be broadened so that they have a deeper understanding of God's world and their place in it. An inclusive curriculum will represent gains, not losses, for all the learners.

4. Social-action approach. Banks' final level of curriculum transformation is designed to prepare students to be active in their communities. The skills to bring about a more just and equitable society do not come naturally, so students need an academically rigorous curriculum that equips them with the knowledge, skills, and dispositions to understand the world around them at a deep enough level of complexity that they can adequately understand and analyze issues, concepts, and events. In addition, they need to learn basic intercultural-communication, conflict-resolution, and problem-solving skills to enable them to make real changes in their school and community. These skills must be built into the curriculum along with the basic skills of literacy, numeracy, and critical thinking.

A social-action approach to curriculum provides students with opportunities to grapple, at developmentally appropriate levels, with challenging issues of justice and injustice. This approach also equips them to address those issues from the perspective of a biblical conceptual framework. Appropriate conversations about how the variables of race, culture, language, class, gender, and ability affect peoples' experiences in the world by privileging some and silencing others are an integral part of the curriculum. Students learn how to work collaboratively with people different from themselves—people whose interaction styles, value systems, and life experiences are different from their own. Students are supported in their learning about how to live with conflict and ambiguity, how to disagree respectfully, and how to engage in problem solving that is based on principled compromise. They learn to share power with others. Above all, they see administrators, teachers, aides, and staff modeling all these behaviors daily.

Guiding questions about curriculum. In order for the curriculum to be transformed to reflect the experiences and perspectives of a global Christian community, the process for choosing and implementing school curriculum has to be collaborative and intentional. Questions that school leaders need to ask about curriculum decision-making processes include the following:

- Who currently makes the decisions about curriculum content? How can a broader range of stakeholders be involved in this process?
- How are decisions made about what to include and what to exclude? How are priorities determined when it is impossible to include everything? How can multiple ethnic and cultural perspectives be represented in the priority-setting process if the school's staff are monocultural?
- Do criteria for determining the quality of already-constructed curricula include the representation of multiple voices in the materials? Does scrutiny extend beyond the illustrations to the substance of the text? For example, do reading materials include authors from multiple ethnic, cultural, and socioeconomic groups? Does content present a balanced and appropriate view of the members of those groups? How can curriculum committees determine whether materials relating to specific cultural groups are accurate, up-to-date, and balanced?
- Where can materials be accessed that foster equity and justice and also fit with the theological and theoretical perspectives and values of the school? How can Christian perspectives be integrated into materials that were not designed with that particular emphasis in mind?
- How are teachers engaged as stakeholders in the curriculum-development process? What orientation and mentoring are provided for new teachers? How can principals ensure that all teachers develop a deep enough understanding of history and multiple perspectives to implement a transformed curriculum effectively?

As is evident from this list of complex questions, the process of critiquing current curriculum and transforming it to be culturally comprehensive and transformative must be carefully designed and implemented. New materials and resources must be accessed, and expert assistance may be needed to facilitate the redesign process.

Instruction: Grounded and connected

Instructional strategies that are grounded in a deep understanding of justice and respect for learners as individuals made in the image of God give students valuable life experiences right in the classroom itself. All too often, instructional strategies are chosen for expediency or efficiency rather than with careful consideration of what the strategies are communicating about the learner, about relationships between teacher and learner, or about relationships among learners. In a culturally inclusive Christian school community, the teaching and learning process must be examined thoroughly to ensure that all students are treated with respect and care and that teachers and school leaders model respect, caring, equity, and justice in their relationships with one another.

Instructional strategies that promote questioning, discussion, critical thinking, and active responses are essential means to help students learn how to be "salt and light" in their communities. Instructional strategies that challenge culturally constructed (rather than biblically informed) gender, cultural, socioeconomic, or ability stereotypes, as well as strategies that encourage leadership among students who are not traditionally considered leaders, or demand servanthood from students traditionally put in places of honor, can also model a society transformed by biblical norms. Who is chosen to lead activities? Who is called on often, and who is not? Who is asked to do a physical or mechanical task versus a verbal or artistic one? What skills and gifts are affirmed, and which are not? Instructional strategies, because they have a powerful impact on learners, must be chosen carefully.

In addition to designing instructional systems that are biblically grounded, Western Christian Academy must implement instructional strategies that connect to the learners *where they are* so that all students develop the skills they need to live effective, empowered lives within their multiple communities of school, family, church, and nation. Instructional strategies, therefore, need to be constructed around the "cultural capital" that students bring to school. For example, narrative and linguistic patterns vary among cultural groups, and these varied patterns have a powerful impact on reading, writing, and approaches to problem solving. Different narrative patterns do not represent a deficit that needs to be remedied; they are rich and sophisticated forms of expression, and teachers who understand alternative narrative patterns well enough to integrate them into instruction empower all students with multiple modes of expressing ideas and knowledge (Heath 1983; Heath and Mangiola 1991).

The cultural capital that students bring to schools also includes a wealth of life experience outside school. In a culturally inclusive teaching environment, teachers connect materials and examples with the life experiences of students in order to challenge them to expand their experiences and vision of the world. Teachers, therefore, need time and resources to learn about their students' lives outside school. Motivations to learn and the kinds of knowledge that are valued vary across cultural groups, so teachers cannot assume that all learners share the same attitudes toward particular content or skills (Gay 2000; Garcia 2002). A curious Chicago educator who wondered why Latino preschoolers so often lacked school "readiness skills" visited with Latino families in their homes and discovered that "preparing children to express themselves verbally, develop fine motor skills, listen and attend to storybooks, partake in structured play activities, amplify vocabulary, or recognize colors was simply not considered a parental responsibility" (Carger 1997, 41). Rather than nurturing their young children's independence or academic skills, Latino parents viewed their primary task as nurturing children within the family to be *"well-bred, mannerly, clean, respectful, responsible, loved, and loving"* (42, emphasis in original). Paradoxically, this researcher discovered that, while Anglos were critical of Latino parents for neglecting the academic preparation of their children, Latinos were equally critical of Anglos for failing to teach their children manners, respect, or the ability to work cooperatively and unselfishly with others. (Which, one might ask, is a more biblical model of parenting?)

Classroom management is another complex part of instruction that needs to be critiqued. What is communicated to students and their families by their classroom and schoolwide management systems? Do those systems recognize students as active agents who have an appropriate voice in how the classroom and school are run? Are management systems based on assumptions about groups of students and their need for "more structure" or "firmer limits"? Where do these assumptions come from? How can the validity of these assumptions be tested? What behaviors are rewarded, and what behaviors are ignored or punished? Do the values behind those choices fit the values and priorities of all members of the community? What is the role of grace in classroom discipline plans (Graham 2003; Wolterstorff 2002)? Above all, are the assumptions about learners and relationships that underlie classroom management systems in conformity with the statements about learners and relationships enshrined in the mission statement of the school, or are mixed messages being sent? Management systems that engage students in determining appropriate rewards and consequences for classroom and school behaviors help them experience what is involved in living equitably and cooperatively with their neighbors.

The learner: Deep respect and dogged determination

History has a powerful impact on how different members of a society view one another. Long-lived, unacknowledged assumptions arise about inferiority and superiority, about privilege and disadvantage; these assumptions are based on skin color, ethnicity, national origin, language, or religion (Takaki 1993; Tatum 2003). It can be very difficult to develop deep respect for every learner when learners from particular ethnic groups have, in the past, been portrayed as inferior in cognitive ability, motivation, linguistic skills, or moral values.

Most Christian school mission statements recognize the image of God in every learner. Some authors refer to "unwrapping" the many unique gifts that God gives to learners (Stronks and Blomberg 1993). However, cultural contexts (past and present) have a powerful effect on how gifts, strengths, and resources (as well as deficits and needs) are defined (Joldersma 2001). In some contexts, the ability to work with one's hands might be more highly valued than the ability to manipulate letters and numbers. Some athletic skills (such as the ability to jump high in basketball) may be valued more than others (such as the ability to perform an intricate step in ballet). The ability to play Mozart on the piano may be valued more highly than the ability to compose synthesized music on a computer or play a guitar. The ability to question authority and stand up for one's rights may be highly valued in some cultures but seen as a problem in others. To develop deep respect for every learner, educators must scrutinize assumptions about gifts and deficits to determine which assumptions are biblically based and which are based on a particular set of cultural traditions. This difficult task requires the thoughtful eyes and persistent voices of people from all the cultural groups represented in the school.

Definitions of gifts and deficits have a particularly powerful impact on expectations and interpretations of student behavior. Whether students look a teacher in the eye when the teacher is speaking to them, what tone of voice they use with one another and with adults, and whether they prefer to work alone or together are all behaviors that must be interpreted within their particular cultural context. When teachers interpret all student behaviors according to the norms of the majority culture, their responses to some students might be inappropriate and could be misinterpreted and misunderstood.

The power of teacher expectations and interpretations was brought home vividly to one author of this chapter a couple of years ago. Her teacher-preparation program places students in a variety of school settings, including urban, suburban, and rural schools. Once, half of her student teachers were placed in an urban school in a working-class neighborhood that had a predominantly African American population. The rest worked in an upper-class suburban school that had a predominantly white population. About six weeks into the experience, they all began to experience the normal round of classroom-management problems faced by beginning teachers. The students' behaviors in each school were virtually the same: they took longer to do basic tasks, engaged in more talking, and "forgot" rules and policies. But the student teachers' interpretations of these challenges and their responses to them varied greatly between the two settings.

In the upper-class, predominantly white setting, the student teachers responded to the management challenges by analyzing their teaching to determine if it was engaging enough or if it met the learners' needs in appropriate ways. They made comments about their need to change tasks to be more interesting or to introduce some new routines or concepts to catch the learners' attention. They also worked to determine if problem behaviors happened at a certain time of day so that they could adjust the curriculum. Most of their energy focused on teaching more effectively.

In the working-class, predominantly African American setting, the student teachers talked about the external factors that affected their students' behavior. For example, the student teachers made comments about a lack of support or structure at home. They focused on being firmer and implementing stricter management guidelines and expectations. They all implemented complex management systems that included material rewards and strong consequences. They ended up spending extensive class time and personal energy on these management systems. There was little talk of how they needed to teach in a more engaging way or rearrange the curriculum to better meet the needs of their students.

When the student teachers from the two settings were asked to share their management challenges and solutions with each other, they were shocked to discover that the behaviors they were addressing in the two settings were very much the same. They had all assumed that the problem behaviors in the urban school would be different. They were also shocked when their responses were described to them. The reporting of these observations led to a number of painful but worthwhile conversations about where their expectations of and responses to their learners came from and how they might address those expectations in the future.

All these new teachers were Christians who cared about their students. They all believed that every learner has worth as a person created in the image of God. But those in the urban setting had not developed that deep respect for the learner, a respect that looks for strengths and gifts and that challenges assumptions about individual or family deficits. They were unable to look beyond the stereotypes perpetuated in the media or in the teachers' lounge about the assumed deficits of particular ethnic or socioeconomic groups. They allowed those perceptions to shape their teaching behaviors in ways that were hurtful to their learners.

Relationships: Built on Trust

In order to develop this deep respect for learners from historically oppressed or marginalized groups, teachers need the dogged determination to develop trusting and caring relationships with all students. It is often easier for teachers to develop trusting relationships with students who share their own behaviors, norms, values, and histories. However, building trusting relationships is an essential step toward developing the kind of deep respect for learners that enables a teacher to overcome destructive historical or cultural perceptions and expectations. Teachers do not thereby become relativists for whom "anything goes." But the thoughtful and careful application of biblical principles to particular cultural practices is a process that can be accomplished only in community with students and their families, in a context of mutual respect.

Now What? Application to Practice

LEARNING TO LIVE together in a multicultural Christian community is no easier for Western Christian Academy today than it was for first-century Jewish and Gentile Christians. It is difficult to restructure systems that have been in place for a long time, that are comfortable, and that have worked quite well for particular populations. It is not natural to welcome the conflict and discomfort that are inevitable during difficult conversations around curriculum, instruction, the learner, and governance. Christian schools often develop a strong identity around a shared set of values held by the original school organizers. When conversations about change come up, fears about the loss of that identity can emerge rapidly. The task of separating applied biblical truths from the traditions and practices of particular cultural communities is a complex and controversial undertaking, and it may be difficult to convince teachers and parents that gains will offset potential losses. Expert facilitation can help the school community embark on conversations about identity and values— conversations that appropriately honor all traditions and backgrounds within the defining context of a biblical worldview. School leaders need to seek appropriate support to lead these challenging but valuable conversations in effective ways.

Christian schools that want to become more inclusive multicultural communities could well begin by integrating the topics addressed in this chapter into their overall school-improvement plan. The integration of multicultural questions and perspectives into an existing plan will help the undertaking become part of everyday school life rather than another thing added to an already-too-full agenda. The task is difficult, but all participants in the Christian schooling process will be enriched by this work.

The challenge of redeeming every square inch of God's creation demands that Christian schools let go of traditions and practices that inhibit their redemptive calling and shrink its vision. Then these schools can demonstrate to a broken and divided world the power of the Holy Spirit to make peace, destroy barriers, and break down dividing walls of hostility (Ephesians 2:14). Educators have the rare and precious opportunity to touch the lives of hundreds of young people and to teach them what it means to transform the world. School leaders have the challenging and invigorating opportunity to lead this process. It is truly an awesome task. However, with the divine power that Christians are promised through Christ, schools can be transformed. The agencies, institutions, and individuals supporting Christian schooling can work together, under God, to accomplish this worthy and essential goal.

References

Banks, James A. 2002. *Teaching strategies for ethnic studies*. 7th ed. Boston: Allyn and Bacon.

———. 2006. *Cultural diversity and education: Foundations, curriculum, and teaching*. 5th ed. Boston: Allyn and Bacon.

Carger, Chris Liska. 1997. Attending to new voices. *Educational Leadership* 54, no. 7 (April): 39–43.

Eyes on the Prize. 1999. PBS home video, directed by Henry Hampton.

Garcia, Eugene. 2002. *Student cultural diversity: Understanding and meeting the challenge*. Boston: Houghton Mifflin.

Gay, Geneva. 2000. *Culturally responsive teaching: Theory, research, and practice*. New York: Teachers College Press.

Graham, Donovan L. 2003. *Teaching redemptively: Bringing grace and truth into your classroom*. Colorado Springs, CO: Purposeful Design Publications.

Heath, Shirley Brice. 1983. *Ways with words: Language, life, and work in communities and classrooms*. New York: Cambridge University Press.

Heath, Shirley Brice, and Leslie Mangiola, eds. 1991. *Children of promise: Literate activity in linguistically and culturally diverse classrooms*. Washington, DC: National Education Association.

Joldersma, Clarence W. 2001. Educating for social justice: Revisiting Stronks & Blomberg's idea of responsive discipleship. *Journal of Education and Christian Belief* 5, no. 2 (Autumn): 105–117.

Nieto, Sonia. 2002. *Language, culture, and teaching: Critical perspectives for a new century*. Mahwah, NJ: Lawrence Erlbaum Associates.

Stronks, Gloria Goris, and Doug Blomberg, eds. 1993. *A vision with a task: Christian schooling for responsive discipleship*. Grand Rapids, MI: Baker Academic.

Takaki, Ronald. 1993. *A different mirror: A history of multicultural America*. Boston: Little, Brown and Company.

Tatum, Beverly Daniel. 2003. *"Why are all the black kids sitting together in the cafeteria?" A psychologist explains the development of racial identity*. Rev. ed. New York: Basic Books.

Van Brummelen, Harro. 2002. *Steppingstones to curriculum: A biblical path*. 2nd ed. Colorado Springs, CO: Purposeful Design Publications.

Wolterstorff, Nicholas P. 2002. *Educating for life: Reflections on Christian teaching and learning*. Ed. Gloria Goris Stronks and Clarence Joldersma. Grand Rapids, MI: Baker Academic.

Other Helpful Resources

The following resources must be used judiciously and with discrimination. The books are helpful guides, and they include samples of culturally inclusive lesson plans in multiple subject areas, but some content will require modification and adaptation for use by Christian teachers and schools.

Books

Grant, Carl A., and Christine E. Sleeter. 2007. *Turning on learning: Five approaches for multicultural teaching plans for race, class, gender and disability.* 4th ed. Hoboken, NJ: John Wiley and Sons.

Irvine, Jacqueline Jordan, Beverly Jeanne Armento, Virginia E. Causey, Joan Cohen Jones, Ramona S. Frasher, and Molly H. Weinburgh. 2000. *Culturally responsive teaching: Lesson planning for elementary and middle grades.* Columbus, OH: McGraw-Hill.

Websites

The Teaching for Change website at www.teachingforchange.org lists multiple publications that focus on social justice in schools. One useful publication is *Beyond Heroes and Holidays: A Practical Guide to K–12 Anti-racist, Multicultural Education and Staff Development.* It includes articles for professional development, examples of culturally inclusive units, and a thirty-page resource guide of anti-racist, multicultural teaching materials.

A Web project of the Southern Poverty Law Center, the Teaching Tolerance website at www.tolerance.org lists multiple resources for anti-racist education, including newsletters, classroom materials, and free teaching kits.

CHAPTER 12

THE ASSESSMENT PROCESS

Evaluating Students for Academic Excellence

❧

By Matthew Lucas

Matthew Lucas is an associate professor of education and the director of graduate studies in education at Corban College. He earned his doctor of arts in English from Idaho State University and taught high school English for six years before starting at Corban College in 2004.

CHAPTER 12

THE ASSESSMENT PROCESS

By Matthew Lucas

WHY A CHAPTER on assessment in a text primarily for educational leaders? Is not assessment largely an instructional issue? Is it not a teacher responsibility? Since the typical context for discussing assessment is public-school reform and accountability, such questions are understandable. However, in today's social and political climate, school administrators must take an active role in this important aspect of children's education.

Since *A Nation at Risk: The Imperative for Educational Reform* was published in 1983, the public has been obsessed with standardized tests as the primary means to assess student knowledge. In the years since, there has been a relentless barrage of media headlines that (1) lament student performance on these tests as compared with students from other developed nations; (2) decry the achievement gaps that occur along racial, economic, and gender lines; or (3) announce modest gains or dips in test scores. Recently, government reports and media hysteria have led to federal legislation, and the tie between standardized testing and assessment has been strengthened. This strengthening has been most evident in the No Child Left Behind Act of 2001, passed in 2002, in which schools are held accountable for student achievement as measured by students' performance each year on standardized "high stakes" tests.

Given this negative and vitriolic climate, it is understandable if some Christian school administrators distance themselves from assessment and regard it as solely a public-school concern. Although Christian school administrators can ignore the reporting mandates handed down by the federal government and disregard their schools' annual yearly progress (AYP) evaluations, they cannot overlook their stakeholders' clamor for evidence of student achievement. In a society in which accountability is paramount, Christian school administrators must demonstrate that their schools are accomplishing their primary mission of educating students, or these administrators will face the possibility of stakeholders' taking their students and money elsewhere. Given this reality, administrators need to turn their attention to sound assessment practice as a means to measure student learning.

The pages that follow will help educational leaders meet this challenge from a specifically biblical context. First, however, a close examination of standardized tests and the administrator's role in the assessment process is in order. Then the focus will turn toward a fuller definition of *assessment*, grounding the definition in a biblical worldview.

Standardized Tests

Assessment is not synonymous with standardized testing. All standardized tests are assessments, but not all assessments are standardized tests. Therefore, leaders must keep current assumptions about standardized tests in perspective and put less emphasis on these tests as the primary means of assessing student learning. This statement is not intended to dismiss the usefulness of standardized tests, since they do provide meaningful information. For several reasons, however, educators should not use these tests as the sole or primary means of measuring student achievement.

First, standardized tests are narrowly focused, and they fail to provide a holistic view of education and the student. Since the content of these tests is restricted to core subject areas, valuable skills that constitute a good education—such as citizenship, physical health, verbal communication, and interpersonal skills—are not tested. Likewise, the manner in which the test is constructed favors a limited range of cognitive skills. Although these tests are useful in measuring knowledge that is easily reduced to right or wrong answers, they do not measure students' ability to solve problems, develop arguments, or think creatively or reflectively. Test content also raises two common concerns when standardized tests are the primary means of assessment. Either teachers reduce the curriculum to match the content of the test—what many refer to as "teaching to the test"—or teachers offer a varied curriculum, and the tests measure only a small slice of the overall content.

For Christian schools, the narrow focus of the tests should pose additional problems. Principally, the emphasis on core academics *can* distort or overshadow the purpose of a Christian education. From a biblical perspective, the primary purpose of education is the same as the primary purpose of humankind: to glorify God and enjoy Him forever (quoted in Graham 2003). This perspective is not intended to suggest that academic achievement is not central to a Christian school. Christian education, however, should educate the whole person by including such spiritual disciplines as righteous living (Galatians 5:16, 22–23), godly decision making (Proverbs 3:5–6), wholehearted devotion to God (Deuteronomy 6:4–5), submission to God and authorities (James 4:7, Romans 13:1–5), a Christlike attitude (Philippians 2:5–8), love for others (Matthew 22:39), and self-sacrifice (Luke 9:23–24)—all of which should figure prominently in instruction and assessment. Not only do standardized tests not measure these Christian disciplines, but attempts to measure them through traditional test items would be ridiculous at best.

Second, standardized tests do not measure just what is learned in the classroom. W. James Popham (1999) identifies three factors that influence test scores: classroom instruction, innate ability, and student background. Only one of these is directly related to what takes place in school. "A meaningful amount of what's measured by today's high-stakes tests is directly attributable not to what students learn in school, but to what they *bring* to school in the form of their families' socioeconomic status or the academic aptitudes they happened to inherit" (2001, 18; emphasis in original). Even though the tests do measure student academic achievement, they are an inadequate tool for identifying the impact of instruction on student learning.

Third, no single administration of an assessment—especially a standardized test, which causes considerable student anxiety—can provide sufficient information about student learning. There are many factors besides student knowledge that influence student performance on a test:

for example, stress from home, unfamiliarity with the test format, lack of sleep, and language and cultural barriers. Thus, no single test gives a full account of a student's ability, skill level, or knowledge. Educators should make decisions about student achievement using multiple pieces of evidence (Taylor and Nolen 2005).

For these reasons, Christian school administrators should avoid relying on standardized tests as their principal means of assessment, even if test scores demonstrate that students from the Christian school are outperforming students from the neighboring public school. This temptation to tout student test scores may be particularly difficult to resist given the market-driven nature of Christian schooling and the prevalent evidence that students from private institutions academically outperform (as defined by standardized-test scores) those who attend public schools. Recently the National Assessment of Educational Progress (NAEP) made these comparisons more useful by disaggregating data for private schools, using three categories: Catholic, Lutheran, and conservative Christian (Perie, Vanneman and Goldstein 2005). Now, it is possible not only to compare public with private but also to compare private with private, and specific private with public. But given the limitations of standardized-test scores, administrators would do well to refrain from such comparisons.

The Administrator's Relationship to Assessment

Thus far, it has been argued that administrators should be concerned with assessment, but is such a presupposition valid? Given the numerous responsibilities of today's school administrators, is it reasonable to expect them to focus on assessment? Furthermore, does focusing on assessment have any appreciable effect on student achievement? In light of the current reality of school administration today and the research on administrator effectiveness, the answer to each of these questions is an unqualified yes.

The nature of school administration has changed profoundly in the past two decades. Administrators are no longer considered managers (Lezotte 1994). It is not enough for administrators merely to manage budgets, administer discipline, oversee building use and maintenance, and develop and maintain community relationships. They must also function as instructional leaders who are accountable for student achievement (Smith and Andrews 1989). Others argue that administrators should primarily focus on improving student learning (Knowles 2003; O'Donnell and White 2005).

Research has shown that administrators have a direct effect on student achievement. A survey of the literature on administrators as instructional leaders shows a continuing and sharpening focus on the behaviors of effective instructional leaders (Blase and Blase 1998; Sheppard 1996; Smith and Andrews 1989). These and other studies culminated in Kathleen Cotton's *Principals and Student Achievement* (2003), in which Cotton summarizes the research on successful principals and identifies twenty-five behaviors that foster student learning. Robert Marzano, Timothy Waters, and Brian McNulty (2005) pare the behaviors to twenty-one responsibilities of an effective school leader. It is this recent study that has the greatest significance for school administrators. While some studies indicate an indirect effect on student outcomes (Hallinger and Heck 1998), Marzano, Waters, and McNulty argue that there is a direct correlation between effective school leadership and student achievement. Using the research methodology known as meta-analysis, they demonstrate that administrators can have a profound effect on student learning. Of the twenty-one behaviors and skills listed in their study, the following three behaviors of educational leaders have a direct relation to assessment:

- The leader is "directly involved in the design and implementation of curriculum, instruction, and assessment practices."
- The leader is "knowledgeable about current curriculum, instruction, and assessment practices."
- The leader "monitors the effectiveness of school practices and their impact on student learning." (2005, 42–43)

The implications of this research are numerous and significant, but the following four bear exploring here because they directly affect the school administrator.

1. Not only are administrators responsible for student achievement, but they are also able to improve it. This statement means that administrators not only must examine their leadership as it relates to assessment and reflect on ways to improve it but must also keep abreast of the latest instructional strategies and the most effective ways to measure student learning.

2. Administrators must develop and articulate a philosophy of sound assessment practice. They need to set the vision for overall school achievement.
3. Administrators must look at a variety of assessments and the resulting data so that they have an accurate understanding of student achievement. So administrators need to be as interested, if not more so, in the types of assessments that occur in the classroom as they typically are in the standardized-test reports they receive each year.
4. Administrators must supervise both teacher instruction and teacher assessment of student learning, as well as the effect that those assessments will have on future instruction.

Definition and Practice Grounded in Biblical Principles

Definitions of *assessment* abound, but all emphasize a few key points: assessment includes tools and processes (Taylor and Nolen 2005), involves collection and interpretation (Airasian 2005; Banks 2005; McMillan 2004), and aids instructional decision making (Airasian 2005; McMillan 2004; Taylor and Nolen 2005). In light of this framework, assessment is the body of information used to interpret students' understanding and learning in order to make future instructional decisions. It is distinguished from evaluation, the process of making informed value judgments about student performance or teacher decisions (Airasian 2005). The distinction between the two is important. Assessment precedes evaluation and serves as the basis of informed and meaningful value judgments.

A simple definition of *assessment*, however, is not enough. Christian educators must base that definition on biblical principles—specifically grace, the image of God, and sin.

Grace

Grace, the unmerited favor of God toward His people, is the defining doctrine of the Christian faith, and it affects every area of the Christian life. It is grace that restores sinners to a right relationship with God (Ephesians 2:8). It is grace that accomplishes sanctification by teaching Christians to live godly lives (Titus 2:11–12), by supplying strength in weakness (2 Corinthians 12:9), and by providing an escape from temptation (Hebrews 4:15–16). Grace also characterizes how Christians should live. It should season conversation (Colossians 4:6), temper grievances

(Matthew 18:21–35), and inform personal conduct (2 Timothy 2:1).

Since grace is such an all-pervasive Christian doctrine, it should be no surprise that it must alter the understanding and application of assessment in the classroom as well. This claim does not mean that assessments lose all sense of rigor and accountability as every student is given unmerited evaluations. Good assessments must be measured against consistent and fair standards. To argue that grace removes standards or makes them meaningless is to misunderstand the concept. Grace is given by God because humans fall short of His standard. Grace does not preclude standards; it presupposes them. Ethically, teachers must strive to be objective by constructing and administering valid (accurate measurement upon which unbiased and appropriate decisions can be made) and reliable (consistent measurement over varied time and place) assessments because without such measurement standards, assessments are meaningless. At the same time, to exclude grace from the assessment process is to ignore the complexities of learning and the needs of individual students.

What is needed is a balanced approach, one that is fair yet gracious. Such an assessment system is informative rather than punitive and comparative. It is not used to identify shortcomings so that students may be punished, nor is it focused on what students do not know or on how much they know compared with their peers. Rather, it is focused on what students have gained and what needs to change in instruction so that students may continue in their growth in a subject. Furthermore, failure in students is a place from which teachers encourage them to try again in a supportive environment (Graham 2003). Assessment correctly understood and implemented has the best interests of the students in mind.

The Image of God

The assessment process involves teachers and students who are made in the image of God. The significance of this truth should not be passed over lightly. The image of God is not just a value judgment attributing dignity and worth to each person, though it certainly does confer both. It is also substantive and functional, meaning that image bearers have essential God-like qualities that enable them to act in specific ways. Following this line of thought, Graham (2003) identifies eleven attributes that are a result of being created in the image of God. While all would contribute to elucidating some aspect of assessment, three are of special significance: the ability to exercise dominion, the ability to think, and the ability to create. Exercising dominion is demonstrated in the human role of steward, which is addressed specifically in Genesis 1. Immediately after creating both man and woman, God placed them as stewards over His creation (Genesis 1:27–30). As stewards, they were to be caretakers as well as rulers who bring about order and meaning in the world. The second and third attributes, rationality and creativity, are manifested as humans bring the world under dominion through the ingenuity of technological advances and the development of culture.

All three attributes must shape the Christian's view of assessment. Students are not repositories of knowledge that merely regurgitate information; rather, they are active learners who desire not only to understand what is already known but also to use that knowledge to make meaning of the world. It is important to create meaningful, challenging, and relevant learning environments and assessments in order to give students opportunities to demonstrate these qualities in their learning (Graham 2003). This also means that students must be allowed to participate in the assessment process. These attributes also have significance for teachers, who are capable of and responsible for creating these significant and relevant assessments. No longer will worksheets, textbook unit tests, or curriculum guides be considered sufficient to guide teaching and learning in the classroom.

Sin

Because of the Fall, these attributes and human nature have been marred by sin; God's image in humans has been distorted and twisted (Romans 1:18–32). The theological term for this human condition is *total depravity*. A correct understanding of this term is in order because it is often interpreted to mean that humans are as sinful as they can be, are incapable of anything good, or engage in every conceivable sin (Erickson 1985). Such a definition is itself a distortion. Total depravity means that all aspects of human nature are affected by sin, and nothing can be done to earn God's favor. The implication is not that sin has completely destroyed human nature or replaced it with an entirely new nature; rather, sin turns humans from their original purpose and perverts their actions.

The teacher must take into account that students struggle and make errors. Since no student is perfect and the Bible does not establish a norm for student achievement, the teacher must account for varied abilities by differentiating learning to meet each student's needs. Furthermore, teachers must reconcile how their own fallibility affects student achievement. Student errors do not all result from student inability; some are the result of poor teaching. Finally, teachers need to be aware of personal bias—intentional or unintentional—and guard against it.

Informed by this definition and these biblical principles, administrators should direct their own and teachers' attention to four key areas: content standards, preassessment, assessment methods, and assessment tools.

Content Standards

In order for teachers to infuse grace into the assessment process, they must first adopt standards that allow them to be fair and ethical in their assessments while holding students accountable. As stated earlier, grace presupposes standards. Adopting standards can be a daunting endeavor; however, because of recent educational-reform efforts, there are several natural places to begin. A number of national subject-area organizations have established content standards for their subjects. For example, the National Council for the Social Studies (1994) identifies ten thematic strands (e.g., culture; time, continuity, and change; global perspectives) and offers standards and performance expectations for elementary, middle school, and high school students. The standards are comprehensive, and they span all the cognitive domains. The states are another source for content standards. Since George H. W. Bush's national Education Summit in 1989, the states have created academic content standards for each grade level. Oregon has a highly developed system that identifies content standards, skill proficiencies, and benchmarks for each grade level. Oregon's third-grade reading standards, for example, identify specific content and skills that students are expected to meet: decoding and word recognition, vocabulary, and reading to perform a task.

Simply adopting these standards wholesale is not enough. Standards must be tempered by a gracious application of them. Not only is it important that the standards appropriately represent the content; they must also be achievable. Rigorous standards for the sake of rigor ignore student needs. It may be more appropriate to lower the standards for the sake of the students, then slowly raise the standards so that students are able to achieve them. Another reason why educators should not blindly adopt standards is the standards themselves. Researchers have shown that standards often suffer from lack of specificity (Marzano 2000). In these instances, the standards do not provide information that can help teachers create meaningful and relevant assessments. Administrators should also refrain from rushing to achieve a standards-based curriculum system by looking for easy solutions. Mark O'Shea identifies three common shortcuts and warns against using them when adopting a standards-based assessment model:

- "aligning curriculum with the standards"
- "adopting standards-aligned curriculum materials"
- "offering professional development programs" (2005, 16–18)

The problem with each of these shortcuts is that they are superficial, and they do not lead to school and faculty ownership of the standards.

Instead, administrators should follow a two-step process. First, they should act as instructional leaders and bring faculty members together to determine the expected standards for their particular school. To facilitate this process, educators should use Catherine Taylor and Susan Nolen's four framing questions for identifying learning goals to guide faculty through this process:

1. "What are the major dimensions of each *subject area?*"
2. "Which aspects of these subject area dimensions are the *most important* for students to learn in *this* term or *this* year, and at what level of sophistication?"
3. "What knowledge and skills within the *discipline(s)* will help students understand *how people work* in the discipline, *what people know* that helps them be successful in this discipline, and *how people think* in the discipline?"
4. "What work do adults do (within the discipline and in daily life) that show[s] they have met these larger goals?" (2005, 30; emphasis in original)

As faculty members meet to answer these questions, they will begin to form a body of standards that are school specific and, hence, will take ownership of the process.

The second step is to ensure that the standards are linked to curriculum and assessment. O'Shea's (2005) Standards Achievement Planning Cycle (SAPC) is an excellent protocol for doing this. Rather than attempting to do this globally so that the curriculum for an entire grade level is done, it is suggested that administrators bring small teams of grade-level-specific teachers together to work on specific lessons. In situations that prevent grade-level-specific teams, multiple-grade-level teams can be just as effective. The protocol consists of a five-step process:

1. Identify standards
2. Analyze standards
3. Describe student performances
4. Select learning activities
5. Evaluate students' work

To begin, teachers identify and analyze the standards for a specific lesson. This step focuses the teachers on key content and skills that students must learn. Next, teachers use the standards to write descriptions of student performances; these descriptions will guide the instruction and assessment of the material. The next step is to turn to the teacher guides, textbooks, activities, and other resources and evaluate the usefulness of these resources in helping students meet the standards. This process may make some teachers uncomfortable because portions of the textbook may not be taught; but it is important that faculty members know that meeting the standards, and not covering the material, is the goal. At this point, teachers have the outline of a standards-based lesson plan. After teaching the lesson, teachers meet again to evaluate the students' work. This step is crucial because it forces teachers to reflect on their instruction and examine whether students succeeded in meeting the standards. Teachers should also use this time to reexamine the entire process and improve their lessons (O'Shea 2005).

Admittedly, this is a time-intensive process; therefore, it may be tempting for administrators to skip the step, adopt already-existing standards, and have teachers incorporate those standards into their lessons. The problem with this strategy is that teachers are not forced to make the standards the basis of their instruction and assessment. A practical solution is to have the teams go through the whole process for one assessment once a quarter. As the faculty members become familiar with the standards, they should be expected to complete the process independently. When administrators review lesson plans, they should check to see that the standards determine the instruction and assessment. Furthermore, administrators should make questions about the protocol a standard part of their yearly faculty evaluations. An additional benefit is that the process can serve as an excellent way of orienting new teachers to the school's curriculum standards and the assessment process.

Preassessment

It is not enough merely to integrate standards into the school's curriculum and teach to those standards; teachers must also have an accurate understanding of students' current knowledge and ability. There is a practical advantage to such preassessments. Rather than determine student understanding on the basis of the teacher's knowledge and experience in working with students, the teacher can use preassessments to gauge present student ability and to plan future instruction (Taylor and Nolen 2005). Preassessments also acknowledge that students bring a wealth of knowledge to classroom learning. This approach is consistent with the biblical view of the student as an image bearer who has the capacity to learn and who has been actively engaged in the learning process. By not basing instruction on assumptions about student learning and by not reteaching learned concepts, teachers honor the God-given abilities of their students.

There are a number of ways teachers can conduct preassessments:

1. *Review the school's scope and sequence.* Since the previous teacher may not have followed the scope and sequence, such a review may not be the most accurate preassessment, but it does help teachers get an overview of what the students were probably taught the previous year. It also helps the teacher make connections between last year's instruction and this year's curriculum. If a scope and sequence does not exist, one must be designed and implemented as soon as possible.

2. *Examine student files.* While the previous year's performances do not necessarily determine current performance, reading a student's file does allow teachers to identify patterns and anomalies, and this information can be useful for the teacher.

3. *Evaluate standardized-test scores.* Like student files, standardized-test scores should not be used as determinative assessments of student ability; however, they can reveal patterns and anomalies that can be useful for the teacher to know.

4. *Initiate discussions with students.* Interviewing students, individually and as a class, about their interests, abilities, and learning can provide valuable information and can place the above three preassessments in meaningful contexts.

5. *Contact parents.* Teachers can send home a parent-friendly copy of the grade-level or subject-area standards and ask parents to identify

strengths and weaknesses of their children. While some parents may not feel qualified to respond, it is a useful means of educating parents about the curriculum.

6. *Use group activities and written assessments.* Although the above five preassessments are usually done at the beginning of the year, teachers should give written preassessments for each new unit. The teacher should use the information gleaned from these to make future instructional decisions.

While preassessment is primarily a teacher responsibility, administrators can play an important role in ensuring that it is done. At the very least, administrators should encourage their faculty to use these and other means of preassessment. However, just encouraging teachers to do preassessment is not enough. Administrators must support this process by providing additional teacher preparation time or release time so that teachers can create and review preassessments.

Assessment Methods

The assessment principles discussed above can revolutionize assessment practices. As these principles are followed, classroom assignments will no longer be student activities that simply keep students busy or that merely supply scores for the grade book; instead, student activities will be seen as opportunities for measuring specific abilities and student understanding. Assessment methods will provide meaningful engagement with the content as teachers no longer rely on "drill and kill" tactics, in which students generate volumes of paperwork derived from workbooks and photocopied teacher guides. Teachers will also be skeptical of traditional test items derived from test banks or textbook publishers. Finally, since students will be seen as rational and creative beings, teachers will give students opportunities to demonstrate understanding in a variety of ways. But because students are fallible and susceptible to outside influences, the teacher must use a variety of assessment methods in evaluating student achievement.

For many administrators the work done in classrooms may look quite different compared with the classroom work they did as children (Stiggins 2001). Even though teachers may use worksheets and tests to guide instruction and decision making, other forms of assessment will also be prevalent. Performance-based or authentic assessments provide opportunities to demonstrate learning holistically as students engage in worth-while and meaningful tasks that represent work done in specific fields (Wiggins 1990). Such assessments require students to apply a number of skills and abilities to real situations. Performances can include essays, speeches, science labs, and other projects that students do in the class-room. Teachers can increase the authenticity of the assessment by having students perform tasks that experts in the field evaluate, or by having audiences for the assessment that reach beyond the classroom. For exam-ple, students can write letters to editors, with the goal of having the letters printed in the local paper; write stories for younger students; or complete a scientific study of contaminated local waterways and present the findings to the city council.

Merely incorporating such performances into the classroom, however, does not necessarily make them performance assessments (Taylor and Nolen 2005). For a task to be a performance assessment, the following four criteria must be met (Airasian 2005, 238):

1. "Have a clear purpose that identifies the decision to be made from the performance assessment."
2. "Identify observable aspects of the pupil's performance or product that can be judged."
3. "Provide an appropriate setting for eliciting and judging the per-formance or product."
4. "Provide a judgment or score to describe performance."

Besides performances, portfolios—collections of student work—pro-vide another means of evaluation. In recent years, there has been an increase in the variety of portfolios. Charlotte Danielson and Leslye Abrutyn (1997) have identified three types of portfolios:

1. In a working portfolio, the student manages a collection of work that is in progress. From this portfolio, students select work they wish to include in the next two types of portfolios. Working port-folios are usually content specific, so a student may have a number of these.
2. In a showcase portfolio, a collection of work demonstrates the stu-dent's best work. While this portfolio is typically focused on work assigned in school, it may include some student-initiated work.
3. An assessment portfolio, sometimes referred to as a growth port-folio, allows the student to document learning. Contents often include reflective essays in which students analyze and assess their

work by identifying strengths and weaknesses in comparison with predetermined standards.

Teachers who use performance assessments will want to use portfolios to provide a holistic picture of student achievement and to include students in the assessment process, thus allowing students take ownership of their own learning.

Administrators can play a vital role in making sure that students are given opportunities to engage in performance-based assessments. Administrators can provide areas and venues for students to display their products or perform their work. Administrators can also invite community leaders and members to be observers or evaluators of these assessments. They should also consider providing teachers with release time so that the teachers can evaluate student portfolios effectively.

Assessment Tools

As a school adopts standards and incorporates assessments that measure student learning, teachers are going to need tools that allow them to make meaningful evaluations and gather useful feedback. One effective tool is a scoring rubric—an assessment tool that identifies specific criteria and explains the levels of quality for each criterion (Andrade 2005). Rubrics are an essential part of the instructional and assessment process. When constructing rubrics, teachers are forced to think—before instruction begins—about the products that students will create.

There are several reasons why administrators should require their teachers to use rubrics. The transparency of a rubric contributes to an ethical assessment process. The students know up front what is expected of them. They are aware of the standards, and they know how the teacher will assess them. Rubrics also help teachers be consistent and fair in evaluation. This statement does not mean that the rubrics are totally bias free or objective. Teachers need to be aware that as fallen beings they are susceptible to bias-based judgments. However, the rubric can help minimize that bias. Teachers can also use rubrics to invite students into the assessment process. Not only can students participate in the creation of the rubrics, but they can also use them as they assess their own and one another's work. Because human beings are rational beings who are created to exercise dominion over what they know, this use of rubrics should not seem like a novel or innovative idea, but rather the natural outgrowth of a biblically informed understanding of people. Finally, the use of rubrics still allows teachers to exercise grace in their interaction with students. Students are and should be held to high academic standards and expectations, but as teachers detect weaknesses in their instruction or shortcomings in their students, they should account for those findings in their assessments.

Rubrics also aid teachers in providing specific and meaningful feedback to students. Research has shown that such feedback positively affects student learning (Black and Wiliam 1998). By using rubrics, teachers are able to identify and isolate specific tasks, abilities, and knowledge; give students recognition for meeting or exceeding expectations; and provide instructive feedback on areas that need improvement. A rubric's usefulness in identifying student weaknesses is a significant benefit. Often, summative scores or grades hide the real problems that students encounter on a given assessment. When areas of weakness are identified, teachers should then reflect on and analyze what is causing the problem in order to prescribe solutions.

Creating rubrics takes time to master. Because of their popularity, it is easy to find examples that can serve as templates and models. However, administrators should be wary of teachers shortcutting the process and uncritically adopting rubrics found in resource packets or on the Web. Rubrics are meaningful and useful only when they are an integral part of the *instructional planning process.* In addition to providing planning time (a practice that has been a theme throughout this chapter), administrators can support teachers' application of rubrics by making rubric construction part of the professional development of their faculty members. The Web also provides many training resources. One site that is of particular help is RubiStar—http://rubistar.4teachers.org/index.php. This site offers instruction on how to create a rubric and has a program that helps teachers create rubrics.

Now What? Application to Practice

ADMINISTRATORS NEED to understand that they play a crucial role in student learning. They cannot abdicate this role and let teachers be solely responsible. As Marzano, Waters, and McNulty (2005) have demonstrated, administrators can make a positive impact on student achievement. Administrators can contribute by giving teachers more time to plan and collaborate so that good assessment practices truly take hold, and by requiring teachers to use assessment to plan future instruction.

Administrators should also examine other ways to use good assessment practices to improve the quality of education in their schools. One area that Christian teachers need to address is the assessment of students' spiritual lives. A possible direction this assessment could take is the use of performance-based assessment, corresponding rubrics, and portfolios to document growth. A final area that bears exploration is the application of the assessment principles delineated here to teacher evaluations. Administrators can model good assessment practices for their teachers. They should collaboratively determine the standards for effective teachers, create rubrics that match these standards, and use the rubrics to assess classroom teachers and provide meaningful and specific feedback so that teachers can improve their practices and identify areas for future professional development.

References

Airasian, Peter W. 2005. *Classroom assessment: Concepts and applications.* 5th ed. Boston: McGraw-Hill.

Andrade, Heidi Goodrich. 2005. Teaching with rubrics: The good, the bad, and the ugly. *College Teaching* 53, no. 1:27–30. Proquest document ID 761703241.

Banks, Steven R. 2005. *Classroom assessment: Issues and practices.* Boston: Allyn and Bacon.

Black, Paul, and Dylan Wiliam. 1998. Inside the black box: Raising standards through classroom assessment. *Phi Delta Kappan* 80, no. 2:139–48.

Blase, Jo, and Joseph Blase. 1998. *Handbook of instructional leadership: How really good principals promote teaching and learning.* Thousand Oaks, CA: Corwin Press.

Cotton, Kathleen. 2003. *Principals and student achievement: What the research says.* Alexandria, VA: Association for Supervision and Curriculum Development.

Danielson, Charlotte, and Leslye Abrutyn. 1997. *An introduction to using portfolios in the classroom.* Alexandria, VA: Association for Supervision and Curriculum Development.

Erickson, Millard J. 1985. *Christian theology.* Grand Rapids, MI: Baker.

Graham, Donovan L. 2003. *Teaching redemptively: Bringing grace and truth into your classroom.* Colorado Springs, CO: Purposeful Design Publications.

Hallinger, Philip, and Ronald H. Heck. 1998. Exploring the principal's contribution to school effectiveness: 1980–1995. *School Effectiveness and School Improvement* 9, no. 2:157–91.

Knowles, Timothy. 2003. The academic imperative: New challenges and expectations facing school leaders. In *A nation reformed? American education 20 years after A Nation at Risk,* ed. David T. Gordon, 39–52. Cambridge, MA: Harvard Education Press.

Lezotte, Lawrence. 1994. The nexus of instructional leadership and effective schools. *The School Administrator* 51, no. 6:20–23.

Marzano, Robert J. 2000. *Transforming classroom grading.* Alexandria, VA: Association for Supervision and Curriculum Development.

Marzano, Robert J., Timothy Waters, and Brian A. McNulty. 2005. *School leadership that works: From research to results.* Alexandria, VA: Association for Supervision and Curriculum Development.

McMillan, James H. 2004. *Classroom assessment: Principles and practice for effective instruction.* 3rd ed. Boston: Allyn and Bacon.

National Council for the Social Studies. 1994. Expectations of Excellence: Curriculum standards for social studies. www.ncss.org/standards.

O'Donnell, Robert J., and George P. White. 2005. Within the accountability era: Principals' instructional leadership behaviors and student achievement. *NASSP Bulletin* 89, no. 645.

Oregon Department of Education. n.d. Available from www.ode.state.or.us.

O'Shea, Mark R. 2005. *From standards to success: A guide for school leaders.* Alexandria, VA: Association for Supervision and Curriculum Development.

Perie, M., A. Vanneman, and A. Goldstein. 2005. *Student achievement in private schools: Results from NAEP 2000–2005.* No. NCES 2006–459. Washington, DC: U. S. Department of Education, National Center for Education Statistics.

Popham, W. James. 1999. Why standardized tests don't measure educational quality. *Educational Leadership* 56, no. 6:8–15.

———. 2001. *The truth about testing: An educator's call to action.* Alexandria, VA: Association for Supervision and Curriculum Development.

RubiStar. n.d. Creating rubrics for your project-based learning activities. http://rubistar.4Teachers .org/index.php.

Sheppard, B. 1996. Exploring the transformational nature of instructional leadership. *Alberta Journal of Educational Research* 42, no. 4:325–44.

Smith, Wilma F., and Richard L. Andrews. 1989. *Instructional leadership: How principals make a difference.* Alexandria, VA: Association for Supervision and Curriculum Development.

Stiggins, Richard J. 2001. The principal's leadership role in assessment. *NASSP Bulletin* 85, no. 621:13–26.

Taylor, Catherine S., and Susan Bobbitt Nolen. 2005. *Classroom assessment: Supporting teaching and learning in real classrooms.* Upper Saddle River, NJ: Pearson Prentice Hall.

Wiggins, Grant. 1990. The case for authentic assessment. *Practical Assessment, Research and Evaluation.* http://PAREonline.net/getvn.asp?v=2&n=2.

CHAPTER 13

COMPASSIONATE DISCIPLINE

The Three Rs of Classroom Management

≈

By James L. Drexler

James L. Drexler is the chair of the education department and the dean of the master of education program at Covenant College. He earned his PhD in educational leadership at Saint Louis University and served for twenty-three years as a middle school and high school teacher, coach, and administrator in St. Louis.

CHAPTER 13

COMPASSIONATE DISCIPLINE

By James L. Drexler

School days, school days,
Dear old golden rule days,
Read-in' and 'rit-in' and 'rithmetic
Taught to the tune of the hick-ry stick,
You were my queen in calico
I was your bashful barefoot beau,
And you wrote on my slate
"I love you, so,"
When we were a couple of kids.

GUS EDWARDS AND Will Cobb collaborated in 1907 to produce the Broadway musical *School Days*, which ran for twenty years at the Circle Theatre. The above lyrics are from the culminating song of their show. A century later, one can appreciate the familiar tune, the joys of adolescent love, and the fond memories of schooling, even though the three Rs themselves are ironically misspelled and the suggested method of classroom management is open to criticism.

Theories of Classroom Management

The purpose of this chapter is to propose three Rs of effective classroom management. Within that framework, an overview of some of the major classroom-management strategies and theories is woven, sometimes for support for the thesis and sometimes for contrast. The goal is to provide a philosophical and biblical basis for classroom management that is rooted in grace, relationships, dignity, and authority.

The number of books and resources with theories, models, advice, and strategies related to classroom management are legion, and this chapter does not provide a comprehensive meta-analysis of this smorgasbord of choices. The following listing of just some of the book titles reveals the variety of both philosophical bases and practical approaches:

The Art of Classroom Management
Assertive Discipline
Authentic Classroom Management
Beyond Behaviorism
Beyond Discipline
Building Classroom Discipline
Classroom Management: A Proactive Approach
Classroom Management That Works
Cooperative Discipline
Discipline and Group Management in Classrooms
Discipline That Develops Self-Discipline
Discipline That Works
Discipline with Dignity
Discipline Without Tears
The Key Elements of Classroom Management
Positive Classroom Discipline
Principles of Classroom Management
Punished by Rewards
The Quality School: Managing Students Without Coercion
Smart Discipline for the Classroom
Teaching with Love and Logic

The three Rs of student behavior and discipline in the Christian school are similar to the three pillars of good health. First, the prudent person will take precautionary steps—regular exercise, yearly physical exams, weight control, adequate rest, and not smoking—in order to avoid serious medical problems. Second, when problems do occur, the person applies corrective procedures immediately—eyeglasses, surgery, hearing aids, medications, and change in habits—to make a bad condition better. Third, following the intervention and correction comes a period of rehabilitation and readjustment during which time things get back to normal.

In the same way, the Christian school practices *realistic prevention and support* with its students, with *rebuke, intervention, and correction* graciously administered as needed, but always within the context of the *repentance* of the offending students and their *restoration* to the broader community—the ultimate goals of biblical discipline.

Realistic Prevention and Support

The Bible teaches that parents have the primary responsibility for the nurture and training of their children. While this is true, at the same time several secondary institutions also exercise authority. For instance, the state has the responsibility—ordained by God—of promoting justice and punishing evildoers. The church has responsibility for children, as evidenced by the vows taken at a child's baptism or dedication. The church also shepherds children through catechism class and church membership. The school has secondary authority for children in its care. On the basis of English common law, and United States law since 1878, teachers and administrators legally stand in loco parentis—"in the place of a parent"—and therefore have responsibilities for discipline (*State ex rel. Burpee v. Burton*, 45 Wis. 150. 1878).

Parents willingly convey their authority to the teacher, but, as Louis Berkhof and Cornelius Van Til (1990, 112–15) note, the school is not simply an extension of the family. The school has original authority of its own as an independent social community to establish rules and policies as it sees fit. The implications of this authority for the teachers are several: the teacher is ruling in the name of God and should teach the students that principle; the teacher must act in conformity with the Bible; discipline should be motivated by love and justice; and teachers should rule with equity, justice, order, and firmness in order that the children learn obedience.

Children of God are still children of Adam, with Adam's will, pride, independence, and waywardness (Bridges 1981, 168). Preventive and supportive discipline realistically acknowledges this sinful nature. The discipline at this level is linked with instruction, a link that is a common feature of Scripture. Students learn—by both the spoken word and the deeds of the teacher—what Jack Fennema calls instruction that is "taught" (formal teaching) and "caught" (informal modeling) (2005, 207–8). The teacher's life is on display before the students, and, by God's grace, a good role model will go far in pointing the child to Christ. It is realistic prevention, however, because the reality of the fallen world means that the prevention and support will not prevent every problem.

Relationships among the staff

Relationships are critical to a whole range of activities in the Christian school: discipline, character education, teaching, advising, coaching, and counseling. Simply put, if students do not know the teacher as a person, and sense that administrators care about them as people, they will not care much about what is being taught.

Good relationships among the faculty and administration, what Roland Barth labels the undiscussed "elephant in the room" (2006, 9), must come first. When educators are "playing together"(11)—talking with each other about practice, sharing with one another concerning the craft of teaching, observing each other teach, and encouraging each other's success—relationships are strong and the school is healthy. By contrast, when relationships are rooted in fear, competition, suspicion, and criticism, the culture of the school is weak. The relative strength or weakness of the relationships among the staff is a good barometer in determining the overall strength or weakness of the relationships and culture in the school (9–11).

Too often, teachers work in isolation with the door closed and window covered. Or, perhaps worse, educators will circle the wagons and train their guns—on each other! The educational leader has a crucially important role to "foster consequential relationships" among the staff (13). Citing the work of Judith Warren Little, Barth exhorts leaders to clearly state expectations for relationships, model collegiality themselves, and reward and protect those who pursue collegial behaviors (13). As baseball manager Casey Stengel once quipped, "Getting good players is easy. Getting 'em to play together is the hard part" (11).

Relationships between students and staff

Rules without relationships lead to rebellion. The reactions to such a statement range from a positive affirmation of something that seems obvious from experience, to a negative and dismissive shake of the head.

The scriptural model endorses the concept that relationships are important. God delivered the Mosaic Law on Mt. Sinai only after He had sovereignly initiated a covenant relationship with the people of Israel. When Jesus preached the Beatitudes in the Sermon on the Mount, He was speaking to people who knew Him personally. The apostle Paul wrote many letters that are filled with rules, rebukes, and imperatives—but to people in churches that he personally helped to start. Additionally, common sense tells us that in other social contexts—family, the military, church, and work—the successful leader is the one who pursues meaningful relationships with the individuals in the group. It stands to reason, therefore, that if educational leaders and teachers are serious about effective classroom management, they must begin by developing strong relationships with students.

In the 2003 report from the Commission on Children at Risk, *Hardwired to Connect: The New Scientific Case for Authoritative Communities*, doctors, research scientists, youth professionals, and others argue that the best way to attack the current crises in childhood—including depression, anxiety, and various emotional, behavioral, and mental disorders—is to create close connections for children with other people and with the moral and spiritual meanings of life. The report argues that humans are "hardwired for meaning, born with a built-in capacity and drive to search for purpose and reflect on life's ultimate ends" (Institute for American Values 2003, 14). Citing the power of relationships to form authoritative communities, the authors state, "In sum, our sense of right and wrong originates largely from our biologically primed need to connect with others. In this sense, moral behavior—good actions—stem at least as much from relationships as from rules" (26). An indispensable key, therefore, for successful classroom management is genuine and loving relationships throughout the school.

Fallen image bearers

All students, teachers, and administrators have two fundamental characteristics that must be kept in proper balance: each person is a unique creation of God who bears the title "image of God," and each person is a fallen, weak, finite sinner who is born in sin—and proves that fact every day! To tip the balance in one direction or the other produces an unrealistic and unbiblical view of human beings and philosophically imbalanced approaches to classroom management. Educational leaders must recognize and appreciate the dignity and uniqueness of each child, maintain a clearheaded view of the realities of sin, and proclaim the promises of redemption in Jesus Christ.

Progressive educators such as John Dewey write frequently of educating the "whole child," an emphasis that tends to celebrate the uniqueness, creativity, and worth of each student. Christians can certainly applaud this stance as far as it goes. But progressive educators often ignore the other side of the ledger: the sinfulness and rebellion of the child. More modern educational theorists such as Elliot Eisner call for a renewed emphasis on holistic education that regards all parts of a child as "interconnected"—emotional, creative, social, and cognitive (2005, 18). Alfie Kohn also celebrates the whole child, and appeals for unconditional acceptance of each one, but again without a biblical understanding of the debilitating effects of the Fall. Kohn offers some provocative and helpful ideas—for example, he questions the common practice of removing a child from a classroom or from the school for misbehavior because such actions promote a conditional membership in the community that "creates an uneasy, uncertain, and ultimately unsafe climate" for children (2005, 22)—but does so without regard for the fallen state of all humans. Student-directed classroom management models such as those proposed by Kohn and others put too much authority and control into the hands of students.

Ironically, classroom management experts such as Lee and Marlene Canter (1992), Fredric Jones (1987) and James Cangelosi (1984), who emphasize control and more teacher-directed theories of classroom management—some of the same ones Alfie Kohn critiques—seem to tip the balance too far in the direction of the fallen nature of children, expecting the worst from students. Advocates of control, those who favor the "systems" approach of classroom management, stress rules and regulations, threats of punishment, and other such methods to coerce and manipulate students into external compliance with expected norms. "Teachers in these classrooms think that the students will take a mile when given an inch and will abuse any freedom and responsibility the teacher gives them. Teachers assume that the students will be disruptive and perhaps destructive. The teacher's job is to control" (Graham 2003, 260). However, classroom management is not a system or program, but a personal relationship built on clear expectations, respect, trust, rebuke, consequences, mercy, grace, and forgiveness. To recognize that students are redeemable image bearers is the best way to love the whole child.

The liberating power of directions, training, and procedures

Even though many may not verbalize it, students want to know what the teacher and the school expect and why. "The seminal research of the 1980s … points to the importance of establishing rules and procedures for general classroom behavior, group work, seat work, transitions and interruptions, use of materials and equipment, and beginning and ending the period or the day" (Marzano and Marzano 2003, 7). Harry and Rosemary Wong emphasize that rules and procedures have to do with managing a classroom, a task that is distinct from disciplining a classroom. The key, these authors argue, is to have clear plans and procedures in place before the school year begins. "Effective teachers spend a good deal of time during the first weeks of school introducing, teaching, modeling, and rehearsing procedures…. Behaviors must be taught, modeled, practiced, monitored, and retaught" (2001, 175).

In addition to providing clear expectations and procedures for routine behaviors and attitudes, it is important to define the mission statement and learning goals for the school. Flowing from these documents are the overall educational objectives for both the school and the various academic departments and programs. From there, individual classroom teachers develop the curriculum for each course, all of which must be created with these goals, objectives, and standards in mind. In order to ensure this conformity, teachers must then develop clear grading rubrics for students. Not only do rubrics guarantee that the classroom instruction is fulfilling the goals for that course, but they also are the best way for students to know how and why they will be evaluated. With all these elements in place, teachers will be in the strongest position to make the best use of each school day. Research consistently demonstrates that when teachers are prepared, when plans and procedures are in place, when teachers are on time and meet deadlines, when relationships are valued, when teachers are fair and flexible, and when faculty and administration take a personal interest in the success of each student, discipline problems are minimized and effective schooling takes place.

> This implies that almost everything a teacher says and does, including the way she stands about when doing nothing, can potentially reveal something that will heighten or diminish an observer's impression of her trustworthiness….
>
> Or picture the high school teacher who stands by his classroom door at the beginning of each period, ushers in the near latecomers, closes

the door promptly at the sound of the bell, and then immediately strides to the center of the room, calling for attention as he launches into the day's lesson.... The abruptness of the teacher's movements conveys a sense of the importance of what is about to take place in that room.... They say that here is a teacher who cares about what he is doing. Here is someone who doesn't have a moment to lose. (Jackson, Boostrom, and Hansen 1993, 34–37)

Love and logic

One promising approach to classroom management and schoolwide discipline is described by Jim Fay and David Funk in *Teaching with Love and Logic: Taking Control of the Classroom* (1995). Schools that have adopted this approach report a sharp decline in discipline incidents along with less of the tension, frustration, and loss of time that are often associated with student discipline. The approach is straightforward, emphasizing three basic rules: (1) use enforceable limits, (2) provide choices within limits, and (3) apply consequences with empathy (26). The authors argue that their approach reduces student misbehaviors, increases students' self-concept, and improves student achievement.

This approach is rooted in strong and positive student-teacher relationships of affirmation and support. Fay and Funk advise teachers to set limits within a framework of compassion and understanding while encouraging them to stay calm and resist the temptation to use strong-arm tactics when students misbehave. By treating students with respect and dignity, they argue, power struggles can be avoided and students can learn to be responsible and accountable. When teachers respond with empathy instead of anger, and offer choices instead of direct consequences, students accept responsibility more readily and experience the effects of their actions. Some "choice" statements—such as the following—reveal that both options actually lead to better classroom control, student responsibility, and teacher control (25–54):

- Would you rather sit and read, or work on your project?
- What would be best for you, to play kickball or watch the others?
- You can play either in the block area or in the home living area. Which do you choose?
- Would you rather play by the rules, or learn about the game by watching the others play?
- Feel free to sit in the chair beside me or remain quiet in your seat.

The love-and-logic method advocates a "principles approach" as opposed to a "systems approach" to discipline. A systems approach is based on specific punishments for specific offenses that are applied equally to all, whereas a principles approach prescribes discipline based on a set of principles that adhere to a predetermined set of values. The principles approach allows for individualization, circumstances, and flexibility while still treating all students fairly. Fay and Funk's model is similar to other collaborative theories such as Richard Curwin and Allen Mendler's (1999) and William Glasser's (1992), in which teachers and students work together out of mutual respect and cooperation. The love-and-logic method is based on four pillars: (1) A student's self-concept needs to be maintained or enhanced, (2) control is shared between the teacher and the student, (3) consequences must be delivered with empathy and understanding, and (4) students need to be encouraged to think about the situation at least as much as the teacher does. To this end, delaying consequences is a way to bring more satisfying results (Fay and Funk 1995, 99–110).

Classroom management that is (1) rooted in realistic prevention and support, (2) characterized by loving and grace-filled relationships, (3) guided by a levelheaded understanding that all people are fallen yet redeemable image bearers, and (4) framed with clearly stated rules, procedures, goals, and standards offers the best formula to prevent many discipline problems so that teachers can be busy with the work of teaching and not policing.

Rebuke, Intervention, and Correction

Not all preventive discipline is successful, however. Educational leaders often refer to the "10 percent," a mythical statistic that suggests that most students abide by most of the rules most of the time. In reality, this statistic is probably more a euphemism than a fact, simply because all are sinners. If realistic preventive discipline is difficult because it requires consistency and dedication, then rebuke is difficult because it involves confrontation, and most educators tend to avoid confrontation whenever possible.

The lost art of confrontation

Donald Guthrie warns, "A *father* who neglects to discipline a *son* is deficient in his capacity as father, and a son who escapes all discipline is losing out on his sonship" (1983, 253; emphasis in original). The absence of corrective discipline is a negative reflection on all involved.

Godly confrontation is rapidly becoming a lost art. This situation is a real travesty for the church and the school. Most Christians are familiar with the Matthew 18 principle, but how many actually confront the brother who sins in order to win him over for the Lord? Many get angry, resort to yelling, or quietly hold grudges, but how many go privately to someone as that person's champion and not a critic, out of a spirit of love and mercy, not revenge or control? Many like to "tell it to the church" by gossiping about a person, and sadly, faculty lounges are notorious in this regard. Loving and gracious rebuke is difficult to deliver and receive—that is why it is an art—but the blessings that will come for the individuals and the community who practice godly rebuke are significant.

Psalm 141:5 declares, "Let a righteous man strike me—it is a kindness; let him rebuke me—it is oil on my head. My head will not refuse it." In commenting on this psalm, John Calvin notes that David was declaring "that he would much rather be awakened to his duty by the severe rod of reproof, than be seduced through pleasing falsehoods" (1981b, 238). If there is a lost art of merciful confrontation, there is an equal overabundance of glad-handing and flattery, and both are dangerous. Schools need educational leaders who, motivated by love, are willing to confront students and teachers when sin is present, and to humbly receive a rebuke when necessary.

It is the hope, of course, that realistic preventive discipline will solve most problems: "The great secret is, to establish authority in the dawn of life; to bend the tender twig, before the knotty oak is beyond our power" (Bridges 1981, 169). Obviously, the key years occur before the child is old enough for school, but the church and the school also play critical roles. If preventive discipline is effective, the need for corrective discipline will be lessened. "Our heavenly Father never stirs the rod with his children, if his gentle voice of instruction prevail" (430).

Natural and imposed consequences

When misbehavior and noncompliance occur, the classroom teacher has several options. First, in some situations there are natural consequences that ensue—for example, a student might waste time in study hall and then fail a math test (negative), or a student knows that he will be hurt if he gets into a fight, so he walks away (positive). Such consequences do not necessarily require further adult interventions.

Second, when consequences are needed, the wise teacher should begin first with nonverbal interventions such as (1) removal of the distraction, (2) eye contact that sends a message, (3) moving physically into closer proximity to the student, (4) prearranged signals, (5) planned ignoring of the problem, or (6) where appropriate, a hand on the shoulder or arm. Many times, these nonverbal cues will eliminate the problem so that no further interventions are needed.

Third, imposed consequences may be necessary. These consequences include a wide range of options such as these: (1) verbal reprimand, (2) sanctions and loss of privileges, (3) removal from the group or class, (4) after-school detentions, (5) office referrals, (6) student-parent meetings, and (7) redirection. Regarding all consequences, whether natural or imposed, teachers and administrators must always remember not to take things personally, not to act out of anger, and to keep in mind the ultimate purposes for discipline: self-discipline and self-management by the student.

Guidelines for biblical rebuke

When rebuke and correction are necessary, there are several guidelines to keep in mind. First, the teacher must remember the admonition of Ephesians 6:4 not to exasperate children. Correction is a medicine to be applied when necessary, not a daily food to force on children. As the body develops immunities to certain medications through frequent use, so children may learn to disobey and resist discipline and to harden their hearts, and the corrective value of the correction will be diminished.

Second, teachers and administrators should realize that each child is unique and each situation different. This is not an argument for situational ethics or relativism, but rather the acknowledgment that children respond in different ways: "Different tempers, like different soils, require corresponding difference of treatment. But discipline there must be; not relaxed in fondness, not pushed in harshness; but authority tempered in love. If a gentle hand cannot control, a stronger hand must be applied" (Bridges 1981).

Third, the teacher must enter into discipline, whether preventive or corrective, realistically. Discipline is often perceived negatively by both teacher and student. In practice, discipline is unpleasant: "No discipline seems pleasant at the time, but painful" (Hebrews 12:11a). In purpose, however, the goal of all discipline is positive: "Later on, however, it produces a harvest of righteousness and peace for those who have been trained by it" (Hebrews 12:11b). The key word in the first part of the verse is *seems*, in the second part, it is *trained*. Students need to learn the benefits of discipline even though it may seem unpleasant at the time. Christian teachers and administrators train by what is taught, but also by what is said and done—or not said or done.

Fourth, the biblical difference between correction and punishment is significant. Chastening and correction are not the same as punishment. As Jack Fennema notes, "Correction is *reformative*; punishment is *retributive*" (2005, 231; emphasis in original). He provides a helpful chart distinguishing the two words.

	Correction	Punishment
Purpose	Redirects towards acceptable and appropriate conduct; a means to an end	Inflicts a penalty for an offense; an end to itself
Focus	On future, acceptable conduct	On past, unacceptable conduct; also, on the child's person
Attitude	Reflects love and concern on the part of the teacher	Reflects hostility, frustration, and, at times, sadism
Resulting emotion in the child	Security	Fear, guilt, resentment, the possibility of rejection

Last, it is important to remember the role of trials and testing in the life of a Christian. While it is true that discipline is difficult, there are at the same time benefits in terms of personal growth. The goal of all correction is to change the heart and will, a positive objective in and of itself. But beyond that, it must be remembered that the Lord will use suffering and difficulties to teach. "God whispers to us in our pleasures, speaks in our conscience, but shouts in our pains: it is His megaphone to rouse a deaf world" (Lewis 1967, 93). In *The Blessing of a Skinned Knee*, Jewish clinical psychologist Wendy Mogel (2001) reinforces the potential value of setbacks and failures for children.

Freedom and accountability
The concept of freedom as it relates to discipline is important to consider. "Biblical freedom and discipline are naturally related such that one directly implies or is complementary to the other. Both concepts must operate harmoniously in biblical Christian schools" (Maffet 1987, 115).

Freedom does not mean the license to do whatever one wants. In fact, real freedom comes only as a product of submission. For students to learn to be responsible adults, they need the freedom to make decisions, even when those choices may bring negative consequences.

> Freedom is, however, much like a river that runs between two banks. One bank is license and anarchy; the other bank is legalism and exter- nalism. One must always function *between* these two extremes in order to remain free. Desiring license is giving in to hedonistic impulses. Desiring the security of legalism, having it all spelled out, is slavery of the opposite type. Conforming to the laws, mores, and expecta- tions of men causes abdication of one's responsibilities and the loss of one's freedom (Mark 2:23–3:5; 7:1–13). Both license and legalism are equally as damaging. (Fennema 1979, 99; emphasis in original)

As Greg Maffet explains, this freedom is necessary so that students can learn to internalize both freedom and discipline:

> The Spirit of God works in the hearts of regenerate students to incline them, by the grace of God, to will to do the will of God. This is internalized, God-conscious, biblical discipline as students exercise responsible freedom in accord with the covenant God has established with them. It is not to be fear or terror, whereby students are forced to obey. Rather, we desire to develop an atmosphere where God's Spirit stimulates His covenant students to do rightly because they love Him in response to God first loving them. (1987, 118–19)

Students should be free to make choices, free to express emotions, free to discover ways to serve, and even free to make mistakes, reminded continually that it is only by God's grace that students and teachers are able to do what is right.

Freedom, of course, produces tension as well as risks. When students are allowed to make choices, they will inevitably make some wrong deci- sions. Pressure will come on the school for conformity, frequently for the less-than-biblical reasons of image and respectability. When students choose wisely, they need to be commended and encouraged. When they choose poorly, it is time for nurture, which includes chastening, and for guidance in the way they should go. Failure is a genuine, and even daily, reality. "Although student performance in the moral arena will often be substandard, we do not sacrifice students on the altar of our respectability. Instead, we nurture those who have made mistakes. We realize that competence in moral living, as in piano-playing or car repair (which are also a part of moral living), develops best when opportunities are plentiful and real, when advice is relevant and sincere, and when forgiveness and a new start are the rewards of grace" (Vryhof et al. 1989, 32).

Repentance and Restoration

The prayerful hope for all discipline is repentance followed by full restoration into the community. Calvin writes, "God, indeed, invites us, and even urges us by external means to repent; for what is the design of punishment, but to lead us to repentance?" (1981a, 100). Not all students will respond positively to discipline. In fact, one of the most unpleasant situations any administrator faces is to reach the point when a student must be asked to leave because of continuing discipline problems.

But the Bible also offers great encouragement to persevere: "Discipline your son, for in that there is hope" (Proverbs 19:18); "Discipline your son, and he will give you peace; he will bring delight to your soul" (Proverbs 29:17); "Moreover, we have all had human fathers who disciplined us and we respected them for it" (Hebrews 12:9). The prayer of every Christian school teacher should be that each student become "one who loves what is good, who is self-controlled, upright, holy and disciplined" (Titus 1:8). The positive potential for a school that is pursuing discipline with restoration in mind is limitless.

> The Christian school community stresses the restorative power of God's grace in individual lives and within the world community. In an age of cynicism and hopelessness, Christian school people focus on redemption, restoration, and "shalom"—as seen in history, as depicted in literature, as celebrated by the church. Because grace transcends the balance-sheet approach to life, cooperation comes before competition, service before self-interest. (Vryhof et al. 1989, 27)

When an administrator sits across the desk from a student who has been sent to the office, or when teachers confront misbehavior, they must always remember that the child will change his behavior and do what is right only by the grace of God working in his heart. Ultimately, the student cannot change his behavior any more than he can save himself. He needs God's grace to save him and to sanctify him. The apostle Paul proclaims this two-sided reality of grace: "For the *grace* of God that *brings salvation* has appeared to all men. It *teaches us* to say 'No' to ungodliness and worldly passions, and to live self-controlled, upright and godly lives in this present age" (Titus 2:11–12; emphasis added).

God's grace through Jesus Christ must be the generative center of discipline efforts. Although it may be tempting to try to manipulate students through guilt, fear, or intimidation, or to use some form of behavior modification to coerce them into correct behavior, ultimately these methods are doomed to fail. External conformity is one thing. A repentant and changed heart is quite another. Students, teachers, and administrators need God's grace, not guilt. All need God's mercy, not manipulation.

The strategy, then, in dealing with students is to focus on Jesus Christ and the need for complete dependence on Him. Jesus describes this daily living by grace and mercy in stark terms:

> Remain in me, and I will remain in you. No branch can bear fruit by itself; it must remain in the vine. Neither can you bear fruit unless you remain in me. I am the vine; you are the branches. If a man remains in me and I in him, he will bear much fruit; apart from me you can do nothing. (John 15:4–5)

The apostle John provides a magnificent glimpse of glory in describing the New Jerusalem: "Now the dwelling of God is with men, and he will live with them. They will be his people, and God himself will be with them and be their God. He will wipe away every tear from their eyes. There will be no more death or mourning or crying or pain, for the old order of things has passed away" (Revelation 21:3–4). When biblical discipline takes place in the Christian school, be it ever imperfect and finite, the community gets a taste of the glory to come, when God's redeemed and restored people will dwell together perfectly.

Now What? Application to Practice

THE FOLLOWING questions are designed to help the reader evaluate personal beliefs and school practices related to classroom management:

1. Are students categorized ("the bad third graders this year") such that

they are labeled for all future teachers? Is this unfair to the students? Does it allow for God's grace to change hearts?

2. Often, educational leaders will refer to "my faculty" or "the teachers who work for me." What signal does this type of language send in terms of relationships and community? Are teachers working for the principal, or are all working for the Lord? What impact does language have on the culture of the school?

3. How important is it for all the teachers in a school to use similar classroom-management models? What can an educational leader do to facilitate schoolwide management procedures and expectations?

4. Are there plans in place for restitution and reconciliation?

As a high school principal, this author developed "Keys for Successful Classroom Management" and introduced them each August with new teachers during the multiday orientation and induction program. Following is a slightly revised and abbreviated version:

1. Get off to a strong start. Be ready on the first day. Set the expectations high. Know where you are going and why.

2. Be specific. Students want to know what is expected and what the consequences are for failure, both for behavior and for academics.

3. Provide positive reinforcements. Catch them being good. Encourage them.

4. Be fixed and firm, but fair and flexible.

5. Remain calm. Do not yell; do not become angry; do not try to "win."

6. Communicate with students, with parents, and with colleagues.

7. Be consistent. Follow through on consequences. Treat students with equity. Do what you say you will do.

8. Seek help when you need it. You will need help at some time; find it when you do!

9. Be honest and open. Build strong, godly, and meaningful relationships. Students will not care what you know unless they know you care. Model saying, "I'm sorry."

10. Pray. Pray for wisdom, for strength, for tenacity, and especially for opportunities to demonstrate your love.

References

Barth, Roland S. 2006. Improving relationships within the schoolhouse. *Educational Leadership* 63, no. 6 (March): 9–13.

Berkhof, Louis, and Cornelius Van Til. 1990. *Foundations of Christian education: Addresses to Christian teachers*. Phillipsburg, NJ: Presbyterian and Reformed Publishing.

Bridges, Charles. 1981. *A Commentary on Proverbs*. Edinburgh, Scotland: Banner of Truth Trust.

Calvin, John. 1981a. *Commentaries on the prophet Jeremiah and the Lamentations*. Vol. 3 of *Calvin's Commentaries*. Trans. John Owen. Repr., Grand Rapids, MI: Baker Books.

———. 1981b. *Commentary on the book of Psalms*. Trans. James Anderson. Vol. 5 of *Calvin's Commentaries*. Repr., Grand Rapids, MI: Baker Books.

Cangelosi, James S. 1984. *Cooperation in the classroom*. Washington, DC: National Education Association of the United States.

Canter, Lee, and Marlene Canter. 1992. *Assertive discipline: Positive behavior management for today's classroom*. Rev. ed. Santa Monica, CA: Lee Canter and Associates.

Charles, C. M. 1999. *Building classroom discipline*. 6th ed. New York: Addison Wesley Longman.

Curwin, Richard L., and Allen N. Mendler. 1999. *Discipline with dignity*. Alexandria, VA: Association for Supervision and Curriculum Development.

Edwards, Clifford H. 2000. *Classroom discipline and management*. 3rd ed. New York: John Wiley and Sons.

Edwards, Gus, and Will Cobb. 1907. *School days*. http://www.niehs.nih.gov/kids/lyrics/schooldays.htm.

Eisner, Elliot. 2005. Back to whole. *Educational Leadership* 63, no. 1 (September): 14–18.

Fay, Jim, and David Funk. 1995. *Teaching with love and logic: Taking control of the classroom*. Golden, CO: Love and Logic Press.

Fennema, Jack. 1979. *Nurturing children in the Lord: A study guide for teachers on developing a biblical approach to discipline*. Repr., Grand Rapids, MI: Baker Books.

———. 2005. *The religious nature and biblical nurture of God's children: A guide for parents and teachers*. Sioux Center, IA: Dordt College Press.

Freiberg, H. Jerome, ed. 1999. *Beyond behaviorism: Changing the classroom management paradigm*. Needham Heights, MA: Allyn and Bacon.

Glasser, William. 1992. *The quality school*. 2nd, exp. ed. New York: HarperCollins.

Graham, Donovan L. 2003. *Teaching redemptively: Bringing grace and truth into your classroom*. Colorado Springs, CO: Purposeful Design Publications.

Guthrie, Donald. 1983. *The letter to the Hebrews: An introduction and commentary.* Grand Rapids, MI: Eerdmans.

Henley, Karyn. 2002. *Child-sensitive teaching: Helping children grow a living faith in a loving God.* Nashville, TN: Child Sensitive Communication.

Henley, Martin. 2006. *Classroom management: A proactive approach.* Upper Saddle River, NJ: Pearson Education.

Hunter, Madeline C. 1990. *Discipline that develops self-discipline.* Thousand Oaks, CA: Corwin Press.

Institute for American Values. 2003. *Hardwired to connect: The new scientific case for authoritative communities.* New York: Institute for American Values.

Jackson, Philip W., Robert E. Boostrom, and David T. Hansen. 1993. *The moral life of schools.* San Francisco: Jossey-Bass.

Jones, Fredric H. 1987. *Positive classroom discipline.* New York: McGraw-Hill.

Koenig, Larry. 2000. *Smart discipline for the classroom: Respect and cooperation restored.* 3rd ed. Thousand Oaks, CA: Corwin Press.

Kohn, Alfie. 1996. *Beyond discipline: From compliance to community.* Alexandria, VA: Association of Supervision and Curriculum Development.

———. 2005. Unconditional teaching. *Educational Leadership* 63, no. 1 (September): 20–24.

Larrivee, Barbara. 2005. *Authentic classroom management: Creating a learning community and building reflective practice.* 2nd ed. Boston, MA: Allyn and Bacon.

Levin, James, and James F. Nolan. 1999. *Principles of classroom management: A professional decision-making model.* 3rd ed. Boston, MA: Allyn and Bacon.

Lewis, C. S. 1967. *The problem of pain.* New York: Macmillan.

Maffet, Gregory J. 1987. *Biblical schools for covenant children.* Middleburg Heights, OH: Signal.

Marzano, Robert J. 2003. *Classroom management that works: Research-based strategies for every teacher.* With Jana S. Marzano and Debra J. Pickering. Alexandria, VA: Association for Supervision and Curriculum Development.

———. Barbara B. Gaddy, Maria C. Foseid, Mark P. Foseid, and Jana S. Marzano. 2005. *A handbook for classroom management that works.* Alexandria, VA: Association for Supervision and Curriculum Development.

Marzano, Robert J., and Jana S. Marzano. 2003. The key to classroom management. *Educational Leadership* 61, no. 1 (September): 6–18.

McEwan, Barbara. 2000. *The art of classroom management: Effective practices for building equitable learning communities.* Upper Saddle River, NJ: Prentice-Hall.

McLeod, Joyce, Jan Fisher, and Ginny Hoover. 2003. *The key elements of classroom management: Managing time and space, student behavior, and instructional strategies.* Alexandria, VA: Association for Supervision and Curriculum Development.

Mogel, Wendy. 2001. *The blessing of a skinned knee: Using Jewish teachings to raise self-reliant children.* New York: Penguin Compass.

Moorish, Ronald G. 2003. *With all due respect: Keys for building effective school discipline.* Colorado Springs, CO: Purposeful Design Publications.

Vryhof, Steven, Joel Brouwer, Stefan Ulstein, and Daniel Vander Ark. 1989. *12 affirmations: Reformed Christian schooling for the 21st century.* Grand Rapids, MI: Baker Books.

Wong, Harry K., and Rosemary T. Wong. 2001. *The first days of school: How to be an effective teacher.* Mountain View, CA: Harry K. Wong Publications.

CHAPTER 14

NEW DIRECTIONS

Changing School Culture Effectively

৵

By David L. Roth
and Jon Keith

David L. Roth, EdD, served for seventeen years as the headmaster of Wheaton Academy in Wheaton, Illinois. Currently, he is the headmaster emeritus and chief education officer of the Wheaton Academy Institute, and his initiative is to extend the values, principles, objectives, and mission of Wheaton Academy into a virtual campus environment.

Jon Keith, MBA, CAS, is the principal and chief operating officer of Wheaton Academy in Wheaton, Illinois, where he has served for the past twenty-five years. Several of his initiatives at Wheaton Academy—including Winterim, the Living Curriculum Teachers, and the "AND" Institution philosophy—have been replicated and modeled across the country.

CHAPTER 14

NEW DIRECTIONS

*By David L. Roth
and Jon Keith*

Frank Gaebelein, the late headmaster of the Stony Brook School, wrote that the old spiritual "Everybody talkin' 'bout heav'n ain't goin' there" might be paraphrased "Everybody talkin' 'bout Christian education ain't doin' it." He explains that "in respect to a thorough-going integration of Christ and the Bible with the whole institution, with all departments of study, with all kinds of student activities, with all phases of administration, there remains much land to be taken" (1968, 15–16). More than fifty years after Gaebelein made these observations (*The Pattern of God's Truth* was first published in 1954), they are still true. A significant number of Christian schools are not providing true Christian education. What is needed to address this problem is a change in the school's culture that extends to the soul of the school.

Change

Before attempting to change a school's culture, leaders should ask a foundational question: Why should we change? The answer to this question is found in a personal faith in Jesus Christ. Regardless of denominational persuasion, the common opinion among Christians is that followers of Jesus are called to a lifelong pursuit of spiritual maturity and Christlikeness. Jesus set a new standard for His disciples in Matthew 5–7. What Jesus proposed in the Sermon on the Mount was change. It was a change to a different and higher standard. For example, when teaching about anger, Jesus said, "You have heard that it was said to the people long ago, 'Do not murder, and anyone who murders will be subject to judgment.' But I tell you that anyone who is angry with his brother will be subject to judgment" (Matthew 5:21–22). It follows logically that Christian organizations are similarly called to grow, improve, and change to a higher standard.

Christian organizations change and grow in ways similar to those Jesus describes in the parable of the sower. The growth of any plant is ultimately dependent on its environment. Likewise, the growth of a Christian school relies heavily on its environment, which is the health of its culture. *Culture* is "the predominating attitude and behavior that characterize the functioning of a group or organization" (*The American Heritage Dictionary of the English Language*, 4th ed.). Therefore, changing or improving the attitudes and behaviors in schools is the beginning focus for effectively changing school culture.

There is a consensus in the popular media and in the professional literature that change and improvement in schools are needed. The theme of change in education is not new. Since the 1960s there have been consistent calls for education reform, improvement, and change. Before looking at the strategy for change at one specific school, Wheaton Academy, it is important to review what some of the writers and researchers have said about culture change in schools and in other organizations.

In *The Fifth Discipline: The Art and Practice of the Learning Organization*, Peter Senge (1990) suggests that the most successful organizations—those that will truly excel in the future—are learning organizations. He further argues that learning cannot be focused on just the top leadership. According to Senge, organizations need to figure out how to get people to learn at all levels in order for the organization to reach its potential.

Mastery of the following disciplines is vital to a learning organization: (1) personal mastery, (2) mental models, (3) building shared vision, and (4) team learning (Senge 1990, 5–13). The fifth discipline, as Michael Fullan cites in *Leadership and Sustainability*, is systems thinking, which integrates the first four disciplines (2005, 41). Because the theme of systems thinking keeps recurring in the literature, the Christian school educator needs to consider its applicability to the Christian school. The value of systems thinking (see chapter 6) is that it allows one to look at an issue or goal in a big-picture context.

Fullan contends that change hinges on identifying ideas and strategies that promote systems thinking, especially as it relates to leadership. He offers eight elements of sustainability, the last of which is "the long lever of leadership" (2005, 14). In the process of assessing the sustainability of change in the Christian school culture, it is imperative to examine the quality of leadership in the school.

In *The Dance of Change*, Senge and colleagues talk about the "myth of the omnipotent CEO" and the "myth of the hero-leader." These myths suggest that leaders are "the few special people blessed with the capability for command and influence." According to these myths, people "become leaders precisely because of their unique mix of skill, ambition, vision, charisma, and no small amount of hubris. They can overcome the blocks that stymie everyone else. They make great things happen. The implication is clear: If you too want to make a difference, you had better be one of these special people" (1999, 11).

Terrence Deal and Kent Peterson believe that "the leadership of principals is key to building a strong school culture." These authors conclude that principals who effect change in a school's culture "must be able to both *read* and *shape* school cultures with the cooperation and support of teachers, students, and community members" (1991, 89; emphasis in original). Just as teaching is both an art and a science, so is school administration. A Christian school administrator should acquire certification and endorsements: the science component. The art component relates to people skills, to understanding the school's culture, and to casting a compelling vision.

Another student of change, Andy Hargreaves, discusses teacher leadership in the classroom and underscores the point that "schools and teachers are being affected more and more by the demands and contingencies of an increasingly complex and fast-paced, postmodern world" (1994, 23). In the Christian school, the teacher is at the heart of the enterprise. Teachers have numerous opportunities to help shape the minds, hearts, and souls of the next generation. Teachers hold the key to changing a school's culture effectively. In the Christian school movement, there are many donors who will not give to "bricks and mortar," but who will give generously to support teachers because they view the work of teachers as the most effective way to bring change.

Richard Elmore and his associates, who wrote *Restructuring Schools,* say that school restructuring "is a complex compound of specialized knowledge about teaching and learning, organizational structure, administrative organization, and political decision making" (1990, 26). Effective pedagogy tends to relate to the organization, the structure, and the administration of the school, which in turn relate to the decision makers.

Most of the research on educational reform or school culture is public-school based. Most private schools have limited interaction with the government at the local, state, and federal levels. However, the other variables mentioned by Elmore and his associates relating to teaching and learning, organizational structure, and administrative organization are germane to the Christian school's understanding of change in a school's culture.

In *The New Meaning of Educational Change*, Michael Fullan presents this word picture: "Two ships have been passing in the night, stopping occasionally to do battle, in the dark. One is named Accountability, the other Professional Learning Community. Both have evil twins. One is called Name and Shame and other Navel Gazing. The future of educational change is very much a matter of whether these two ships will learn to work through the discomfort of each other's presence until they come to respect and draw on each other's essential resources" (2001, 267).

Fullan's two-ships analogy has direct bearing on a major cultural flaw in the Christian school. Some Christian schools contend that if they are truly spiritual or God-honoring, they can't be excellent academically— that is, a professional learning community. Other Christian schools, in their attempt to excel academically, often retreat from a biblical and Christ-centered approach to education, making accountability their goal. The Christian school must be both: a God-honoring, biblically based school and an excellent professional learning community.

Worldview

Given the often low view of Christian scholarship held by the non-Christian public, effecting change in Christian schools in a way that prepares students to articulate and live out a Christian worldview is very important. Arthur Holmes writes of the importance of understanding the term *Christian worldview*. It is a topic of much discussion in that "worldview disagreements continue in international affairs, culture wars, bioethics, and all the academic disciplines, and for that matter in everything we think and do. For it is the very nature of world and life views to be all-inclusive" (2002, xiii).

Further, Charles Colson and Nancy Pearcey demonstrate through their discussion of a Christian worldview that "the way we *see* the world guides the way we work to *change* the world" (1999, 477; emphasis in original). Colson and Pearcey help keep the big picture in mind: the goal is not merely to effect change in a school's culture but to effect change in the hearts and minds of the students served, who in turn will become countercultural, high-impact Christians who change the world.

Worldview by definition leads to the integration and application of one's faith. Cornelius Plantinga takes educators beyond the classic and sometimes esoteric discussion of integration of faith and learning to the living part—the application of faith and learning. Plantinga pushes Christian school educators to the edge of their comfort zones when he says that if they intend to change or reform culture, they need to get close enough to secular culture "to understand it, to witness to it, to try in some ways to reform it" (2002, 150).

Tools for Change

In order to find an appropriate starting point for change, several good tools are suggested. Analyzing strengths, weaknesses, opportunities, and threats (the SWOT process) will help (see chapter 9). Conducting regular surveys of multiple constituents and maintaining an open-door policy will also help leaders describe the school's culture and monitor its changes. An accreditation process will provide benchmarks of generally accepted educational standards by which to evaluate the school.

Another tool in assessing a school's potential for change is the *Board Evaluation of the Chief Educational Officer in the Christian School* (Miller and Schimmer 2005). Representatives from the Association of Christian Schools International (ACSI) brought together Christian school educators and formed a task force to develop a framework for Christian schools to use in the board's evaluation of the administrator. The authors state that one of the essential job functions of the chief educational officer is to demonstrate "leadership that is an agent for educational change and innovation" (18).

Answering these questions can help leaders assess a school's culture:
- What percentage of everything that goes on at this school comes under the authority of Scripture?
- How fully is the school partnering with the church and the Christian home?
- How can students and parents at this school have a thoroughly Christian education without sacrificing excellence (or academics, athletics, or fine arts)?
- How extraordinary are the teachers?
- How is this school being a good steward of every resource God has provided?

Effective school change requires that leaders identify the school's starting point, the school's ultimate destination, the school's distinctives, and how one will know when the goal has been achieved. For example, the Wheaton Academy mission statement describes the overall educational process:

> Nurturing growth in students through excellence, relationships, and service, to the glory of God. Our goal is to partner with Christian parents to produce graduates who are becoming mature disciples of Christ, equipped for college and life. Specifically, our graduates should have
> - a growing and personal relationship with Christ
> - a thoroughly biblical worldview
> - begun to discover and practice their God-given gifts
> - acquired the necessary knowledge, understanding, and wisdom for their life calling

Every school needs to articulate both its starting point and destination, and this important work must be done before moving on to the business of implementing Jesus' method of cultural change.

Wheaton Academy's Story

What follows is a story of a particular private Christian college-preparatory high school. In 1989 the new leadership articulated a vision for Wheaton Academy. They wanted the school to become a professional learning organization that was committed to sustainable change in its culture. They intended to accomplish this goal by addressing the issues of systems thinking, leadership, curriculum, and the role of the teachers. Because Wheaton Academy is a 150-year-old faith-based school, the leaders made a conscious effort to use Jesus as a model for effecting change in the school's culture.

Wheaton Academy has undergone significant cultural change over the past fifteen years. While it has by no means achieved perfection, the school's culture has produced some positive indicators. Students are taking what they have learned about God and Scripture and are reaching out to the needy in tangible ways. Graduates are academically well prepared for the colleges of their choice. Student participation in cocurricular activity is up. School spirit is passionate, and parents actively recruit others to join the school community. The number of donors has risen. New state-of-the-art facilities continue to be built. Innovative programs regularly start. Employee morale is high, and the school is respected throughout the community. Of course, Wheaton Academy still has all those teen-related, parent-related, and teacher-related problems common to school life. However, there are some positive trends in the school culture.

Jesus as Model Change Agent

Jesus came to this world to bring about great changes in every area of life. However, Jesus is not often used as a model for educational leadership—or at least, not as often as He should be. Jesus used specific principles and methods, and they worked. His principles are available to all educators interested in changing their school culture. Jesus' methods for changing culture include the following:

1. Jesus resisted distractions and temptations.
2. Jesus articulated a new standard.
3. Jesus modeled what He taught.
4. Jesus invited and empowered partners.
5. Jesus defined His partners' roles and equipped His partners for success.
6. Jesus had a prioritized plan that kept the big picture in mind.

When Jesus came into this world, He had a distinct advantage. He knew His starting point and destination. He also knew His job was to influence the world for thirty-three years and then make the ultimate impact on His culture by dying on the Cross. In Christian education, such clarity is not always present. The culture of a school, as well as its mission and vision, may often be opaque and subject to change. Day-to-day priorities, the business of work, and the tyranny of the urgent can cloud the big-picture strategies.

After spending its first 110 years of existence as a cohort of Wheaton College, Wheaton Academy became independent in 1970. For the next few decades, the Academy experienced the growing pains that many Christian schools are familiar with: spurts of growth and pockets of excellence along with setbacks and corners of mediocrity. A change in culture was needed. The following discussion relates some of those changes to the change principles modeled by Jesus in His earthly ministry.

1. Jesus resisted distractions and temptations.

In the fourth chapter of Matthew, we read about Jesus' temptation. Using the allure of something too good to be true, Satan tried to entice Jesus to sin. Early in Wheaton Academy's cultural change, the school was faced with a difficult and tempting financial situation. Some donations were available, but they had strings attached. Those conditions would have diverted the school from its new vision. It took prayer, faith, and resolve to turn down those donations.

In the late 1800s, D. L. Moody attended a speech by Wheaton College's first president, Jonathan Blanchard. President Blanchard had spoken in a direct and passionate way about a number of controversial subjects. Sensing the audience's discomfort, Moody came to the platform and stated, "Some of you don't like what Dr. Blanchard has been saying. A man told me today that we could not get money for our schools if we continued to admit this subject to our platform. That's all right. God can get on without our schools very well, but our schools cannot get on without God, and we cannot have God if we are not faithful" (Wheaton Academy archives). Satan will tempt Christian school leaders in similar ways to distract them from the educational tasks at hand. Whatever the temptation, educational leaders must remain focused—just as Jesus was—on the calling to lead in a nonnegotiable, biblically consistent way.

2. Jesus articulated a new standard.

In Matthew 5:28, Jesus declared that if a man looks at a woman impurely he has already committed adultery. Elsewhere in the Sermon on the Mount, He redefined the standards for love, divorce, oaths, and murder. He refused to let people get away with following only the letter of the Law. Jesus taught that the spirit of the Law matters, and in doing so He set a new standard.

What about Christian teachers? Can teachers be obeyed, respected, and even liked by their students? Can those same teachers be interesting and inspirational, or are some topics just dry and boring? Jesus' example tells us to set the bar high. Most of us have had one or two outstanding teachers—teachers who changed lives, whom students knew as well as they knew the content of their courses—and the impact has been remarkable. A teacher's job description at Wheaton Academy is a document titled "The Living Curriculum Teacher." This document outlines what the school expects from its teachers, including 100 specifically identifiable traits and beliefs. This description was intended to set a new standard for teaching. (To read the complete document, see www.wheatonacademy.org.) The first year it was unveiled, one veteran teacher commented, "Only Jesus could be like that and do all those things!"

Harry Blamires wrote, "To think secularly is to think within a frame of reference bounded by the limits of our life on earth: it is to keep one's calculations rooted in this-worldly criteria. To think christianly is to accept all things with the mind as related, directly or indirectly, to man's eternal destiny as the redeemed and chosen child of God" (1963, 44). The standard for Christian schools is to enable students to view all of life, including each academic discipline and each cocurricular activity, through the lens of Scripture.

3. Jesus modeled what He taught.

In the game of basketball, coaches teach players to watch their opponents' stomachs when playing defense—not their heads, arms, legs, or even the basketball. The reason is that the stomach can't fake out the defender. Opponents can create all kinds of distracting movements, but not with the stomach. Similarly, what a person really believes is revealed not by words but by actions.

Jesus understood the need to model what He taught. Jesus had clear standards, such as going the extra mile, having patience, showing humility, putting others first, and turning the other cheek. And He modeled what He preached through a life of service.

The ability to change school culture hinges on the desire of leaders to follow Christ and humbly model Christlike choices. If the local newspaper prints a critical article that misinterprets a difficult personnel or student discipline situation, how should the leader respond? When an angry parent explodes in a conference, the leader can become defensive and fight fire with fire or model a soft answer that turns away wrath. When it is time to clean up after the banquet, does the leader help stack chairs or let others do the work? Faculty, staff, and students listen and watch the leaders and will follow the articulated high standards only to the extent that actions match words.

Christian school teachers must serve as role models. Richard Riesen contends that "no education takes place in a vacuum. Every teacher teaches from a point of view, a point of view determined by his fundamental convictions, philosophical, theological, psychological, scientific, and so on" (2002, 85). It is important that a teacher model the Christ-centered and Bible-centered mission of the Christian school. This is true because "everyone who is fully trained will be like his teacher" (Luke 6:40). Jesus modeled what He taught, and so must the Christian teacher.

4. Jesus invited and empowered partners.

" 'Come, follow me,' Jesus said, 'and I will make you fishers of men.' At once they left their nets and followed him" (Matthew 4:19–20). Jesus found some folks who understood what He was asking of them and who were willing to be part of His team. A critical part of culture change is expanding the presence of the new norm. People who represent the new models are needed. Philosophical alignment between the school and its employees is one of the most overlooked yet important ingredients of a healthy school.

When Wheaton Academy began its cultural change, the leaders began an aggressive search for people who could model the new philosophy. At the same time, no apologies were made to those teachers who found that they no longer had a good philosophical fit with the school. When announcing her intention to leave, one teacher stated, "The students are no longer afraid of me!" She did not believe she could be effective any longer because the new culture would no longer allow fear and intimidation as primary tools of motivation. Wheaton Academy sought mature and growing people, people who were happy and optimistic, people who loved students as much as their subjects, people who valued parents, people who admitted when they were wrong, people who had high standards and knew how to help students reach them, and people who did not believe that Christian education and excellence are mutually exclusive. Jesus found disciples and empowered them to spread His message. Administrators and boards can further culture change in their schools by finding and empowering partners who are a good philosophical fit for the school.

Hudson T. Armerding writes about the criteria Moses was given in Exodus 18:21 for finding partners. Moses looked for partners who "(1) feared God, (2) were men of truth, and (3) hated covetousness or dishonest gain" (1992, 115–16). The selection of trustees and the appointment of teachers who will be partners for change is dependent on biblical criteria for leadership such as those found in Exodus 18:21, 1 Timothy 3, Proverbs 3:1–6, and Titus 2.

5. Jesus defined His partners' roles and equipped His partners for success.

Jesus made the roles of His followers clear. Just as the Sermon on the Mount clearly articulated desired qualities (being merciful, being pure in heart, being peacemakers), admonishments (being salt), contrasts (not abolishing the Law but fulfilling it), and calls to action (praying, fasting), educational leaders need to articulate clearly what is expected of everyone in the school. Students are expected to read and understand the student handbook that lays out biblical guidelines for Christian living and community norms. Teachers are expected to be "living curriculum teachers." Jesus showed us it is important to have a definitive standard, and He taught this standard to His disciples. In the same way, administrators must take the time to teach and illustrate standards and to measure how effectively those standards are being met.

Jesus was not content to just define roles; He equipped His followers to do their jobs. He explained to His disciples how to give, how to pray, how to fast, and how to focus on what is important. He also took the time to teach what not to do—do not worry, do not judge, do not forget to ask. Likewise, as leaders of change, principals need to take the time to teach specifics and to illustrate new methods. Role-playing typical student-teacher interactions is a useful teaching tool—an exercise that provides both humorous and powerful illustrations of how common situations can be handled in a variety of ways with very different results. Providing teachers with resources such as to-do lists and the "Top 20 Dumb Things to Say to Parents" can be effective. These tools provide valuable methods and tools that will make the school more effective.

Equipping partners in the culture change is critical for success.

As part of an effort to be a professional learning community, Wheaton Academy is committed to building a strengths-based organization, as described by Marcus Buckingham and Donald O. Clifton: "Most organizations take their employees' strengths for granted and focus on minimizing their weaknesses." The paradigm Buckingham suggests is based on two assumptions: (1) "Each person's talents are enduring and unique," and (2) "Each person's greatest room for growth is in the areas of his or her greatest strength" (2001, 8). Wheaton Academy leaders are shown this paradigm and encouraged to determine whose talent fits into which role and to focus each teacher's performance on outcomes rather than on a preconceived mold. Clifton, using research from the Gallup Organization, developed a Web-based assessment instrument called StrengthsFinder. Each Wheaton Academy teacher and staff person takes the online assessment. The director of spiritual life then facilitates the interpretation and application of the findings from the StrengthsFinder assessment for the faculty, staff, and student body. The purpose of this process is to more clearly define teacher and staff roles and to better equip them for success by capitalizing on each employee's strengths.

6. Jesus had a prioritized plan that kept the big picture in mind.

Jesus knew He had only a certain amount of time on earth to accomplish His mission. Accordingly, whenever He faced a decision about allocation of time or resources, He made the choice that most closely matched His central purpose. When the legalistic Pharisees challenged Jesus about feeding His hungry disciples, Jesus responded, "It is lawful to do good on the Sabbath" (Matthew 12:12). In explaining the cost of discipleship, Jesus proclaimed, "What good will it be for a man if he gains the whole world, yet forfeits his soul?" (Matthew 16:26). When the Pharisees asked Jesus to rank the many commandments of the Jewish law, Jesus said, " 'Love the Lord your God with all your heart and with all your soul and with all your mind.' This is the first and greatest commandment. And the second is like it: 'Love your neighbor as yourself.' All the Law and the Prophets hang on these two commandments" (Matthew 22:37–40). Jesus clearly had a plan that kept the big picture in mind. He made and kept priorities. Educational leaders must do the same by developing an orderly plan and then making decisions that follow the stated priorities.

The administration of Wheaton Academy, with board endorsement, created a five-year strategic plan composed of nine key result areas. Each of these key result areas—leadership, teachers, curriculum, students, parents, communication, stewardship, finances, and property and facilities—includes a current status and a five-year goal. In the area of finances, for example, the percentage of annual budget monies that came from giving needed to be lower. The target of less than 10 percent (from a starting point of 35 percent) provided a guide for planning tuition rates and expense budgets from year to year. In the curriculum area, targets were set and progress measured by adding honors tracks and advanced placement courses. It is crucial for school leaders to set goals, prioritize plans, and make good decisions that align with the starting point and intended target. What matters is not the specific plan, but the fact that the plan works for the individual school and is followed.

Now What? Application to Practice

THE AUTHORS HAVE observed, in over four decades of ministry in Christian schools, that positive changes in a school's culture are few and far between, and tend to be slow. A dramatic exception at Wheaton Academy is the ongoing Zambia Project. Over a four-year period, Wheaton Academy students built a schoolhouse in a remote village in Zambia; provided food, fresh water, and spiritual guidance; and helped build a wing for a medical clinic. The students raised over $400,000 for the project. The students have also begun to raise awareness of the AIDS pandemic. Wheaton Academy students have targeted 1,000 schools, colleges, and universities to solicit student support for addressing global issues such as hunger, poverty, and poor health conditions. Local and national media and World Vision have all cited the change in the school's culture that produced such a proactive involvement by high school students. Students in this affluent western suburb of Chicago experienced this schoolwide culture change because the student and faculty leaders were able to teach the student body the relevance of helping the "poor and needy" and the biblical admonishment do that (Deuteronomy 15:11). The results of the Zambia Project are evidence of a learning institution embracing culture change.

The Change Over Time? study, which examined eight schools in New York and Ontario over the last three decades of the twentieth century, suggests that the most comprehensive findings and understandings of school-culture change will emerge when longitudinal studies of a number of schools occur (Labaree 2006). With the regular turnover of families, teachers, and administrators in Christian schools, longitudinal studies are a challenge, but such studies are a challenge worth taking on. The findings of a longitudinal study of several Christian schools could yield much more understanding than the results of a one-time survey or the minutes of one focus group. Andy Hargreaves and Ivor Goodson report the five change forces found in the Change Over Time? study: (1) waves of reform, (2) changing student demographics, (3) teacher generations, (4) leadership succession, and (5) school interrelations (2006, 3). The middle three forces—relating to students, teachers, and leaders—are directly applicable to culture change in a Christian school. Reform, the first force cited, generally comes from within the administration or the board of trustees in a Christian school, whereas reform in public schools is usually introduced through legislation or mandates at the local, state, and federal levels. School interrelations, the last of the five change forces cited, have less or little effect on change in a private school because of the school's independence and direct parent or trustee governance.

Returning to Senge's theme of a learning organization, Michael Fullan gives his own "action guidelines for 'What's Worth Fighting For in Your School' ... practical advice for the principal committed to building learning schools." Fullan advocates the following (1993, 72):

- Understand the culture of the school.
- Value your teachers: promote their professional growth.
- Extend what you value.
- Express what you value.
- Promote collaboration, not cooptation.
- Make menus, not mandates.
- Use bureaucratic means to facilitate, not to constrain.
- Connect with the wider environment.

What is worth fighting for in the Christian school must be clearly articulated by the key stakeholders. At Wheaton Academy, the "Wheaton Academy Immutables" or "What We Believe" statements help to draw those battle lines.

Wheaton Academy Immutables: What We Believe
1. Total integration of biblical truth in all areas of our school (no exception)
2. Partnering with parents (valuing, supporting, encouraging)

3. Having specific outcomes/identifiable targets

4. The enormous impact of "living curriculum teachers" and staff

5. A dynamic, exciting, and mature culture (discipline designed for the 90 percent)

6. The principles of the "AND Institution" (high standards AND relationships)

7. Understanding students individually ("Ladder of Maturity")

8. Top-notch academics (basics and higher-level thinking)

9. Comprehensive extracurriculars (opportunities and excellence)

10. Good stewardship (time, resources, people, heritage)

11. Powerful communication (intentional, timely, accurate, effective)

12. Experiencing great joy as we serve God together (this ought to be fun!)

"Rethinking Educational Change with Heart and Mind" was the theme of the 1997 ASCD Yearbook. Andy Hargreaves, editor and contributor to that yearbook, writes that schools are becoming "more and more permeable." Schools must interface with the community in which they exist, Hargreaves says: "The struggle for positive educational change must now move beyond the school in order to enrich what goes on within it" (1997, 22). The Christian school does not deal with a publicly elected school board or taxpayer sensitivity regarding referenda, but biblically and practically it is important that the Christian school practice being a "good neighbor" in the fullest sense of the term. Communities exert great control over the Christian school through ordinances and other regulations. It is wise to develop good, solid, and long-lasting "good neighbor" relations with the local community. The Christian school is also dependent on the local Christian community for student enrollment and financial support. Hargreaves' comments also apply to the Christian school: "Openness, informality, care, attentiveness, lateral working relationships, reciprocal collaboration, candid and vibrant dialogue, and a willingness to face uncertainty together are the basic ingredients of effective school-community collaboration, not merely the emotional icing that adorns it" (22).

A learning organization is exciting and growing inside, but it must be tied in to the larger context. Fullan states, "In order to improve learning situations that one cares about, it is necessary to become involved in ideas and matters outside the immediate setting—the school in addition to the classroom, the environment in addition to the school—and to do this without losing focus on the core mission of teaching and learning" (1993, 83). Educational leaders must look for ways to accomplish this task while still engaging in the important job of educating children.

To the Christian educator who seeks to be involved in a professional learning community with accountability, the overarching message is not only to create a dynamic school culture inside the classroom, but also to recognize that in order to experience change in the total school culture, one must do so in conjunction with the entire school community, the homes represented by each family, and the churches attended by the students, teachers, staff, and parents. It is from an understanding of and a partnership with the home, the church, and the school that a consensus emerges from the sponsoring Christian tradition. That consensus results in what Duane Litfin calls the systemic institution: "As the name suggests, [systemic institutions] seek to make Christian thinking systemic throughout the institution, root, branch, and leaf. Their curriculum is typically all-encompassing. Their goal is to engage any and all ideas from every perspective, but they attempt to do so from a particular intellectual location, that of the sponsoring Christian tradition. Thus they draw their faculty exclusively from those who know what it means to live and work from that tradition—indeed, from those who embody it.... They seek to live and work *as Christians*" (2004, 18; emphasis in original).

Educational leaders work on culture growth, and they change schools, because as followers of Christ they seek to emulate Him. Jesus used identifiable principles to change His world for eternity—principles that are readily available to all: He resisted distractions and temptations, He articulated a new standard, He modeled what He taught, He invited and empowered partners, He defined His partners' roles and equipped them for success, and He had a prioritized plan that kept the big picture in mind.

Subsequent steps are unique to each school, but there might be some common elements. As leaders seek to transform the school's culture, they may consider these three steps:

1. Use assessment tools to find out where the school is today (starting point).

2. Take the time to define where the school should go (destination).

3. Implement the six principles that Jesus used to change His culture (cultural change).

After a rigorous critique of Christian schools, Frank Gaebelein writes in *Christian Education in a Democracy*, "After all, Christian education is more than a human enterprise" (1995, 205). Even though this pioneer in the modern Christian school movement spent his long career advocating changes in the culture of Christian schools through lectures, the writing of books, and his work at the Stony Brook School, he never forgot whose school system it is. It is God's school system. Gaebelein frames the issue this way: "If the Christian educator may not consider even a single failure with complacency, neither should he look at the success with anything but humility. In the face of God's holiness and man's imperfection, in view of the depth of human need and the inability of human effort, however benevolent, to meet it, he can only exclaim with the Psalmist: 'This is the Lord's doing, and it is marvelous in our eyes' " (205).

References

Armerding, Hudson T. 1992. *The heart of godly leadership.* Wheaton. IL: Crossway Books.

Blamires, Harry. 1963. *The Christian mind: How should a Christian think?* Repr., Ann Arbor, MI: Servant Publications, 1978.

Buckingham, Marcus, and Donald O. Clifton. 2001. *Now, discover your strengths.* New York: Free Press.

Colson, Charles, and Nancy Pearcey. 1999. *How now shall we live?* Wheaton, IL: Tyndale House Publishers.

Deal, Terrence E., and Kent D. Peterson. 1991. *The principal's role in shaping school culture.* Washington, DC. U.S. Department of Education, office of Educational Research and Improvement.

Elmore, Richard F., and associates. 1990. *Restructuring schools: The next generation of educational reform.* San Francisco: Jossey-Bass.

Fullan, Michael. 1993. *Change forces: Probing the depths of educational reform.* Bristol, PA: Falmer Press.

———. 2001. *The new meaning of educational change.* 3rd ed. New York: Teachers College Press.

———. 2005. *Leadership and sustainability: System thinkers in action.* Thousand Oaks, CA: Corwin Press.

Gaebelein, Frank E. 1968. *The pattern of God's truth: The integration of faith and learning.* Chicago, IL: Moody Press.

———. 1995. *Christian education in a democracy.* Colorado Springs, CO: Association of Christian Schools International.

Hargreaves, Andy. 1994. *Changing teachers, changing times: Teachers' work and culture in the postmodern age.* New York: Teachers College Press.

———. 1997. Rethinking educational change: Going deeper and wider in the quest for success. In *Rethinking educational change with heart and mind*, ed. Andy Hargreaves, 1–26. ASCD Yearbook. Alexandria, VA: Association of Supervision and Curriculum Development.

Hargreaves, Andy, and Ivor Goodson. 2006. Educational change over time? The sustainability and non-sustainability of three decades of secondary school change and continuity. *Educational Administration Quarterly* 42, no. 1:3–41.

Holmes, Arthur F. 2002. Foreword to *Worldview: The history of a concept*, by David K. Naugle. Grand Rapids, MI: Eerdmans.

Labaree, David F. 2006. Innovation, nostalgia, and the politics of educational change. *Educational Administration Quarterly* 42, no. 1:157–64.

Litfin, A. Duane. 2004. *Conceiving the Christian college*. Grand Rapids, MI: Eerdmans.

Miller, Robert, and John Schimmer Jr. 2005. *Board evaluation of the chief educational officer in the Christian school*. Ed. Derek Keenan. Colorado Springs, CO: Purposeful Design Publications.

Plantinga, Cornelius, Jr. 2002. *Engaging God's world: A Christian vision of faith, learning, and living*. Grand Rapids, MI: Eerdmans.

Riesen, Richard A. 2002. *Piety and philosophy: A primer for Christian schools*. Phoenix, AZ: ACW Press.

Senge, Peter M. 1990. *The fifth discipline: The art and practice of the learning organization*. New York: Currency.

Senge, Peter, Art Kleiner, Charlotte Roberts, Richard Ross, George Roth, and Bryan Smith. 1999. *The dance of change: The challenges to sustaining momentum in learning organizations*. New York: Currency.

Weber, Jeremy. 2005. Raising the compassion bar. *Christianity Today* (August).

PART FOUR

Building Community
with Others

CHAPTER 15

THE COLLABORATIVE SCHOOL COMMUNITY

Building Meaningful Relationships Among Stakeholders

෴

By Bruce Young

Bruce Young, EdD, is an associate professor for early childhood education and the master of education programs at Covenant College. He earned his doctorate in learning and instruction at the University of San Francisco. He has thirty years of experience in teaching and administration in Christian elementary schools.

CHAPTER 15

THE COLLABORATIVE SCHOOL COMMUNITY

By Bruce Young

THERE IS A STORY about a country pastor who was about to begin his sermon one stormy night when lightning struck the power pole outside the church. Immediately the lights went out and the congregation began to get worried. Sensing their concern, the pastor called out to his parishioners, "Don't be afraid. I want everyone to raise their hands and shout 'hallelujah!'" The congregation members raised their hands and shouted "hallelujah!" Immediately the lights came back on. The parishioners were amazed. "It's a miracle!" they cried. The country pastor simply replied, "Well, I thought everyone knew that *many hands make light work.*"

Collaboration does sometimes produce miraculous results. There is probably no sphere of life in which collaboration is more necessary than in the field of education. A variety of people and agencies are involved in the educational enterprise, making cooperation vital for success. The collaborators in education include parents, teachers, school administrators, pastors, neighbors, local businesspeople, publishers of curriculum materials, and government officials. These participants function in the home, school, church, community, and government. Education is most successful when all the stakeholders are working together toward a common end.

One of the greatest challenges in education is the relationship of home and school. Parents often distrust schools, and schools often distrust parents (Sanders 2001; Comer 2004). The result is a competitive rather than a collaborative community. Only when the home and the school share a common end developed from a common worldview will they develop a relationship of unity and trust. Doug Blomberg addressed this problem in a presentation at the International Symposium of the Association for Reformational Philosophy in 2005 by stating, "The very problem of schools in relation to families and societies in our postmodern era is that there is no consensus." Blomberg continued to state that conflicts between home and school are inevitable if there is no consensus about what is normative because schooling cannot be neutral. When differing values of home and school collide, the results are often fear, mistrust, and an unhealthy competition for the hearts and minds of the children.

The same unhealthy competitive community can develop among the other participants in the schooling process. Wherever there is disagreement about what is pedagogically normative, there is potential for conflict. In a fallen world it is even difficult to reach consensus in a homogeneous community, whether it be secular or religious (Blomberg 2005).

The brokenness found in a fragmented and competitive schooling community can be reformed. The aim of this chapter is to explore the nature of the relationships among the collaborators in schooling and to uncover biblical directives that can guide the formation of a truly collaborative schooling community.

The Importance of a Collaborative Community in Schooling

There is abundant research concerning the positive relationship between student performance and the involvement of family and community in schools. Research indicates that the involvement of parents at school results in increased student attendance, decreased discipline problems, increased achievement, better self-esteem, and improved attitudes about school and learning (Mapp 1997; National Committee for Citizens in Education 1994; Olmstead and Rubin 1982; Hrabowski, Maton, and Greif 1998). A meta-analysis of 66 studies conducted by the National Committee for Citizens in Education (1994) found that a supportive, involved home was a more accurate predictor of student achievement than any other factor investigated in the studies.

The development of "learning communities"—schools where students, teachers, parents, and community members collaborate in the students' learning experience—has resulted in increased academic achievement for students (Schaps 2003). These learning communities foster success for students regardless of ethnicity or socioeconomic status. In a review of fifty-one studies concerning the relationship of parents and community to student outcomes, the results are clear (Henderson and Mapp 2002, 24):

> Taken as a whole, these studies found a positive and convincing relationship between family involvement and benefits for students, including improved academic achievement. This relationship holds across families of all economic, racial/ethnic, and educational backgrounds and for students at all ages. Although there is less research on the effects of community involvement, it also suggests benefits for schools, families, and students, including improved achievement and behavior.

James Comer, a professor of psychiatry at Yale and the director of the collaborative School Development Program, believes that the mantra for successful child development and learning is "relationships, relationships, relationships" (2004, 2).

The importance and necessity of a collaborative community effort in the educational process has a biblical basis. God created people to live in relationships. We read in Genesis 2:18 that God said, "It is not good for the man to be alone." Dutch theologian Herman Bavinck emphasizes this point when discussing the importance of the community of believers. Bavinck states, "A human being is a companionable creature, and he does not like being alone" (1956, 515). God has created humans to have relationships that are both dependent and interdependent. People need the support of one another as they fulfill the cultural mandate to care for and cultivate the resources that God has embedded in creation.

God's intention from eternity is to create a community of people who would be holy and blameless before Him "for the praise of his glory" (Ephesians 1:12). In 1 Corinthians 12 Paul compares this community, the Church, to a body. No one part is independent; rather, each part is dependent upon the other parts. Each part serves an important role in the working of the whole body. Similarly, all the members of the learning community—parents, teachers, businesspeople, church leaders, and government representatives—serve important roles in educating students.

These roles are most effective when performed collaboratively toward a common end (Epstein 1992, 1995; Ballen and Moles 1994; Strike 2004).

A Collaborative Community Works to Achieve a Common End

Schools are places for learning, but learning is not the same in all schools. For this reason, parents must identify the purpose and vision of a school before engaging in a collaborative relationship with it. The task of finding a school with which to partner would be simplified if education were neutral, since schools would then differ only regarding how well education was implemented. However, education varies in numerous value-laden and content-specific ways that are determined by beliefs, philosophies, and worldviews. Christian educators generally agree that learning is not a neutral activity:

- "Education is always religious in the sense that it cannot but lead forth according to our faith commitments and ideals" (Van Brummelen 1988, 5).
- "Every school—public or private, Christian or non-Christian—is a religious school actively involved in the teaching of religion" (Harper 1981, 62).
- "Education has never been neutral, nor can it ever be" (Edlin 1994, 40).
- "The truth is that we can never get out of a philosophic position in education.... It cannot be neutral, for Christ has said, 'He that is not with me is against me: and he that gathereth not with me scattereth'" (De Jong 1974, 39).
- "No one can teach out of a philosophical vacuum. Their beliefs and values will come out and these will help shape the beliefs and values of those whom they teach" (Schultz 2003, 166).
- "Public education has a faith commitment to which a Christian cannot adhere" (Van Brummelen 1972, 71).
- "Facts are never neutral" (Greene 1990, 72).

Because education is not a neutral process, school administrators must answer these three important questions from parents:

1. *To what extent and in what manner is learning going on in the school?* If schools are for learning, then anything else about the school that appeals to the parents must be subservient to the issue of learning.

Administrators should be prepared to provide evidence of learning in the school (for example, test scores, student projects, work
samples, classroom visits).

2. *Do the school and the home share a common end?* Parents should
   avoid forming partnerships with schools that will direct their children toward an end that conflicts with the parents' end. Administrators must be able to articulate the vision of the school clearly and
   winsomely.

3. *Is the learning at school able to equip and prepare students to love and
   serve God and their neighbors?* Administrators need to identify for
   parents how love is manifested in the school community.

The issue of love is primary in education. If the end of education is
the same as the end of all of life—"to glorify God and to enjoy Him
forever" (Williamson 1973, 1)—and if God is most glorified, and our
greatest joy is found, through loving and obeying Him (1 John 5:1–2,
Matthew 22:36–40, Galatians 5:14), then education is the process of
equipping and preparing students through the learning of knowledge
and the development of skills to glorify and enjoy God by loving Him
and their neighbors.

It is the role of the school administrator to keep the stakeholders
focused on the end of glorifying and enjoying God. "Effective schools
are ones where there is a perception that board and committee members, the principal, teachers, parents and students share a common vision
and are working unitedly to implement that vision" (Van Brummelen
1988, 15). While some major philosophical rifts between secular and
Christian educators exist, one area in which both find agreement is the
necessity of having shared goals and a common vision among schooling
participants to bring about effective collaboration (Epstein 1992; Ballen
and Moles 1994; Funkhouser and Gonzales 1997). Education is most
powerful when the home, school, church, community, and government
work together toward a common end, particularly the end of glorifying
and enjoying God.

A Collaborative Community as the Model for Schooling

Urie Bronfenbrenner's Ecological Theory of Development (1995) is
helpful in explaining the effect of a range of societal influences on a child's
learning and development. Bronfenbrenner's theory proposes five envi-

ronmental systems that interact with and influence the development of a child. These five systems, known as the microsystem, mesosystem, exosystem, macrosystem, and chronosystem, range from proximal systems where the child has direct interaction with others to distal systems where cultural and socioeconomic conditions indirectly influence the child's development and learning. Bronfenbrenner's ecological theory expands traditional views of child development to incorporate the influences of multiple contexts for determining development and learning.

Bronfenbrenner's model emphasizes the important and collaborative influence the five systems have on the educational process. It is interesting to note that while proximal systems (family, peers, community, and church) will have the greatest and most immediate influence on the student, distal systems (school boards, government agencies, and businesses) can also have significant effects on learning (1995). For example, the desegregation of public schools in the mid-1950s had a great effect on the learning opportunities for African American students. Even though the home and the church provided support and encouragement to students within the African American community, an educational ceiling existed that did not allow the majority of African American students the opportunity to rise to their fullest academic potential—until the government removed that ceiling.

Christian educators have long acknowledged the significant roles that different agencies play in students' education. The importance of collaboration among the home, church, and school has been espoused by Christian educators for centuries. The Canons of Dordt, written almost four centuries ago for the Dutch Reformed Church in the Netherlands, acknowledge the collaborative roles of parents, schools, and churches (Lockerbie 1994). Concerning the role of parents, the Canons state that "the office of Parents is diligently to instruct their children and their whole household in the principles of the Christian religion, in a manner adapted to their respective capacities" (200). Regarding schools, "the schoolmasters shall instruct their scholars according to their age and capacity" (201). Finally, the church's role in a the education of students is to "explain familiarly to them, the articles of the Christian faith, and catechise them according to the circumstances of their different capacities, progress, and knowledge" (201). The argument can be made that the practice of having the community involved in the training of children dates back to the days of Moses, when God told the whole nation to pass on His commands and promises (Deuteronomy 6:4–9, 32:7).

Models have been constructed to show the interrelationship of the home, church, and school. The "three-legged stool" model emphasizes how the home, church, and school provide the support for the students' education by working cooperatively (Fennema 2005). If one leg is missing, the whole educational structure is compromised (Van Brummelen 1988). Also, the "cord of three strands" model (based on Ecclesiastes 4:12) emphasizes not only how education is strengthened by the collaboration of home, church, and school, but also how all three must be intertwined in their educational efforts to provide the most effective schooling (Schultz 2003).

Although the stool and cord models are helpful in explaining the value of collaboration among the home, church, and school, a new model is needed that not only accounts for the increasing influences of the community and government on a child's education in a postmodern world but also acknowledges the sovereignty of God over the entire process. Proposed here is a three-dimensional model that incorporates the community, the government, and God's sovereign and loving rule over it all, into the traditional model of home, school, and church (figure 1).

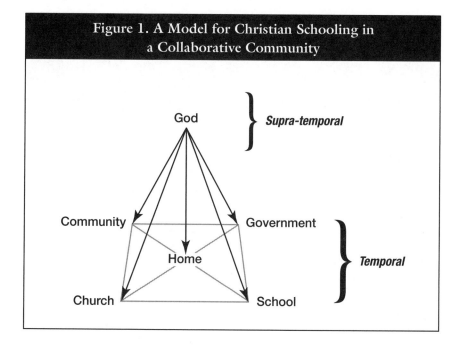

Figure 1. A Model for Christian Schooling in a Collaborative Community

A Collaborative Community as the Model for Christian Schooling

The model for Christian schooling in a collaborative community draws from Bronfenbrenner's insights (1995). The model acknowledges the presence of a wide range of influences on learning and shows how these influences relate to one another. In the model, God grants authority to each influential agency in the temporal plane and superintends their relationships. In the temporal plane, the family is placed at the center because the home has been given the primary responsibility by God to educate the child (Ephesians 6:4, Proverbs 22:6). All other agencies in the temporal plane interact with the child through the mediation of the family.

The agencies on the perimeter of the temporal plane have an educational relationship with the child directly from God and indirectly from God through the parents. Each agency is involved according to the normative laws that God has embedded in the created structure of that agency's domain (Dooyeweerd 1997). Each agency in the model has a unique role and a relationship with the student in the schooling process (table 1). Although there is some overlapping of tasks, no agency may usurp the authority of another agency. The roles and relationships of the various agencies are established and governed by God, who oversees the process for His glory and for the good of the community.

Table 1. Roles and Relationships of Various Agencies in the Schooling of a Student		
Agency	**Role**	**Relationship**
Home	Incubates	Parental
School	Integrates	Pedagogical
Church	Inculcates	Ecclesiastical
Community	Initiates	Cultural
Government	Insulates	Legal

The home's role and relationship

Parents have the primary responsibility for educating the children whom God has placed under their care (Ephesians 6:4). This does not mean, however, that parents may educate their children in any way they choose. God has given parents the authority to educate their children in a particular way for a particular purpose. As Martin Luther (1530) writes, God "has not given you children and the means to support them, only that you may do with them as you please, or train them for worldly glory. You have been earnestly commanded to raise them for God's service." Regarding the particular way and purpose of educating children, God has mandated that parents should "bring them up in the training and instruction of the Lord" (Ephesians 6:4). Paul's charge to fathers connects to several Old Testament passages. Psalm 78:5–6 states, "He decreed statutes for Jacob and established the law in Israel, which he commanded our forefathers to teach their children, so the next generation would know them, even the children yet to be born, and they in turn would tell their children." In Proverbs 22:6 the direction is given to "train a child in the way he should go, and when he is old he will not turn from it." Clearly, God holds parents ultimately responsible for educating their children.

The role of the home in educating children has been described by D. Bruce Lockerbie as one that "*incubates* a child's character, providing those moral and spiritual conditions favorable to the child's healthy development as a believer" (1980, 129; emphasis in original). In the home, children can be nurtured in a loving, accepting family context. In the home, children first learn who they are, what they can do, and why they are in this world. In the home, children experience the first context for their relationship with God, others, and the world. Community is practiced and learned in the family for application outside the protective walls of the home.

While the parents have the primary responsibility to God for how their children are educated, they may enlist the help of others who possess expert content knowledge and pedagogical knowledge. In a technological society, many parents may need the support of experts with the knowledge and skills necessary to equip children for living and working in the world; therefore, parental responsibility may be shared with gifted, godly, and competent teachers. Christian school administrators have the role of assisting parents in understanding the biblical mandates established by God to guide educational decision making for their children.

The school's role and relationship

"The Christian school *integrates* every element of human knowledge and experience into a view of life that can be whole and wholly Christian" (Lockerbie 1980, 129; emphasis in original). The integrative role

307

of the school defines its uniqueness. Schools are concerned with helping students understand and develop their relationships with God, others, the world, and themselves. The knowledge and skills needed to develop these relationships form the content of the school's curriculum within its cultural context.

Schools, acting in loco parentis, have many of the same God-given responsibilities as parents; however, the school's relationship to the child is a pedagogical, not a parental, one. This distinction means that the discipline, instruction, and nurturing that take place in schools happen in the context of pedagogical authority. Pedagogy is primarily concerned with instructional activities, a role that distinguishes the school from other societal agencies in which instruction is of secondary importance.

The school administrator has the leadership role in organizing and coordinating collaboration between the school and its educational partners. The administrator is responsible for inviting potential collaborators to participate with the school and for creating a welcoming school atmosphere (Steyn 1993; Swymer 1986). In order to have an inviting school, the administrator must get away from the desk and serve as a role model by spending time forming relationships both inside and outside the school. The relational tasks can be as simple as greeting parents as they drop off their students in the morning or hosting breakfast for volunteers or leading a tour of the campus for local community and civic leaders.

Another important task of the school administrator is to communicate the vision of the school to the stakeholders. In the most effective schools, the stakeholders share a common vision. Administrators need to use the most effective means of communicating the vision with their learning community. Personal contact, whether through "fireside chats" in homes or evening discussions at school, builds meaningful relationships. Other means of communication are email, principal blogs, newsletters, and websites (table 2). Home visits, especially when made by both a school staff person and a parent representative, have been successful in increasing parent involvement (Epstein 2005).

Table 2. Kinds of Involvement	
Agency	**Kinds of Involvement**
Parent	Attending parent-teacher conferences, supervising and assisting with homework, classroom volunteering, student tutoring, chaperoning field trips, attending school events (sports, open house), supervising lunch and recess, helping with fund-raising events, participating in school governance (committees, boards, planning sessions), participating in school work days, attending parent training sessions, participating in home visits, praying, making financial donations
School	Holding special events (back-to-school nights, family and community picnics, school fairs), building channels of communication (class- and administration-level vehicles, newsletters, email, website, principal blogs), conducting workshops (homework tips, effective discipline), providing school orientations (kindergarten, middle school, high school), providing family math and science nights, scheduling "fireside talks" with the principal (on campus and in homes), conducting home visits (visiting team of one parent and one staff person), hosting PTA/PTO meetings, forming governance teams
Church	Making donations (money, food, services), providing volunteers (after-school tutoring), providing counseling, supplying chapel speakers, participating in school governance (committees, boards, planning sessions), providing scholarships, providing prayer support, sharing facilities, providing mercy ministries to families
Community	Providing internships, making donations (money, expertise, food, training), conducting mock job interviews, advertising in school publications, serving as guest speakers and instructors (local artists, musicians, mechanics, bankers, CEOs), job shadowing, one-on-one mentoring, providing community information (chamber of commerce), participating in school governance (committees, boards, planning sessions), providing volunteer opportunities (hospitals, senior centers), conducting field trips (museums, musical events, businesses), collaborating with college and university departments of education, establishing business partnerships
Government	Providing guest speakers (police officers, firefighters, council members, politicians, armed forces personnel), conducting mock trials, providing health department support, providing locations for field trips (parks, historic sites, zoos), funding various programs, promoting legislation to improve education, passing and enforcing health and safety regulations

The church's role and relationship

"The church *inculcates* a knowledge of its creeds and doctrines. By preaching and teaching, by observance of the holy sacraments, and by being a community held together in common worship, fellowship, and service, the church impresses the child with his responsibility to participate in the Body of Christ" (Lockerbie 1980, 129; emphasis in original). The teaching roles of the church and school may overlap, but they differ in terms of their relationship to the child. Although the school's relationship to the child is based on pedagogical authority, the church's relationship to the child is based on ecclesiastical authority—the church focuses on teaching biblical doctrine and its application.

The church collaborates with the school in numerous ways. It may provide the school with chapel speakers, assistance in family or child counseling, staff training in peacemaking, consultation in decision making, financial assistance for needy families, mercy ministries for school families, service opportunities for students, devotionals for faculty meetings, guidance in the selection of Bible curriculum, after-school tutoring and childcare, representation on committees and the board, and support through teaching and preaching biblical directives concerning education (table 2).

Because the roles of church and school overlap at times, each must be careful not to usurp the other's authority. The school must be careful not to let activities such as chapel become confused with the church's worship assembly, which is under the leadership of elders and deacons. In the case of parochial schools, the church must be careful to respect the authority of the educational experts regarding pedagogical decisions.

The community's role and relationship

The role the community plays in education has expanded in recent years. School partnerships with businesses and community groups have increased (University of Oregon College of Education n.d.). Schools are making a greater effort to arrange student internships at businesses, service organizations, and nonprofit organizations. The increased collaboration between community groups and schools makes it necessary to add another participant, the community, to the model of a collaborative community.

The role of the community in the student's education is *initiation*. The community helps initiate the student into the culture. The enculturation process happens as students observe people at work and play within the context of daily living. It is important for students to be involved in the community because they will internalize the norms of a community as they experience the caring and acceptance of community members (Strike 2004). Christian students learn how to live Christianly as they observe other Christians carrying out their callings. Within the community context, students learn that "This is how we do business," "This is how we help one another," "This is how we play," "This is how we solve problems." Students will experience real-life problems and solutions through community interaction. Theory transforms into praxis within the context of community.

The school administrator has a leadership role in establishing and maintaining partnerships with a variety of groups, organizations, and businesses within the community (Sanders and Lewis 2005; Steyn 1993). To accomplish this important task, the administrator should organize a committee of parents and teachers to investigate opportunities for col-laboration (Sanders 2001). There are numerous ways the school and community can collaborate, including the following: internships, dona-tions of money and expertise, guest speakers, participation on school committees and boards, and field-trip opportunities (table 2). Authentic learning takes place when students participate in business practicums and service projects. Community members can provide students with role models to follow as well as opportunities to experience caring relation-ships as faith and academic learning are integrated with vocations.

The government's role and relationship

The increased involvement of the government in education, most noticeably in such legislation as No Child Left Behind (2002), warrants giving the government a place in the model. The proper role of the gov-ernment is to *insulate* or protect its citizens. This insular role is carried out through a legal relationship with families, students, and schools as established by God (Romans 13:1). When the government is acting in its God-ordained role of administering justice and protecting the pub-lic good, it has the authority to legislate compulsory education and to accredit schools (Harper 1981).

These legal actions can serve to protect parents and children. Requir-ing children to receive an education is good and necessary in an advanced technological society. Through education, citizens develop and refine skills and abilities that they can direct toward loving God and their neigh-bors by being productive and contributing members of society. School accreditation serves to inform parents about how the school is meeting accepted educational norms. It is the responsibility of the school administrator to seek accreditation with agencies that emphasize norms that do not compromise or inhibit the school's ability to carry out its mission.

The government usurps its God-given authority if it legislates compulsory government education. This was the case in 1925 when the state of Oregon, prompted by the Ku Klux Klan's concern about the increasing influence of immigrants and the Catholic Church, passed a Compulsory Education Act, making it illegal to send children to nonpublic schools. Those favoring the act referred to students as "the state's children." In a judgment overturning the law, the Supreme Court stated, "The fundamental theory of liberty upon which all governments in this Union repose excludes any general power of the state to standardize its children by forcing them to accept instruction from public teachers only" (*Pierce v. Society of Sisters* 1925). The government also usurps its authority if it requires, as a condition of accreditation, a curriculum that excludes God.

The government can play a collaborative role in Christian schooling when it fulfills its role of administering justice. For example, rather than excluding funding from all religious education except the religious secular humanism of the public schools, the government could make an equitable distribution of taxpayer funds to all schools serving its citizens. The funds could be distributed through vouchers or partial government funding as is the case in Canada. Dependency on government funding does not necessarily result in educational compromise or loss of a school's Christian distinctiveness, as demonstrated in a study of independent schools in British Columbia (Van Brummelen 1993).

The sovereignty of God and the collaborative community

"We are responsible to God for how we act with respect to God. We are responsible to God for how we act with respect to ourselves and our fellow human beings. We are responsible to God for how we act with respect to nature" (Wolterstorff 1980, 9). God is not the grand watchmaker who set a mechanistic universe into motion but is no longer intimately involved in its operations. On the contrary, God demonstrates His care of creation by feeding the birds and clothing the lilies, and He cares even more for the needs of those made in His image (Matthew 6:26–30). Out of His love, God supervises and empowers those agencies involved in the education of His children. If not for God's grace at work in the world, sin would go unrestrained, making it impossible to have a collaborative learning community.

Now What? A Collaborative Community in the Present and Future of Schooling

An AFRICAN PROVERB states, "It takes a village to raise a child" (Scheven 1981, 123). This concept is not new to the Christian community. In a very real sense, "It takes an *ecclesia* to raise a child." The term *ecclesia* is used in several biblical passages (for example, Ephesians 1:22, Hebrews 2:12, Acts 7:38), where it can be translated as a "community of believers" (Bavinck 1956, 517). The Christian school, as an integral part of the community of believers, should not stand alone or in competition with other agencies in the community. The school has the unique task of integrating knowledge and skills in order to teach students how all the agencies—home, school, church, community, and government—work together to glorify God by lovingly serving Him and one another. In order to carry out this task, the school administrator must take a leadership role as the coordinator within the collaborative learning community.

Present application to practice

Robert Illman, former superintendent at Contra Costa Christian Schools in Walnut Creek, California, implemented several programs that serve as good models for how collaboration can work in the learning community. Three programs in particular are briefly reviewed here. Each program demonstrates what school administrators can do to involve the family, church, and community in the educational process.

Illman believes that the entire covenant community is responsible for the education of the covenant children. For this reason he established the Independent Study Program (ISP) for homeschooling families. Often, homeschoolers find themselves isolated from the broader educational community. To help connect homeschoolers to the school community, the ISP allows homeschooled students to follow the school's curriculum, take courses on campus, and participate in school-sponsored activities. The homeschooling parents are invited to attend training sessions, take advantage of special services, and have their children participate in the school's standardized-testing program. The homeschooled students are invited to go on field trips, join sports teams, and participate in graduation ceremonies. Through the ISP, families who had been isolated from

313

the larger Christian learning community are able to collaborate with the school in meaningful ways.

Inter-session is another program that Illman instituted to take learning outside the walls of the school. Inter-session takes place between the first and second semesters at the high school level. Teachers are asked to create an interesting and educational weeklong course that draws on each teacher's particular interests and passions. Through the Inter-session experience, students are able to relate to their teachers in a broader context than that of the classroom. Some Inter-session courses involve trips abroad. One teacher took a group of students to Scotland to study castles. Another teacher took students to visit different churches to study how faith influenced the architecture of the churches. One teacher stayed on campus and taught hip-hop dance along with studying, from a biblical perspective, the culture that produced the dance style. The course culminated in a public performance at a local theme park. Parents with specialized skills team-taught courses, and local artists were brought in to teach art. For one week the school is the collaborative community.

Another program, Pastors Day, is designed to foster partnerships with the local churches. Students invite the pastors from their churches to a breakfast served by students at the school. The event gives pastors an opportunity to network with pastors of other churches and denominations in "neutral" territory. The pastors hear about opportunities to collaborate with the school, visit classes, and interact with students from their church. In addition to being invited to participate in Pastors Day, local pastors are invited to speak in weekly chapels, serve as advisors to the board, consult with the school regarding discipline and family issues, and sit on school committees.

Future application to practice

If the end of education is to glorify and enjoy God forever through loving service to Him and others, then the activities of the school conducted toward this end will have eternal value. The apostle Paul states, "Each man's work will become evident; for the day will show it because it is to be revealed with fire, and the fire itself will test the quality of each man's work. If any man's work which he has built on it remains, he will receive a reward" (1 Corinthians 3:13–14, NASB). The work that survives will be what was done in faith, hope, and love (1 Corinthians 13:13).

The collaborative or "one another" community that God is building is an eternal community. What students learn in schools today and practice in their lives has double value. First, the acts of love—such as a skilled surgeon repairing a damaged heart valve, a wise company owner making a business decision that increases the wages of his employees, a judge using expert judicial knowledge to bring justice to the oppressed, a computer programmer using skills that were refined over years of study to simplify a program and make it more user friendly, or a stay-at-home mother wisely managing the family resources—all have redemptive value in the present temporal world. The gifts and abilities developed and refined in the schooling process expand the opportunities one has for love-motivated service.

Second, those same acts, performed in God's service, are stored as "treasure in heaven" (Matthew 19:21, Luke 12:33). In some real and mysterious way, the sacrifices of love made in obedience to God have both a present and a future value. One day the collaborative community, by God's love and grace, will become the consummated community that will forever glorify and enjoy God in loving service before the throne of the Lamb (Revelation 7:15–17).

References

Ballen, Jennifer, and Oliver Moles. 1994. Strong families, strong schools: Building community partnerships for learning September. U.S. Department of Education, National Family Initiative.

Bavinck, Herman. 1956. *Our reasonable faith*. Grand Rapids, MI: Baker.

Blomberg, Doug. 2005. Panel: Education and family. Paper presented at the International Symposium of the Association for Reformational Philosophy, Hoeven, Netherlands.

Bronfenbrenner, Urie. 1995. Developmental ecology through space and time: A future perspective. In *Examining lives in context: Perspectives in the ecology of human development*, ed. Phyllis Moen, Glen H. Elder Jr., and Kurt Lüscher, with the assistance of Heather E. Quick, 599–618. Washington, DC: American Psychological Association.

Comer, James P. 2004. *Leave no child behind: Preparing today's youth for tomorrow's world*. New Haven, CT: Yale University Press.

De Jong, Norman. 1974. *Education in the truth*. Phillipsburg, NJ: Presbyterian and Reformed Publishing.

Dooyeweerd, Herman. 1997. *A new critique of theoretical thought: The necessary presuppositions of philosophy*. Ser. A, vol. 1. Lewiston, NY: Edwin Mellen Press.

Edlin, Richard J. 1994. *The cause of Christian education*. Northport, AL: Vision Press.

Epstein, Joyce L. 1992. School and family partnerships. In *Encyclopedia of educational research*. 6th ed. Vol. 4, ed. by Marvin C. Alkin, with the assistance of Michele Linden, Jana Noel, and Karen Ray, 1139–48. New York: Macmillan.

———. 1995. School/family/community partnerships: Caring for the children we share. *Phi Delta Kappan* 76, no. 9 (May): 701–12.

———. 2005. A case study of the partnership schools comprehensive school reform (CSR) model. *The Elementary School Journal* 106, no. 2 (November): 151–70.

Fennema, Jack. 2005. *The religious nature and biblical nurture of God's children: A guide for parents and teachers*. Sioux Center, IA: Dordt College Press.

Funkhouser, Janie E., and Miriam R. Gonzales. 1997. *Family involvement in children's education: Successful local approaches*. U.S. Department of Education. http://www.ed.gov/PDFDocs/97-7022.pdf.

Greene, Albert E., Jr. 1990. *Thinking Christianly: New patterns for new people.* Medina, WA: Alta Vista College Press.

Harper, Norman E. 1981. *Making disciples: The challenge of Christian education at the end of the 20th century.* Memphis, TN: Christian Studies Center.

Henderson, Anne T., and Karen L. Mapp. 2002. *A new wave of evidence: The impact of school, family, and community connections on student achievement.* Austin: Southwest Educational Development Laboratory. http://www.sedl.org/connections/resources/evidence.pdf.

Hrabowski, Freeman A., Kenneth I. Maton, and Geoffrey L. Greif. 1998. *Beating the odds: Raising academically successful African American males.* New York: Oxford University Press.

Lockerbie, D. Bruce. 1980. *Who educates your child? A book for parents.* Repr., Grand Rapids, MI: Zondervan.

———. 1994. *A passion for learning: The history of Christian thought on education.* Chicago: Moody Press.

Luther, Martin. 1530. A sermon on keeping children in school. God Rules International. http://www.godrules.net/library/luther/NEW1luther_d12.htm.

Mapp, Karen. 1997. Making the connection between families and schools. *Harvard Education Letter* 13, no. 5 (September/October): 1–3.

National Committee for Citizens in Education. 1994. *A new generation of evidence: The family is critical to student achievement.* Ed. Nancy Berla and Anne Henderson. Washington, DC: Center for Law and Education.

No Child Left Behind. 2002. http://www.whitehouse.gov/news/reports/no-child-left-behind.html.

Olmstead, Patricia P., and Roberta I. Rubin. 1982. Linking parent behaviors to child achievement: Four evaluation studies from the parent education follow-through programs. *Studies in Educational Evaluation* 8, no. 3:317–25.

Pierce v. Society of Sisters. 268 U.S. 510. 1925. http://caselaw.lp.findlaw.com/scripts/printer_friendly.pl?page=us/268/510.html.

Sanders, Mavis G. 2001. The role of "community" in comprehensive school, family, and community partnership programs. *The Elementary School Journal* 102, no. 1 (September): 19–34.

Sanders, Mavis G., and Karla C. Lewis. 2005. Building bridges toward excellence: Community involvement in high schools. *The High School Journal* 88, no. 3 (February/March): 1–9.

Schaps, Eric. 2003. Creating a school community. *Educational Leadership* 60, no. 6 (March): 31–33.

Scheven, Albert. 1981. *Swahili proverbs.* Washington, DC: University Press of America.

Schultz, Glen. 2003. *Kingdom education: God's plan for educating future generations.* 2nd ed. Colorado Springs, CO: Purposeful Design Publications.

Steyn, Trudie. 1993. The manifestation of invitational theory in inviting schools. *Journal of Invitational Theory and Practice.* Vol. 2, no. 1 (Winter): 19–28.

Strike, Kenneth A. 2004. Community, the missing element of school reform: Why schools should be more like congregations than banks. *American Journal of Education* 110, no. 3 (May): 215–32.

Swymer, Stephen. 1986. Creating a positive school atmosphere: The principal's responsibility. *NASSP Bulletin* 70, no. 493 (November): 89–91.

University of Oregon College of Education. n.d. *Corporate involvement in school reform.* http://cepm.uoregon.edu/publications/policy_reports/corporate_involvement.

Van Brummelen, Harro. 1972. Towards a radical break with public school curriculum. In *To prod the "slumbering giant": Crisis, commitment, and Christian education.* Toronto, Canada: Wedge Publishing Foundation.

———. 1988. *Walking with God in the classroom.* Seattle, WA: Alta Vista College Press.

———. 1993. The effects of government funding on private schools: Appraising the perceptions of long-term principals and teachers in British Columbia's Christian schools. *Canadian Journal of Education* 18, no. 1:14–28.

Williamson, G. I. 1973. *The shorter catechism.* Vol. 1. Phillipsburg, NJ: Presbyterian and Reformed Publishing.

Wolterstorff, Nicholas P. 1980. *Educating for responsible action.* Grand Rapids, MI: Eerdmans.

CHAPTER 16

THE LEADER AND THE BOARD

Roles, Relationships, and Responsibilities

め

By James C. Marsh Jr.

James C. Marsh Jr., MA, is the head of school at Westminster Christian Academy in St. Louis, Missouri. He has twenty-seven years of experience as a head of school and currently serves as the board chair of Christian Schools International. He is also a member of the board and executive committee of the Independent Schools Association of the Central States.

CHAPTER 16

THE LEADER
AND THE
BOARD

By James C. Marsh Jr.

THE RELATIONSHIP BETWEEN those God has called to govern the Christian school (the board of trustees) and the leader of the school (the head of school) is arguably the most important and effectual element in the Christian school community. God clearly states in His Word that He gives His people different gifts for service and leadership and that although "these members do not all have the same function, so in Christ we who are many form one body, and each member belongs to all the others" (Romans 12:4–5). The board and the head of school—those charged with upholding the school's mission and keeping the vision for the school—must belong to each other in order for the school to thrive and fulfill its God-given purpose.

A recent research report claims that disconcerting trends in school leadership have developed in recent years. The report states that "almost seventy percent of all heads of schools are fired. They do not leave of their own volition. Thirty years ago many heads served long terms of office and most left under their own steam" (Littleford 2005, 1). Leadership volatility has also surfaced as a matter of critical concern for the Christian school community. According to the Association of Christian

Schools International (ACSI) and Christian Schools International (CSI), there are an unfortunate number of terminated heads, schools without a head, schools seeking an interim head to mark time while a suitable new leader is recruited, and schools with debilitating tension between the head and the board.

Christian schools are positively affected by strong, consistent leadership, and adversely affected by frequent leadership transitions and the instability and insecurity that they bring. Thriving, growing Christian school communities tend to have long-term heads, cohesive relationships between the board and the head of school, and little attrition in the leadership ranks of the faculty and staff. Christian schools must work prayerfully and diligently to establish strong, God-glorifying personal and professional relationships between the board and the head of school. Such relationships will provide a strong foundation for the schools and will serve as models for the entire Christian school community.

The Linchpin: Trust and Confidence

It is fitting that those called to govern the Christian school are called "trustees," because that is exactly what they must do—hold the school in trust: "Now it is required that those who have been given a trust must prove faithful" (1 Corinthians 4:2). Fulfilling this mandate is the single most important responsibility of the work of the head of school and the board, and it is the heart of their relationship.

Strong, successful Christian school communities, like all communities, are bound together by strong ties of trust and confidence among all constituencies—board, parents, faculty, staff, administrators, students, alumni, and friends of the school. Trust and confidence are of critical importance because schools deal with a most treasured possession: God's children. Parents trust the school to provide safety for their children; to nurture and care for them; to treat them fairly and with respect; to extend mercy when appropriate and apply justice when necessary; and, most essential, to give them an education that will develop their minds, touch their hearts, and lead them to lives of serving and following Jesus. Christian school leaders and teachers are human and frail; they will make mistakes and disappoint from time to time. But if a foundation of trust and confidence is in place, parents will approach the school with a cooperative and respectful spirit, expecting positive outcomes and biblical resolutions. Without trust and confidence, relationships can easily fracture and diminish the home-school partnership, which is at the core of the Christian school community.

In the school community, trust and confidence must begin in the boardroom. The head of school and the trustees set the tone, exemplify the model, and ensure the foundation upon which the school fulfills its mission and advances its cause. Faculty will quickly lose confidence in their leaders if the head and the board are not "on the same page" regarding the school's mission, vision, policy, and working environment. The school will not be well served if the board loses confidence in the head and believes it must go beyond appropriate boundaries and direct day-to-day operations. Parents will lose trust if the head of school says one thing and the board says another. If mistrust and lack of confidence persist, sooner or later the foundation begins to crumble and the school suffers. Then, if trust and confidence cannot be restored, inevitably the head is terminated, and the result is volatility and insecurity from an unexpected leadership transition.

Christian school leaders must establish and maintain the trust and confidence of the board they serve in order to be effective stewards of the leadership role to which God has called them. The relationship between the board and the head of school must be founded on a clear understanding of roles and responsibilities and on a commitment to nonnegotiable principles—from the day of appointment and continuing throughout the head's tenure. A foundation built with ambiguity regarding these principles is like the house built on sand: it will not last (Matthew 7:26–27).

Building Trust and Confidence: Standing on the Same Foundation

Thomas Sergiovanni, noted author and lecturer on the importance of community in the life of a school, states, "*Communities* are collections of individuals who are bonded together by natural will and who are together bound to a set of shared ideas and ideals" (1996, 48; emphasis in original). The importance of the strength of this bond around core values and beliefs is especially important in the relationship between the board and the head of school. Before accepting a call to lead a Christian school, a prospective school head should thoroughly understand the board's core values. Lack of congruence in foundational areas will lead to fissures in the working relationship, especially when challenging and important decisions must be made involving mission, vision, philosophy, and policy. In order for the school leaders to work in unity, they must be like-minded in foundational areas.

One of the foundational areas that leaders must understand is the governance structure of the school. The governance structure determines the roles and responsibilities of the board and the head of school. Most Christian schools follow one of these three governance structures: (1) *church-run* (parochial), (2) *parent-run or association-run*, and (3) *board-run* (a self-perpetuating board of trustees). In order for the board and the head of school to have a healthy and productive relationship, the board members and the head must have a common understanding of the school's governance structure.

Church-run schools

Church-run schools typically are governed by school boards that are under the authority of a church's ruling body and pastor. The church views the school as a part of the church's ministry, establishes the mission and vision of the school, and provides facilities and financial support. The autonomy of the school board will vary from school to school, depending on the wishes of the church leadership. The senior pastor may or may not play a significant role in the life of the school, depending on his commitment to Christian schooling and the impact of the school on the life of the church. The church ruling body may either delegate the operation of the school to a separate school board or directly oversee the school's day-to-day events. At times the senior pastor, church leadership, and school board may have different views and understandings of respective roles and responsibilities. Such differences can lead to decision-making ambiguity and role confusion, impeding the pursuit of the school's mission and goals.

Where does the head of school fit into the church-run school governance structure? It is crucial that a prospective head of school clearly understand the perception and understanding of each member of the school leadership—senior pastor, church ruling body, and school board—before accepting a call to service. The effectiveness of the head can be quickly and dramatically compromised if he views his role through a different lens from that of any of the three leadership entities to which he reports. Who will direct his leadership and service: the pastor, the church elders, or the school board? Does each one of these leadership groups clearly know its own roles—and the roles of the other members—and carry out its own responsibilities? Who sets the agenda for the school? Where does the school stand in relation to other church ministries, such as the youth program and the Sunday school? The head of school must clearly grasp the nuances of this structure in order to determine if he or she can comfortably and successfully lead within that organization.

Parent-run or association-run schools

Many Christian school communities believe that the mandate for Christian education is given by God specifically to parents (Deuteronomy 6:6–7); therefore, they have established parent-run or association-run schools. Association members are primarily parents of current students. These parents may meet several times each year to receive reports and vote on the annual budget, elect new board members, enact bylaw changes, and make curriculum decisions. Board members are predominantly current parents, whose frame of reference might often be colored by what they hear from their own children or from other parents in the bleachers or in the parking lot. Many association-run schools have delegated significant authority to their boards, but others are characterized by strong parental influence in day-to-day operations, either through direct contact with teachers and administrators or through the influence they have in and through their elected board representatives. Association-run schools have the advantage of a parent community that is deeply committed to the school and its daily operations.

The head of a parent- or association-run Christian school should both understand and be committed to this philosophy of governance because this philosophy will have a significant impact on the nature of the head's leadership. Clearly and consistently communicating, involving parents in the decision-making process, implementatng a parent volunteer program, and working with a board primarily made up of current parents will be the head's priorities—priorities that will be used by the board and the parents to measure the success of the head's leadership. Strategic thinking and long-range decision making could be a challenge for the association-governed school because parents will be more focused on current realities and their impact on the students. The head of school must be responsive to the broader parent community, the board, the faculty, the current students, the school's alumni, and the school's financial supporters—a balancing act that will test his or her relational and diplomatic skills.

Board-run schools

The self-perpetuating-board form of school governance, typical of most independent or private schools, is gaining adherents in the Christian school community. A self-perpetuating board recruits and selects its own members, enabling the board to profile the skills and qualifications needed on the board and to recruit new members who fulfill these requirements. Self-perpetuating boards are free to go beyond a church or parent body to include talented, committed individuals who will be free from the explicit or implicit expectations of particular interest groups (for example, church pastor, elder board, parents). Self-perpetuating boards can therefore address many critical issues more independently than is possible under other governance structures. These issues include advancing and supporting the school's mission and vision, ensuring the strategic future of the school, and hiring the head of school. Heads of these schools serve as the chief executive officers (CEOs). They are charged with the responsibility of hiring and supervising the faculty and staff, implementing the annual budget, fulfilling annual objectives outlined in the school's strategic plan, soliciting gifts in support of annual and capital needs, and telling the school's story to internal and external constituencies.

Heads of schools governed by self-perpetuating boards must be comfortable with the CEO role and responsibilities. Within this form of government, the head shares few decision-making responsibilities with board members and committees. The head has direct responsibility for recruiting, interviewing, and enrolling students; recruiting, hiring, and firing staff; establishing and implementing curricular programs; and managing the annual budget. Since the board will likely not meet every month and will implement task forces and ad hoc committees (rather than standing committees) to complete much of its work, the head must be able to fulfill these responsibilities without the type of direct oversight and involvement provided by board members at church-run and association-run Christian schools.

Jack Postma, principal of Unity Christian High School in Hudsonville, Michigan, states that "at the core of an administrator's effectiveness is his understanding of the organization, its mission, its decision-making levels, and having the facilitating skills to make it happen" (email communication, March 23, 2006). Each of the three governance structures detailed above has advantages and disadvantages, and it is not the purpose of this chapter to advance or critique any of these structures in particular. However, it is important for the Christian school leader to fully understand the characteristics and distinctions of each structure; identify the one that is the best fit for his or her skills, experience, and philosophy; and make sure that the board and community of the school have a like-minded understanding of each member's roles and responsibilities. A head of school who seeks to serve as a CEO in a church-run Christian school is almost certain to encounter conflicts. A head of an association-run school who is not adept at connecting with parents and including them meaningfully in the life of the school will stumble.

Mission and Philosophy: The Glue for the Board-and-Head Relationship

Regardless of the governance structure, the head and the board must be of the same mind and heart regarding the school's mission (who we are and whom we serve) and core values (what we believe). If the school is covenantal in design and thus is committed to enrolling the children of Christian families, the head and the board must set and implement policies and practices that uphold this foundational belief. Marketing, recruitment, public relations, hiring, and decision making must communicate this belief—without ambiguity or equivocation—to the constituency that the school seeks to serve. Board policy and the head's leadership must affirm, support, and advance the school's foundational premise. A head with a heart for an evangelistic mission and philosophy would be ill suited for leadership of a covenantal Christian school.

The Christian school's philosophy regarding its role in teaching and training young people according to the truth of God's Word also directs the working relationship of the head of school and the board. A school that strives to protect children from the sin and temptation of a secular world will not be well served by a head who believes that Christian schooling should primarily prepare students to be "salt and light" in a dark world. The school's view of its primary role will have an impact on policies and practices regarding issues such as dress, literature, drama, music, and discipline. The board and the head must be of one mind regarding this core belief as they help prepare students to be in the world but not of it (John 17:15–16).

Mutual trust and confidence between the board and the head of school require strong agreement regarding the school's mission, vision, and philosophy. Such agreement will help prepare the school's leaders for the challenging questions and issues that they are likely to face. Trust and confidence will be quickly—and, in some cases, irreparably—compromised if the board and the head are not like-minded in these key areas.

Traveling on the Same Road: Strategic Planning

Once the board and the head are on common ground in understanding and upholding the mission, core values, and philosophy of the school, a strategic plan is the next crucial element in building a strong and effective leadership team. A comprehensive strategic plan serves as a road map that helps the school fulfill its mission and realize its vision. The goals, objectives, and specific action plans that are part and parcel of a well-conceived strategic plan should serve as the primary planning instruments for the board and the head, providing annual goals and plans and serving as the basis of the annual performance evaluations for both the board and the head of school. The strategic plan also enables key constituencies—parents, students, faculty, alumni, and friends—to understand fully the school's short-term and long-term goals. A vibrant, up-to-date strategic plan keeps the board and the head of school united in vision, preventing them from pursuing different priorities and projects.

An effective strategic plan should include the input of a broad range of constituents in order to ensure schoolwide support and cooperation in implementing the plan. Surveys, focus groups, and town-hall meetings can serve as effective information-gathering vehicles. If the school is accredited by a Christian, independent, or regional accrediting agency, the prescribed self-evaluation protocols and the accreditation report can serve as important sources for determining priority issues that should be included in the school's strategic plan. It is important, however, that the board take ownership of the strategic plan and that the head of school view implementation of the strategic plan as the most important measure of his or her leadership success. God tells us that "where there is no vision, the people perish" (Proverbs 29:18, KJV).

The Game Plan: Clearly Defining Roles and Responsibilities

The roles and responsibilities of the board and the head of a Christian school, although distinct in some areas, are entwined in the area of spiritual leadership. The biblical and spiritual foundation of the school must be the first and foremost priority of the board and the head, exemplified in the boardroom and in the leadership life of the head. Many Christian communities have traveled far from their spiritual and biblical roots because boards and heads of school did not properly uphold their mandate to serve as vision keepers and spiritual leaders.

In order to provide spiritual leadership, the board and the head must work diligently to stand for and articulate the kingdom purposes inherent in the mission of the school (for example, "to act justly and to love mercy and to walk humbly with your God," Micah 6:8). Care must be taken to view every aspect of the school program through the lens of God's Word, making sure that biblical principles define what the school does and why. The board and the head must define, embrace, and integrate biblical principles in areas such as admissions, financial aid, staffing, and stewardship. When conflicts arise, the board must affirm the school's commitment to the Matthew 18 principle by refusing to deal with issues brought forward by constituents who have not followed this principle. The school must be a place of prayer, and board members and the head of school should lead the way. Board meetings should begin with Bible reading, devotions, and a season of prayer to thank God for His provision and to bring the specific needs and praises of the school and its people before Him. Board members and the head should exemplify the practice of prayer by attending prayer meetings, pausing to pray before significant issues are voted on, and thanking the Lord in all circumstances.

While spiritual leadership is shared between the board and the head, other areas of responsibility must be distinct. A successful and harmonious working relationship between the board and the head in many Christian schools is often compromised by a lack of clarity regarding roles and responsibilities. A newly appointed head must be sure that he or she clearly understands the board's expectations regarding the work of the board as distinct from the work of the head.

The specific job description of the head of school should include the following tasks (Stratton 2006):

- Implement board policies and initiatives
- Advise the board on all matters under board jurisdiction
- Recommend policies, strategic-plan initiatives, and programs for board consideration
- Implement the strategic plan
- Oversee financial planning and control

- Establish organizational roles for staff
- Supervise and evaluate the organization's operations, and report to the board on performance
- Appoint or select supervisors
- Report annually to constituents on organizational performance
- Act as an advocate
- Report to the board on organizational accomplishments and achievements
- Maintain professional relationships with staff, administrators, the population the school serves, and other community individuals, groups, and organizations
- Share information openly

A Christian school is served well by a board that is attentive to the appropriate lines of decision-making authority that are distinct from those of the head of school. The following board job description focuses the Christian school board on roles and responsibilities appropriate to its leadership (Stratton 2006):

- Establish and communicate the mission, core values, and strategic goals of the organization
- Develop and approve policies to guide the organization.
- Approve the annual budget
- Establish support and recognition systems and a monitoring and evaluation system
- Evaluate the effectiveness of the board in achieving established goals
- Report annually to constituents on organizational performance.
- Act as an advocate
- Hire, supervise, evaluate, and, if necessary, fire the head of school.
- Know and follow its own policies
- Share information openly

A careful analysis of the roles and responsibilities of the board and the head reveals that there are areas of obvious overlap and, therefore, opportunities for confusion and misunderstanding. The role of the head of school has evolved over the years because of the growth and complexity of Christian schools, the increased demands placed on the head in the areas of institutional advancement and fund-raising, and the increased professionalism of school leaders. Therefore, various models in place today define the often contradictory and sometimes competing ideas about what the role of the head of school is and how boards and heads should interact. Models in place today include the following:

1. Strong board, subordinate executive. This model was more prevalent in the past, but it continues to persist in some Christian school communities, especially in new Christian schools. The head is subservient to the board, and the board views supervising and controlling the head as its responsibility. Heads tend to be passive in this model, and boards micromanage the day-to-day operation of the school.

2. Strong executive, ornamental board. A long-term, charismatic head is at the helm in this model, which can be an effective model as long as the head is leading with vision and energy. The board is not developed and used to its maximum potential in this model, and leadership changes can be traumatic.

3. Equal partners. Peter Drucker advocates a model that views the board and the CEO as equal partners who work collaboratively. This model can work if the chemistry between the board and the head is sound. However, ambiguity in regard to roles and responsibilities can result in disagreement and confusion.

4. Partners with clear boundaries. This model typifies a structure that calls for executive limitations and defines specifically what the head of school cannot do. Although this model removes ambiguity, it can result in lack of flexibility.

5. Servant leaders. This model, articulated by Robert Greenleaf, states that leaders must first seek to serve and then lead as a way to expand their service to the school. Servant leaders encourage collaboration, trust, empathy, and the ethical use of power. The servant-leadership model is also consistent with the level-five leadership model that Jim Collins describes in his book *Good to Great* (Moyers 2006).

A Christian school board and its head of school should identify which model describes the board-head relationship at their school in order to be sure that the model in place is the best fit for their school. Difficult decisions and challenging issues will test the strength and effectiveness of the organizational framework that guides the leadership and decision-making functions. A board and a head who clearly understand and support their respective roles will be able to provide the strong and consistent leadership the school needs to deal with hard times and tough decisions.

The board chair plays the most vital role in making sure that the board and the head are exercising appropriate leadership and decision-making authority. The board chair, in conjunction with the head, sets the meeting agenda; keeps the board focused on the mission, core values, and strategic vision for the school; assigns the work of the board to committees and task forces; and ensures effective communication.

The following steps, which the author learned mainly from the reflections of a former school-board chair, provide helpful guidelines for chairs:

Clarify expectations. Sometimes board members do not understand the obligations of trustees, or a board member may disregard or deemphasize a part of the job description (for example, "I don't do fund-raising").

Make sure trustees know and accept their roles. Trustees do their best when they can work on things that most interest them.

Do not be power hungry. Remember that all trustees are equal; all are called to the board under the same criteria.

Serve as an advocate. Praise in public; debate in private.

Practice visibility. Many schools suffer from board anonymity; there is no substitute for your presence.

Take the lead in fund-raising. As the chair, you should be the first donor to the annual fund and should articulate the unequivocal expectations that 100 percent of the board members will give at whatever level they are capable and that they will do so at the beginning of the campaign.

Educate the board about trusteeship. Lead an orientation for new board members. Educator Santo D. Marabella (2006) says that this orientation should include three components: interactive training (for example, role playing, discussions, and case studies), dialogue about needs, and responsiveness to needs.

Provide for succession. A board-chair-in-waiting who knows well in advance that he or she will be chair can help ensure the consistency and effectiveness of school leadership (Kotkins 2003).

Remember that trustees are volunteers. The following may help trustees feel that their service is important and valued:

- *Do not waste their time.* Start meetings promptly, even if a number of people are not there yet.
- *Promote a relaxed, warm, collegial atmosphere.* The application of

Robert's Rules of Order, although necessary at times, should not inhibit a free exchange of ideas and opinions.

- *Appreciate board members.* Take the time to express appreciation for and to recognize exemplary service.
- *Make a personal connection with each trustee,* especially the newest ones.
- *Deal with "problem trustees."* Check in with the no-shows and the nonparticipators. Rein in the parent-trustees who cannot separate those roles.
- *Handle the sensitive stuff.* Most effective boards have a well-established culture of confidentiality. It is up to the chair to balance the trustees' "need to know" with the need to protect the school from unnecessary disruption, liability, or both.

Nonnegotiable: Board and Head Evaluation

Assessment and evaluation help leaders discover if students are effectively learning, if teachers are effectively teaching, and if the school is fulfilling its overall mission and reaching its objectives. Assessment and evaluation enable the school to determine if its philosophy, curriculum, and programs are helping students reach desired outcomes. Assessment and evaluation are also crucial for the board and the head of school in order to clearly determine whether expectations are being met and roles and responsibilities are being successfully carried out.

An annual self-assessment and evaluation of the board will help members focus on their roles and responsibilities, determine their success in advancing the school's strategic-planning efforts, and set new goals and strategies for the subsequent school year and beyond. The board assessment will evaluate performance and progress in areas such as spiritual leadership, application of biblical principles in leadership, mission, vision, philosophy, strategic planning and thinking, fund-raising, fiscal management, relationship between the board and the staff, support of the head, orientation of new members, and risk-management policies.

The annual evaluation of the head of school by the board will enable board members to clarify and define performance expectations, express support and encouragement for the head, set performance goals for the head for the subsequent school year, and ensure clarity in communicating the board's satisfaction with the work of the head. The board's evaluation of the head should focus on annual performance goals that are connected to the school's strategic plan, core competencies identified in the head's position description, and overall leadership performance.

Righting the Ship

The strength of the relationship between the head of school and the board will inevitably be put to the test at some point in the head's tenure. The head might be reluctant to fire a faculty member even though the board has given the teacher a less-than-satisfactory rating. The board might intervene in a disciplinary matter, compromising the head's authority and credibility with the faculty. The head and the board might come into conflict regarding a decision to implement a major expansion and capital-fund drive. If appropriate intervention is not implemented, such conflicts could irrevocably fracture the relationship between the board and the head.

The role of the board chair is crucial when the head and the board enter troubled waters. The chair must take the initiative to bring the head and key board members together in an effort to identify the issues that are causing conflict and to establish a plan of action for reconciling differences and reestablishing trust and confidence. This process might include regular meetings of the head and the executive committee. The board chair might also call in a trusted counselor such as a past board chair or a pastor to serve as a mediator between the head and the board. These proactive steps can effectively help refocus the head and the board on common goals and outcomes, paving the way toward restored relationships.

If initial interventions are not successful and the leadership of the school begins to suffer, the board might consider employing a professional mediator or counselor. There are times when the head and the board are so close to the conflict that they lose objectivity. Consultants from Christian school organizations such as ACSI, CSI, and other Christian agencies can provide the skills, experience, and objectivity necessary to address relational issues, thus averting a bitter resignation or termination.

The Matthew 18 model can help heads and boards work through differences of opinion in times of crisis. If boards and heads work diligently, prayerfully, and intentionally to apply biblical means of resolving conflicts and restoring trust, many separations will be avoided.

Leadership for the Future: Succession Planning

In their book *Built to Last* (1994), Jim Collins and Jerry Porras show how successful businesses and organizations have developed succession plans for the CEO and other key leaders. The same practice can greatly benefit Christian schools. A shortage of qualified and interested applicants for head-of-school leadership positions has resulted in a large number of Christian schools without a head, and many other schools take longer than expected or desired to find a new head. D. Bruce Lockerbie, noted author and school consultant, states, "One of the most insidious weaknesses in not-for-profit enterprises—whether educational institutions, helping agencies of all types, or performing arts groups—is this common failure of current leadership to prepare for the future after their time has ended" (2006, 2). Christian schools should plan for leadership changes and not merely react to these changes.

Establishing and maintaining a community culture that effectively advances and supports the mission and vision of the school must begin at the top of the organization. Heads of schools and boards of trustees must work and pray diligently to establish and maintain a leadership tone and environment that will inspire trust and confidence, enabling the school to prosper in a quickly changing, complex world. Establishing a strong leadership team cannot be left to chance; it must be pursued with intentionality, sound philosophy and practice, and generous amounts of nurture and prayer.

Now What? Application to Practice

THE HEAD OF school and the board might discuss the following questions to evaluate the strength of the school's leadership community and to identify steps that will support leadership development in the school. (Questions 1 through 3 come from the thoughtful leadership of principal Jack Postma, cited above.)

1. Are the board and the head focused on the school's mission? The following questions must be asked before voting on a recommendation:
   - Is it appropriate for the school's mission?
   - Is it the most effective means to accomplish the school's mission?
   - Is it the most efficient means to accomplish the school's mission?
   - Does it maintain or build the organization's morale (esprit de corps) or sense of community?

2. How do trustees work toward achieving a consensus for what is the best way to achieve the school's mission?

- Are our decisions based on valid information—directly verifiable, minimally attributive, and minimally evaluative? (Argyris and Schön 1974)
- Do our decisions provide a free and informed choice for each trustee? (Argyris and Schön 1974)
- Do our decisions lead to internal commitment by each trustee for that decision? (Argyris and Schön 1974)
- Are our decisions made with compassion for those affected? (Schwarz 2002)

3. What process is used to reach consensus? The following process is helpful to model, evaluate, and guide the process. Trustees best achieve consensus when the following are true:

- They have opportunity to engage in dialogue—seek first to understand, then to be understood (Senge 1990).
- Dialogue is followed by skillful conversation to identify the best decision (Senge 1990).
- Devotion to prayerful decision making is practiced.

4. Do we understand the benefits and challenges associated with our governance structure (church-run, parent- or association-run, board-run)?

5. Are the head of school and the board of trustees operating within the roles, responsibilities, and expectations associated with the school's governance structure?

6. Can all board members and the head of school recite the mission statement and illustrate ways and means to integrate the mission into the life of the school and the decision-making process of the board?

7. Do the board members and the head have a well-conceived and clearly articulated vision of where they believe the school will be five years from now? Ten years from now? Twenty-five years from now?

8. Is an up-to-date, operational strategic plan guiding the work of the board and the head of school? Is this strategic plan, along with the

status of its implementation, regularly communicated to the school constituency?

9. Are position descriptions and policy manuals in place that clearly define the roles, responsibilities, and expectations of the board and the head of school? Do board members and the head of school understand their prescribed roles, responsibilities, and expectations? Is there clear evidence that the board members and the head of school are carrying out their distinct roles and responsibilities respectfully and appropriately?

10. Of the options discussed in this chapter, choose the one that best describes the school's board: (1) strong board, subordinate executive; (2) strong executive, ornamental board; (3) equal partners; (4) partners with clear boundaries; (5) servant leaders. What tangible evidence exists that supports this description?

11. Does the board of trustees annually complete a comprehensive evaluation of the head of school that is focused on performance goals relating to the school's strategic plan, core competencies identified in the position description, and overall leadership performance?

12. Does the board evaluate itself each year?

13. Is a defined succession plan in place for the board chair? Head of school? Other key leadership positions?

14. Are board meetings efficient and productive, as well as respectful of the time and needs of individual board members, and do the meetings fully use the skills and resources of each board member?

15. Do all board members give to the annual fund? To the capital campaign?

Although the questions and processes outlined above involve hard work and thoughtful discussion for the board and the head of school, attention to these matters will create a strong foundation for the Christian school—a foundation upon which children can be nurtured, educated, and helped to live out their God-given potential.

References

Argyris, Chris, and Donald A. Schön. 1974. *Theory in practice: Increasing professional effectiveness.* San Francisco: Jossey-Bass.

Collins, Jim. 2001. *Good to great: Why some companies make the leap ... and others don't.* New York: HarperCollins.

Collins, Jim, and Jerry I. Porras. 1994. *Built to last: Successful habits of visionary companies.* New York: HarperCollins.

Kotkins, Henry L. 2003. Nine steps to being the best board chair. *Carney, Sandoe, and Associates Newsletter* (Spring). http://www.carneysandoe.com.

Littleford, John. 2005. The longevity of heads and the effectiveness of schools: What the latest research tells us. *Littleford and Associates Newsletter* (April). http://www.jlittleford.com/articles/longevity.html.

Lockerbie, D. Bruce. 2006. Who succeeds your present leader? *The Paideia Letter* 17, no. 3 (Winter): 2.

Marabella, Santo D. 2006. Reaping the benefits of improved orientation. *Board Member* 15, no. 1 (January/February): 6–7.

Moyers, Richard L. 2006. *The nonprofit chief executive's ten basic responsibilities.* Washington, DC: BoardSource.

Schwarz, Roger. 2002. *The skilled facilitator: A comprehensive resource for consultants, facilitators, managers, trainers, and coaches.* San Francisco: Jossey-Bass.

Senge, Peter M. 1990. *The fifth discipline: The art and practice of the learning organization.* New York: Currency.

Sergiovanni, Thomas J. 1996. *Leadership for the schoolhouse: How is it different? Why is it important?* San Francisco: Jossey-Bass.

Stratton, Jeff, ed. 2006. Roles and responsibilities chart gives guidance. *Board and Administrator* 22, no. 7:2.

CHAPTER 17

CONTINUAL SCHOOL IMPROVEMENT

Evaluation in Reflective Communities

ço

By Scot Headley
and Stephen Cathers

Scot Headley, PhD, is a professor of education, the chair of the educational foundations and leadership department, and the director of the doctor of education program at George Fox University in Newberg, Oregon. He previously served as a high school agriculture teacher and career educator in Aurora, Colorado.

Stephen Cathers, MS, is an assistant professor at George Fox University and the director of administrative licensure. He is a retired school administrator and was named Alaska State Superintendent of the Year in 2002 while serving in Valdez, Alaska. He teaches courses in educational leadership and administration.

CHAPTER 17

CONTINUAL SCHOOL IMPROVEMENT

By Scot Headley
and Stephen Cathers

THIS STORY CAN serve as a cautionary tale for Christian schools.

The school, which was started by a local church, has grown over time and now serves 300 students. During this time of growth, virtually all direction for the school came from the pastor, a strong and visionary man. The school principal was interviewed and hired by the pastor three years ago. Since coming to the school, however, the principal has seen signs of trouble, such as repeated conflicts with a particular teacher and a number of parents mysteriously withdrawing their children from school without giving reasons. He tried to get to the bottom of the problems, but was told by the pastor to "just let it go." His ideas for surveying the parents and for starting some advisory committees were overruled. A week ago, a parent made a complaint of physical abuse of their child by a teacher in the school—the one who had been involved in repeated conflicts. Following the allegations of abuse, several other parents came forward with similar complaints. Every day, several parents have withdrawn their children from the school. So far, the school has lost thirty-two students. The school now faces a crisis. The principal wonders what went wrong and why he didn't long ago insist on investigating the problems he had observed.

When there is no purposeful ongoing evaluation of an organization, the leaders may remain unaware of forces at work below the surface. Catastrophic events such as those that happened at this fictional school do not happen in a moment; pressures build over time, and when they erupt, the unprepared leader gets a shocking surprise.

An ongoing process of gathering information and soliciting feedback can not only prevent major upheavals but also help leaders shape and improve the school's program. This intentional activity of systematically seeking data to provide an accurate view of the institution's health is important for a variety of reasons. It is a sound and wise management behavior that can prevent catastrophic declines such as that experienced by the school in this story. This evaluation practice also reflects principles found in Scripture and in the nature of God.

Many use the terms *evaluation* and *assessment* interchangeably. However, the authors make a distinction between the two terms. *Evaluation* is a process for making a judgment; *assessment* is a process for measuring or collecting information. An evaluation system based on meaningful assessments is the proper work of a school administrator. Assessment in education is often tied to the need to be accountable for the effectiveness of schools. This accountability may be viewed as a political concern; if a school is assessed poorly, some negative judgment will result. It may also be viewed as a business concern; parents will choose whether to send their children to the school on the basis of such an evaluation. However, a Christian school should view evaluation in the spiritual sense of being influenced by and accountable to God and to the community of God's people.

Creation and Community

When we view evaluation in this spiritual sense, it becomes an exercise of continually reflecting on the goodness and meaning—and in some cases the failures and remedies—of the work of the school and on how that work brings, or should bring, honor to God. A Christian school has a legal responsibility to the state for some aspects of its operation, a contractual obligation to its employees, a covenantal relationship with its parents and students, and in many cases must meet the professional requirements of an accrediting body. At the core, however, assessing the meaning and goodness of the work of the school is a reflection of the school's commitment to model itself on the original work of God Himself. In Genesis 1, at five key points in the process of creating, the text says that "God saw that it was good." Indeed, at the conclusion of the sixth day the text states, "God saw all that he had made, and it was very good" (Genesis 1:31, NIV). In addition to doing the work of creating, God was purposeful in evaluating His own work. God's pattern of creating was an ongoing cycle of work and reflection on the goodness of the work. At the conclusion of the process of work, He made a final judgment on the work—followed by a time of rest. This pattern is one that the Christian school would do well to adopt in its work of education: work, reflection, judgment, and rest. In this manner, institutional assessment can be modeled on the most basic pattern, the one established by God at the beginning.

Another basic pattern to be considered by Christian school educators is that of community. As pointed out by a number of authors, our Christian faith is built on relationships and is best lived and nurtured within community. Stanley Grenz states that God purposes the creation of community, "a reconciled people who enjoy fellowship with him, with one another, and ultimately with all of creation" (1998, 23). As both Dallas Willard (2002) and Grenz discuss in their books, with community come joy, growth, and accountability. Nicholas Wolterstorff (2002) and Parker Palmer (1998) have written that living within community is especially needful for Christians in education, while Thomas Sergiovanni (1992), in his book *Moral Leadership*, promotes the leadership work of community building and warns that it should not be supplanted by assessment activities.

Most school effort characterized as assessment relates to assessment of student achievement (see chapter 12). While assessing students is a central and unavoidable part of the instructional process, organizational evaluation is an essential leadership activity that is often neglected. In the press of day-to-day demands, many school leaders push the need to take the pulse of the overall school program lower and lower on the agenda. In many schools, this effort is buried under many urgent demands and never takes place. Effective school leaders will make time for organizational evaluation, recognizing that it is out of this effort that meaningful improvement is possible. A reflective approach to evaluating the health of a school is the first step in developing a sound evaluation process and is central to the principles of servant leadership (Spears 2002). Reflection, then, forms the basis for self-assessment and must serve as a foundation for all evaluation of school programs.

Mission, Outcomes, and Improvement

School leaders must know how their schools are doing. When parents or board members ask principals about school matters, principals typically give positive reports that include elements such as good test scores, happy children, anecdotal information about recent successful activities, and maybe a sports result. This haphazard assessment data, while valid, may not reflect the real health of the school and may sow seeds of uncertainty in those who know of contrary evidence. It is not uncommon for teachers to sense that leadership is moving forward without the guidance of sufficient, accurate, and thoughtful assessment. John Van Dyk points to a resulting disconnect between the leader's activities and the school's real needs: "Needed and missing ... are sustained programs to help Christian teachers analyze their teaching methodology and to encourage communal self-evaluation" (2000, 17). Sound, reflective evaluation of the school's work must begin with and be promoted by the leadership of the school.

So, what is the starting point for designing school evaluation? Good school-program evaluation must be rooted in the school's mission and must be an ongoing process. If the principal's reports regarding test scores, happy children, and basketball results look like snapshots of the organization, then a portrait must also be developed with some care to ensure an accurate representation.

The first evaluation focus must always be the mission of the school, since the foremost evaluation question to be answered is, "Is the school achieving its central purpose for existing?" W. Edwards Deming, founder of Total Quality Management, established as the first of his "fourteen points" the principle that quality requires commitment to "constancy of purpose" (1986). The mission—the statement of purpose for the organization—is the most important standard against which the school's program should be compared. Most organizations understand the need to have clarity about their purpose and to have that purpose expressed in a mission statement. It is wise for a school leader to reflect early in the evaluation process on the school's mission to determine whether the established mission is appropriate and shared by the school's learning community. If a school leader senses that there is not a clear and shared understanding of the school's mission, it is time to reflect as a community and seek that cohesive purpose. Similar commitment to reflection on the vision of the school is just as important. Stephen Covey emphasizes this truth in his book *Principle-Centered Leadership*, urging that we "begin with the end in mind" (1991, 42). Ultimately, program evaluation should address whether outcomes reflect the mission of the school, and outcomes can't reflect the mission if the mission is unclear.

The second attribute of a quality school-evaluation program is that it should be continuous, resulting in a pattern of improvement. The Malcolm Baldrige National Quality Award is given annually to organizations that exemplify quality. One of the key criteria for the Baldrige award is a system for collecting relevant data, interpreting it, and using the findings for continuous improvement. One of the first educational organizations to receive the Baldrige award was Chugach School District, a small public-school district in rural Alaska with predominantly Native American students. Superintendent Richard DeLorenzo came to Chugach School District in 1994. Over the next eight years he transformed the district into a national phenomenon, with scores on standardized tests improving from the 28th to the 71st percentile. He made a commitment to the Baldrige requirement to "translate organizational *performance* review findings into priorities for continuous and breakthrough improvement and into opportunities for *innovation*" (Baldrige National Quality Program 2006, 23; emphasis in original). To do this, DeLorenzo created a simple continuous-improvement process he dubbed PDER, which integrated a cycle of Plan-Do-Evaluate-Refine into everything the district did. Harvard researcher Tony Wagner visited schools in the district and declared the results "revolutionary" (2002, 71). Organizations that wish to achieve quality must shape their evaluation into a continuous improvement-process rather than onetime or occasional activities.

Purposes for Evaluation

Consider the following scene. Two parents who serve on the board of a Christian school are having coffee together:

> "I read about that state report card in the paper this morning. The local government schools had low test scores again this year. It made me wonder how our school matches up."

"Oh? I thought we had strong scores."

"Don't you remember, we don't participate in the state testing program. Christian schools are exempt."

"Really? Well, I think we ought to be testing. How do we know how the school is doing?"

"That annual report makes it seem like things are going well."

"I think we ought to be taking a closer look at how well the kids are doing!"

There are a number of reasons for evaluating a school and its programs. This conversation between board members illustrates that questions about student success on standardized tests are often cited as a reason for assessment. A basic purpose of school evaluation is to determine the value of the school's operation. However, there are a number of specific reasons for institutional evaluation. The most common are (1) to determine whether the school's objectives are being met, (2) to give direction for school improvement, (3) to provide information for decision makers and constituents, (4) to help determine whether products such as textbooks, curriculum materials, and professional services should be purchased, (5) to make professional judgments about the quality of a school or program, and (6) to learn about the culture and operation of a school (adapted from Fitzpatrick, Sanders, and Worthen 2004).

While there are a number of reasons to conduct an evaluation of a Christian school, it is important to remember that administrators, board members, and others who care about the success and quality of the school should be clear about their purpose in choosing to undergo the evaluation process. Consider the differing purposes of these three evaluations: participating in an accreditation review (which is designed to make a professional judgment about the quality of a school and its programs), providing test results to a state agency charged with monitoring student outcomes, and seeking to determine if the school's mission to prepare students to serve Christ and His people is being fulfilled. While the most important evaluation is based on determining the alignment with the school's internal standards, including its mission and goals, there is also an important purpose for evaluating a school's alignment with external standards.

Evaluation using external standards provides a unique mirror for gaining self-awareness and perspective that is not possible with an internal evaluation process. The most common evaluation of this type is an accreditation process. Christian schools must decide whether to seek accreditation and, if so, what type best fits the purposes of the school. This is not a decision to be taken lightly since the process is demanding. Furthermore, the process chosen should be philosophically consistent with the mission and goals of the school. Many schools move quickly into an accreditation process, only to find that the standards demanded by the accrediting body require significant changes in their programs. If accreditation is a way for schools to look in a mirror and see themselves more clearly, then a likely reaction to the resulting picture is that they may not like everything they see. Of course, if the school is undertaking accreditation for the purpose of improvement, this requirement to change can only be seen as a desired, though uncomfortable, result. School leaders should find some appropriate way to measure themselves against external standards—whether through accreditation or other appropriate processes—to avoid falling into the error of believing there is nothing they can learn from the work of others!

When schools do commit to an evaluation process, they should count the costs and be willing to continue the process until they experience beneficial results. Activities that gather information to be used in evaluating the school can be time consuming and challenging. Some schools may even wonder if the process is worth the effort. As pointed out by Posavac and Carey (2003), the fundamental reason for carrying out evaluation efforts is to aid in the improvement of the activities of the organization. Clearly, if a school is not committed to or interested in or able to make improvements in the operation and outcomes of the school, evaluation becomes a waste of time. However, it is likely that when the focus is placed on improvement, the time and effort expended will be worthwhile.

Accountability and the Broader Community

Another important evaluation perspective requires school leaders to recognize the external political and social forces that can influence their schools. No school operates in a vacuum, although it is tempting to desire that when outside demands complicate the already difficult work of the school. John Van Dyk describes three worlds in which educators work: the classroom, the school, and the "ambient world" outside the school (2000, 113). Christian schools occasionally want to ignore the ambient world, but that is increasingly difficult. Indeed, the trend is toward more interaction with the world at large because of technology and communication advances. Thomas Friedman, in his best seller *The World Is Flat*, describes an irreversible and "unprecedented new level of people-to-people communication" caused by technologies such as Internet browsing, email, cell phones, handheld computing devices, and other media (2005, 80). This interaction seems unavoidable. On a local level, school leaders must consider the importance of community perceptions and relationships, which often create problems that are not easily resolved.

Consider the following case:

A small Christian school had operated in a growing community for many years and had kept to itself successfully. However, a conflict with an assertive neighbor irked the school's administrator, and he walked out of a meeting without resolving the issue. Since he did not believe it was really the school's problem, he refused to meet again with the neighbor. Three years later, the school needed a zoning variance in order to build a small addition, and the administrator filed the necessary paperwork. The application that should have been routinely approved was denied with little explanation except that the school could reapply. When the administrator tried to meet with the planning director to get some help, the director did not show up for the appointment. Every time the administrator tried to improve the request and resubmit it, there were delays leading to another denial. The delays were creating a crisis for the school. Finally, a clerk in the office confided in him. She revealed that the neighbor from the three-year-old conflict was best friends with the planning director, and two of the planning commissioners had attended high school with the neighbor and planning director and had played football together. They all still attended games as a group and were good friends. Those responsible for processing and approving the variance had a clear impression that the Christian school was full of arrogant people who would not even listen to their neighbors.

This situation illustrates the risks of being too insular, discounting local networking, and not maintaining relationships in the larger community. In other words, politics matter! In addition to inviting a problem that would be time consuming to resolve, the administrator found that his school was not representing Christ in the community very well.

In the political realm, the school was being evaluated by others on a regular basis, and there was very little information provided to the planning director or the planning commission to balance one bad impression held by a neighbor. This kind of negative judgment does not just come from people at a distance. In most schools an informal assessment practice—what might be called "parking lot evaluation"—takes place daily. Parents who see each other regularly often visit and exchange comments about the school. One disgruntled parent can influence the views of many parents through this informal but very real exchange in the parking lot of the school.

One way to combat wrong impressions and inaccurate information about an organization is to provide regular and credible positive information. Since school reputation is a valuable commodity, one purpose for evaluation of programs is to generate information that can help those who are not in the school to have an accurate concept of the school's quality. An absence of such information, regrettably, often results either in imagined problems or in generalizations made from a single negative report such as that of the unhappy neighbor. A standard way to validate a school program and provide sound information for constituents is to undertake an accreditation process. Accreditation is a formalized school evaluation, based on established external standards, with the benefit of providing a widely recognized certificate of quality.

Christian schools often are accredited through the Association of Christian Schools International (ACSI) or Christian Schools International (CSI). Many schools seek accreditation to gain credibility with their constituents and to become more marketable. This purpose is less than ideal. Undertaking the process with the clear intent of program improvement is likely to be more helpful in terms of developing quality. An honest and reflective process based on a desire for improvement leads to effective assessment and evaluation efforts.

Another primary source of external assessment for United States schools is regional accreditation. This type of accreditation is a stamp of approval that the secular world respects and, in some cases, rewards. These rewards can include offering qualification for grants, allowing teacher experience to count toward advanced licenses or certificates, giving formal state approval, or adding status to student diplomas. In a number of regions, ACSI and CSI cooperate with regional accrediting bodies through dual accreditation agreements.

Other external standards to evaluate schools include state educational standards, national standards, and the Baldrige criteria. Many independent schools voluntarily evaluate their programs and curriculum according to the standards of the state or country in which they operate. This effort often requires a purposeful selection of relevant state or national standards rather than a comparison with every standard. For example, a school may choose to assess its alignment with state math standards but not state health standards. While assessing alignment with state and national standards is less common as an external measure for independent schools than accreditation alone, it should be considered as a way to maintain integrity and to be assured that one's school is maintaining standards that meet or exceed those of public schools. Two fringe benefits of this use of official school standards are to reduce any perceptions that independent-school education is inferior to public-school education, and to discourage governmental temptation to interfere with independent schools.

The No Child Left Behind Act of 2001 (NCLB) has increased this awareness of standards-based accountability. The highly publicized NCLB debate has strengthened the desire of parents for data-driven measurement to validate the schools that teach their children. All independent schools should have those data available for their constituents so that school leaders have good answers to questions such as "Is our school meeting and exceeding the standards public schools have to meet?" and "How do we know that our school is meeting those standards?" Under the NCLB, schools that do not meet adequate yearly progress (AYP) are publicly identified each year and labeled as schools needing improvement. Heavy sanctions may follow, including the right for students to transfer to other schools at district expense. Because of the technical requirements of the law, many if not most public schools may eventually be sanctioned under NCLB guidelines, and parents may consider options such as local independent schools. This possibility provides a practical reason why Christian schools should pay attention to external secular standards.

A Model for Evaluation

As was discussed above, the basic purpose for school evaluation should be to determine value with the intent to improve a school and its program. Consider the following:

While participating in a board-administrator retreat for a Christian school, the principal observed, "I am still getting a lot of feedback from parents and students that they just don't see the purpose in our service-learning program. I am concerned that we don't have commitment for the program and that our people don't see how it is tied to our school's mission. I think it is time we take a look at this."

In reply, a new board member stated, "Maybe the kids need to spend less time on those service projects and more time in the class-room. Our SAT scores were not as high as similar schools. I am hearing a lot of talk about that."

The assistant principal added, "I wish we could get more buy-in from our staff for those community workdays. The fellowship is incredible, and I have seen kids' hearts changed."

"Well, if you ask me, that new curriculum is the reason why our math scores are low. Back in my day, we had several hours of homework a night in trigonometry," replied a longtime board member.

Though these folks are not in agreement as to what is most important for their school, each one expresses a need for evaluation. There are a number of factors to consider in choosing to conduct a school evaluation. Some of those factors are (1) the needs and concerns of the school constituents, (2) the desired levels of accountability, (3) the resources available for conducting the evaluation, (4) the school culture, and (5) the willingness of school personnel to participate in the evaluation process. As stated previously, a well-defined mission and a strong and broad commitment to that mission are important prerequisites for meaningful evaluation that leads to improvement.

Figure 1 is a model for school evaluation. The model is based on two premises: that improvement is the goal and that evaluation is a process, not an event. It assumes that reflection, judgment, and adjustment are integral parts of the work of education. Consisting of four major components—planning, action, assessment, and reflection—the model is helpful in examining classroom practices, school programs, and schoolwide institutional evaluation.

This model presents the relationships among the four key components of the evaluation cycle. The school's mission, vision, and objectives (planning) shape the school's educational, spiritual-development, and character-development activities (action). Measuring student perfor-

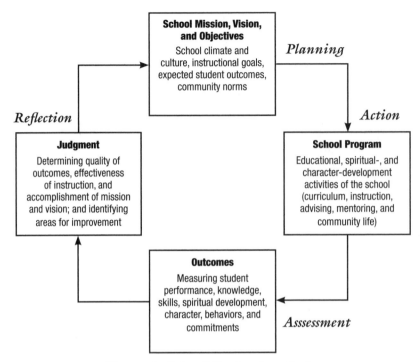

Figure 1. School Evaluation Cycle

mance, behaviors, skills, and knowledge (assessment) provides feedback about the effectiveness of the school's program and provides information by which the school's efforts may be judged or evaluated (reflection). Judgments made through reflecting on the information obtained in assessment lead to further planning and adjustments in the programs of the school. In a school evaluation system as proposed here, assessment leads to judgment for the purpose of adjusting and improving school efforts. By contrast, in an accountability system, assessment leads to judgments for the purpose of providing rewards or administering sanctions.

As the school works with existing assessment information in order to examine specific programs within the school, a long-term goal should be to develop a broad-based evaluation system that is continuous, comprehensive, and focused on improvement. It is important to examine the relationships among planning, actions, assessment, and reflection. As this model illustrates, evaluation is a process, not an event.

Procedures

A general set of procedures for evaluation are presented in figure 2. These procedures may be adapted for use in assessing specific programs within the school or in conducting organizational assessment.

Figure 2. Evaluation Procedures	
Step	**Emphasis**
Describe the program	Present a complete and accurate picture
Determine the purpose of evaluation	Reach broad agreement on the purpose
Develop evaluation questions	Prioritize by importance and practicality
Determine information sources	Consider constraints
Collect and analyze information	Make judgments on program quality
Report results	Use results for improvement

Describe the program to be evaluated

If you cannot describe a program, you cannot evaluate it. Contextual information about the school, its students, and the community must be included in the evaluation process. The school and its particular mission and vision must be clear, and the relationships among the mission, vision, and activities of the school must be described. Posavac and Carey (2003) encourage the use of program theory in describing the program. Program theory requires school personnel to develop a picture of the intended relationships among the purposes and plans for a program, the activities carried out, and the expected outcomes. Having teachers, administrators, board members, and other stakeholders carefully develop this type of framework for the school will greatly enhance assessment and improvement efforts.

Determine the purpose of evaluation

If the school seeks to establish an ongoing, continuous system of evaluation, there must be agreement among stakeholders about why the evaluation is being done and what is being evaluated. It is helpful to begin the evaluation process with specific programs such as math instruction, chapel program, athletics, student leadership, and Bible instruction. As time goes on, other programs should be added to the evaluation process with the aim of developing an overall institutional evaluation process. Leaders should assign responsibility and authority for the evaluation activities. Some leaders decide to recruit external help for the evaluation process.

Develop evaluation questions

Developing questions has both a divergent and a convergent phase (Cronbach 1982). In the divergent phase, the goal is to involve the key stakeholders of the school in considering many possible questions to be addressed. According to Fitzpatrick, Sanders, and Worthen, stakeholders are "various individuals and groups who have a direct interest in and may be affected by the program being evaluated" (2004, 54). These stakeholders include teachers, board members, parents, students, administrators, alumni, and community members. A broad group of stakeholders should be involved in determining what types of questions to answer in evaluating the school.

Different stakeholders will have different questions they want answered. In the convergent phase, the goal is to reduce the number of questions to a manageable list of the most important and practically answerable questions. As questions are developed, they become the criteria by which the program will be evaluated. Standards for judging the quality of programs should be established as well. Different stakeholders will also have different criteria and, therefore, may have different standards. These differences can be problematic, but they can also lead to important discussions about school mission and about what is important to different stakeholders.

Determine information sources

Once the evaluation questions are developed, the next step is to determine the information needed to answer those questions, the information sources to be used, and the methods needed for gathering the information. What standard testing instruments will be used? Will new tests and other measures of student performance be developed? What information will be gathered by surveying or interviewing stakeholders (teachers, students, parents, and others)? What information will be gathered through a review of documents? Some questions will require multiple methods of information gathering. This process can become complex and costly.

Keeping the information-collection system as simple as possible will lead to a workable evaluation process.

Collect and analyze information

For some types of information, collection may involve reviewing information that already exists, such as attendance records, test scores, student work, and teacher evaluations. For other types of information, new collection methods will need to be devised. If surveys and interviews are used or if some assessment of behavior or attitudes is required, school personnel should obtain instruments—such as questionnaires, interview guides, scoring guides and rubrics, and observation records—to collect the needed information. If appropriate instruments do not exist, school personnel will need to create their own. Instruments must be constructed carefully to ensure that accurate and trustworthy information is obtained.

After collection, the information must be analyzed. This analysis could be as simple as comparing average test scores on a yearly basis or as complex as making examinations by using statistical methods, financial analysis, and prayerful review of behaviors and attitudes. After a time of reflection on the meaning of the findings, judgments should be made. With improvement as a key goal, judgments should center not just on how the school is doing but also on how it can be improved. It is not enough to merely examine outcomes and judge that the results are less than desired. It is also necessary to determine what is lacking in the school, and what contributed to the gap between expected and actual outcomes.

Report results

This step should inform school personnel and others of the evaluation findings and provide the type of information that will be helpful in the next round of planning. To make the best use of evaluation findings for program improvement, it is important not to view evaluation as an opportunity to take punitive action for substandard results. Rather, evaluation findings should be viewed as diagnostic information to contribute to a plan for helping the school improve. Therefore, results should be shared broadly and in forms that are easy for various stakeholders to access and understand. Lengthy reports may not be useful for staff and parents. On the other hand, a one-paragraph summary to board members may leave questions unanswered, causing concern.

The assessment process can be modified in a variety of creative ways. Michael Fullan (2001) describes an assessment practice he calls a "Learning Fair," which came out of a project called the Assessment for Learning initiative. This example demonstrates strong commitment to reporting and using evaluation findings. In this assessment model, a school schedules staff time to collaboratively organize assessment data, collect artifacts, and draw conclusions. Instead of treating evaluation as a secret, behind-the-scenes process, a school gathers as a learning community to create a body of evidence that demonstrates—and celebrates—the school's achievements. In *Leading in a Culture of Change*, Fullan describes such a learning fair held at the eight-four schools of the Edmonton Catholic School District. They conducted these fairs at intervals of about a year. The fairs produced not only helpful assessment feedback for the schools but also a community learning experience that provided a "multiplier effect" (102). While this is a less traditional type of assessment with inadequate research to support its findings, it has merit in that it serves the additional functions of staff development and community building.

Now What? Application to Practice

IN THE WHOLE scope of a school leader's work, evaluation is an often neglected yet essential responsibility. Not only is the school evaluation process a reflection of God's evaluation of His creative work, but it is also the means to improving the school over time. While assessment has often been seen as a disjointed series of measurements, a school leader should strive to develop a cohesive system using multiple assessments from which to draw information that leads to a fair and balanced evaluation of the school. The judgments that come from this evaluation process should become part of a cycle of continuous improvement that is the basis for school quality.

The following steps are recommended:
- The school leader must design and implement an evaluation system for the school programs.
- The school leader must focus on the school's central mission and purpose.
- The school leader must clarify and articulate the purpose, or purposes, for the school's evaluation process.

- The school leader must seek appropriate external validation, such as accreditation.
- All assessment should fit within a school evaluation cycle, resulting in continuous improvement for the school.

The result will be an integrated system that assesses appropriate school behaviors and allows for a balanced evaluation leading to continuous improvement for the school and its programs.

Resources for Institutional Assessment

A. Books: General texts on program evaluation and assessment

Fitzpatrick, Jody L., James R. Sanders, and Blaine R. Worthen. 2004. *Program evaluation: Alternative approaches and practical guidelines.* 3rd ed. Boston, MA: Allyn and Bacon.

Posavac, Emil J., and Raymond G. Carey. 2003. *Program evaluation: Methods and case studies.* 6th ed. Upper Saddle River, NJ: Prentice Hall.

Sanders, James R., and Carolyn D. Sullins. 2005. *Evaluating school programs: An educator's guide.* 3rd ed. Thousand Oaks, CA: Corwin Press.

B. Web-based resources

Baldrige Award Program: http://www.quality.nist.gov.

Chugach Schools: http://www.chugachschools.com.

Government Accountability Office Publications: http://www.gao.gov/special.pubs/erm.html.

Greenleaf Center: http://www.greenleaf.org.

C. Regional accrediting agencies and state agencies and standards

Education Resource Organizations Directory: http://wdcrobcolp01.ed.gov/Programs/EROD/.

Northwest Commission on Colleges and Universities: http://www.nwccu.org (see "related links").

United States Department of Education Office of Non-Public Education: http://www.ed.gov/pubs/RegPrivSchl/index.html.

References

Baldrige National Quality Program. 2006. *Criteria for performance excellence.* http://www.quality.nist.gov.

Covey, Stephen R. 1991. *Principle-centered leadership.* New York: Summit Books.

Cronbach, Lee J. 1982. *Designing evaluations of educational and social programs.* San Francisco: Jossey-Bass.

Deming, W. Edwards. 1986. *Out of the crisis.* Cambridge, MA: Massachusetts Institute of Technology.

Fitzpatrick, Jody L., James R. Sanders, and Blaine R. Worthen. 2004. *Program evaluation: Alternative approaches and practical guidelines.* Boston, MA: Allyn and Bacon.

Friedman, Thomas L. 2005. *The world is flat: A brief history of the twenty-first century.* New York: Farrar, Straus and Giroux.

Fullan, Michael. 2001. *Leading in a culture of change: Being effective in complex times.* San Francisco: Jossey-Bass.

Grenz, Stanley J. 1998. *Created for community: Connecting Christian belief with Christian living.* 2nd ed. Grand Rapids, MI: BridgePoint Books.

Palmer, Parker J. 1998. *The courage to teach: Exploring the inner landscape of a teacher's life.* San Francisco: Jossey-Bass.

Posavac, Emil J., and Raymond G. Carey. 2003. *Program evaluation: Methods and case studies.* 6th ed. Upper Saddle River, NJ: Prentice Hall.

Sergiovanni, Thomas J. 1992. *Moral leadership: Getting to the heart of school improvement.* San Francisco: Jossey-Bass.

Spears. Larry C. 2002. *On character and servant-leadership: Ten characteristics of effective, caring leaders.* The Robert K. Greenleaf Center for Servany-Leadership. http://www.greenleaf.org.

Van Dyk, John. 2000. *The craft of Christian teaching.* Sioux Center, IA: Dordt Press.

Wagner, Tony. 2002. *Making the grade: Reinventing America's schools.* New York: RoutledgeFalmer.

Willard, Dallas. 2002. *Renovation of the heart: Putting on the character of Christ.* Colorado Springs, CO: NavPress.

Wolterstorff, Nicholas P. 2002. *Educating for life: Reflections on Christian teaching and learning.* Ed. Gloria Goris Stronks and Clarence W. Joldersma. Grand Rapids, MI: Baker Books.

CHAPTER 18

EDUCATING
FOR
SHALOM

Missional School Communities

ↄ

By Brian Fikkert

Brian Fikkert is an associate professor of economics and the director of the Chalmers Center for Economic and Community Development at Covenant College. He received a PhD from Yale University, specializing in third-world development, and he focuses on equipping college students, churches, and Christian ministries to work with the poor.

CHAPTER 18

EDUCATING FOR SHALOM

By Brian Fikkert

"WHEN ARE WE ever going to talk about the most important thing?" Brenda asked. She and her classmates were being debriefed by three professors about the twelve-week internships they had just completed in locations ranging from squatter towns in Manila to slums in Uganda to a poor community in Appalachia. It was late at night, and everyone was tired, so it was a bit disappointing to learn that Brenda felt that the most important topic had not yet been addressed. Brenda continued, "Last night we students met without you professors present. As we shared our experiences with one another, we discovered something. Even though we had gone to very different places and had had quite diverse experiences, all of us had one thing in common: Each one of us felt that we had been spiritually transformed by the process. There was something about being so totally unable to control our environment, about having to rely so completely on God, and about seeing the poor faithfully praising God under such difficult circumstances that made us grow in ways we had never experienced before. And *that* is the most important thing."

The classroom is a powerful place to shape students' minds and hearts. But it was clear from listening to Brenda and seeing the nods of agreement from her classmates that God had not used a "wise man," a "scholar," or a "philosopher of this age" to transform these young people (1 Corinthians 1:20, NIV). Rather, God had used the least academic people on the earth—the "foolish," the "weak," the "lowly," the "despised," and the "things that are not"—to accomplish remarkable growth in these students (1 Corinthians 1:27–28).

Communities are necessarily exclusive. Some are in the community, and some are not. The communities that Christian schools create typically exclude from their membership the very people who—through no merit of their own—dwell on center stage of Christ's redemptive work: the poor. In the process, teachers, administrators, and students can become distantly removed from observing, encountering, and partaking in the community chosen by God to "nullify the things that are" (1 Corinthians 1:28). Therefore, educational leaders desiring to seek first the kingdom of God must undertake bold, creative, and, yes, radical measures to engage with communities that the world—and all too often the church—despise. A failure to cross this vast socioeconomic and cultural divide places the entire school community in peril of becoming part of the establishment that Christ's kingdom and community are in the business of "nullifying."

This chapter provides a framework to enable school communities to engage with despised communities without doing harm to either community. The likelihood that such engagement will do significant damage to both communities is very real; however, with God's help and the proper approach, such engagement can bring about a powerful transformation for all the parties involved. After laying out this framework, the chapter briefly describes specific models for engagement in the hope that readers will seek to implement these concepts in their own schools. Before doing so, however, the chapter makes the case that engaging with despised communities is a biblical imperative that educational leaders must take seriously.

Why Did Jesus Come to Earth?

Most evangelical Christians believe they know why Jesus came to the earth. But there are nuanced differences in how evangelicals think about this most basic issue, and those small differences have dramatic consequences for all endeavors, including the educational task.

Jesus' earthly ministry began one Sabbath day in a synagogue in Nazareth. For years Jews had gathered in this synagogue to worship under the chafing yoke of the Roman Empire. Cognizant of Old Testament prophecy, these worshippers were longing for God to fulfill His promise to send a Messiah who would reign on David's throne and would restore the kingdom to Israel forever. But this Sabbath day would be like none other before or since, for on this day the son of a carpenter from that very town stood up and was handed a scroll from the prophet Isaiah.

> Unrolling it, he found the place where it is written:
> "The Spirit of the Lord is on me, because he has anointed me to preach good news to the poor. He has sent me to proclaim freedom for the prisoners and recovery of sight for the blind, to release the oppressed, to proclaim the year of the Lord's favor."
> …The eyes of everyone in the synagogue were fastened on him, and he began by saying to them, "Today this scripture is fulfilled in your hearing." (Luke 4:17–21)

A shiver must have gone down the spines of the worshippers that day. Could it be that Isaiah's prophecies were really about to come true? Could it really be that a kingdom whose domain would increase without end was about to begin (Isaiah 9:7)? Was it really possible that justice, peace, and righteousness were about to be established forever (Isaiah 9:7)? Would this king really bring healing to the parched soil, the feeble hands, the shaky knees, the fearful hearts, the blind, the deaf, the lame, the mute, the brokenhearted, the captives, and the sinful souls; and would He ultimately proclaim the year of Jubilee for the poor (Isaiah 35:1–6, 53:5, 61:1–2)? Would the Messiah really come (in the words of the Isaac Watts hymn "Joy to the World") to "make His blessings flow far as the curse is found?"

Why did Jesus come to the earth? Shortly after His dramatic announcement in the synagogue, Jesus answers that question: "I must preach the good news of the kingdom of God to the other towns also, because that is why I was sent" (Luke 4:43).

The kingdom of God is not a peripheral issue in Scripture. As Herman Ridderbos states, "It may be rightly said that the whole of the preaching of Jesus Christ and his apostles is concerned with the kingdom of God" (1962, xi). And what is this kingdom? Timothy Keller summarizes the biblical concept of the kingdom as "the renewal of the whole world through the entrance of supernatural forces. As things are brought back under Christ's rule and authority, they are restored to health, beauty, and freedom" (1997, 52–53).

The author has asked thousands of evangelical Christians in numerous contexts this most basic of questions: Why did Jesus come to the earth? The majority answer by stating that Jesus came to "die on the Cross to save souls from sin." Although this answer is true, saving souls is only a subset of the comprehensive healing of the entire cosmos that Jesus' kingdom brings and that is the centerpiece of His message (Romans 8:18–21, Colossians 1:15–20, Revelation 21:1–5).

One of the most remarkable features of this kingdom is that it is upside down. Unlike earthly princes, the Prince of Peace was born in a smelly stable. Rather than dwelling in an elaborate palace, the King of Kings had no place to lay His head. Instead of socializing with the aristocracy, the Great Physician spent His time with the lepers, the crippled, the blind, the deaf, and the poor (Luke 4:18–21, 7:18–22).

Given the focus of Jesus' ministry, it is not surprising that James makes the following observation about the early Church: "Listen, my dear brothers: Has not God chosen those who are poor in the eyes of the world to be rich in faith and to inherit the kingdom he promised those who love him?" (James 2:5).

Similarly, Paul drives this point home in his letter to the unloving Corinthian church when he says the following:

> Brothers, think of what you were when you were called. Not many of you were wise by human standards; not many were influential; not many were of noble birth. But God chose the foolish things of the world to shame the wise; God chose the weak things of the world to shame the strong. He chose the lowly things of this world and the despised things—and the things that are not—to nullify the things that are, so that no one may boast before him. (1 Corinthians 1:26–29)

Commenting on these passages, Mark Gornik states, "Here then from both James and Paul is a central witness drawn from all of Scripture: God has sovereignly chosen to work in the world by beginning with the weak who are on the 'outside,' not the powerful who are on the 'inside'" (2002, 73).

The claim here is not that the poor are inherently more righteous or sanctified than the rich. There is no place in the Bible that indicates that poverty is a desirable state or that material things are evil. In fact, wealth is viewed as a gift from God. The point is simply that God has chosen—for His own glory—to reveal His kingdom in the place where the world, in all its pride, would least expect it: the communities of the despised.

What Is the Task of the Church?

The task of God's people is rooted in Christ's mission. In the Old Testament, God's chosen people, the nation of Israel, pointed forward to the coming King by foreshadowing what He would be like (Matthew 5:17; John 5:37–39, 45–46; Colossians 2:16–17). Since the King would preach good news to the poor, it is not surprising that God wanted Israel, the foreshadowing of Jesus, to care for the poor as well. In fact, God told Israel, "There should be no poor among you" (Deuteronomy 15:4). Toward that end, God gave Moses numerous commands instructing Israel to care for the poor, including the Gentiles, in order to eradicate poverty from the land (Exodus 23:10–12; Leviticus 19:9–10, 25:8–55; Deuteronomy 14:28–29, 15:1–18).

Unfortunately, Israel did not fulfill its task, and God sent the Israelites into captivity. Even though most evangelicals are aware that God was angered by Israel's worship of idols, few North American evangelicals recognize that one of the central reasons for Israel's exile was her failure to care for the poor and the oppressed (Isaiah 1:10–23, 5:8–9, 58:1–12; Amos 2:6–7, 4:1, 5:11–12). Ezekiel goes so far as to say that Israel was worse than Sodom, whose sin was that "she and her daughters were arrogant, overfed and unconcerned; they did not help the poor and needy" (Ezekiel 16:49).

In the New Testament, God's people, the Church, are more than just a picture of Jesus. The Church is the very body, bride, and fullness of Jesus Christ (Ephesians 1:18–23, 4:7–13, 5:32). When people look at the Church, they should see Jesus Himself. People should see the one who declared in word and in deed to the poor that He is bringing healing to every square inch of the universe. It is not surprising, then, that the early Church was concerned for the poor, since there is no poverty in the kingdom of Jesus Christ. In the first passage describing the New Testament Church, Luke notes, "There were no needy persons among them" (Acts 4:34). Dennis Johnson (1997) explains that Luke is intentionally repeating the language of Deuteronomy 15:4 to indicate that God's people have been reinstated to their proper role as the embodiment of the kingdom, a kingdom in which there is no poverty. Indeed, throughout the New Testament, care of the poor is central to the Church's task (Matthew 25:31–46; Galatians 2:1–10, 6:10; James 1:27; 1 John 3:16–17).

Mark Gornik cautions that when the Church embodies Jesus' concern for the poor it cannot do so in an arms-length fashion. Rather, the Church is to be a "fellowship amidst the hurting and harmed, the excluded and the suffering" (2002, 73). God's people are told to "seek first his kingdom" (Matthew 6:33), a kingdom whose primary manifestation is in a community that consists, although not exclusively so, of those who are the least likely to have the opportunity to attend Christian schools.

The Expansion of the Upside-Down Kingdom

It is strange to place the despised at the center of a kingdom's strategy for invasion and conquest, but history indicates that this unusual plan has been quite successful. Sociologist Rodney Stark (1997) documents that the early Church's engagement with the suffering was crucial to its explosive growth. Cities in the Roman Empire were characterized by poor sanitation, contaminated water, high population densities, open sewers, filthy streets, unbelievable stench, rampant crime, collapsing buildings, and frequent illnesses and plagues. "Life expectancy at birth was less than thirty years—and probably substantially less" (1997, 155). The only way for cities to avoid complete depopulation from mortality was for there to be a constant influx of immigrants, a very fluid situation that contributed to urban chaos, deviant behavior, and social instability.

Rather than fleeing these urban cesspools, the early Church found its niche there. Stark explains that the Christian concept of self-sacrificial love of others, emanating from God's love of them, was a revolutionary concept to the pagan mind, which viewed the extension of mercy as an emotional act to be avoided by rational men. Hence, paganism provided no ethical foundation to justify caring for the sick and the destitute, who were being trampled by the teeming urban masses. In contrast, Stark (1997, 161) describes Christianity's impact as follows:

> Christianity revitalized life in Greco-Roman cities by providing new norms and new kinds of social relationships able to cope with many urgent urban problems. To cities filled with the homeless and impov-

erished, Christianity offered charity as well as hope. To cities filled with newcomers and strangers, Christianity offered an immediate basis for attachments. To cities filled with orphans and widows, Christianity provided a new and expanded sense of family. To cities torn by violent ethnic strife, Christianity offered a new basis for social solidarity. And to cities faced with epidemics, fires, and earthquakes, Christianity offered effective nursing services.

Jesus' kingdom strategy of ministering to and among the suffering is so powerful that other kings have taken note. In the fourth century A.D., the Roman emperor Julian tried to launch pagan charities to compete with the highly successful Christian charities that were attracting so many converts. Writing to a pagan priest, Julian complained, "The impious Galileans [the Christians] support not only their poor, but ours as well, everyone can see that our people lack aid from us" (Stark 1997, 84).

As Christianity exploded into the Roman world, the urban poor were on center stage of the drama. And the same is true today. Historian Philip Jenkins (2002) documents that Christianity is experiencing explosive growth in Africa, Latin America, and parts of Asia. For example, by 2025, in terms of numbers of adherents, Africa will have replaced Europe and the United States as the center of Christianity. By 2050, Uganda alone is expected to have more Christians than the largest four or five European nations combined. And like the early Church, the growth in the Church in the developing world is taking place primarily with the poor on center stage. Jenkins observes, "The most successful new denominations target their message very directly at the have-nots, or rather, the have-nothings" (2002, 92).

Schools, Camels, and the Eye of a Needle

Schools generally admit and focus on students who are financially and intellectually capable. Public funding partially overcomes the financial constraints in many societies, but this fact generally does not apply to Christian schools. Special programs can assist those who are intellectually less gifted or who are from disadvantaged educational backgrounds, but such programs are in short supply, especially in financially challenged Christian schools.

It is unreasonable to expect an individual school to be able to solve all the historical and contemporary social problems that contribute to the gap between the school community and the communities of the despised, but this gap creates an enormous challenge. If the primary locus of the revelation of the kingdom is in despised communities that are isolated from the school community, how is the school community to "seek first the kingdom"? The argument here is not that the gap is damaging to the despised communities, although it is. Rather, the problem is that the school community is severely hindered from observing and experiencing a significant manifestation of Christ's redemptive work because of its lack of contact with despised communities. Christian schools should be seeking first the kingdom; hence, it is unfortunate that they need binoculars to see the center stage of that kingdom from their vantage point in the back row.

Jesus said, "I tell you, it is easier for a camel to go through the eye of a needle than for a rich man to enter the kingdom of God" (Matthew 19:24). Given that Christian schools tend to be enclaves for the relatively privileged, what might Jesus have said about the challenges that members of these exclusive communities face in entering the kingdom of heaven? Fortunately, "with God all things are possible" (Matthew 19:26).

Beyond the Three Rs: Educating for Shalom

What is the purpose of a Christian education? Consistent with the earlier discussion, philosopher Nicholas Wolterstorff (2004) argues that the central concern of both the Old and New Testament writers is that the kingdom of God has burst onto the earthly scene in the person of Jesus Christ. The primary benefit of this kingdom for redeemed individuals is that they experience shalom, the human flourishing that comes from living according to God's design. In particular, God has established four key relationships for each individual: with God, with others, with creation, and with oneself. When humans take delight in the proper functioning of these relationships, they experience the shalom that God intends. Wolterstorff asserts that since Jesus revealed His shalom primarily among the despised, so Christian education must include an emphasis on justice for the poor and oppressed, a justice that cries out for these four foundational relationships to be reconciled.

The shalom-based educational model is concerned with movement. Success is not achieved when students simply accumulate knowledge. Rather, the entire educational endeavor is geared toward equipping and motivating students to become ministers of reconciliation (2 Corinthians 5:11–21), transforming agents who will passionately promote shalom by seeking to restore people's foundational relationships. The implications of this model for the educational process are quite profound, requiring schools to move beyond training minds to equipping hands and transforming hearts. Wolterstorff (2004, 34) argues that a shalom-based educational model will be

> far more concerned than ever before with building bridges from theory to practice. Throwing some abstract political science at the student along with some abstract economics and sociology will not do the trick. The goal is not just to understand the world but to change it. The goal is not just to impart to students a Christian world-and-life-view but to equip and motivate them for a Christian way of being and acting in the world. There is not a shred of evidence that simply putting abstract theory in front of them will alter their actions.

Clearly, many schools will need to learn some new methods if they want to impart to their students not just knowledge but dispositions to live and act justly in a broken world. Drawing on the literature from psychology, Wolterstorff (2004, 1980) discusses such methods, emphasizing the use of audio-visual resources to confront students with the suffering of the oppressed.

Wolterstorff's (2004) educational model is consistent with the kingdom motif that is central to Scripture, and his pedagogical methods are compelling. However, two additional points need to be made. First, even though it is legitimate to draw on any valid insights from psychology, the type of dispositional changes that Wolterstorff seeks require the sanctifying work of the Holy Spirit. Transformative education—education for shalom—requires a miracle to take place in the hearts of the students and teachers. Without the work of the Holy Spirit, it is simply impossible to create the dispositions that Wolterstorff rightly seeks. Hence, praying for miracles must become one of the primary tools in educators' kits.

Second, although confronting students with visual images of the oppressed can be powerful, it is no substitute for directly engaging students with despised communities. While this statement is generally true, it is especially the case for today's students, who have been numbed by the constant stream of images from the media throughout their lives (Postman 1985). As will become clear in the next section, students and the despised both need relationships if they are to experience the shalom of the kingdom, and relationships cannot be built through a television screen.

A Framework for Effective Engagement

It is one thing to talk about engaging schools with despised communities; it is quite another thing to do so in a productive manner that avoids doing harm to students and to the poor. The central question that must be considered is this: What is poverty? How one answers this question will largely determine the solutions that one takes to alleviating poverty. For example, most Americans typically define poverty as a lack of material things. Not surprisingly, these Americans often see the giving or lending of material things as the solution to poverty. On the other hand, some Christians believe that people are poor as a result of some personal sin such as laziness. Such Christians believe that the solution for poverty is to evangelize the poor so that they will accept Jesus as Lord, change their behavior, and get out of poverty. Still others believe that the global economic system is exploiting the poor. The solution, they say, is to reform the international trade and financial systems so that the poor will no longer be victims of the global economy.

As these examples illustrate, how one diagnoses the cause of poverty determines the medicine one prescribes. If the diagnosis is wrong, the medicine will be wrong, and the medicine could actually do more harm than good.

What, then, is the proper diagnosis? Bryant Myers (1999), a Christian development practitioner with World Vision International, argues that one must consider the fundamental nature of reality in order to get at the ultimate causes of poverty. Myers notes that God is a relational being who established several foundational relationships for humans at the point of Creation. Each person has a relationship with self, with others inside and outside the person's community, with nature, and with God. These foundational relationships express themselves in many ways, including the social, political, and economic systems that humans develop at the local, national, and global levels. Sin has marred all these relationships and the behaviors and systems that emanate from them. The damage caused by sin leads to Myers' description of the fundamental causes of poverty: "Poverty is a result of relationships that do not work, that are not just, that are not for life, that are not harmonious or enjoyable. Poverty is the absence of shalom in all its meanings" (1999, 86). Consistent with Wolterstorff's framework, Myers argues that the goal in working with the poor is to seek shalom by helping to reconcile these fundamental relationships.

There are a number of implications from Myers' conception of poverty. First, everyone is poor in the sense that all are suffering from broken relationships. For some this brokenness manifests itself in economic poverty, while for others it manifests itself in other ways. For example, the lazy have a broken relationship with nature, failing to use their gifts to have dominion over the creation and to support themselves in the process. Workaholics also have a broken relationship with nature, idolizing their work at the expense of leisure and other responsibilities, the result being stress-induced health problems, troubled marriages, and neglected children. These considerations should lead the relatively rich to a greater sense of humility as they engage with low-income people, because all are suffering from the same fundamental problems, and all are in need of shalom. Rather than trying to be messiahs to the economically poor, the rich should see themselves as walking hand in hand with low-income people, as both encourage each other to experience the fullness of Christ's reconciling work. From this perspective, working with the economically poor is as much about the transformation of the economically rich as it is about the transformation of those typically considered the poor.

Second, the solution to economic poverty is rooted in restoring relationships, not in giving material things to low-income people. In fact, such gifts are likely to do more harm than good to both the giver and the recipient. Myers (1999) argues that the primary feature of poor people's brokenness with themselves is that they feel inferior to the rest of society. This assertion is confirmed by interviews with thousands of low-income people in which they often express overwhelming feelings of shame and worthlessness (Narayan et al. 2000; Narayan et al. 2001). In contrast, Myers (1999) asserts that the primary feature of the rich's broken relationship with themselves tends to be God complexes in which the rich see themselves as superior to others. When the rich give material things to the economically poor, both parties suffer. The rich are affirmed in their belief that they are superior and that the poor need them, thereby increasing their pride. The poor are affirmed in their belief that they are inferior and dependent upon the rich. Both the economically rich and poor are more broken as a result of the gift than they would be without it.

Third, engagement with the economically poor should focus more on processes than on products. A short-term missions trip in which the relatively rich outsiders build ten houses for low-income people might very well harm the low-income people by further marring their self-image. An alternative approach in which the outsiders simply support the economically poor as the poor design and direct the housing project might result in fewer houses getting built, but have the positive result of helping the economically poor see their own gifts of management and leadership.

The Traditional Service-Learning Model: Santa Claus Is Coming to Town?

Schools are increasingly adding to their curriculum a service-learning model, which may be defined as "a teaching and learning approach that integrates community service with academic studies to enrich learning, teach civic responsibility and strengthen communities. It engages students in addressing real unmet needs or issues in a community and actively involves them in decision-making at all levels of the process" (Pritchard and Whitehead 2004, 4).

Classroom instruction introduces students to the issues and literature pertaining to some existing problem or civic cause and allocates class time to allow students to dialogue among themselves and with community organizations or members. Students are then expected to design and implement some related form of community service and subsequently to reflect on their experiences along the lines of David Kolb's (1984) action-reflection model of experiential learning. A host of information and resources for designing and implementing service-learning for students at all age levels can be obtained from the National Service-Learning Clearinghouse at www.servicelearning.org.

Drawing on constructivist learning theory, Florence Pritchard and George Whitehead III (2004) argue that by engaging students in group-based, real-world problem solving, service-learning is likely to enhance students' intellectual, social, and motivational development; and there is some empirical support for their assertions. Shelley Billig (2000) reviews evidence from numerous studies and concludes that service-learning helps students acquire academic skills and knowledge and increases their motivation to learn.

Although these results are encouraging, the previous discussions should give the reader some pause about the service-learning model as applied to engaging with despised communities. How is the marred self-identity of the economically poor likely to be restored by a herd of relatively rich students invading a low-income community for a short period of time in order to fix it? And how are the God complexes of the economically rich students likely to be overcome by placing them in the position of Santa Claus vis-à-vis the less fortunate? These concerns have been raised by a number of educators who see the traditional service-learning model as inherently paternalistic in that it degrades the poor and strokes the egos of teachers and students (Illich 1990; Sigmon 1990; Souza 1999). Karen Grady (1997) provides evidence from one service-learning project suggesting that prejudicial attitudes of many students toward low-income, minority people were actually exacerbated by the project. Unfortunately, there do not appear to be any empirical studies examining the effects of the traditional service-learning model on the economically poor.

What is needed is a model of engagement that eschews short-term, commodity-focused, paternalistic projects in favor of creating relationships between students and the despised—relationships that can result in the holistic transformation of both.

Learning from the Poor as Service to the Poor

The past two decades have seen the emergence of participatory approaches to poverty alleviation, approaches which assume that the poor have considerable knowledge, creativity, and analytical abilities to contribute to their own development. Rather than doing something *to* the poor or *for* the poor, many practitioners have started to do things *with* the poor—both because the poor have remarkable insights and because such an approach builds the self-respect that is so often lacking in the poor.

One of the central methods in this approach is Participatory Learning and Action (PLA), a set of tools that enable an outsider to facilitate conversations in which members of a poor community share their knowledge and construct their own solutions to the problems they are facing (Chambers 1997; Myers 1999). Inherent to PLA is a revolutionary dynamic in which the outsiders are the learners and the poor are the teachers. This role reversal leads to a natural process in which the outsiders affirm the dignity of the poor by simply listening to them, and the poor help the outsiders overcome their God complexes by teaching the outsiders things they never knew. When the Holy Spirit shows up, transformation often happens for both the poor and the students.

In contrast to the traditional service-learning model, in this approach the students are not producing some commodity *for* the poor or doing something *to* the poor. Rather, the students are learners *from* the poor, which, in the upside-down kingdom, ends up reconciling broken relationships for both the poor and the students. The students' willingness to learn is the service they provide.

Although they do not use PLA tools, a number of educators have placed their students in the position of learners as they engage with poor communities in service-learning programs (Brabant and Hochman 2004; Novek 2000; Soukup 1996). R. L. Sigmon (1990) outlines principles for service-learning programs that are consistent with those advocated here.

For the past four years, the author has been privileged to teach in an undergraduate major in community development. One of the goals of this major has been to implement the developmental approach to service-learning. The students typically come from middle-class to upper-middle-class suburban American backgrounds and from families and evangelical churches that stress doctrinal purity and a fairly cerebral approach to Christianity.

Students are prepared with the proper knowledge, attitudes, and skills to engage in cross-cultural learning, including assistance with designing a research project that they develop in dialogue with a host organization that is ministering in a low-income community. Students then live in that community for three to six months between their junior and senior years. The students go as learners, using PLA and other techniques to listen to the low-income people who are now their next-door neighbors.

In addition to conducting research, the students complete a number of reflective essays and keep weekly logs in which they respond to a series of questions about their surroundings and themselves. In particular, students are required to listen for evidence of shalom in the lives of the economically poor and to look for such evidence in themselves.

The stories of Christ's kingdom being revealed among the economically poor are abundant in the students' reports, and the results of this learning process on the students themselves are quite profound. Consider the following example from the log of one student about a church she attended in a slum in the Philippines (Luther 2005):

> I came expecting to see a small church with many doctrinal issues and not a full understanding of what it truly means to be a Christian. How wrong I was! I have been humbled and challenged in so many ways to see the passion and purpose that these people have in living their life to and for the Lord…. Instead of me thinking that I have understood God's Word fully, I find myself searching the Scriptures for a better understanding of what it means to worship the Lord in His sanctuary and lift His name on high. I have had to repent of my lack of understanding about God, His people, and His work in their lives. As Pastor Ephraim says, "Poor people have a bigger God because they have bigger problems." In the midst of such hardships and poverty, God's promises come alive and the Word becomes a treasure.

There is also some evidence suggesting that the students' learning posture has been an encouragement to the low-income communities and has provided useful information to the host organizations. The entire educational process has had a lasting impact on the students: the vast majority of the graduates of this program are engaged in full-time work among the despised.

Now What? Application to Practice

1. Instruction in the gospel of the kingdom

Students need to be constantly reminded that the central theme of Scripture is the kingdom of God and that the poor are on center stage of the revelation of this kingdom. Helpful resources include *To Live in Peace: Biblical Faith and the Changing Inner City* (Gornik 2002), *Ministries of Mercy: The Call of the Jericho Road* (Keller 1997), *Walking with the Poor: Principles and Practices of Transformational Development* (Myers 1999), and *Good News and Good Works: A Theology for the Whole Gospel* (Sider 1999).

2. Instruction in the causes of poverty and its solutions

Students need to be confronted with the multifaceted and relational nature of poverty and see themselves as suffering from the same problems as the economically poor. They also need an introduction to the solutions to poverty that move beyond dependency-creating, paternalistic handouts. Helpful resources include *Walking with the Poor* by Bryant Myers (1999) and a distance-learning course based on Myers' book called Foundations and Principles of Holistic Ministry, taught by community-development experts at the Chalmers Center for Economic and Community Development at Covenant College (www.chalmers.org).

3. Instruction in tools for learning from the poor

Students need to be equipped with tools to learn from and listen to low-income people. A number of outstanding PLA manuals and tools are available from de Negri et al. (1998), the Peace Corps (2000), and the World Bank (1996).

4. Development of a relationship with a Christian ministry in a low-income community

It is important to link arms with those organizations that are already working with the poor because they can often advise schools about appropriate ways and opportunities to develop relationships with low-income people in those communities. Often these organizations are ministering to the children of low-income families, providing opportunities for younger students to develop friendships.

5. The leading of students through a planning, action, and reflection cycle

Class time must be allocated both to allow students to plan how they will engage with the poor and to give them time to reflect about their experiences together. Students should consider the following reflective questions:

- What did you learn from the people in the community?
- What gifts has God given to these people and to their community?
- Is there evidence that people are growing in their relationships with God, themselves, others, and nature?
- How are you growing in those relationships?
- How did you see God working in this community?
- How do you see God working in your life?

References

Billig, Shelley H. 2000. Research on K–12 school-based service-learning: The evidence builds. *Phi Delta Kappan* 81, no. 9:658–64.

Brabant, Margaret, and Arthur Hochman. 2004. What are schools for? Crossing institutional boundaries for the sake of learning. *Educational Studies* 36, no. 2:159–77.

Chambers, Robert. 1997. *Whose reality counts? Putting the first last.* 2nd ed. London, England: Intermediate Technology Publications.

de Negri, Bérengère, Elizabeth Thomas, Aloys Ilinigumugabo, Ityai Muvandi, and Gary Lewis. 1998. *Empowering communities: Participatory techniques for community-based programme development.* Vols. 1 and 2. Nairobi, Kenya: Centre for African Family Studies. http://pcs.aed.org/empowering.htm.

Gornik, Mark R. 2002. *To live in peace: Biblical faith and the changing inner city.* Grand Rapids, MI: Eerdmans.

Grady, Karen. 1997. *Constructing the other through community service learning.* Unpublished paper. Indiana University.

Illich, Ivan. 1990. To hell with good intentions. In *Combining service and learning, A resource book for community and public service,* vol. 1, ed. Jane C. Kendall and associates, 314–20. Raleigh, NC: National Society for Internships and Experiential Education.

Jenkins, Philip. 2002. *The next Christendom: The coming of global Christianity.* New York: Oxford University Press.

Johnson, Dennis E. 1997. *The message of Acts in the history of redemption.* Phillipsburg, NJ: P&R Publishing.

Keller, Timothy J. 1997. *Ministries of mercy: The call of the Jericho road.* 2nd ed. Phillipsburg, NJ: P&R Publishing.

Kolb, David A. 1984. *Experiential learning: Experience as the source of learning and development.* Upper Saddle River, NJ: Prentice Hall.

Luther, Ashleigh. 2005. Student logs for research internship in community development. Covenant College, Lookout Mountain, GA.

Myers, Bryant L. 1999. *Walking with the poor: Principles and practices of transformational development.* Maryknoll, NY: Orbis Books.

Narayan, Deepa, Robert Chambers, Meera K. Shah, and Patti Petesch. 2001. *Crying out for change.* Voices of the Poor series, vol. 2. New York: Oxford University Press.

Narayan, Deepa, Raj Patel, Kai Schafft, Anne Rademacher, and Sarah Koch-Schulte. 2000. *Can anyone hear us?* Voices of the Poor series, vol 1. New York: Oxford University Press.

Novek, Eleanor M. 2000. *Tourists in the land of service-learning: Helping middle-class students move from curiosity to commitment.* Paper presented at the 86th annual convention of the National Communication Association, Seattle, WA (November).

Peace Corps. 2000. *Promoting powerful people: A process for change.* ICE Publication no. T0104. Washington, DC: Center for Field Assistance and Applied Research.

Postman, Neil. 1985. *Amusing ourselves to death: Public discourse in the age of show business.* New York: Penguin Books.

Pritchard, Florence Fay, and George I. Whitehead III. 2004. *Serve and learn: Implementing and evaluating service-learning in middle and high schools.* Mahwah, NJ: Lawrence Erlbaum Associates.

Ridderbos, Herman. 1962. *The coming of the kingdom.* Trans. H. de Jongste. Ed. Raymond O. Zorn. Philadelphia, PA: Presbyterian and Reformed Publishing.

Sider, Ronald J. 1999. *Good news and good works: A theology for the whole gospel.* Grand Rapids, MI: Baker Books.

Sigmon, Robert L. 1990. Service-learning: Three principles. In *Combining service and learning: A resource book for community and public service,* vol. 1, ed. Jane C. Kendall and associates, 56–64. Raleigh, NC: National Society for Internships and Experiential Education.

Soukup, Paul. A. 1996. Inviting others to take the helm: Service-learning and the marginated community. Paper presented at the 82nd annual meeting of the Speech Communication Association, San Diego, CA (November).

Souza, Tasha. 1999. Service-learning and interpersonal communication: Connecting students with the community. In *Voices of strong democracy: Concepts and models for service-learning in communication studies*, ed. David Droge and Bren Ortega Murphy, 77–86. Service-Learning in the Disciplines series. Washington, DC: Stylus Publishing.

Stark, Rodney. 1997. *The rise of Christianity: How the obscure, marginal Jesus movement became the dominant religious force in the Western world in a few centuries.* New York: HarperCollins.

Wolterstorff, Nicholas. 1980. *Educating for responsible action.* Grand Rapids, MI: Eerdmans.

———. 2004. *Educating for shalom: Essays on Christian higher education.* Ed. Clarence W. Joldersma and Gloria Goris Stronks. Grand Rapids, MI: Eerdmans.

World Bank. 1996. *The World Bank participation sourcebook.* Environmental Management series. Washington, DC: World Bank.

CONCLUSION

THE LORD'S NAME AND RENOWN

By James L. Drexler

IN THE MIDST of announcing judgment on the people of Israel, the prophet Isaiah pauses to praise the Lord. Anticipating the time when Israel returns to God, the prophet writes, "In that day this song will be sung in the land of Judah:... The path of the righteous is level; O upright One, you make the way of the righteous smooth. Yes, Lord, walking in the way of your laws, we wait for you; your name and renown are the desire of our hearts" (Isaiah 26:1, 7–8, NIV). If the prophet could sing this song even in the darkness of judgment, what better mission statement for educational leaders and Christian schools could there be than to affirm confidently that the Lord's "name and renown are the desire of our hearts"?

As the preceding chapters have elucidated, the Christian school must not be motivated by unbiblical standards of success, influence, and prestige—and these will be ever-present temptations—but rather, by God's grace, motivated by the dogged pursuit of God's kingdom and the truth of His eternal Word. It is the task of the educational leader to get the focus right, then to humbly lead the school toward righteousness, justice, faithfulness, and peace.

The comfort of Isaiah 26 is the promise that the Lord Himself will make the path of the righteous smooth, for otherwise the feeble efforts of leaders will certainly fail. In effect, then, this passage is calling educational leaders to make God the leader of the school—to follow Jesus, who will safely guide His people. The Christian school—its leadership, faculty, and students—must avoid the temptation to boast about what *they* have accomplished, but instead regularly acknowledge, as Jeremiah does, "I know, O Lord, that a man's life is not his own; it is not for man to direct his steps" (Jeremiah 10:23).

Steven Vryhof (2004–2005) provides an inspiring description of Christian school effectiveness when he contrasts the "thornbushes" and "briers" of unbiblical goals and philosophies of education with the "pine tree" and "myrtle" (Isaiah 55:12–13) of an educational philosophy that is consistent with God's Word. A Christian school that is pursuing God's kingdom and purposes will, according to Vryhof, do the following:

- Reflect and imitate unconditional love instead of conditional love based on human achievements
- Celebrate the wholeness of each student instead of holding to a "constricted, learning-machine view of students" (7)
- Offer through its curriculum a deep and rich appreciation for all facets of humanity instead of appreciating just high scores on standardized tests
- Provide community—with meaningful and supportive relationships—instead of keeping people rushed, fragmented, and fearful
- Inspire calm instead of a constant striving and busyness
- Be deeply rooted in the wisdom of God instead of "hydroplaning on the shallowest understandings of the purpose of life" (8)
- Advocate higher expectations, humility, and the peace of God instead of superficial definitions of the Christian life
- Encourage a life of obedience, gratitude, honesty, and hope instead of a life of self-indulgence, self-serving, and self-importance

> The effectiveness of a Christian school is measured by graduates who spread out through the world and leave behind forests of pine trees and fields of myrtle. This will be for the Lord's renown, for an everlasting sign, which will not be destroyed. (Vryhof 2004–2005, 9)

The Lord's renown and name must be the eternal ambition for effective educational leaders and the Christian schools they lead.

Reference

Vryhof, Steven C. 2004–2005. The measure of Christian school effectiveness. *Christian School Education* 8, no. 3:6–9.

INDEX OF NAMES

INDEX OF SUBJECTS